D0208634

Jiffy
Phrasebook
GERMAN

Langenscheidt
NEW YORK

Edited by the Langenscheidt Editorial Staff and Donald Arthur

Phonetic transcriptions: Walter Glanze Word Books
(The Glanze Intersound System)

Jiffy Phrasebooks are also available for many other languages.

*Jiffy Travel Packs combine the Jiffy Phrasebooks with a
travel-oriented 60-minute cassette. Each can be used independently
of the other.*
(Jiffy Travel Pack German ISBN 0-88729-977-6)

*For detailed information please contact
Langenscheidt Publishers, Inc.
46-35 54th Road, Maspeth, NY 11378
(718) 784-0055*

INFORMATION

GUIDE TO THE USE OF THE PHRASEBOOK

This German phrasebook offers you all the important words and phrases you may need on a visit to Germany. The phonetic transcriptions which follow the German expressions are designed as an aid to correct pronunciation, and the systematic arrangement of the phrasebook will help you to find what you are looking for in the shortest possible time.

Structure of the phrasebook

The phrasebook is divided into 20 chapters. It begins with general words and phrases, followed by sections on transportation, accommodations, food and drink, and many other important aspects of travel abroad. There are chapters on shopping, health, cultural activities, and entertainment; the appendix gives you lists of common signs and abbreviations, weights and measures, and colors. For easy reference, English words and phrases are printed in heavy black type, while the German translations are in blue. Following these are the phonetic transcriptions of the German phrases in normal black type.

Occasionally two or more phrases have been combined and the interchangeable elements given in italics. For example, the sentence "Is it going to *rain (snow)?*" corresponds to the German „Wird es *regnen (schneien)?*". Thus "Is it going to rain?" is translated „Wird es regnen?" and "Is it going to snow?" becomes „Wird es schneien?".

In the boxes you will find help on certain language difficulties, tips on general etiquette, and information on travel, eating out, using the telephone, etc., which will help you get by in everyday situations you may encounter while traveling abroad.

An asterisk at the beginning of a sentence indicates that this is something someone else might say to you.

German pronunciation

On pp. 8–11 you will find a detailed guide to German pronunciation. Most of the symbols used in the phonetic system are taken from the Latin alphabet, so you should have no difficulty getting accustomed to the transcriptions.

German grammar

If you would like to get to know some important aspects of German grammar, the brief survey on pp. 195–202 will give you a basic grounding. Apart from offering you an insight into the structure of the German language and helping you to understand the expressions in the phrasebook, this grammatical survey will also enable you to form simple sentences of your own.

Traveler's Dictionary and Index

The glossary at the end of the book is 52 pages long and is for quick reference to words and phrases. The translations are followed by phonetic transcriptions and page references, so that this glossary serves as an index as well.

Carry this phrasebook with you all the time to make the most of your stay.

CONTENTS

PRONUNCIATION GUIDE

When you begin to learn German, not only the grammatical rules may seem rather complicated to you, but German pronunciation may also cause you difficulty. This is due on the one hand to the unfamiliar spelling of German words. On the other hand, while many German sounds come quite close to English sounds, there are a number which do not exist at all in English. In spoken German the tongue and lips are generally not quite as loose as in English, and lip movement is more pronounced.

In order to help you pronounce the words and sentences in this phrasebook without having to learn the somewhat demanding phonetic symbols and rules of the "International Phonetic Association", we have decided on a compromise. Our phonetic transcriptions read largely like English words, since we have used almost exclusively letters from the Latin alphabet. The table below, together with the cassette containing specimen phrases, will enable you to understand and pronounce correctly the phonetic symbols in italics as well.

In the phonetic transcriptions you will find two different stress marks, which have been placed **after** the syllables to be emphasized. ['] indicates a main stress, while ['] denotes a secondary stress, which is weaker than a main stress. Words consisting of one syllable only have not been given stress marks.

To avoid ambiguity as to phonetic syllabication, a dot has been placed between two consecutive vowels or consonants where they are pronounced separately:

Jugendherberge [yo͞o'gənt·her'bergə]

A. Vowels and Diphthongs

Symbol	Pronunciation	German Example
ä	long vowel, similar to **a** in father and the identical sound in American English watch, doll, box	Vater [fä'tər], Straße [shträ'sə]
ä	short vowel, similar to **u** in butter, rust	Mann [män], an [än], kalt [kält]

ā	1. long vowel, similar to **ai** in fair 2. long vowel, nearest English equivalent: **a** in fate, **ai** in rain	1. Universität [ōōn'iver-zitāt'], später [shpā'tər] 2. zehn [tsān], See [zā]
ā	long vowel, nearest English equivalent: **ea** in heard, **i** in bird (see also phonetic symbol *e* below)	Öl [*ā*l]
e	short vowel, similar to **e** in met, bed or **ai** in said	Bett [bet], ändern [en'dərn]
e	short vowel, nearest English equivalent: **ea** in heard, **i** in bird, but shorter and opener (with the lips less rounded) than phonetic symbol *ā*	möchte [m*e*sh't*ə*], öffnen [*e*f'nən]
ē	long vowel, similar to **ee** in see, **e** in we, **ea** in read	die [dē], ihnen [ē'nən]
ē	long vowel, similar to **ue** in the French word revue; think of phonetic symbol ē but round your lips as much as you can!	prüfen [pr*ē*'fən], für [f*ē*r]
i	short vowel, very much like **i** in fit, hidden	bitte [bit'ə]
i	short vowel, similar to, but shorter than, phonetic symbol *ē*	stürmisch [sht*i*r'mish], fünf [f*i*nf]
ī	diphthong like **i** in white	zwei [tsvī], leihen [lī'ən]
ō	long vowel, similar to **o** in nose but rather a monophthong	holen [hō'lən], wohnen [vō'nən]
ô	short vowel, similar to **aw** in law but much shorter (like the **o** in British English got)	oft [ôft], morgen [môr'gən]
o͞o	long vowel, like the **u** in rule, the **ou** in route or the **oo** in boot	Schule [sho͞o'lə], Ruhe [ro͞o'ə]
o͝o	short vowel, similar to **oo** in book	Leitung [lī'to͝ong], Mutter [mo͝ot'ər]
oi	diphthong, similar to **oy** in boy, **oi** in void	Freund [froint], Fräulein [froi'līn]

ou	diphthong, similar to **ou** in house, **ow** in powder	Haus [hous], genau [gənou']
ə	unstressed vowel, similar to **a** in alone, fatigue	bitte [bit'ə], Abend [ä'bənt], Meter [mā'tər]
äN	nasalized vowel like in French **en**	Pension [päNsyōn']
eN	nasalized vowel like in French **pain**	Cousin [kōōzeN']
ôN	nasalized vowel like in French **on**	Salon [zälôN']

B. Consonants

Symbol	Pronunciation	German Example
b	like **b** in bell	Bett [bet], bin [bin]
d	like **d** in deep	du [dōō], Nudeln [nōō'dəln]
f	like **f** in fat	fahren [fä'rən], viel [fēl]
g	like **g** in go	geben [gā'bən], Glas [gläs]
h	like **h** in hand	haben [hä'bən], Herbst [herpst]
h	like **ch** in Scottish Lo**ch**, **J** in Spanish **J**uan	Nacht [nä*h*t], Buch [bōō*h*], Koch [kô*h*], rauchen [rou*h*'ən]
j	like **g** in gem, **j** in jealous	Gin [jin]
k	like **c** in can, **k** in kind, **ck** in pickles	kann [kän], wecken [vek'ən], Flughafen [flōōk'-häfən], genug [gənōōk'], Weg [vāk]
l	like "clear" **l** in long, lip	holen [hō'lən], Unfall [ōōn'fäl], Liter [lē'tər]
m	like **m** in more	mehr [mār], Nummer [nōōm'ər]
n	like **n** in no	nein [nīn], Panne [pän'ə]
ng	like **ng** in sing	bringen [bring'ən], Dank [dängk], Zeitung [tsī'tōong]
p	like **p** in pen	Paß [*p*äs], Abfahrt [*ä*p'-färt], gibt [gēpt], gib [gēp]

r	quite different from the usual **r** in English, though everybody will understand you if you use the **r**-sound you're familiar with. Most Germans use an **r** formed, as it seems, deep in the throat, similar to a "French **r**". Others prefer to roll their **r**'s with the tip of their tongues.	vo**r**gestern [fōr'gestərn], **R**eifen [rī'fən], Moto**r** [mō'tôr]
s	like **s** in **s**end	Au**s**fahrt [ous'färt], e**ss**en [es'ən], An**s**chluß [än'shlo͞os]
sh	like **sh** in **sh**e	**Sch**ule [sho͞o'lə], Stra**ß**e [shträ'sə], **S**port [shpôrt]
sh	similar to **h** in Hugo; if you have trouble pronouncing this unfamiliar sound, replace it by **sh**.	i**ch** [i*sh*], mö**ch**te [m*esh*'tə], dur**ch** [do͞or*sh*], geräu**ch**ert [gəroi*sh*'ərt], Ferngesprä**ch** [fern'-gəshprä*sh*]
t	like **t** in **t**ea	**T**ee [tā], Ra**d**kappe [rät'käpə], Ke**tt**e [ket'ə], Win**d** [vint]
ts	like **ts** in cu**ts**, **tes** in bi**tes**	**Z**oll [tsôl], Über**s**etzung [ēʹbərzets'o͞ong], Re**z**eption [rätseptsyōn']
tsh	like **ch** in mu**ch**	deu**tsch** [doitsh], Que**tsch**ung [kvetsh'o͞ong]
v	like **v** in **v**est	**W**agen [vä'gən], wievie**l** [vēfēl'], Ge**w**ürze [gəvirts'ə]
y	like **y** in **y**et	**j**etzt [yetst], **j**a [yä]
z	like **z** in **z**eal	**s**ind [zint], **s**agen [zä'gən], Be**s**atzung [bəzäts'o͞ong]
zh	like **s** in mea**s**ure	Orange [ōräN'zhə]

GENERAL WORDS AND PHRASES

Greetings

Good morning!	**Good afternoon!**	**Good evening!**
Guten Morgen!	Guten Tag!	Guten Abend!
goo'tən môr'gən	goo'tən täk	goo'tən ä'bənt

Hello!	**Hi!**
Guten Tag!	Hallo!
goo'tən täk	hälō'

Hello! (*in Southern Germany or Austria*)
Grüß Gott! (Grüß Sie!, Grüß dich!)
grēs gôt (grēs zē, grēs dish)

> Normally, Germans will shake hands each time they meet and each
> time they say good-bye.

*Welcome! (Glad to see you!)
Herzlich willkommen!
herts'lish vilkôm'ən

*Did you have a good trip?
Hatten Sie eine gute Reise?
hät'ən zē ī'nə goo'tə rī'zə

I'm delighted to see you.	**How are you?**
Es freut mich, *Sie (dich)* zu sehen.	Wie geht es *Ihnen (dir)?*
es froit mish, zē (dish) tsoo zā'ən	vē gāt es ē'nən (dēr)

How're you doing?	**And you?**	**How's the family?**
Wie geht's?	Und *Ihnen (dir)?*	Wie geht es Ihrer Familie?
vē gāts	oont ē'nən (dēr)	vē gāt es ē'rər fämē'lē·ə

My ... is sick.	**Did you sleep well?**
Mein(e) ... ist krank.	Haben Sie gut geschlafen?
mī'n(ə) ... ist krängk	hä'bən zē goot gəshlä'fən

Thanks, just fine.	**We're feeling fine.**
Danke, (recht) gut.	Wir fühlen uns ausgezeichnet.
däng'kə, (resht) goot	vēr fē'lən oons ousgətsīsh'nət

Thanks for your cordial welcome.
Ich danke (Wir danken) für den herzlichen Empfang.
ish däng'kə (vēr däng'kən) fēr dān herts'lishən empfäng'

Forms of Address

Mr. *(name)*	Herr *(Name)*	her (nä'mə)
sir	mein Herr	mīn her
Mrs. *(name)*	Frau *(Name)*	frou (nä'mə)
Madam	Madame, gnädige Frau	mädäm', gnä'digə frou
Miss	Fräulein	froi'līn
Ladies!	Meine Damen!	mī'nə dä'mən
Gentlemen!	Meine Herren!........	mī'nə her'ən
Ladies and Gentle-men!	Meine Damen und Her-ren!	mī'nə dä'mən ōont her'ən
Your wife	Ihre *Frau (Gattin)*	ē'rə frou (gät'in)
Your husband	Ihr *Mann (Gatte)*	ēr män (gät'ə)
Doctor *(when addressing him or her)* ...	*Herr (Frau)* Doktor ...	her (frou) dôk'tôr

Letters

Mr. Johann Schmidt .	Herrn Johann Schmidt	hern yō'hän shmit
Mrs. Barbara Schmidt	Frau Barbara Schmidt	frou bär'bärä shmit
Miss Beate Schmidt .	Fräulein (Frl.) Beate Schmidt	froi'līn bā·ä·'tə shmit
Dear Mr. Schmidt, ..	Sehr geehrter Herr S., .	zär gə·är'tər her shmit
Dear Mrs. Schmidt, .	Sehr geehrte Frau S.,	zär gə·är'tə frou shmit
Dear Miss Schmidt, .	Sehr geehrtes Frl. S., ..	zär gə·är'təs froi'līn shmit
Dear Sirs, Gentlemen, ...	Sehr geehrte Damen und Herren, ...	zär gə·är'tə dä'mən ōont her'ən
Dear Mr. Koch, *(to a respected friend)* ..	Lieber Herr Koch, ...	lē'bər her kôh
Dear Peter, ...	Lieber Peter, ...	lē'bər pä'tər
Dear Mrs. Koch, *(to a respected friend)* ..	Liebe Frau Koch, ...	lē'bə frou kôh
Dear Miss Koch, *(to a respected friend)* ..	Liebes Fräulein Koch, .	lē'bəs froi'līn kôh
Yours sincerely, Cordially yours, Kindest regards, ...	Mit freundlichen Grüßen, ...	mit froint'lishən grē'sən

Introductions

My name is ...
Ich heiße (Mein Name ist) ...
i*sh* hī'sə (mīn nä'mə ist) ...

This is my husband (my wife).
Das ist *mein Mann (meine Frau).*
däs ist mīn män (mī'nə frou)

my son	mein Sohn	mīn zōn
my daughter	meine Tochter	mī'nə tôh'tər
my friend *(male)*	mein Freund	mīn froint
my friend *(female)* ..	meine Freundin	mī'nə froin'din
my friends	meine Freunde	mī'nə froin'də

> *In German, a man will speak of his girl friend – and only his girl friend*
> *– as „meine Freundin". A woman will speak of her boy friend – and*
> *only her boy friend – as „mein Freund". They will refer to non-*
> *intimate friends as „mein Bekannter" [mīn bəkän'tər] (male) or*
> *„meine Bekannte" [mī'nə bəkän'tə] (female).*

my fiancé	mein Verlobter	mīn ferlōp'tər
my fiancée	meine Verlobte	mī'nə ferlōp'tə

Pleased to meet you. (How do you do?)
Freut mich sehr. (Sehr erfreut.)
froit mi*sh* zār (zār erfroit')

Do you live here?
Wohnen Sie hier?
vō'nən zē hēr

Are you Mr. (Mrs., Miss) Schmidt?
Sind Sie *Herr (Frau, Fräulein)* Schmidt?
zint zē her (frou, froi'līn) shmit

What is your name, please?
Wie ist Ihr Name, bitte?
vē ist ēr nä'mə, bit'ə

What's your name?
Wie heißen Sie (Wie heißt du?)
vē hī'sən zē (vē hīst dōō)

Where are you from?
Woher kommen Sie?
vō'hār kôm'ən zē

Have you been here long?
Sind Sie schon lange hier?
zint zē shōn läng'ə hēr

Do you like it here?
Gefällt es *Ihnen (dir)* hier?
gəfelt' es ē'nən (dēr) hēr

I (We) like it very much.
Mir (uns) gefällt es sehr.
mēr (ōōns) gəfelt' es zār

Are you here alone?
Sind Sie (Bist du) allein hier?
zint zē (bist dōō) älīn' hēr

I'm here on vacation.
Ich verbringe hier meinen Urlaub.
i*sh* ferbring'ə hēr mī'nən ōōr'loup

Where do you work?
Wo *arbeiten Sie (arbeitest du)?*
vō är′bītən zē (är′bītəst dōō)

What do you do for a living?
Was sind Sie von Beruf?
väs zint zē fôn bərōōf′

What are you studying? (What's your major?)
Was studieren Sie?
väs shtōōdē′rən zē

Germans differentiate between school pupils – „Schüler" [shē′lər] – and students at an institute of higher learning – „Studenten" [shtōōden′tən]. The word „studieren" (to study) applies only to university students – pupils do not study, they learn (lernen [ler′nən]).

Got some time?
Haben Sie noch etwas Zeit?
hä′bən zē nôh et′väs tsīt

Shall we go to the …?
Wollen wir *zum (zur)* … gehen?
vôl′ən vēr tsōōm (tsōōr) … gā′ən

What time shall we meet?
Wann treffen wir uns?
vän tref′ən vēr ōōns

Please leave me alone!
Lassen Sie mich bitte in Ruhe.
läs′ən zē mish bit′ə in rōō′ə

A Visit

Is Mr. (Mrs., Miss) … at home?
Ist *Herr (Frau, Fräulein)* … zu Hause?
ist her (frou, froi′līn) … tsōō hou′zə

Could I speak to Mr. (Mrs., Miss) …?
Kann ich *Herrn (Frau, Fräulein)* … sprechen?
kän ish hern (frou, froi′līn) … shpresh′ən

Does Mr. (Mrs., Miss) … live here?
Wohnt *Herr (Frau, Fräulein)* … hier?
vōnt her (frou, froi′līn) … hēr

I'm looking for …
Ich suche …
ish zōō′hə …

When will he (she) be home?
Wann ist *er (sie)* zu Hause?
vän ist ār (zē) tsōō hou′zə

I'll drop by again later.
Ich komme später noch einmal wieder.
ish kôm′ə shpā′tər nôh īn′mäl vē′dər

When can I (shall we) come?
Wann *kann ich (sollen wir)* kommen?
vän kän ish (zôl′ən vēr) kôm′ən

I'd (We'd) love to come.
Ich komme (Wir kommen) sehr gerne.
i*sh* kôm′ə (vēr kôm′ən) zär ger′nə

*Come in!	***Please have a seat!**	***Come right in.**
Herein!	Bitte nehmen Sie Platz!	Treten Sie näher.
herīn′	bit′ə nä′mən zē pl*ä*ts	trä′tən zē nä′ər

*Just a minute, please.   **Thanks so much for the invitation.**
Einen Augenblick, bitte.   Vielen Dank für die Einladung.
ī′nən ou′gənblik, bit′ə   fē′lən d*ä*ngk fēr dē īn′lädoong

Am I bothering you?   **Please don't go to a lot of trouble.**
Störe ich?   Bitte machen Sie sich keine Umstände.
sht*ä*′rə i*sh*   bit′ə m*ä*′hən zē zi*sh* kī′nə oom′shtendə

*What'll you have? (What may I offer you?)   ***Would you like …?**
Was darf ich Ihnen anbieten?   Möchten Sie …?
väs därf i*sh* ē′nən *ä*n′bētən   m*esh*′tən zē …

Mr. (Mrs.) Schmidt sends you *his (her) regards (love)*.
Ich soll Sie von *Herrn (Frau)* Schmidt grüßen.
i*sh* zōl zē fôn hern (frou) shmit gr*ē*′sən

I'm afraid I've got to go now.
Ich muß jetzt leider gehen.
i*sh* moos jetst lī′dər gā′ən

Thanks so much for *a lovely evening (coming)*.
Vielen Dank für *den netten Abend (Ihren Besuch)*.
fē′lən d*ä*ngk fēr dān net′ən *ä*′bənt (ē′rən bəzooh′)

Please give *Mr. (Mrs.)* … my best regards.
Grüßen Sie bitte *Herrn (Frau)* … schön von mir.
gr*ē*′sən zē bit′ə hern (frou) … sh*ä*n fôn mēr

I'll tell *him (her)* you said hello.
Ich werd's *ihm (ihr)* ausrichten.
i*sh* verts ēm (ēr) ous′ri*sh*tən

I hope we'll meet again soon!
Ich hoffe, wir sehen uns bald wieder!
i*sh* hôf′ə, vēr zä′ən oons bält vē′dər

Farewells

*German farewells vary from region to region. „Auf Wiedersehen"
[ouf vē'dərzā·ən] is always acceptable, but Northern Germans are
more likely to say „Tschüß" [tshis], Southern Germans and Austrians „Servus" [zer'vōōs] when they say good-bye to a good friend.*

Good-bye!
Auf Wiedersehen!
ouf vē'dərzā·ən

See you soon!
Bis bald!
bis bält

Good night!
Gute Nacht!
gōō'tə näht

See you tomorrow!
Bis Morgen!
bis môr'gən

All the best!
Alles Gute!
äl'əs gōō'tə

*Have a good trip!
Gute Reise!
gōō'tə rī'zə

I'd like to say good-bye!
Ich möchte mich verabschieden!
ish mesh'tə mish feräp'shēdən

I'm afraid we have to go.
Wir müssen leider gehen.
vēr mis'ən lī'dər gā'ən

Thanks so much for coming.
Ich danke für Ihren Besuch.
ish däng'kə fēr ē'rən bəzōōh'

Come again soon!
Kommen Sie bald wieder!
kô'mən zē bält vē'dər

When can we get together again?
Wann sehen wir uns wieder?
vän zā'ən vēr ōōns vē'dər

I'll give you a call tomorrow.
Ich rufe morgen an.
ish rōō'fə môr'gən än

Can I give you a lift home?
Darf ich Sie nach Hause bringen?
därf ish zē näh hou'zə bring'ən

It's pretty late.
Es ist schon spät.
es ist shōn shpät

Give ... my best!
Grüßen Sie ...!
grē'sən zē ...

Thanks very much.
Vielen Dank!
fē'lən dängk

I had a lovely time.
Es war sehr schön.
es vär zār shän

I enjoyed myself very much.
Es hat mir sehr gut gefallen.
es hät mēr zār gōōt gəfäl'ən

I'll *take you to (give you a lift to)* the ...
Ich bringe *Sie (dich)* noch *zum (zur)* ...
ish bring'ə zē (dish) nôh tsōōm (tsōōr) ...

General Questions

When?	Why?	What?	What kind of ...?
Wann?	Warum?	Was?	Was für ...?
vän	väroom'	väs	väs fēr ...

Which?	To whom?	With whom?	Whom?
Welche(r)?	Wem?	Mit wem?	Wen?
vel'shə(r)	vām	mit vām	vān

Who?	Why? (How come?)	How?	How long?
Wer?	Weshalb?	Wie?	Wie lange?
vār	ves·hälp'	vē	vē läng'ə

How much (many)?	Where?	Where from?	Where to?	What for?
Wieviel? (Wie viele?)	Wo?	Woher?	Wohin?	Wozu?
vēfēl' (vē fēl'ə)	vō	vōhār'	vōhin'	vōtsoo'

Is ... allowed here?	Can I ...?	Do you need ...?
Darf man hier ...?	Kann ich ...?	Brauchen Sie ...?
därf män hēr ...	kän ish ...	brou'hən zē ...

Have you (got) ...?	When can I get ...?
Haben Sie ...?	Wann kann ich ... bekommen?
hä'bən zē ...	vän kän ish ... bəkôm'ən

What time do you open (close)?	What would you like? (What can I do for you?, May I help you?)
Wann wird geöffnet (geschlossen)?	Was wünschen Sie?
vän virt gə·ef'nət (gəshlôs'ən)	väs vin'shən zē

What's that?	What happened?	What does that mean?
Was ist das?	Was ist geschehen?	Was bedeutet das?
väs ist däs	väs ist gəshā'ən	väs bədoi'tət däs

How much does that cost?	What are you looking for?
Was (Wieviel) kostet das?	Was suchen Sie (suchst du)?
väs (vē'fēl) kôs'tət däs	väs zoo'hən zē (zoohst doo)

Whose is that?	*Whom do you wish to see?
Wem gehört das?	Zu wem möchten Sie?
vām gəhärt' däs	tsoo vām mesh'tən zē

Who's there?	Who can (Can anyone) ...?	What do you call ...?
Wer ist da?	Wer kann ...?	Wie heißt ...?
vār ist dä	vār kän ...	vē hīst ...

What's your name?
Wie *heißen Sie (heißt du)?*
vē hī'sən zē (hīst doo)

How do I get to ...?
Wie komme ich *nach (zum, zur, bis)* ...?
vē kôm'ə i*sh* näh (tsoom, tsoor, bis) ...

How does that work?
Wie funktioniert das?
vē foongk'tsyōnērt' däs

How long does it take?
Wie lange dauert es?
vē läng'ə dou'ərt es

How much do I get?
Wieviel bekomme ich?
vē'fēl bəkôm'ə i*sh*

How much is it?
Wieviel ist es?
vē'fēl ist es

Where *can I find* ... *(is ... located)?*
Wo befindet sich ...?
vō bəfin'dət zi*sh* ...

Where *is (are)* ...?
Wo *ist (sind)* ...?
vō ist (zint) ...

Where's the nearest ...?
Wo ist *der (die, das)* nächste ...?
vō ist dār (dē, däs) nä*sh*'stə ...

Where can I ...?
Wo kann ich ...?
vō kän i*sh* ...

Where can I get (find) ...?
Wo bekomme ich ...?
vō bəkôm'ə i*sh* ...

Where *is (are)* there ...?
Wo gibt es ...?
vō gēpt es ...

Where do you live?
Wo *wohnen Sie (wohnst du)?*
vō vō'nən zē (vōnst doo)

Where are we?
Wo sind wir?
vō zint vēr

Where do you come from?
Woher *kommen Sie (kommst du)?*
vō'hār kôm'ən zē (kômst doo)

Where are you going?
Wohin *gehen Sie (gehst du)?*
vō'hin gā'ən zē (gāst doo)

„Gehen" – *to go" always refers to getting somewhere on foot. If
you want to know where someone is going in a car, train, bus, or
other ground vehicle, you should ask:* „Wohin fahren Sie?" [vō'hin
fä'rən zē].

Where does this *road (path)* lead?
Wohin führt *diese Straße (dieser Weg)?*
vō'hin fērt dē'zə shträ'sə (dē'zər vāk)

Wishes, Requests

> *The German word „bitte" [bit'ə], like the English "please", is one of those all-purpose words that can mean many things. Probably the most important meanings are "please", "excuse me!", "here you are!" and "you're welcome". Generally the context makes the meaning clear – but remember, „Bitte" is also a noun – meaning "request".*

Would you please *bring (give, show)* me ...?
Bringen (Geben, Zeigen) Sie mir bitte ...
bring'ən (gā'bən, tsī'gən) zē mēr bit'ə ...

Would you please tell me ...?
Sagen Sie mir bitte ...
zä'gən zē mēr bit'ə ...

Would you please *get (fetch)* ...?
Holen Sie bitte ...
hō'lən zē bit'ə ...

Beg your pardon? (Say what?)
Wie bitte?
vē bit'ə

What can I do for you? (May I help you?)
Was wünschen Sie?
väs vin'shən zē

I'd (We'd) like ...
Ich hätte (Wir hätten) gern ...
ish het'ə (vēr het'ən) gern ...

I need ...
Ich brauche ...
ish brou'hə ...

I'd rather have ...
Ich möchte lieber ...
ish mesh'tə lē'bər ...

Could I *have (get)* ...?
Kann ich ... *haben (bekommen)?*
kän ish ... hä'bən (bəkôm'ən)

Please help me!
Bitte helfen Sie mir!
bit'ə hel'fən zē mēr

Certainly!
Bitte sehr.
bit'ə zār

Allow me? (Excuse me?)
Gestatten Sie?
gəshtät'ən zē

Get well soon!
Gute Besserung!
gōō'tə bes'ərōōng

All the best!
Alles Gute!
äl'əs gōō'tə

Have *a good time (fun)*!
Viel *Vergnügen (Spaß)*!
fēl fergnē'gən (shpäs)

I wish you ...
Ich wünsche *Ihnen (dir)* ...
ish vin'shə ē'nən (dēr) ...

Thanks

Thanks (Thank you) very much!
Danke *sehr (schön)!*
däng′kə zār (shän)

Thanks a lot!
Vielen (herzlichen) Dank!
fē′lən (herts′lishən) dängk

Thank you too!
Danke, gleichfalls!
däng′kə, glīsh′fäls

No, thanks.
Nein, danke.
nīn, däng′kə

I'm very grateful to you.
Ich bin *Ihnen (dir)* sehr dankbar.
ish bin ē′nən (dēr) zār dängk′bär

You're welcome.
Bitte sehr.
bit′ə zār

Thanks very much for *your help (all your trouble)!*
Vielen Dank für *Ihre Hilfe (Ihre Bemühungen)!*
fē′lən dängk fēr ē′rə hil′fə (ē′rə bəmē′ōōngən)

***I (We)* thank you so much for ...**
Ich danke (Wir danken) Ihnen *sehr (vielmals)* für ...
ish däng′kə (vēr däng′kən) ē′nən zār (fēl′mäls) fēr ...

Thanks a million!
Tausend Dank!
tou′zənt dängk

Don't mention it.
Keine Ursache.
kī′nə ōōr′zähə

Glad to do it.
Gern geschehen.
gern gəshā′ən

Yes and No

Yes.
Ja.
yä

Certainly.
Gewiß.
gəvis′

Of course.
Selbstverständlich.
zelpst′fershtent′lish

I'd be glad to.
Sehr gern.
zār gern

Good! (Fine!)
(Sehr) Gut!
(zār) gōōt

Right!
Richtig!
rish′tish

Terrific!
Prima!
prē′mä

With pleasure!
Mit Vergnügen!
mit fergnē′gən

No.
Nein.
nīn

Never.
Niemals!
nē′mäls

Nothing.
Nichts!
nishts

Certainly not! (No way!)
Auf keinen Fall!
ouf kī′nən fäl

Out of the question!
Kommt gar nicht in Frage!
kômt gär nisht in frä′gə

I'd rather not!
Lieber nicht.
lē′bər nisht

I *don't want to (can't)*.
Ich *will (kann)* nicht.
ish vil (kän) nisht

***Perhaps (Maybe)*.**
Vielleicht.
filīsht′

Probably.
Wahrscheinlich.
värshīn′lish

Pardon

Excuse me!
Entschuldigung!
entshŏŏl′digŏŏng

I beg your pardon!
Verzeihung!
fertsī′ŏŏng

Please excuse me!
Entschuldigen Sie bitte!
entshŏŏl′digən zē bit′ə

I'm very sorry.
Es tut mir sehr leid.
es tōōt mēr zār līt

I'm extremely sorry.
Es ist mir sehr unangenehm.
es ist mēr zār ōōn′än·gənäm`

I must apologize to you.
Ich muß mich bei *Ihnen (dir)* entschuldigen.
ish mōōs mish bī ē′nən (dēr) entshŏŏl′digən

Please don't be angry!
Nehmen Sie es bitte nicht übel!
nā′mən zē es bit′ə nisht ē′bəl

Please forgive me!
Bitte verzeihen Sie mir!
bit′ə fertsī′ən zē mēr

Regrets

What a pity! (Too bad!)
(Wie) Schade!
vē shä′də

To my (great) regret ...
Zu meinem (großen) Bedauern ...
tsōō mī′nəm (grō′sən) bədou′ərn ...

I'm so very sorry about that.
Ich bedauere das sehr.
ish bədou′ərə däs zär

What a shame that ...
Es ist sehr schade, daß ...
es ist zär shä′də, däs ...

I'm afraid that isn't possible.
Es ist leider unmöglich!
es ist lī′dər ōōnmäg′lish

I'm afraid that can't be done.
Das geht leider nicht.
däs gāt lī′dər nisht

Congratulations and Condolences

Congratulations!
Ich gratuliere *Ihnen (dir)*.
ish grä′tŏŏlē′rə ē′nən (dēr)

I congratulate you ...
Ich beglückwünsche *Sie (dich)* ...
ish bəglik′vinshə zē (dish) ...

on your birthday .... zum Geburtstag ...... tsōōm gəbŏŏrts′täk
on your marriage .... zur Vermählung ...... tsōōr fermä′lŏŏng

---

Northern Germans prefer „Glückwunsch" [glik′vŏŏnsh] *to Southern German* „Gratulation" [grä′tōōlätsyōn′], *and* „beglückwünschen" [bəglik′vinshən] *to* „gratulieren" [grä′tōōlē′rən].

All the best! (Best wishes!)
Herzlichen Glückwunsch!
herts'lishən glĭk'vōōnsh

Happy birthday!
Herzlichen Glückwunsch zum Geburtstag!
herts'lishən glĭk'vōōnsh tsōōm
gəbōōrts'täk

Merry Christmas!
Frohe Weihnachten! (Frohes Fest!)
frō'ə vī'nähtən (frō'əs fest)

Happy New Year!
Ein glückliches neues Jahr! (Prosit Neujahr!)
īn glĭk'lishəs noi'əs yär (prō'zit noi'yär)

I (We) wish you ...
Ich wünsche (Wir wünschen) Ihnen (dir) ...
ish vin'shə (vēr vin'shən) ē'nən (dēr) ...

Good luck!
Viel Glück!
fēl glĭk

Much success!
Viel Erfolg!
fēl erfôlk'

All the best!
Alles Gute!
äl'əs gōō'tə

My sincerest condolences.
Mein aufrichtiges Beileid.
mīn ouf'rishtigəs bī'līt

Our warmest sympathy.
Unsere herzliche Anteilnahme.
ōōn'zərə herts'lishə än'tīlnä'mə

Complaints

I'd like to register a complaint.
Ich möchte mich beschweren.
ish mesh'tə mish bəshvār'ən

I'd like to speak to the manager.
Ich möchte den Geschäftsführer sprechen.
ish mesh'tə dān gəshefts'fērər shpresh'ən

I'm afraid I'll have to make a complaint about ...
Ich muß mich leider über ... beschweren.
ish mōōs mish lī'dər ē'bər ... bəshvār'ən

... is (are) missing ...
Es *fehlt (fehlen)* ...
es fält (fā'lən) ...

I haven't got any ...
Ich habe kein(e, -en) ...
ish hä'bə kīn (kī'nə, kī'nən) ...

... is broken.
... ist kaputt.
... ist käpōōt'

... doesn't work.
... funktioniert nicht.
... fōōngk'tsyōnērt' nisht

... is *not in order (out of order)*.
... ist *nicht in Ordnung (außer Betrieb)*.
... ist nisht in ôrd'nōōng (ou'sər bətrēp')

Communication

Do you speak English?
Sprechen Sie Englisch?
shpre*sh*' ən zē eng'lish

German?
Deutsch?
doitsh

French?
Französisch?
fränts*ā*' zish

Can you understand me?
Verstehen Sie mich?
fershtā' ən zē mi*sh*

I understand.
Ich verstehe.
i*sh* fershtā' ə

I can't understand a thing.
Ich verstehe nichts.
i*sh* fershtā' ə ni*sh*ts

Would you please speak a little slower?
Sprechen Sie bitte etwas langsamer.
shpre*sh*' ən zē bit' ə et' väs läng' zämər

What do you call ... in German?
Was heißt ... auf Deutsch?
v*ä*s hīst ... ouf doitsh

How do you say that in German?
Wie heißt das auf Deutsch?
vē hīst d*ä*s ouf doitsh

What does that mean?
Was bedeutet das?
v*ä*s bədoit' ət d*ä*s

I beg your pardon? (Say what?)
Wie bitte?
vē bit' ə

How do you pronounce this word?
Wie spricht man dieses Wort aus?
vē shpri*sh*t m*ä*n dē' zəs vôrt ous

Would you please translate this for me?
Könnten Sie mir das bitte übersetzen?
k*en*' tən zē mēr d*ä*s bit' ə *ē*bərzets' ən

Would you please write that down for me?
Schreiben Sie mir das bitte auf.
shrī' bən zē mēr d*ä*s bit' ə ouf

Would you spell that, please?
Buchstabieren Sie das bitte.
bōō*h*' sht*ä*bēr' ən zē d*ä*s bit' ə

Weather

How's the weather going to be?
Wie wird das Wetter?
vē virt däs vet'ər

What's the weather report?
Was meldet der Wetterbericht?
väs mel'dət dār vet'ərbərisht

The barometer's *rising (falling)*.
Das Barometer *steigt (fällt)*.
däs bärōmā'tər shtīkt (felt)

We're going to have ...
Wir bekommen ...
vēr bəkôm'ən ...

fine weather	schönes Wetter	shȫ'nəs vet'ər
bad weather	schlechtes Wetter	shlesh'təs vet'ər
changeable weather ..	wechselhaftes Wetter ..	vek'səlhäf'təs vet'ər

It's going to stay nice.
Es bleibt schön.
es blīpt shȫn

Is it going to *rain (snow)*?
Wird es *regnen (schneien)*?
virt es rāg'nən (shnī'ən)

How are the road conditions between here and ...?
Wie ist der Straßenzustand nach ...?
vē ist dār shträ'səntsoo'shtänt näh ...

It's very slippery.
Es ist sehr glatt.
es ist zār glät

– very hot.
– sehr heiß.
– zār hīs

– *foggy (misty)*.
– neblig.
– nāb'lish

– very muggy.
– sehr schwül.
– zār shvēl

– very windy.
– sehr windig.
– zār vin'dish

– stormy.
– stürmisch.
– shtir'mish

What's the temperature?
Wieviel Grad haben wir?
vē'fēl grät hä'bən vēr

It's ... *above (below)* zero.
Es ist ... Grad *über (unter)* Null.
es ist ... grät ē'bər (oon'tər) nool

It's *cold (hot)*.
Es ist *kalt (warm)*.
es ist kält (värm)

I'm *cold (hot)*.
Mir ist *kalt (warm)*.
mēr ist kält (värm)

Often, Germans will say „warm" rather than „heiß" (hot) when discussing meals or the weather.
***Careful:** Don't ever say „ich bin kalt" [ish bin kält] when you mean „mir ist kalt" [mēr ist kält]. You may find yourself unwittingly telling your partner about your love life!*

The weather's going to change.	**It'll be nice again.**
Das Wetter wird sich ändern.	Das Wetter wird wieder schön.
däs vet′ər virt zish en′dərn	däs vet′ər virt vē′dər shän

The wind has dropped.	**The wind has changed.**
Der Wind hat sich gelegt.	Der Wind hat sich gedreht.
där vint hät zish gəläkt′	där vint hät zish gədrāt′

We're going to have a thunderstorm.	**There's going to be a storm.**
Wir werden ein Gewitter bekommen.	Es gibt Sturm.
vēr vär′dən īn gəvit′ər bəkôm′ən	es gēpt shtoorm

Is the fog going to lift?	**It's stopped raining.**
Wird sich der Nebel auflösen?	Es hat aufgehört zu regnen.
virt zish där nā′bəl ouf′lāzən	es hät ouf′gəhärt tsoo rāg′nən

The sun is shining.	**The sun is burning hot.**	**The sky is clear.**
Die Sonne scheint.	Die Sonne brennt.	Der Himmel ist klar.
dē zôn′ə shīnt	dē zôn′ə brent	där him′əl ist klär

German temperatures are always measured in degrees Celsius [tsel′sē·oos] *Here's a handy conversion table:*

> Fahrenheit to Celsius: $(x-32)$ $5/9 = °C$
> Celsius to Fahrenheit: $32 + 9/5 x = °F$

---

air	die Luft	looft
atmospheric pressure	der Luftdruck	looft′drook
barometer	das Barometer	bärōmā′tər
blizzard	der Schneesturm	shnā′shtoorm
climate	das Klima	klē′mä
cloud	die Wolke	vôl′kə
cloudburst	der Wolkenbruch	vôl′kənbrooh
cloud cover,		
cloudy skies	die Bewölkung	bəvel′koong
cloudy	bewölkt	bəvelkt′
dawn	die (Morgen)Däm-merung	(môr′gən)dem′ə-roong
dew	der Tau	tou
draft	der Luftzug	loof tsook
dusk	die (Abend)Dämmerung	(ä′bənt)dem′əroong

fog	der Nebel	nä′bəl
frost	der Frost	frôst
hail	der Hagel	hä′gəl
heat	die Hitze	hits′ə
high pressure (system)	das Hoch	hō*h*
ice	das Eis	īs
icy road	das Glatteis	glät′īs
it's freezing	es friert	es frērt
it's hailing	es hagelt	es hä′gəlt
it's raining	es regnet	es rāg′nət
it's snowing	es schneit	es shnīt
it's thawing	es taut	es tout
it's windy	es ist windig	es ist vin′di*sh*
lightning	der Blitz	blits
low pressure (system)	das Tief	tēf
mist	der Nebel	nä′bəl
moon	der Mond	mōnt
north (east) wind	*Nord(Ost)*wind	nôrt′(ôst′)vint
precipitation	der Niederschlag	nē′dərshläk
road conditions	der Straßenzustand	shträ′səntsoō′shtänt
shower	der Regenschauer	rā′gənshou′ər
snow	der Schnee	shnā
snow flurries	das Schneegestöber	shnā′gəsht*ā*bər
south (west) wind	*Süd(West)*wind	s*ē*t′(vest′)vint
star	der Stern	shtern
storm	der Sturm	shtoōrm
sun	die Sonne	zôn′ə
sunrise	der Sonnenaufgang	zôn′ənouf′gäng
sunset	der Sonnenuntergang	zôn′ənoōn′tərgäng
temperature	die Temperatur	tempər*ä*toōr′
thaw	das Tauwetter	tou′vetər
thunder	der Donner	dôn′ər
thunderstorm	das Gewitter	gəvit′ər
weather	das Wetter	vet′ər
weather prediction	die Wettervorhersage	vet′ərfōrhär′zägə
weather report	der Wetterbericht	vet′ərbəri*sh*t
wind	der Wind	vint

Numbers

Cardinal Numbers

0	.... null	.....	noōl
1	.... eins	.....	īns
2	.... zwei	....	tsvī
3	.... drei	.....	drī
4	.... vier	.....	fēr

5	.... fünf	.....	fĭnf
6	.... sechs	....	zeks
7	.... sieben	..	zē'bən
8	.... acht	.....	*ä*ht
9	.... neun	....	noin

10	.... zehn	tsān
11	.... elf	elf
12	.... zwölf	tsvelf
13	.... dreizehn	drī'tsān
14	.... vierzehn	fēr'tsān
15	.... fünfzehn	fĭnf'tsān
16	.... sechzehn	ze*sh*'tsān
17	.... siebzehn	zēp'tsān
18	.... achtzehn	*ä*h'tsān
19	.... neunzehn	noin'tsān
20	.... zwanzig	tsv*ä*n'tsi*sh*
21	.... einundzwanzig	īn'ŏŏntsv*ä*n'tsi*sh*
22	.... zweiundzwanzig	tsvī'ŏŏntsv*ä*n'tsi*sh*
23	.... dreiundzwanzig	drī'ŏŏntsv*ä*n'tsi*sh*
30	.... dreißig	drī'si*sh*
40	.... vierzig	fēr'tsi*sh*
50	.... fünfzig	fĭnf'tsi*sh*
60	.... sechzig	ze*sh*'tsi*sh*
70	.... siebzig	zēp'tsi*sh*
80	.... achtzig	*ä*h'tsi*sh*
90	.... neunzig	noin'tsi*sh*
100	.... (ein)hundert	(īn)hŏŏn'dərt
200	.... zweihundert	tsvī'hŏŏndərt
1 000	.... (ein)tausend	(īn)tou'zənt

When writing numbers in German, the function of periods and commas is reversed from the English function. Commas are used in decimals, and periods in numbers of four or more digits. Thus 1,000 – one thousand – becomes 1.000 – eintausend – in German, and 1.5 – one point five–is translated as 1,5 – eins-komma-fünf [īns kôm'ä fĭnf].

2.000	zweitausend	tsvī'touzənt
10.000	zehntausend	tsān'touzənt
1.000.000	eine Million	ī'nə milyōn'
1.000.000.000	eine Milliarde	ī'nə milyär'də

Ordinal Numbers

> German expresses ordinal numbers by tacking on a period after the number, thus 1st (first) becomes German 1. (erste [ers'tə]).

1.	...... erste	ers'tə	**6.**	..... sechste ..	zeks'tə
2.	...... zweite ...	tsvī'tə	**7.**	..... siebte ...	zēp'tə
3.	...... dritte	drit'ə	**8.**	..... achte	äh'tə
4.	...... vierte ...	fēr'tə	**9.**	..... neunte ...	noin'tə
5.	...... fünfte ...	fīnf'tə	**10.**	..... zehnte ...	tsān'tə

11.	.... elfte	elf'tə
12.	.... zwölfte	tsvelf'tə
13.	.... dreizehnte	drī'tsäntə
14.	.... vierzehnte	fēr'tsäntə
15.	.... fünfzehnte	fīnf'tsäntə
16.	.... sechzehnte	zesh'tsäntə
17.	.... siebzehnte	zēp'tsäntə
18.	.... achtzehnte	äh'tsäntə
19.	.... neunzehnte	noin'tsäntə
20.	.... zwanzigste	tsvän'tsishstə
21.	.... einundzwanzigste	īn'ŏontsvän'tsishstə
22.	.... zweiundzwanzigste	tsvī'ŏontsvän'tsishstə
23.	.... dreiundzwanzigste	drī'ŏontsvän'tsishstə
30.	.... dreißigste	drī'sishstə
40.	.... vierzigste	fēr'tsishstə
50.	.... fünfzigste	fīnf'tsishstə
60.	.... sechzigste	zesh'tsishstə
70.	.... siebzigste	zēp'tsishstə
80.	.... achtzigste	äh'tsishstə
90.	.... neunzigste	noin'tsishstə
100.	.... hundertste	hŏon'dərt·stə
200.	.... zweihundertste	tsvī'hŏon'dərt·stə
1.000.	.... tausendste	tou'zənt·stə
2.000.	.... zweitausendste	tsvī'tou'zənt·stə
10.000.	.... zehntausendste	tsān'tou'zənt·stə
1.000.000.	.... millionste	milyōn'stə

Time

What time is it?
Wie spät ist es?
vē shpät ist es

Have you got the exact time?
Haben Sie die genaue Zeit?
hä'bən zē dē gənou'ə tsīt

It's one o'clock.
Es ist ein Uhr.
es ist īn ōōr

It's about two o'clock.
Es ist ungefähr zwei Uhr.
es ist ōōn'gəfār tsvī ōōr

It's exactly three o'clock.
Es ist genau drei Uhr.
es ist gənou' drī ōōr

It's quarter past five.
Es ist Viertel nach fünf.
es ist fir'təl näh fïnf

It's half past seven.
Es ist halb acht.
es ist hälp äht

It's quarter to nine.
Es ist drei Viertel neun.
es ist drī fir'təl noin

It's five (minutes) past four.
Es ist fünf (Minuten) nach vier.
es ist fïnf (minōō'tən) näh fēr

It's ten (minutes) to eight.
Es ist zehn (Minuten) vor acht.
es ist tsän (minōō'tən) fōr äht

In German, fractions generally relate to the coming hour rather than the past one. Thus "half past seven" in German is expressed as „halb acht". "Quarter past seven" can be expressed as „Viertel acht", but „Viertel nach sieben" is more idiomatic. "Quarter to nine" can be expressed either as „Viertel vor neun" or „drei Viertel neun".

When?	**At *ten o'clock (10 : 00)*.**	**At eleven sharp.**
Wann?	Um *zehn Uhr (10.00)*.	Pünktlich um elf.
vän	ōōm tsän ōōr	pïngkt'lish ōōm elf

At *half-past nine (nine-thirty)*.
Um *halb zehn (neun Uhr dreißig)*.
ōōm hälp tsän (noin ōōr drī'sish)

At eight-fifteen P.M.
Um *Viertel nach acht abends
(zwanzig Uhr fünfzehn)*.
ōōm fir'təl näh äht ä'bənts
(tsvän'tsish ōōr fïnf'tsän)

From eight to nine A.M.
Von acht bis neun Uhr morgens.
fôn äht bis noin ōōr môr'gəns

At five P.M.
Um fünf Uhr nachmittags.
ōōm fïnf ōōr näh'mitäks'

Between ten and twelve A.M.
Zwischen zehn und zwölf Uhr vormittags.
tsvish'ən tsän ōont tsvelf ōor fōr'mitäks'

At seven P.M.
Um sieben Uhr abends.
ōom zē'bən ōor ä'bənts

In two hours.
In zwei Stunden.
in tsvī shtōōn'dən

Not before seven.
Nicht vor sieben Uhr.
nisht fōr zē'bən ōor

It's still too early.
Es ist noch zu früh.
es ist nôh tsōō frē

In a half an hour.
In einer halben Stunde.
in ī'nər häl'bən shtōōn'də

Shortly after eight.
Kurz nach acht Uhr.
kōorts näh äht ōor

It's (too) late.
Es ist (zu) spät.
es ist (tsōō) shpāt

Is this clock right?
Geht diese Uhr richtig?
gāt dē'zə ōor rish'tish

It's too *fast (slow)*.
Sie geht *vor (nach)*.
zē gāt fōr (näh)

Times of the Day

During the day.
Am Tage.
äm tä'gə

In the morning.
Morgens.
môr'gəns

During the morning.
Vormittags.
fōr'mitäks

At noon.
Mittags.
mit'äks

Around noon.
Gegen Mittag.
gā'gən mit'äk

In the afternoon.
Nachmittags.
näh'mitäks

In the evening.
Abends.
ä'bənts

At night.
Nachts.
nähts

At midnight.
Um Mitternacht.
ōom mit'ərnäht

Daily (Every day).
Täglich.
tāk'lish

Hourly (Every hour).
Stündlich.
shtint'lish

The day before yesterday.
Vorgestern.
fōr'gestərn

Yesterday.
Gestern.
ges'tərn

Today.
Heute.
hoi'tə

Tomorrow.
Morgen.
môr'gən

Tomorrow morning.
Morgen früh.
môr'gən frē

The day after tomorrow.
Übermorgen.
ē'bərmôrgən

A week from now.
In einer Woche.
in ī'nər vô'hə

A week from Wednesday.
Mittwoch in acht Tagen.
mit'vôh in äht tä'gən

Two weeks from now.
In vierzehn Tagen.
in fēr'tsän tä'gən

This *morning (afternoon, evening)*.
Heute *morgen (nachmittag, abend)*.
hoi'tə môr'gən (näh'mitäk, ä'bənt)

Tonight.
Heute nacht.
hoi'tə näht

This noon.	**A month ago.**	**For the last ten days.**
Heute Mittag.	Vor einem Monat.	Seit zehn Tagen.
hoi'tə mit'äk	fõr ī'nəm mō'nät	zīt tsän tä'gən

Within a week.	*Last (Next) year.*
Innerhalb einer Woche.	*Voriges (Nächstes) Jahr.*
in'ərhälp ī'nər vô'hə	fõr'igəs (näsh'stəs) yär

Every year (Annually).	**Every week (Weekly).**	**From time to time.**
Jedes Jahr.	Jede Woche.	Von Zeit zu Zeit.
yā'dəs yär	yā'də vô'hə	fôn tsīt tsoo tsīt

Now and then.	**About this time.**	**At the moment.**
Ab und zu.	Um diese Zeit.	Zur Zeit.
äp oont tsoo	oom dē'zə tsīt	tsoor tsīt

During this time (Meanwhile).	**This coming weekend.**
Während dieser Zeit.	Am kommenden Wochenende.
vä'rənt dē'zər tsīt	äm kôm'əndən vô'hənen'də

a little while ago	vor kurzem	fõr koor'tsəm
any time	jederzeit	yä'dərtsīt'
earlier	früher	frē'ər
later	später	shpä'tər
now	jetzt	yetst
on time	pünktlich	pingkt'lish
previously (before) ...	vorher	fõr'här
recently	neulich	noi'lish
since	seit	zīt
sometimes	manchmal	mänsh'mäl
soon	bald	bält
temporarily (for the time being)	vorläufig	fõr'loi'fish
until	bis	bis
second	die Sekunde	zəkoon'də
minute	die Minute	minoo'tə
hour	die Stunde	shtoon'də
day	der Tag	täk
week	die Woche	vô'hə
month	der Monat	mō'nät
year	das Jahr	yär
half year	halbes Jahr	häl'bəs yär
quarter, three months	Vierteljahr	fir'təlyär'

Days of the Week, Months

English	German	Pronunciation
Monday	Montag	mōn′täk
Tuesday	Dienstag	dēns′täk
Wednesday	Mittwoch	mit′vô*h*
Thursday	Donnerstag	dôn′ərstäk
Friday	Freitag	frī′täk
Saturday *(North Germany)*	Sonnabend	zôn′äbənt
(South Germany and Austria)	Samstag	zäms′täk
Sunday	Sonntag	zôn′täk
January	Januar	yän′ōō·är
February	Februar	fā′brōō·är
March	März	merts
April	April	äpril′
May	Mai	mī
June	Juni	yōō′nē
July	Juli	yōō′lē
August	August	ougōōst′
September	September	septem′bər
October	Oktober	ôktō′bər
November	November	nōvem′bər
December	Dezember	dātsem′bər

Seasons

English	German	Pronunciation
Spring	der Frühling	fr*e*̄′ling
Summer	der Sommer	zôm′ər
Fall/Autumn	der Herbst	herpst
Winter	der Winter	vin′tər

Holidays

English	German	Pronunciation
New Year's Eve	Silvester	zilves′tər
New Year's Day	Neujahr	noi′yär
Good Friday	Karfreitag	kärfrī′täk
Easter	Ostern	ōs′tərn
Christmas	Weihnachten	vī′nä*h*tən

The Date

What's the date today?
Den wievielten haben wir heute?
dān vēfēl'tən hä'bən vēr hoi'tə

It's the second of July.
Heute ist der zweite Juli.
hoi'tə ist dār tsvī'tə yoo'lē

On *the fifteenth of May (May fifteenth)*, 19 ...
Am fünfzehnten Mai, neunzehnhundert(und) ...
äm fínf'tsäntən mī, noin'tsänhoon'dərt(oont) ,..

On the fifth of *this (next)* **month.**
Am fünften *dieses (nächsten)* Monats.
äm fínf'tən dē'zəs (näsh'stən) mō'näts

Until the 10th of March.
Bis zum zehnten März.
bis tsoom tsän'tən merts

On April first of *this (last)* **year.**
Am ersten April *dieses (vergangenen) Jahres.*
äm ers'tən äpril' dē'zəs (fergäng'ənən) yä'rəs

We leave on *the twentieth of September (September twentieth).*
Wir reisen am zwanzigsten September ab.
vēr rī'zən äm tsvän'tsishstən septem'bər äp

We arrived on *the twelfth of August (August the twelfth).*
Wir sind am zwölften August angekommen.
vēr zint äm tsvelf'tən ougoost' än'gəkômən

The letter was mailed on the ninth of June.
Der Brief wurde am neunten Juni abgeschickt.
dār brēf voor'də äm noin'tən yoo'nē äp'gəshikt

Thank you for your letter of February 2nd.
Vielen Dank für Ihr Schreiben vom zweiten Februar.
fē'lən dängk fēr ēr shrī'bən fôm tsvī'tən fā'broo·är

Age

How old are you?
Wie alt *sind Sie (bist du)?*
vē ält zint zē (bist doo)

How old is *he (she)?*
Wie alt ist *er (sie)?*
vē ält ist ār (zē)

I'm twenty years old.
Ich bin zwanzig Jahre alt.
ish bin tsvän'tsish yä'rə ält

I'm over 18.
Ich bin über achtzehn (Jahre alt).
ish bin ē'bər äh'tsän (yä'rə ält)

Children under 14.
Kinder unter vierzehn Jahren.
kin'dər oon'tər fēr'tsän yä'rən

I was born on the ...
Ich bin am ... geboren.
ish bin äm ... gəbō'rən

He's *younger (older).*	**– under age.**	**– grown up.**
Er ist *jünger (älter).*	– minderjährig.	– erwachsen.
är ist ying'ər (el'tər)	– min'dəryä' rish	– erväk' sən

At the age of ...	**At my age.**
Im Alter von ...	In meinem Alter.
im äl'tər fôn ...	in mī'nəm äl'tər

Family

aunt	die Tante	tän'tə
boy	der Junge	yŏong'ə
brother	der Bruder	brŏo'dər
brother-in-law	der Schwager	shvä'gər
cousin *(female)*	die *Cousine (Kusine)*	kŏozē'nə
cousin *(male)*	der *Cousin (Vetter)*	kŏozeN' (fet'ər)
daughter	die Tochter	tôh'tər
family	die Familie	fämē'lē-ə
father	der Vater	fä'tər
father-in-law	der Schwiegervater	shvē'gərfä'tər
girl	das Mädchen	mād'shən
grandchild	der Enkel,	eng'kəl
	die Enkelin	eng'kəlin
granddaughter	die *Enkelin*	eng'kəlin
	(Enkeltochter)	(eng'kəltôhtər)
grandfather	der Großvater	grōs'fätər
grandmother	die Großmutter	grōs'mŏotər
grandparents	die Großeltern	grōs'eltərn
grandson	der Enkel	eng'kəl
husband	der *Ehemann (Mann)*	ā'əmän (män)
mother	die Mutter	mŏot'ər
mother-in-law	die Schwiegermutter	shvē'gərmŏotər
nephew	der Neffe	nef'ə
niece	die Nichte	nish'tə
parent	der Elternteil	el'tərntīl
parents	die Eltern	el'tərn
sister	die Schwester	shves'tər
sister-in-law	die Schwägerin	shvä'gərin
son	der Sohn	zōn
uncle	der Onkel	ông'kəl
wife	die *Ehefrau (Frau)*	ā'əfrou (frou)

Occupations

apprentice	der Lehrling	lār'ling
artist	der Künstler	kinst'lər
auto mechanic	der Autoschlosser	ou'tōshlôs'ər
baker	der Bäcker	bek'ər
bank teller	der Bankbeamte	bängk'bə-ämtə
bookkeeper	der Buchhalter	bōō*h*'hältər
bookseller	der Buchhändler	bōō*h*'hendlər
bricklayer	der Maurer	mou'rər
butcher	der *Fleischer*	flī'shər
	(Metzger)	(mets'gər)
cabinetmaker	der Schreiner	shrī'nər
carpenter	der *Tischler*	tish'lər
	(Zimmermann)	(tsim'ərmän)
chef	der Koch	kô*h*
civil servant	der Beamte	bə-äm'tə
clergyman	der *Pfarrer*	pfär'ər
	(Geistliche)	(gīst'lishe)
cobbler	der Schuster	shōō'stər
confectioner	der Konditor	kôndēt'ôr
cook	der Koch,	kô*h*
	die Köchin	ke'shin
dentist	der Zahnarzt,	tsän'ärtst
	die Zahnärztin	tsän'ärts'tin
doctor	der Arzt,	ärtst
	die Ärztin	ärts'tin
dressmaker	die Schneiderin	shnī'dərin
driver	der Kraftfahrer	kräft'färər
driving instructor	der Fahrlehrer	fär'lārər
druggist *(pharmacist)*	der Apotheker	äpōtā'kər
druggist		
(drugstore owner)	der Drogist	drōgist'
electrician	der Elektriker	älek'trikər
engineer *(scientific)*	der Ingenieur	in'zhenyär'
engineer *(railroad)*	der Lokführer	lôk'fērər
farmer	der *Landwirt*	länt'virt
	(Bauer)	(bou'ər)
fisherman	der Fischer	fish'ər
forester	der Förster	fers'tər

gardener	der Gärtner	gert'nər
glazier	der Glaser	glä'zər
interpreter *(translator)*	der Dolmetscher	dôl'metshər
journalist	der Journalist	zho͞ornälist'
judge	der Richter	ri*sh*'tər
lawyer	der Rechtsanwalt	re*sh*ts'änvält
librarian	der Bibliothekar	bib'lē-ōtäkär'
locksmith	der Schlosser	shlôs'ər
mailman	der Briefträger	brēf'trägər
mechanic	der Mechaniker	me*sh*ä'nikər
metalworker	der Schlosser	shlôs'ər
midwife	die Hebamme	häb'əmə
miner	der Bergmann	berk'män
musician	der Musiker	mo͞o'zikər
notary	der Notar	nōtär'
nurse *(female)*	die Krankenschwester	kräng'kənshves'tər
nurse *(male)*	der Krankenpfleger	kräng'kənpflä'gər
optician	der Optiker	ôp'tikər
painter	der Maler	mä'lər
pastry chef	der Konditor	kôndē'tôr
pharmacist	der Apotheker	äpōtä'kər
plumber	der *Installateur*	in'stälätär'
	(Klempner)	(klemp'nər)
postal clerk	der Postbeamte	pôst'bə·ämtə
pupil *(including high school students)*	der Schüler	shē'lər
railroad man	der Eisenbahner	ī'zənbänər
retailer	der Kaufmann	kouf'män
retiree	der Rentner	rent'nər
salesperson	der Verkäufer	ferkoi'fər
scholar	der Wissenschaftler	vis'ənshäft'lər
scientist	der Wissenschaftler	vis'ənshäft'lər
sculptor	der Bildhauer	bilt'hou·ər
secretary *(male)*	der Sekretär	zekrätär'
shoemaker	der Schuster	sho͞o'stər
storekeeper	der Kaufmann	kouf'män
student *(college or university only)*	der Student	shto͞odent'
tailor	der Schneider	shnī'dər
teacher	der Lehrer	lā'rər

technician	der Techniker	te*sh*'nikər
trainee	der *Lehrling*	lār'ling
	(Auszubildende)	(ous'tsoobil'dəndə)
translator	der Übersetzer	*ē*bərzets'ər
truck driver	der LKW-Fahrer	el'kävä'fä'rər
veterinarian	der Tierarzt,..........	tēr'ärtst
	die Tierärztin.........	tēr'ärts'tin
waiter	der *Kellner (Ober)*	kel'nər (ō'bər)
waitress	die Kellnerin	kel'nərin
watchmaker	der Uhrmacher	ōōr'mä*h*ər
wholesaler	der Großhändler	grōs'hendlər
worker	der Arbeiter	är'bītər
writer	der Schriftsteller	shrift'shtelər

Most of these occupations are practiced by both men and women. When referring to female doctors, lawyers or whatever in German, you should always use the feminine form of the noun, which, in most cases, is formed by adding the suffix „-in".

Education

Where are you studying? (What college or university do you attend?)
Wo studieren Sie?
vō shtōōdēr'ən zē

I'm at ... *college (university)*.
Ich studiere am ... College (an der ... Universität).
i*sh* shtōōdēr'ə äm ... kôl'ij (*ä*n dār ... ōōn'iverzität')

I'm *studying (majoring in)* ...
Ich studiere ...
i*sh* shtōōdēr'ə ...

I *go to (am attending)* (the) ... school.
Ich besuche die ... Schule.
i*sh* bəzōō'hə dē ... shōō'lə

lecture	die Vorlesung	fōr'lāzōōng
major	das Studienfach.......	shtōō'dē·ənfä*h*
school	die Schule............	shōō'lə
– boarding school ...	das Internat	in'tərnät'
– business school	die Handelsschule	hän'dəls·shōō'lə
– grammar school ...	die Volksschule	fôlks'shōōlə

– high school (*academic*)	das Gymnasium	gimnä'zē-ōom
– high school (*general*)	die Oberschule	ō'bərshōō'lə
– vocational school	die Berufsschule	bərōōfs'shōōlə
subject	das Studienfach	shtōō'dē-ənfäh
– American studies	Amerikanistik	ämär'ikänis'tik
– archaeology	Archäologie	är'shä-ōlōgē'
– architecture	Architektur	är'shētektōōr'
– art history	Kunstgeschichte	kōōnst'gəshishtə
– biology	Biologie	bē'ōlōgē'
– business administration	Betriebswirtschaft	bətrēps'virtshäft
– chemistry	Chemie	shämē'
– dentistry	Zahnmedizin	tsän'mäditsēn'
– economics	Wirtschaftswissenschaft	virt'shäftsvis'ənshäft
– education	Pädagogik	pä'dägō'gik
– English	Anglistik	änglis'tik
– geology	Geologie	gä'ōlōgē'
– German	Germanistik	ger'mänis'tik
– history	Geschichte	gəshish'tə
– journalism	Publizistik	pōōb'litsis'tik
– law	Jura	yōō'rä
– mathematics	Mathematik	mä'tämätēk'
– mechanical engineering	Maschinenbau	mäshē'nənbou
– medicine	Medizin	mä'ditsēn'
– musicology	Musikwissenschaft	mōōzēk'vis'ənshäft
– painting	Malerei	mä'lərī'
– pharmacy	Pharmazie	fär'mätsē'
– physics	Physik	fizēk'
– political science	Politologie	pōl'itōlōgē'
– psychology	Psychologie	psish'ōlōgē'
– Romance languages	Romanistik	rō'mänis'tik
– Slavic languages	Slawistik	slävis'tik
– sociology	Soziologie	zō'tsē-ōlōgē'
– veterinary medicine	Tiermedizin	tēr'mäditsēn'
– zoology	Zoologie	tsō'ōlōgē'
technical college	die Technische Hochschule	tesh'nishə hōh'shōōlə
university	die Universität	ōōn'iverzität'

ON THE ROAD

Asking the Way

Where *is (are)* ...?
Wo *ist (sind)* ...?
vō ist (zint) ...

How do I get to ...?
Wie komme ich nach ...?
vē kôm'ə i*sh* nä*h* ...

How many kilometers is it to the next town?
Wieviel Kilometer sind es bis zur nächsten Stadt?
vē'fēl kēlōmā'tər zint es bis tsōōr nä*sh'*stən sht*ä*t

> 8 kilometers = 5 miles

Is this the road to ...?
Ist das die Straße nach ...?
ist d*ä*s dē shträ'sə nä*h* ...

Is this the right way to ...?
Bin ich hier richtig nach ...?
bin i*sh* hēr ri*sh'*ti*sh* nä*h* ...

Do I have to go ...?
Muß ich ... fahren?
mōōs i*sh* ... fär'ən

Right.	**Left.**	**Straight ahead.**	**Back.**
Rechts.	Links.	Geradeaus.	Zurück.
re*sh*ts	lingks	gərä'də·ous'	tsōōrik'

Here.	**There.**	**This way.**	**As far as ...**
Hier.	Dort.	In dieser Richtung.	Bis zu ...
hēr	dôrt	in dē'zər ri*sh'*tōōng	bis tsōō ...

How long?	**Where (to)?**	**How far is it to ...?**
Wie lange?	Wo(hin)?	Wie weit ist es nach ...?
vē läng'ə	vō(hin')	vē vīt ist es nä*h* ...

Would you please show me that on the map?
Zeigen Sie mir das bitte auf der Karte.
tsī'gən zē mēr d*ä*s bit'ə ouf dār kär'tə

Vehicles

camping trailer	der *Wohnwagen*	vōn'vägən
	(Campingwagen)	kem'pingvä'gən
car	das Auto, der Wagen ..	ou'tō, vä'gən

– **delivery truck**	der Lieferwagen	lē′fərvä′gən
– **passenger car**	der Personenwagen	perzōn′ənvä′gən
– **ranch (station) wagon**	der Kombiwagen	kôm′bēvä′gən
– **truck**	der Lastwagen	läst′vägən
bicycle	das Fahrrad	fä′rät
horse cart	der Pferdewagen	pfär′dəvä′gən
moped	das Moped	mō′pet
motorcycle	das Motorrad	mō′tōrät
motor scooter	der Motorroller	mō′tôrôl′ər
trailer	der Anhänger	än′hengər
vehicle	das Fahrzeug	fär′tsoik

Renting a Car

Where can I rent a car?
Wo kann ich ein Auto mieten?
vō kän ish īn ou′tō mē′tən

I'd like to rent a car.
Ich möchte ein Auto mieten.
ish mesh′tə īn ou′tō mē′tən

... with chauffeur.
... mit Fahrer.
... mit fä′rər

... for 2 (6) people.
... für zwei (sechs) Personen.
... fēr tsvī (zeks) perzō′nən

... for one day (one week, two weeks).
... für einen Tag (eine Woche, zwei Wochen).
... fēr ī′nən täk (ī′nə vô′hə, tsvī vô′hən)

How much will it cost?
Wieviel kostet es?
vē′fēl kôs′tət es

... including full coverage insurance?
... einschließlich Vollkaskoversicherung?
... īn′shlēslish fôl′käs′kōferzish′ərooong

Will I have to pay for the gasoline myself?
Muß ich das Benzin selbst bezahlen?
moos ish däs bentsēn′ zelpst bətsä′lən

How much will I have to deposit?
Wieviel muß ich bei Ihnen hinterlegen?
vē′fēl moos ish bī ē′nən hintərlā′gən

When (Where) can I pick up the car?
Wann (Wo) kann ich den Wagen abholen?
vän (vō) kän ish dān vä′gən äp′hōlən

Will somebody be there when I bring the car back?
Ist jemand da, wenn ich das Auto zurückbringe?
ist yā′mänt dä, ven ish däs ou′tō tsoorik′bringə

On a Drive

I'm *going (driving)* to ...		**Are you going to** ...?
Ich fahre nach ...		Fahren Sie nach ...?
i*sh* fä′rə nä*h* ...		fä′rən zē näh ...

		Fast.	**Slow.**
To go by *car (motorcycle, bicycle).*			
Mit dem *Auto (Motorrad, Fahrrad)* fahren.		Schnell.	Langsam.
mit däm ou′tō (mō′tôrät, fä′rät) fä′rən		shnel	läng′zäm

access road	die Einfahrt	īn′färt
automobile club	der Automobilklub	ou′tōmōbēl′klo͞op
bike lane	der Radfahrweg	rät′färväk
bridge	die Brücke	brĭk′ə
center strip	der Mittelstreifen	mit′əlshtrī′fən
city limits sign	die Ortstafel	ôrts′täfəl
curve	die Kurve	ko͞or′fə
detour	die Umleitung	o͞om′līto͞ong
direction sign	der Wegweiser	väk′vīzər
driver's license	der Führerschein	fē′rərshīn
driveway	die Einfahrt	īn′färt
exit	die Ausfahrt..........	ous′färt
falling rocks	der Steinschlag	shtīn′shläk
highway	die Autobahn	ou′tōbän
highway patrol	die Verkehrspolizei	ferkärs′pôlitsī′
intersection	die Kreuzung........	kroi′tso͞ong
lane	die Fahrspur	fär′shpo͞or
limited parking zone .	die Kurzparkzone	ko͞orts′pärktsō′nə
maximum speed	die Höchstgeschwindig-	hö͞oḥst′gəshvin′di*sh*-
	keit	kīt
(mountain) pass	der Paß	päs
no parking	das Parkverbot	pärk′ferbōt′
no passing	das Überholverbot	ē′bərhōl′ferbōt′
no stopping	das Halteverbot	häl′təferbōt′
parking disk	die Parkscheibe	pärk′shībə
parking lot	der Parkplatz	pärk′pläts
parking meter	die Parkuhr	pärk′o͞or
path	der Weg	väk
– footpath	der Fußweg	fo͞os′väk
railroad crossing	der Bahnübergang	bän′ē′bərgäng′

registration	die Zulassung	tsōō'läsōōng
right of way	die Vorfahrt..........	fōr'fàrt
road	die Straße	shträ'sə
– coastal road	die Küstenstraße.....	kis'tənshträ'sə
– country road	die Landstraße	länt'shträ'sə
– cross road	die Querstraße.......	kvär'shträ'sə
– main *road (street)* .	die Hauptstraße	houpt'shträ'sə
road sign	das Verkehrsschild	ferkärs'shilt
road under construc-		
tion	Baustelle	bou'shtelə
route	die Fahrtroute	fàrt'rōōtə
side wind	der Seitenwind........	zī'tənvint
slippery road		
(literally: danger of		
sliding)	die Rutschgefahr	rōōtsh'gəfär
speed limit	die Geschwindigkeits-	gəshvin'dishkīts-
	begrenzung...........	bəgren'tsōōng
steep downgrade	das Gefälle	gəfel'ə
steep upgrade	die Steigung	shtī'gōōng
traffic	der (Straßen)Verkehr ..	(shträ'sən)ferkär'
traffic circle	der Kreisverkehr......	krīs'ferkär'
traffic light	die Ampel............	äm'pəl
traffic regulations ...	die Verkehrsregeln	ferkärs'rā'gəln
trip (journey)	die Fahrt	fàrt
– brake	bremsen	brem'zən
– drive	fahren	fà'rən
– get in lane	(sich) einordnen	(zish) īn'ordnən
– get out (of the car)	aussteigen...........	ous'shtīgən
– hitch-hike	per *Anhalter*	per än'hältər
	(Autostopp) fahren	(ou'tōshtôp') fä'rən
– park	parken	pär'kən
– pass (on the road) .	überholen	ēbərhō'lən
– stop.............	(an)halten	(än')häl'tən
– turn (the car)	wenden	ven'dən
– turn (into a road) ..	einbiegen	īn'bēgən
– turn off (a road) ...	abbiegen	äp'bēgən
winding road	die Serpentine	zer'pentē'nə
zebra crossing	der Zebrastreifen	tsā'brästrī'fən

Garage, Parking Lot

Where can I leave my car? *(for safekeeping)*
Wo kann ich meinen Wagen unterstellen?
vō kän ish mī'nən vä'gən ōōn'tərshtel'ən

Is there a garage near here?
Ist hier in der Nähe eine Garage?
ist hēr in där nä'ə ī'nə gärä'zhə

Have you still got a vacant *garage (parking space)*?
Haben Sie noch eine *Garage (Box)* frei?
hä'bən zē nôh ī'nə gärä'zhə (bôks) frī

Where can I leave the car?
Wo kann ich den Wagen lassen?
vō kän ish dän vä'gən läs'ən

Can I leave it here?
Kann ich ihn hier lassen?
kän ish ēn hēr läs'ən

Can I park here?
Kann ich hier parken?
kän ish hēr pär'kən

Is this parking lot guarded?
Ist der Parkplatz bewacht?
ist där pärk'pläts bəväht'

Is there a space free?
Ist noch ein Platz frei?
ist nôh īn pläts frī

How long can I park here?
Wie lange kann ich hier parken?
vē längə kän ish hēr pär'kən

How much does it cost to park here *overnight (until ...)*?
Was kostet das Unterstellen *pro Nacht (bis ...)*?
väs kôst'ət däs ōōn'tərshtel'ən prō näht (bis ...)

Is the garage open all night?
Ist die Garage die ganze Nacht geöffnet?
ist dē gärä'zhə dē gän'tsə näht gə•ef'nət

When do you close?
Wann schließen Sie?
vän shlē'sən zē

I'll be leaving *this evening (tomorrow morning at eight)*.
Ich fahre *heute abend (morgen früh um acht)* weiter.
ish fä'rə hoi'tə ä'bənt (môr'gən frē ōōm äht) vī'tər

I'd like to take my car out of the garage.
Ich möchte meinen Wagen aus der Garage holen.
ish mesh'tə mī'nən vä'gən ous där gärä'zhə hō'lən

Gas Station, Car Repair

Where's the nearest gas station?
Wo ist die nächste Tankstelle?
võ ist dē näsh'stə tängk'shtelə

How far is it?
Wie weit ist es?
vē vīt ist es

Fifteen liters of *regular (high test, premium)*, **please.**
Geben Sie mir bitte fünfzehn Liter *Normalbenzin (Super)*.
gā'bən zē mēr bit'ə fīnf'tsän lē'tər nôrmäl'bentsēn' (zoō'pər)

---

1 gallon = approx. 4 liters

I'd like 20 liters of diesel, please.
Ich möchte zwanzig Liter Diesel.
ish mesh'tə tsvän'tsish lē'tər dē'zəl

Fill her up, please.
Bitte volltanken.
bit'ə fôl'tängkən

I need *water (coolant)*.
Ich brauche Kühl*wasser(-flüssigkeit)*.
ish brou'hə kēl'väsər(flisishkīt')

A road map, please.
Eine Straßenkarte, bitte.
ī'nə shträ'sənkärtə, bit'ə

Would you please fill up the radiator?
Füllen Sie bitte Kühlwasser nach.
fil'ən zē bit'ə kēl'väsər näh

Would you please check the brake fluid?
Prüfen Sie bitte die Bremsflüssigkeit.
prē'fən zē bit'e dē brems'flisishkīt'

anti-freeze	das Frostschutzmittel..	frôst'shoōtsmit'əl
attendant	der Tankwart	tängk'värt
brake fluid	die Bremsflüssigkeit ...	brems'flisishkīt'
car repair service	der Kundendienst	koōn'dəndēnst'
coolant	die Kühlflüssigkeit	kēl'flisishkīt'
(cooling) water	das Kühlwasser	kēl'väsər
gasoline	das Benzin	bentsēn'
gasoline can	der Benzinkanister	bentsēn'känis'tər
gas station	die Tankstelle	tängk'shtelə
oil	das Öl	āl
reserve tank	der Reservetank	rəzer'vətängk
spark plug	die Zündkerze	tsint'kertsə
water	das Wasser	väs'ər
– distilled water	destilliertes Wasser	destilēr'təs väs'ər

Oil

Please check the oil.
Prüfen Sie bitte den Ölstand.
prē′fən zē bit′ə dān āl′shtänt

Have I got enough oil?
Ist noch genug Öl da?
ist nôh gənoōk′ āl dä

I need *motor oil (gear oil)*.
Ich brauche *Motoröl (Getriebeöl)*.
ish brou′hə mō′tôrāl′ (gətrē′bə·āl′)

. . . liters of oil, please.
. . . Liter Öl, bitte.
. . . lē′tər āl, bit′ə

> 1 Liter = approx. 2 pints

Please fill up the oil tank.
Füllen Sie bitte Öl nach.
fil′ən zē bit′ə āl näh

Please change the oil.
Wechseln Sie bitte das Öl.
vek′səln zē bit′ə däs āl

gear oil	das Getriebeöl	gətrē′bə·āl′
lubrication	der Abschmierdienst . .	äp′shmērdēnst′
motor oil	das Motoröl	mō′tôrāl′
oil	das Öl	āl
– special/standard . . .	spezial/normal	shpetsē·äl′/nôrmäl′
oil can	die Ölkanne	āl′känə
oil change	der Ölwechsel	āl′veksəl
oil level	der Ölstand	āl′shtänt

Tires ·

Can you *repair (retread)* this tire?
Können Sie diesen Reifen *reparieren (runderneuern)?*
ken′ən zē dē′zən rī′fən repärē′rən (ro͞ont′ernoi′ərn)

Can this inner tube be patched?
Können Sie diesen Schlauch flicken?
ken′ən zē dē′zən shlouh flik′ən

One of my tires had a blow-out.
Ein Reifen ist mir geplatzt.
īn rī′fən ist mēr gəplätst

Please change this tire.
Wechseln Sie bitte diesen Reifen.
vek′səln zē bit′ə dē′zən rī′fən

A new inner tube, please.
Einen neuen Schlauch, bitte.
ī′nən noi′ən shlouh, bit′ə

Would you please check the tire pressure?
Prüfen Sie bitte den Reifendruck.
prē′fən zē bit′ə dān rī′fəndro͞ok′

The front tires are 22.7, and the rear ones are 28.4.
Vorn 1,6, hinten 2,0 atü.
fôrn īns kôm′ä zeks, hin′tən tsvī kôm′ä no͞ol ätē′

Tire Pressure Conversion Table					
lbs./sq. in.	atü	lbs./sq. in.	atü	lbs./sq. in.	atü
17.0	1,2	22.7	1,6	28.4	2,0
18.5	1,3	24.2	1,7	29.9	2,1
19.9	1,4	25.6	1,8	31.3	2,2
21.3	1,5	27.1	1,9	32.7	2,3

atü = Atmosphärenüberdruck = *atmosphere excess pressure*
ätē' = ätmôsfär'ənēb'ərdro͞ok

blow-out	die Reifenpanne	rī'fənpänə
inner tube	der Schlauch	shlou*h*
jack	der Wagenheber	vä'gənhā'bər
puncture	die Reifenpanne	rī'fənpänə
tires *(in general)*	die Bereifung	bərī'fo͞ong
tire	der Reifen	rī'fən
– tubeless	– schlauchloser	shlou*h*'lōzər
tire change	der Reifenwechsel	rī'fənvek'səl
tire pressure	der Reifendruck	rī'fəndro͞ok
valve	das Ventil	ventēl'
wheel	das Rad	rät
– back wheel	das Hinterrad	hin'tərät'
– front wheel	das Vorderrad	fôr'dərät'
– reserve wheel	das Reserverad	rezer'vərät'
– wheels	die Räder	rā'dər

Car Wash

Please wash *the windshield (the windows).*
Waschen Sie bitte *die Windschutzscheibe (die Scheiben).*
väsh'ən zē bit'ə dē vint'sho͞ots·shī'bə (dē shī'bən)

I'd like my car washed, please.
Waschen Sie mir bitte den Wagen.
väsh'ən zē mēr bit'ə dän vä'gən

Please clean out the inside too.
Reinigen Sie mir den Wagen bitte auch innen.
rī'nigən zē mēr dän vä'gən bit'ə ou*h* in'ən

Breakdown, Accident

I've (We've) had a breakdown.
Ich habe (Wir haben) eine Panne.
i*sh* hä'bə (vēr hä'bən) ī'nə pän'ə

... is *busted (not working)*.
... ist defekt.
... ist däfekt'

I've had an accident.
Ich habe einen Unfall gehabt.
i*sh* hä'bə ī'nən oon'fäl gəhäpt'

May I use your phone?
Kann ich bei Ihnen telefonieren?
kän i*sh* bī ē'nən tālāfōnē'rən

Would you please call the police?
Verständigen Sie bitte die Polizei.
vershten'digən zē bit'ə dē pôlitsī'

Please help me!
Bitte helfen Sie mir.
bit'ə hel'fən zē mēr

Call an ambulance quickly!
Rufen Sie schnell einen Krankenwagen!
roo'fən zē shnel ī'nən kräng'kənvä'gən

Get a doctor!
Holen Sie einen Arzt!
hō'lən zē ī'nən ärtst

I need bandages.
Ich brauche Verbandszeug.
i*sh* brou'hə ferbänts'tsoik

Could you lend me ...?
Können Sie mir ... leihen?
ken'ən zē mēr ... lī'ən

Could you ...?
Könnten Sie ...?
ken'tən zē ...

– look after the injured?
– sich um die Verletzten kümmern?
– zi*sh* oom dē ferlets'tən kim'ərn

– give me a lift?
– mich ein Stück mitnehmen?
– mi*sh* īn shtĭk mit'nā'mən

– tow my car?
– meinen Wagen abschleppen?
– mī'nən vä'gən äp'shlep'ən

– get me a *mechanic (a tow truck)?*
– mir einen *Mechaniker (Abschleppwagen)* schicken?
– mēr ī'nən mesh*ä*'nikər (äp'shlepvä'gən) shik'ən

Where is there a *service station (repair shop)?*
Wo ist eine Reparaturwerkstatt?
vō ist ī'nə rep*ä*rätoor'verk'sht*ä*t

Would you please give me your name and address?
Bitte geben Sie mir Ihren Namen und Ihre Adresse an.
bit'ə gā'bən zē mēr ē'rən nä'mən oont ē'rə ädres'ə än

It's your fault.
Es ist Ihre Schuld!
es ist ē'rə shoolt

You've damaged ...
Sie haben ... beschädigt.
zē hä'bən ... bəshä'di*sh*t

I had the right of way.
Ich hatte Vorfahrt.
i*sh* hät′ə fōr′färt

Nobody's hurt.
Es ist niemand verletzt.
es ist nē′mänt ferletst′

Will you be my witness?
Können Sie mein Zeuge sein?
k*en*′ən zē mīn tsoi′gə zīn

. . . is (badly) injured.
. . . ist (schwer) verletzt.
. . . ist (shvär) ferletst′

Thanks very much for your help.
Vielen Dank für Ihre Hilfe.
fē′lən dängk fēr ē′rə hil′fə

Where is your car insured?
Wo ist Ihr Wagen versichert?
vō ist ēr vä′gən ferzi*sh*′ərt

accident	der Unfall	ŏŏn′fäl
ambulance	der Krankenwagen	kräng′kənvä′gən
bandages	das Verbandszeug	ferbänts′tsoik
body and fender damage	der Blechschaden	ble*sh*′shä′dən
breakdown	die Panne	pän′ə
careful!	Vorsicht!	fōr′zi*sh*t
collision	der Zusammenstoß	tsŏŏzäm′ənshtōs
damage	der Unfallschaden	ŏŏn′fälshä′dən
danger!	Vorsicht!	fōr′zi*sh*t
dealership garage	die Vertragswerkstatt	ferträks′verk′shtät
emergency ward	die Notstation	nōt′shtätsyōn′
fire department	die Feuerwehr	foi′ərvār
first aid station	die Unfallstation	ŏŏn′fälshtätsyōn′
head-on collision	der Frontalzusammenstoß	frôntäl′tsŏŏzäm′ənshtōs
help	die Hilfe	hil′fə
hospital	das Krankenhaus	kräng′kənhous
impact	der Aufprall	ouf′präl
injury	die Verletzung	ferlets′ŏŏng
insurance	die Versicherung	ferzi*sh*′ərŏŏng
mechanic	der Mechaniker	me*sh*ä′nikər
police	die Polizei	pôlitsī′
rear-end collision	der Auffahrunfall	ouf′färŏŏn′fäl
repair shop	die Reparaturwerkstatt	rep*ä*rätŏŏr′verk′shtät
service station	die Reparaturwerkstatt	rep*ä*rätŏŏr′verk′shtät
towing service	der Abschleppdienst	*ä*p′shlepdēnst′
tow line	das Abschleppseil	*ä*p′shlepzīl′
tow truck	der Abschleppwagen	*ä*p′shlepvä′gən

Repair Workshop

Where's the nearest garage (Volkswagen garage)?
Wo ist die nächste Reparaturwerkstatt (Vertragswerkstatt von Volkswagen)?
vō ist dē näsh'stə repärätōōr'verk'shtät (ferträks'verk'shtät fôn fôlks'-
vä'gən)

. . . isn't working right.
. . . ist nicht in Ordnung.
. . . ist nisht in ôrd'nŏŏng

. . . is out of order (isn't working).
. . . ist defekt.
. . . ist dāfekt'

Can you fix it?
Können Sie das machen?
ken'ən zē däs mäh'ən

Where can I have this fixed?
Wer kann das machen?
vār kän däs mäh'ən

Would you please check . . .
Prüfen Sie bitte . . .
prē'fən zē bit'ə . . .

Would you please give me . . .
Geben Sie mir bitte . . .
gā'bən zē mēr bit'ə . . .

Would you please fix this.
Reparieren Sie das bitte.
repärē'rən zē däs bit'ə

Have you got manufacturer's spare parts for . . .?
Haben Sie Original-Ersatzteile für . . .?
hä'bən zē ōriginäl'-erzäts'tīlə fēr . . .

How soon can you get the spare parts?
Wann bekommen Sie die Ersatzteile?
vän bəkôm'ən zē dē erzäts'tīlə

I need a new . . .
Ich brauche eine neue (einen neuen, ein neues) . . .
ish brou'hə ī'nə noi'ə (ī'nən noi'ən, īn noi'əs) . . .

Can I still drive it?
Kann ich damit noch fahren?
kän ish dä'mit nôh fä'rən

Just do the essentials, please.
Machen Sie bitte nur die nötigsten Reparaturen.
mäh'ən zē bit'ə nŏŏr dē nä'tishstən repärätōō'rən

When will it be ready?
Wann ist es fertig?
vän ist es fer'tish

How much does (will) it cost?
Wieviel kostet es (wird es kosten)?
vē'fēl kôs'tət es (virt es kôs'tən)

Car Parts, Repairs

accelerator	das Gaspedal	gäs'pədäl
– accelerate	Gas geben	gäs gā'bən
– slow down	Gas wegnehmen	gäs vek'nāmən
air filter	der Luftfilter	lōōft'filtər
anti-freeze	das Frostschutzmittel	frôst'shōōtsmit'əl
automatic transmission	die Automatik	ou'tōmä'tik
axle	die Achse	äk'sə
backfire	die Fehlzündung	fāl'tsindoong
ball bearings	das Kugellager	kōō'gəlä'gər
battery	die Batterie	bätərē'
bearing	das Lager	lä'gər
blinker	der Blinker	bling'kər
body	die Karosserie	kärôsərē'
bolt	die Schraube	shrou'bə
– nut	die Schraubenmutter	shrou'bənmōōtər
brake drum	die Bremstrommel	brems'trôməl
brake fluid	die Bremsflüssigkeit	brems'flisishkīt'
brake lights	die Bremslichter	brems'lishtər
brake lining	der Bremsbelag	brems'bəläk
brake pedal	das Bremspedal	brems'pədäl
brakes	die Bremsen	brem'zən
– disc brake	die Scheibenbremse	shī'bənbremzə
– foot brake	die Fußbremse	fōōs'bremzə
– hand brake	die Handbremse	hänt'bremzə
bulb	die Birne	bir'nə
– change the bulb	die Birne auswechseln	bir'nə ous'veksəln
bumper	die Stoßstange	shtōs'shtängə

The battery *has run down (needs charging)*.
Die Batterie ist leer (muß aufgeladen werden).
dē bätərē' ist lār (mōōs ouf'gəlädən ver'dən)

The brakes aren't working right.
Die Bremsen sind nicht in Ordnung.
dē brem'zən zint nisht in ôrd'nŏōng

They're *slack (too tight)*.
Sie sind locker (zu fest).
zē zint lôk'ər (tsōō fest)

The brake drums are getting too hot.
Die Bremstrommeln werden zu heiß.
dē brems'trôməln ver'dən tsōō hīs

cable	das Kabel	kä′bəl
camshaft	die Nockenwelle	nôk′ənvelə
carburetor	der Vergaser	fergä′zər
carburetor jet	die Vergaserdüse	fergä′zərdēzə
car door	die Wagentür	vä′gəntēr
car keys	die Autoschlüssel	ou′tōshlisəl
chain	die Kette	ket′ə
– **snow chains**	die Schneeketten	shnä′ketən
chassis	das Fahrgestell	fär′gəshtel
clutch	die Kupplung	kōōp′lōōng
– **clutch pedal**	das Kupplungspedal	kōōp′lōōngspədäl′
compression	die Kompression	kômpresyōn′
condenser	der Kondensator	kôndenzä′tôr
connecting rod	die Pleuelstange	ploi′əlshtängə
– **connecting rod bearing**	das Pleuellager	ploi′əlägər
contact	der Kontakt	kôntäkt′
crankshaft	die Kurbelwelle	kōōr′bəlvelə
cylinder	der Zylinder	tsilin′dər
– **cylinder head**	der Zylinderkopf	tsilin′dərkôpf′
– **cylinder head gasket**	die Zylinderkopf- dichtung	tsilin′dərkôpf- dish′tōōng
diesel nozzle	die Dieselmotordüse	dē′zəlmōtôrdē′zə
differential	das Differential	difərentsyäl′
dip stick	der Ölmeßstab	äl′mes-shtäp
distributor	der Verteiler	fertī′lər
door lock	das Türschloß	tēr′shlôs
drive shaft	die Kardanwelle	kärdän′velə
dynamo	die Lichtmaschine	lisht′mäshē′nə
exhaust	der Auspuff	ous′pōōf

The dynamo isn't charging.
Die Lichtmaschine gibt keinen Strom.
dē lisht′mäshē′nə gēpt kī′nən shtrōm

It won't stay in ... gear.
Der ... Gang springt raus.
dār gäng shpringt rous

The gearshift needs to be checked over.
Die Gangschaltung muß nachgesehen werden.
dē gäng′shältōōng mōōs näh′gəzā′ən ver′dən

There's oil leaking out of the gear-box.
Aus dem Getriebe tropft Öl.
ous dām gətrē′bə trôpft äl

fan	der Ventilator	ventilä'tôr
fan belt	der Keilriemen	kīl'rēmən
fender	der Kotflügel	kōt'flēgəl
fire extinguisher	der Feuerlöscher	foi'ərleshər
float	der Schwimmer	shvim'ər
free wheel (hub)	der (die) Freilauf(nabe)	frī'louf(nä'bə)
fuel injector	die Einspritzpumpe	īn'shpritspoom'pə
fuel lines	die Benzinleitung	bentsēn'lītoong
fuel pump	die Benzinpumpe	bentsēn'poompə
fuse	die Sicherung	zish'əroong
gas	das Gas	gäs
gasket	die Dichtung	dish'toong
gear	der Gang	gäng
– neutral	der Leerlauf	lār'louf
– reverse	der Rückwärtsgang	rīk'vertsgäng'
– to put it in gear	den Gang einlegen	gäng īn'lāgən
gear box	das Getriebe	gətrē'bə
gear lever	der Schalthebel	shält'hābəl
gearshift	die Gangschaltung	gäng'shältoong
grease	das Fett	fet
handle	der Griff	grif
headlight	der Scheinwerfer	shīn'verfər
– dipped headlights	das Abblendlicht	äp'blentlisht
– full beam	das Fernlicht	fern'lisht
– parking lights	das Standlicht	shtänt'lisht
– rear lights	Schlußlichter	shloos'lishtər
heating system	die Heizung	hī'tsoong
hood	die (Motor)Haube	(mō'tôr)hou'bə
horn	die Hupe	hoo'pə
– flashing signal	die Lichthupe	lisht'hoopə
hub	die Nabe	nä'bə
hub cap	die Radkappe	rät'käpə

The heating doesn't work.
Die Heizung geht nicht.
dē hī'tsoong gāt nisht

The radiator has sprung a leak.
Aus dem Kühler tropft Wasser.
ous dām kē'lər trôpft väs'ər

The clutch *slips (won't disengage).*
Die Kupplung *rutscht durch (trennt nicht).*
dē koop'loong rootsht doorsh (trent nisht)

ignition	die Zündung	tsin'dŏong
– ignition cable	das Zündkabel	tsint'käbəl
– ignition key	der Zündschlüssel	tsint'shlisəl
– ignition lock	das Zündschloß	tsint'shlôs
– ignition system	das Zündsystem	tsint'sistām`
indicator light	die Kontrollampe	kôntrô'lämpə
insulation	die Isolierung	izōlēr'ŏong
interrupter	der Unterbrecher	ŏontərbresh'ər
lamp	die Lampe	läm'pə
license plate	das Nummernschild	nŏom'ərnshilt
lighting system	die Beleuchtung	bəloish'tŏong
lubricant	der Schmierstoff	shmēr'shtôf
mileage indicator	der Kilometerzähler	kēlōmā'tər·tsā'lər
motor	der Motor	mō'tôr
– diesel motor	der Dieselmotor	dē'zəlmōtôr
– rear motor	der Heckmotor	hek'mōtôr
– two-stroke motor	der Zweitaktmotor	tsvī'täktmō`tôr
nationality plate	das Nationalitätskenn-zeichen	nät'syōnälitäts'ken`-tsīshən
oil filter	der Ölfilter	äl'filtər
oil pump	die Ölpumpe	äl'pŏompə
paint job	die Lackierung	läkē'rŏong
pedal	das Pedal	pədäl'
piston	der Kolben	kôl'bən
– piston ring	der Kolbenring	kôl'bənring
pipe	die Leitung	lī'tŏong
power brake	die Servobremse	zer'vōbrem`zə
power steering	die Servolenkung	zer'vōleng`kŏong
radiator	der Kühler	kē'lər
– radiator grill	der Kühlergrill	kē'lərgril

The motor lacks power.	**– is overheating.**
Der Motor zieht nicht.	– läuft sich heiß.
`där mō'tôr tsēt nisht	– loift zish hīs

– knocks.	**– suddenly stalls.**	**– misses.**
– klopft.	– setzt plötzlich aus.	– stottert.
– klôpft	– zetst plets'lish ous	– shtôt'ərt

rear view mirror	der Rückspiegel	rĭk'shpēgəl
repair	die Reparatur	repärätoōr'
reserve fuel can	der Reservekanister	rezer'vəkänis'tər
roof	das Verdeck	ferdek'
screw	die Schraube	shrou'bə
seat belt	der Sicherheitsgurt	zish'ərhītsgoōrt'
shock absorber	der Stoßdämpfer	shtōs'dempfər
short circuit	der Kurzschluß	koōrts'shloōs
sliding (sun) roof	das Schiebedach	shē'bədäh
solder	löten	lā'tən
speedometer	der Tachometer	tähōmā'tər
spoke	die Speiche	shpī'shə
seat	der Sitz	zits
– back seat	der *Rücksitz (Fond)*	rĭk'zits (fōN)
– driver's seat	der Fahrersitz	fä'rərzits
– front seat	der Vordersitz	fôr'dərzits
– front passenger seat	der Beifahrersitz	bī'färərzits'
spare part	das Ersatzteil	erzäts'tīl
spare wheel	das Ersatzrad	erzäts'rät
spark	der Funke	foōng'kə
spark plug	die Zündkerze	tsĭnt'kertsə
spring	die Feder	fä'dər
starter	der Anlasser	än'läsər

The windshield wiper *smears (is broken off)*.
Der Scheibenwischer *schmiert (ist abgebrochen)*.
där shī'bənvishər shmērt (ist äp'gəbrôhən)

This screw needs *tightening (loosening)*.
Diese Schraube muß *angezogen (gelockert)* werden.
dē'zə shrou'bə moōs än'gətsōgən (gəlôk'ərt) ver'dən

The fuse has blown.
Die Sicherung ist durchgebrannt.
dē zish'əroōng ist doōrsh'gəbränt

steering	die Lenkung	leng'kōōng
– **steering wheel**	das Lenkrad	lengk'rät
switch	der Schalter	shäl'tər
thermostat	der Thermostat	ter'mōstät'
(screw) thread	das Gewinde	gəvin'də
top	das Verdeck	ferdek'
transmission	das Getriebe	gətrē'bə
trunk	der Kofferraum	kô'fəroum
tube	der Schlauch	shlou*h*
valve	das Ventil	ventēl'
warning triangle	das Warndreieck	värn'drī`ek
washer	die Dichtung	di*sh*'tōōng
wheel	das Rad	rät
windshield	die Windschutzscheibe	vint'shōōts·shī`bə
windshield washer . . .	die Scheibenwasch- anlage	shī'bənväsh`änlä`gə
windshield wiper	der Scheibenwischer . . .	shī'bənvishər

Would you please straighten out my bumper?
Biegen Sie bitte die Stoßstange gerade.
bē'gən zē bit'ə dē shtōs'shtängə gərä'də

Would you please *check (clean)* the carburetor?
Würden Sie bitte den Vergaser *überprüfen (reinigen)?*
vir'dən zē bit'ə dān fergä'zər ē'bərprē'fən (rī'nigən)

Would you please change the spark plugs?
Wechseln Sie bitte die Zündkerzen aus.
vek'səln zē bit'ə dē tsint'kertsən ous

Tools

Can you loan me ...?
Können Sie mir ... leihen?
ken'ən zē mēr ... lī'ən

I need ...
Ich brauche ...
ish brou'hə ...

air pump	die Luftpumpe	lo͞oft'poͦompə
bolt	die Schraube	shrou'bə
– nut	die Schraubenmutter ..	shrou'bənmoͦotər
cable	das Kabel	kä'bəl
chisel	der Meißel	mī'səl
cloth	das Tuch	too͞oh
drill	der Bohrer	bō'rər
file	die Feile	fī'lə
funnel	der Trichter	trish'tər
hammer	der Hammer	häm'ər
inspection light	die Prüflampe	prēf'lämpə
jack	der Wagenheber	vä'gənhäbər
pincers	die Kneifzange	knīf'tsängə
pliers	die Zange	tsäng'ə
rag	der Lappen	läp'ən
sandpaper	das Schmirgelpapier ...	shmir'gəlpäpēr'
screw	die Schraube	shrou'bə
screwdriver	der Schraubenzieher ...	shrou'bəntsē'ər
socket wrench	der Steckschlüssel	shtek'shlisəl
string	der Bindfaden	bint'fädən
tool	das Werkzeug	verk'tsoik
– tool box (kit)	der Werkzeugkasten ...	verk'tsoik·käs'tən
wire	der Draht	drät
– a piece of wire	ein Stück Draht	shtik drät
wrench	der Schraubenschlüssel	shrou'bənshlisəl

TRAFFIC SIGNS

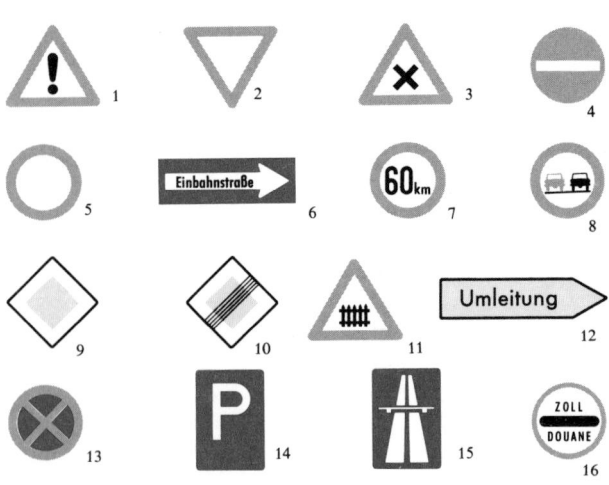

1 DANGER Gefahrenstelle · 2 YIELD RIGHT OF WAY Vorfahrt gewähren · 3 INTERSECTION Kreuzung · 4 DO NOT ENTER Einfahrt verboten · 5 NO VEHICLES ALLOWED Verbot für Fahrzeuge aller Art · 6 ONE WAY STREET Einbahnstraße · 7 SPEED LIMIT (kilometers) Zulässige Höchstgeschwindigkeit (in Kilometer) · 8 NO PASSING Überholverbot · 9 PRIORITY ROAD Vorfahrt · 10 END OF PRIORITY ROAD Ende der Vorfahrtsstraße · 11 RAILROAD CROSSING Beschrankter Bahnübergang · 12 DETOUR Umleitung · 13 NO STOPPING Halteverbot · 14 PARKING Parkplatz · 15 EXPRESSWAY/FREEWAY Autobahn · 16 CUSTOMS Zoll

---

Road signs are color and shape-coded. Triangular signs with a red rim are *warning signs*; round blue signs are *regulatory signs*; round signs with a red rim are *prohibit movement signs*; rectangular yellow signs with a black rim are *destination signs*; rectangular blue signs with white letters are *destination signs* on highways.

ON THE BUS

Where is the next bus stop?
Wo ist die nächste Bushaltestelle?
vō ist dē nāsh'stə bōos'hältəshtelə

Where do the buses to . . . stop?
Wo halten die Busse nach . . .?
vō häl'tən dē bōos'ə näh . . .

Is that far?
Ist das weit?
ist däs vīt

When does *a (the first/last)* bus leave for . . .?
Wann fährt *ein (der erste/letzte)* Bus nach . . .?
vän färt īn (dār ers'tə/lets'tə) bōos näh . . .

Which bus goes to . . .?
Welcher Bus fährt nach . . .?
vel'shər bōos färt näh . . .

Where does the bus go?
Wohin fährt der Bus?
vōhin' färt dār bōos

Is there a bus (Does this bus go) to . . .?
Fährt *ein (dieser)* Bus nach . . .?
färt īn (dē'zər) bōos näh . . .

When do we get to . . .?
Wann sind wir in . . .?
vän zint vēr in . . .

Do I have to change buses for . . .?
Muß ich nach . . . umsteigen?
mōos ish näh . . . ōom'shtīgən

Where do I have to change?
Wo muß ich umsteigen?
vō mōos ish ōom'shtīgən

One (Two) round-trip ticket(s), please.
Eine (Zwei) Rückfahrkarte(n) bitte.
ī'nə (tsvī) rik'färkär'tə(n) bit'ə

One full-fare and one half-fare to . . ., please.
Einmal und ein Kind nach . . . bitte.
īn'mäl ōont īn kint näh . . . bit'ə

bus	der Bus	bōos
bus terminal	der Busbahnhof	bōos'bänhöf
conductor	der Schaffner	shäf'nər
direction	die Richtung	rish'tŏong
driver	der Fahrer	fä'rər
last stop	die Endhaltestelle . . .	ent'hältəshtel'ə
luggage	das Gepäck	gəpek'
route	die Linie	lē'nē-ə
stop	die Haltestelle	häl'təshtel'ə
ticket	der Fahrschein	fär'shīn
transfer	der Umsteigefahr- schein	ōom'shtīgəfär'shīn

BY TRAIN

At the Station

Where is the *station (main station)?*
Wo ist der *Bahnhof (Hauptbahnhof)?*
vō ist dār bän'hōf (houpt'bänhōf)

Where is (are) ...?
Wo ist (sind) ...?
vō ist (zint) ...

the first aid station ..	der Sanitätsraum	zänitäts'roum
the information office	das Auskunftsbüro	ous'koonftsbēro'
the money exchange .	die Wechselstube	vek'səlshtoo'bə
Platform 2	Bahnsteig 2	bän'shtīk tsvī
the rest room	die Toilette	tō·älet'ə
the restaurant	das Restaurant	restôränt'
the room referral office	der Zimmernachweis ..	tsim'ərnäh' vīs
the ticket window ...	der Fahrkartenschalter	fär'kärtənshäl'tər
a time table	ein Fahrplan	fär'plän
the waiting room	der Wartesaal	vär'təzäl

Time Table

arrival/departure	Ankunft/Abfahrt	än'koonft/äp'färt
connection	der Anschlußzug	än'shloos·tsook'
couchette sleeper	der Liegewagen	lē'gəvä'gən
dining car	der Speisewagen	shpī'zəvä'gən
express train	der *Schnellzug (D-Zug)*	shnel'tsook (dā'-tsook)
fast train	der Eilzug	īl'tsook
long distance express	der Fernschnellzug	fern'shnel'tsook
motorail service	der Autoreisezug	ou'tōrī'zətsook'
platform	das Gleis, der Bahnsteig	glīs, bän'shtīk
rail car	der Triebwagen	trēp'vägən
sleeper, sleeping car .	der Schlafwagen	shläf'vägən

> *A couchette car provides overnight travelers with a simple bench and blanket to stretch out during the night. A sleeping car contains little bedrooms complete with private washing facilities.*

suburban train	der Vorortzug	fōr'ôrt·tsook'
supplemental fare payable	zuschlagpflichtig	tsoo'shläkpflish'tish

system time table ...	das Kursbuch	kōōrs'bōōh
through car	der Kurswagen	kōōrs'vägən
track	das Gleis	glīs

Information

When is there a *local (express)* train to ...?

Wann fährt ein *Personenzug (Schnellzug)* nach ...?
vän fārt īn perzō'nəntsōōk (shnel'tsōōk) näh ...

Where is the train to ...?

Wo ist der Zug nach ...?
vō ist dār tsōōk näh ...

Is this the train to ...?

Ist das der Zug nach ...?
ist däs dār tsōōk näh ...

Does this train go by way of ...?

Fährt dieser Zug über ...?
fārt dē'zər tsōōk ē'bər ...

Does this train stop in ...?

Hält dieser Zug in ...?
helt dē'zər tsōōk in ...

Is the train from ... late?

Hat der Zug aus ... Verspätung?
hät dār tsōōk ous ... fershpā'tōōng

How late?

Wieviel?
vēfēl'

Can we make a connection to ...?

Haben wir Anschluß nach ...?
hä'bən vēr än'shlōōs näh ...

When does it get to ...?

Wann ist er in ...?
vän ist ār in ...

Do we have to change trains?

Müssen wir umsteigen?
mis'ən vēr ōōm'shtīgən

Where?

Wo?
vō

Is there a *dining car (Are there sleepers)* on the train?

Hat der Zug *einen Speisewagen (Schlafwagen)?*
hät dār tsōōk ī'nən shpī'zəvä'gən (shläf'vägən)

Can I interrupt the trip in ...?

Kann ich die Fahrt in ... unterbrechen?
kän ish dē färt in ... ōōntərbresh'ən

What platform does the train from ... come in on?

Auf welchem Bahnsteig kommt der Zug aus ... an?
ouf vel'shəm bän'shtīk kômt dār tsōōk ous ... än

What platform does the train for ... leave from?

Von welchem Bahnsteig fährt der Zug nach ... ab?
fôn vel'shəm bän'shtīk fārt dār tsōōk näh ... äp

Tickets

One ticket (Two full fares and two half fares) to . . ., please.
Bitte *eine Karte (zweimal und zwei Kinder)* nach . . .
bit'ə ī'nə kär'tə (tsvī'mäl ōont tsvī kin'dər) näh . . .

– round trip.	– one way.	– first class.	– second class.
– hin und zurück.	– einfach.	– erster Klasse.	– zweiter Klasse.
– hin ōont tsōōrík'	– īn'fäh	– ers'tər kläs'ə	– tsvī'tər kläs'ə

I'd like to reserve a seat on the twelve o'clock train to . . .
Ich möchte eine Platzkarte für den Zwölf-Uhr-Zug nach . . .
ish mesh'tə ī'nə pläts'kärtə fēr dän tsvelf'ōōr' tsōōk näh . . .

How long is the ticket valid?
Wie lange ist die Karte gültig?
vē läng'ə ist dē kär'tə gil'tish

I'd like to interrupt the trip in . . .
Ich möchte die Fahrt in . . . unterbrechen.
ish mesh'tə dē färt in . . . ōontərbresh'ən

I'd like to reserve . . .	**Please reserve two seats.**
Ich möchte . . . vorbestellen.	Reservieren Sie bitte zwei Plätze.
ish mesh'tə . . . fōr'bəshtelən	räzervē'rən zē bit'ə tsvī ple'tsə

How much is the fare to . . .?
Was kostet die Fahrt nach . . .?
väs kôs'tət dē färt näh . . .

fare	der Fahrpreis	fär'prīs
group fare ticket	der Sammelfahrschein .	zäm'əlfär'shīn
half fare	die Kinderfahrkarte . . .	kin'dərfär'kärtə
one-day round-trip . .	die Tagesrückfahrkarte	tä'gəsrík'färkär'tə
platform ticket	die Bahnsteigkarte	bän'shtīk·kär'tə
round-trip ticket	die Rückfahrkarte	rík'färkär'tə
seat reservation	die Platzkarte	pläts'kär'tə
sleeper reservation . .	die Schlafwagenkarte . .	shläf'vägənkär'tə
supplemental fare		
ticket	die Zuschlagkarte	tsōō'shläk·kär'tə
ticket	die Fahrkarte	fär'kär'tə
– **one-way ticket**	die einfache Fahr-	īn'fähə fär'kär'tə
	karte	
– **reduced fare**	die ermäßigte Fahr-	ermä'sishtə fär'-
ticket	karte	kär'tə

Baggage

> *In European countries, you can check your bag with the railroad, just as you do with an airline, and then pick it up at your destination. If you are checking your baggage to be forwarded, you should go to the Gepäckabfertigung. If you are simply checking your luggage within the station, go to the Gepäckannahme or the Gepäckaufbewahrung.*

I'd like to ... — **send this luggage on to ...**
Ich möchte .... — dieses Gepäck nach ... aufgeben.
i*sh* mesh' tə ... — dē' zəs gəpek' nä*h* ... ouf gäbən

— **leave this luggage here.** — *insure (claim) my luggage.*
— dieses Gepäck hierlassen. — mein Gepäck *versichern (abholen)*.
— dē' zəs gəpek' hēr' *läs*ən — mīn gəpek' ferzi*sh*' ərn (äp' hōlən)

Here's my claim check. **These aren't mine.**
Hier ist der Gepäckschein. Das sind nicht meine Sachen.
hēr ist dār gəpek' shīn däs zint ni*sh*t mī' nə zäh' ən

There are two suitcases and a traveling bag. **One suitcase is missing.**
Es sind zwei Koffer und eine Tasche. Es fehlt ein Koffer.
es zint tsvī kôf' ər ōont ī' nə täsh' ə es fält īn kôf' ər

Will my baggage be on the same train? **When does it get to ...?**
Geht mein Gepäck mit demselben Zug ab? Wann ist es in ...?
gät mīn gəpek' mit dämzel' bən tsōok äp vän ist es in ...

baggage	das Gepäck	gəpek'
baggage check area ..	die Gepäckaufbewah-rung	gəpek' oufbəvä'-rōong
baggage claim area ..	die Gepäckausgabe ...	gəpek' ousgä' bə
baggage deposit area	die Gepäckannahme ..	gəpek' än·nä' mə
claim check	der Gepäckschein	gəpek' shīn
hand luggage	das Handgepäck	hänt' gəpek
luggage	das Gepäck	gəpek'
luggage forwarding office	die Gepäckabfertigung	gəpek' äpfer' tigōong
luggage locker	das Schließfach	shlēs' fäh
suitcase	der Koffer	kôf' ər
traveling bag	die Tasche	täsh' ə

Porter

porter	der Gepäckträger	gəpek'trä'gər

Please bring this *luggage (suitcase)* ...
Dieses Gepäck (Diesen Koffer) bitte ...
dē'zəs gəpek' (dē'zən kôf'ər) bit'ə ...

– to the ... train.
– zum Zug nach ...
– tsoom tsook näh ...

– to Platform 2.
– zum Bahnsteig zwei.
– tsoom bän'shtīk tsvī

– to the baggage check area.
– zur Aufbewahrung.
– tsoor ouf'bəvä'roong

– to the exit.
– zum Ausgang.
– tsoom ous'gäng

– to a taxi.
– zum Taxi.
– tsoom täk'sē

– to the ... bus.
– zum Bus nach ...
– tsoom boos näh ...

How much does that cost?
Wieviel bekommen Sie?
vē'fēl bəkôm'ən zē

On the Platform

Is this the train *to (from)* ...?
Ist das der Zug *nach (aus)* ...?
ist däs där tsook näh (ous) ...

Where is ...?
Wo ist ...?
vō ist ...

– first class?
– die erste Klasse?
– dē ers'tə kläs'ə

– the through car to ...?
– der Kurswagen nach ...?
– där koors'vägən näh ...

> *European express trains are frequently reassembled at major stations with different cars going to different destinations. Make sure before you get aboard that your car will take you where you want to go.*

– the couchette car?
– der Liegewagen?
– där lē'gəvä'gən

– the sleeping car?
– der Schlafwagen?
– där shläf'vägən

– the dining car?
– der Speisewagen?
– där shpī'zəvä'gən

– the luggage car?
– der Gepäckwagen?
– där gəpek'vägən

– car number ...?
– Wagen Nummer ...?
– vä'gən noom'ər ...

There.	**Up front.**	**In the middle.**
Dort.	Vorn.	In der Mitte.
dôrt	fôrn	in dār mit'ə

At the rear.
Am Ende.
*ä*m en'də

What time does the train arrive?
Wann kommt der Zug an?
vän kômt dār tsōōk *ä*n

AUFSICHT		AUSKUNFT
Station Master		**Information**

AUSGANG	ZU DEN BAHNSTEIGEN	ERFRISCHUNGEN
Exit	**To Trains**	**Refreshments**

GEPÄCKANNAHME	GLEIS
Baggage Checking	**Platform (Track)**

SANITÄTSRAUM	TRINKWASSER
First Aid	**Drinking Water**

TOILETTEN	HERREN	DAMEN
Rest Rooms	**Gentlemen**	**Ladies**

ÜBERGANG	WARTESAAL	UNTERFÜHRUNG
Overpass	**Waiting room**	**Underpass**

On the Train

Is this seat taken?
Ist dieser Platz besetzt?
ist dē'zər pläts bəzetst'

That's my seat.
Das ist mein Platz.
däs ist mīn pläts

Mind if I *open (close)* the window?
Darf ich das Fenster *öffnen (schließen)?*
därf i*sh* däs fens'tər *e*f'nən (shlē'sən)

Allow me (to get past you).
Gestatten Sie?
gəshtät'ən zē

Could you please help me?
Können Sie mir bitte helfen?
ken'ən zē mēr bit'ə hel'fən

I don't like riding backwards.
Ich kann nicht rückwärts fahren.
ish kän nisht rĭk'verts fä'rən

Would you mind changing places?
Können wir die Plätze tauschen?
ken'ən vēr dē plets'ə tou'shən

*Tickets, please.
Die Fahrkarten bitte.
dē fär'kärtən bit'ə

I'd like to pay the excess fare (pay the supplement, pay now).
Ich möchte *zuzahlen (nachlösen).*
ish mesh'tə tsōō'tsälən (näh'lāzən)

How many stations before . . . ?
Wieviele Stationen noch bis . . . ?
vē'fēlə shtätsyō'nən nôh bis . . .

How long do we stop here?
Wie lange haben wir Aufenthalt?
vē läng'ə hä'bən vēr ouf'enthält

Will we get to . . . on time?
Sind wir pünktlich in . . . ?
zint vēr pĭngkt'lish in . . .

Where are we now?
Wo sind wir jetzt?
vō zint vēr yetst

Will I make it on time to change trains for . . . ?
Erreiche ich den Zug nach . . . noch?
erī'shə ish dān tsōōk näh . . . nôh

*All change, please!
Umsteigen, bitte!
ŏŏm'shtīgən, bit'ə

*Passengers for . . . change at . . .
Reisende nach . . . in . . . umsteigen.
rī'zəndə näh . . . in . . . ŏŏm'shtīgən

*Passengers for . . . get on the *front (rear)* of the train!
Kurswagen nach . . . *im vorderen Teil (am Ende)* des Zuges.
kŏŏrs'vägən näh . . . im fôr'dərən tīl (äm en'də) des tsōō'gəs

NICHTRAUCHER	RAUCHER	NOTBREMSE
No smoking	Smoking	Emergency Brake

SPEISEWAGEN	SCHLAFWAGEN
Dining Car	Sleeping Car

TOILETTE	FREI	BESETZT
Rest Room	Vacant	Occupied

*all aboard! . . . . alles einsteigen! . . . . äl'əs īn'shtīgən
arrival . . . . die Ankunft . . . . än'kŏŏnft
arrive . . . . ankommen . . . . än'kômən
baggage . . . . das Gepäck . . . . gəpek'

baggage car	der Gepäckwagen	gəpek' vägən
barrier	die Sperre	shper'ə
car	der *Wagen (Waggon)*	vä' gən (vägôN)
car door	die Wagentür	vä' gəntēr'
change trains	umsteigen	ōōm' shtīgən
compartment	das Abteil	äptīl'
conductor	der Schaffner	shäf' nər
– head conductor	der Zugführer	tsōōk' fērər
connection	der Anschluß	än' shlōōs
depart	abfahren	äp' färən
departure	die Abfahrt	äp' färt
engine	die Lokomotive	lôkōmōtē' və
– engineer	der Lokführer	lôk' fērər
entrance	der Eingang	īn' gäng
exit	der Ausgang	ous' gäng
fare	der Fahrpreis	fär' prīs
– discount	die Ermäßigung	ermä' sigōōng
get *in (aboard)*	einsteigen	īn' shtīgən
get off	aussteigen	ous' shtīgən
heating	die Heizung	hī' tsōōng
– cold	kalt	kält
– warm	warm	värm
information	die Auskunft	ous' kōōnft
locomotive	die Lokomotive	lôkōmōtē' və
luggage	das Gepäck	gəpek'
luggage rack	das Gepäcknetz	gəpek' nets
passenger	der Fahrgast	fär' gäst

(There is no female form of Fahrgast.)

platform	der *Bahnsteig (das Gleis)*	bän' shtīk (glīs)
railroad	die Eisenbahn	ī' zənbän
route	die Strecke	shtrek' ə
station	der Bahnhof	bän' hôf
station master	der Bahnhofsvorsteher	bän' hôfsfôr-shtä·ər
stop	der Aufenthalt	ouf' enthält'
system time table	das Kursbuch	kōōrs' bōōh
ticket	die Fahrkarte	fär' kärtə
track	das Gleis,	glīs,
	der Bahnsteig	bän' shtīk
train	der Zug	tsōōk
window seat	der Fensterplatz	fens' tərpläts

BY PLANE

Information and Reservations

Is there a (direct) flight to . . . ?
Gibt es eine (direkte) Flugverbindung nach . . . ?
gēpt es ī′nə (direk′tə) flook′ferbin′doong näh . . .

When is there a plane *today (tomorrow)* to . . . ?
Wann fliegt *heute (morgen)* eine Maschine nach . . . ?
vän flēkt hoi′tə (môr′gən) ī′nə mäshē′nə näh . . .

When is the next plane to . . . ?
Wann fliegt die nächste Maschine nach . . . ?
vän flēkt dē näsh′stə mäshē′nə näh . . .

Does the plane make a stopover in . . . ?
Hat die Maschine in . . . eine Zwischenlandung?
hät dē mäshē′nə in . . . ī′ne tsvish′ənländoong

Is there a connection to . . . ?
Habe ich Anschluß nach . . . ?
hä′bə ish än′shloos näh . . .

How long is the ticket valid?
Wie lange ist der Flugschein gültig?
vē läng′ə ist dār flook′shīn gil′tish

When do we get to . . . ?
Wann sind wir in . . . ?
vän zint vēr in . . .

Are there still seats available?
Sind noch Plätze frei?
zint nôh plets′ə frī

How much is a (round-trip) flight to . . . ?
Was kostet ein Flug nach . . . (und zurück)?
väs kôs′tət īn flook näh . . . (oont tsoorík′)

What's the luggage allowance?
Wieviel Gepäck ist frei?
vē′fēl gəpek′ ist frī

How much does excess baggage cost?
Was kostet das Übergepäck?
väs kôs′tət däs ē′bərgəpek′

How much is the airport service charge?
Wie hoch ist die Flughafengebühr?
vē hōh ist dē flook′häfəngəbēr′

How do I get to the airport?
Wie komme ich zum Flughafen?
vē kôm′ə ish tsoōm flook′häfən

When is check-in time?
Wann muß ich dort sein?
vän moos ish dôrt zīn

I'd like to reserve a seat on the Friday flight to …
Bitte für Freitag einen Flug nach …
bit'ə fẽr frī'täk ī'nən flōōk näh…

I'd like to reserve a round-trip ticket to … on the 8th of May.
Bitte für den achten Mai einen Hin- und Rückflug nach …
bit'ə fẽr dān äh'tən mī ī'nən hin- ōōnt rĭk'flōōk näh …

– **First Class.**	– **Business Class.**	– **Economy Class.**
– Erste Klasse.	– Business-Klasse.	– Economy-Klasse.
– ers'tə kläs'ə	– biz'nis-kläs'ə	– ikôn'əmi-kläs'ə

I have to *cancel (change)* my reservation.
Ich muß diesen Flug *annullieren (umbuchen)*.
ish mōōs dē'zən flōōk *änōōlēr'ən (ōōm'bōōhən)*

What is the cancellation fee?
Wie hoch ist die Annullierungsgebühr?
vē hōh ist dē *änōōlēr'ōōngsgəbẽr'*

At the Airport

Can I take this along as hand luggage?
Kann ich das als Handgepäck mitnehmen?
kän ish däs äls hänt'gəpek mit'nāmən

How much does it cost?
Was muß ich zahlen?
väs mōōs ish tsä'lən

Where is *the waiting room (Exit B, Gate B)*?
Wo ist *der Warteraum (Ausgang B, Flugsteig B)*?
vō ist dār vär'təroum (ous'gäng bā, flōōk'shtīk bā)

Where is the information counter?
Wo ist der Informationsschalter?
vō ist dār in'fôrmätsyōns'shältər

Where's the duty-free shop?
Wo gibt es hier zollfreie Waren?
vō gēpt es hēr tsôl'frī-ə vä'rən

Is the plane to … late?
Hat die Maschine nach … Verspätung?
hät dē mäshē'nə näh … fershpā'tōōng

Has the plane from … already landed?
Ist die Maschine aus … schon gelandet?
ist dē mäshē'nə ous … shōn gəlän'dət

On the Plane

*Would you please fasten your seat belts and refrain from smoking.
Wir bitten Sie nun, sich anzuschnallen und das Rauchen einzustellen.
vēr bit'ən zē nōon, zish än'tsōoshnäl'ən ōont däs rouh'ən īn'tsōoshtel'ən

How high are we flying?
Wie hoch fliegen wir?
vē hōh flē'gən vēr

Where are we now?
Wo sind wir jetzt?
vō zint vēr yetst

What *mountains are those (river is that)*?
Was ist das für ein *Gebirge (Fluß)*?
väs ist däs fēr īn gəbir'gə (flōos)

Can I have …?
Kann ich … haben?
kän ish … hä'bən

Have you got an air sickness remedy?
Haben Sie ein Mittel gegen Luftkrankheit?
hä'bən zē īn mit'əl gā'gən lōoft'krängk·hīt

I feel sick.
Mir ist schlecht.
mēr ist shlesht

When do we land?
Wann landen wir?
vän län'dən vēr

How's the weather in …?
Wie ist das Wetter in …?
vē ist däs vet'ər in …

aircraft	das Flugzeug	flōok'tsoik
air jet *(over the seat)*	die Frischluftdüse	frish'lōoftdē'zə
airline	die Fluggesellschaft	flōok'gəzel'shäft
airline passenger	der Fluggast	flōok'gäst
airport	der Flughafen	flōok'häfən
airport service charge	die Flughafengebühr	flōok'häfəngəber'
air sickness	die Luftkrankheit	lōoft'krängk·hīt
approach	der Anflug	än'flōok
arrival	die Ankunft	än'kōonft
charter plane	die Chartermaschine	tshär'tərmäshē'nə
climb	aufsteigen	ouf'shtīgən
crew	die Besatzung	bəzäts'ōong
destination	der Zielflughafen	tsēl'flōok·häfən
duty-free goods	zollfreie Waren	tsōl'frī·ə vä'rən
emergency chute	die Notrutsche	nōt'rōotshə
emergency exit	der Notausgang	nōt'ousgäng
emergency landing	die Notlandung	nōt'ländōong

engine	das Triebwerk	trēp'verk
excess baggage	das Übergepäck	ē'bərgəpek'
exit	der Ausgang	ous'gäng
flight	der Flug	flōok
flight attendant	der Steward,	styōo'ərt
	die Stewardeß	styōo'ərdes
fly	fliegen	flē'gən
flying time	die Flugzeit	flōok'tsīt
fog	der Nebel	nā'bəl
gate	der Flugsteig	flōok'shtīk
hand luggage	das Handgepäck	hänt'gəpek'
helicopter	der Hubschrauber	hōop'shroubər
information	die Auskunft	ous'kōonft
information counter	der Informations-schalter	in'fôrmätsyōns'-shäl'tər
intermediate landing	die Zwischenlandung	tsvish'ənländōong
jet	die Düse	dē'zə
jet plane	das Düsenflugzeug	dē'zənflōok'tsoik
land	landen	län'dən
landing	die Landung	län'dōong
landing gear	das Fahrwerk	fär'verk
life jacket	die Schwimmweste	shvim'vestə
pilot	der Pilot	pilōt'
plane	das Flugzeug,	flōok'tsoik,
	die Maschine	mäshē'nə
reservation	die Buchung	bōo'hōong
return flight	der Rückflug	rīk'flōok
route	die Strecke	shtrek'ə
scheduled flight	der Linienflug	lē'nē·ənflōok
seat belt	der Anschnallgurt	än'shnälgōort'
– fasten seat belts	bitte anschnallen	bit'ə än'shnälən
stopover	die Zwischenlandung	tsvish'ənländōong
system timetable	der Flugplan	flōok'plän
take-off	der Abflug	äp'flōok
thunderstorm	das Gewitter	gəvit'ər
ticket	der Flugschein,	flōok'shīn,
	das Ticket	tik'ət
waiting room	der Warteraum	vär'təroum
weather	das Wetter	vet'ər
wing	die Tragfläche,	träk'fleshə,
	der Flügel	flē'gəl

BY SHIP

Information, Tickets

When does *a ship (the ferry)* leave for …? **Where?**
Wann fährt *ein Schiff (die Fähre)* nach …? Wo?
vän färt īn shif (dē fär'ə) näh … vo

How often does the car ferry go to …?
Wie oft geht die Autofähre nach …?
vē ôft gāt dē ou'tōfä'rə näh …

How long does the crossing (from …) to … take?
Wie lange dauert die Überfahrt (von …) nach …?
vē läng'ə dou'ərt dē ē'bərfärt (fôn …) näh …

How far is the railroad station from the harbor?
Wie weit ist der Bahnhof vom Hafen entfernt?
vē vīt ist där bän'hōf fôm hä'fən entfernt'

What are the ports of call?
Welche Häfen werden angelaufen?
vel'shə hä'fən vär'dən än'gəloufən

When do we *dock (land)* at …? **Can I get a connection to …?**
Wann legen wir in … an? Habe ich Anschluß nach …?
vän lā'gən vēr in … än hä'bə ish än'shlōos näh …

Can we go ashore at …? **For how long?**
Kann man in … an Land gehen? Wie lange?
kän män in … än länt gā'ən vē läng'ə

Will there be any land excursions?
Werden Landausflüge gemacht?
vär'dən länt'ousflē'gə gəmäht'

When do we have to be back on board?
Wann müssen wir wieder an Bord sein?
vän mis'ən vēr vē'dər än bôrt zīn

Where can we get tickets?
Wo bekommt man Karten?
vō bəkômt' män kär'tən

I'd like ...	– to book passage to ...
Ich möchte ...	– einen Schiffsplatz nach ...
ish mesh'tə	– ī'nən shifs'pläts näh ...

– two tickets on the ... to ... tomorrow.
– für morgen zwei Plätze auf der ... nach ...
– fĕr môr'gən tsvī plets'ə ouf dār ... näh ...

– a round-trip ticket from ... to ... and back.
– eine Rundreisekarte von ... nach ... und zurück.
– ī'nə rōont'rīzəkär'tə fôn ... näh ... ōont tsōorĭk'

– a ticket for a *car (motorcycle, bicycle)*.
– einen Beförderungsschein für ein *Auto (Motorrad, Fahrrad)*.
– ī'nən bəfĕr'dərōongs·shīn fĕr īn ou'tō (mō'tôrät, fä'rät)

– a single cabin.	**– an *outside (inside)* cabin.**
– eine Einzelkabine.	– eine *Außen- (Innen-)*Kabine.
– ī'nə īn'tsəlkäbē'nə	– ī'nə ou'sən- (in'ən-)käbē'nə

– a double cabin.	**First Class.**	**Tourist Class.**
– eine Zweibettkabine.	Erste Klasse.	Touristenklasse.
– ī'nə tsvī'betkäbē'nə	ers'tə kläs'ə	tōoris'tənkläs'ə

In the Harbor

Where is the "..." lying?	**Where does the "..." dock?**
Wo liegt die „..."?	Wo legt die „..." an?
vō lēkt dē ...	vō lākt dē ... *än*

Does this ship sail to ...?	**When does she sail?**
Fährt dieses Schiff nach ...?	Wann legt es ab?
fārt dē'zəs shif näh ...	vän lākt es *ä*p

Where is the *shipping company's office (harbor police station, customs office)*?
Wo ist die *Reederei (Hafenpolizei, Zollverwaltung)*?
vō ist dē rādərī' (hä'fənpōlitsī', tsôl'ferväl'tōong)

Where can I pick up my luggage?
Wo erhalte ich mein Gepäck?
vō erhäl'tə ish mīn gəpek'

I come from the "...".
Ich komme von der „...".
ish kôm'ə fôn dār ...

On Board

I'm looking for cabin no. ...	**Where's my baggage?**
Ich suche Kabine Nr. ...	Wo ist mein Gepäck?
i*sh* zōo'hə käbē'nə nōom'ər ...	vō ist mīn gəpek'

Have you got ... on board?	**Please, where is ...?**
Haben Sie ... an Bord?	Bitte, wo ist ...?
hä'bən zē ... än bôrt	bit'ə, vō ist ...

the bar	die Bar	bär
the *barber shop*		
(beauty parlor)	der Friseursalon	frizär'zälôN
the dining room	der Speisesaal	shpī'zəzäl
the lounge	der Aufenthaltsraum ..	ouf'enthältsroum'
the purser's office ...	das Zahlmeisterbüro ..	tsäl'mīstərbērō'
the radio room	der Funkraum	fōongk'roum
the reading room	der Leseraum	lā'zəroum
the ship's photo-		
grapher	der Bordfotograf......	bôrt'fōtōgräf'
the sick bay	das Schiffshospital	shifs'hôspitäl'
the swimming pool ..	der Swimmingpool	svim'ingpōol'
the tour guide's		
office	die Reiseleitung	rī'zəlī`tōong

I'd like to speak to the ...
Ich möchte den ... sprechen.
i*sh* me*sh*'tə dān ... shpre*sh*'ən

– **captain**	Kapitän	käpitän'
– **chief steward**	Obersteward	ō'bərstyōo·ərt
– **deck officer**	Deckoffizier	dek'ôfitsēr'
– **luggage master**	Gepäckoffizier	gəpek'ôfitsēr'
– **purser**	Zahlmeister	tsäl'mīstər
– **ship's doctor**	Schiffsarzt	shifs'ärtst
– **tour guide**	Reiseleiter	rī'zəlī'tər

Steward, please bring me ...
Steward, bringen Sie mir bitte ...
styōo'ərt, bring'ən zē mēr bit'ə ...

Please call the ship's doctor!
Bitte rufen Sie den Schiffsarzt!
bit′ə roo̅′fən zē dān shifs′ärtst

Have you got anything for seasickness?
Haben Sie ein Mittel gegen Seekrankheit?
hä′bən zē īn mit′əl gā′gən zā′krängk·hīt

What is the voltage here?
Welche Stromspannung ist hier?
vel′shə shtrōm′shpän′oong ist hēr

air conditioning	die Klimaanlage	klē′mä·änlä′gə
anchor	der Anker	äng′kər
bank	das Ufer	oo̅′fər
barge	der Kahn	kän
bay	die Bucht	boo̅ht
blanket	die Wolldecke	vôl′dekə
board	Bord	bôrt
– on board	an Bord	än bôrt
boat	das Boot	bōt
– fishing trawler	das Fischerboot	fish′ərbōt
– launch	die Barkasse	bärkäs′ə
– lifeboat	das Rettungsboot	ret′oo̅ongsbōt
– motorboat	das Motorboot	mō′tôrbōt
– sailboat	das Segelboot	zā′gəlbōt
bow	der Bug	boo̅k
breeze	die Brise	brē′zə
bridge	die Kommandobrücke	kômän′dōbrĭk′ə
buoy	die Boje	bō′yə
cabin	die Kabine	käbē′nə
cable	das Kabel	kä′bəl
call (at port)	anlaufen	än′loufən
canal	der Kanal	känäl′
captain	der Kapitän	käpitän′
captain's table	der Kapitänstisch	käp′itäns′tish
coast	die Küste	kis′tə
course	der Kurs	koo̅rs
crew	die Mannschaft	män′shäft
crossing	die Überfahrt	ē′bərfärt
cruise	die Kreuzfahrt	kroits′färt

deck	das Deck	dek
– boat deck	das Bootsdeck	bōts'dek
– fore deck	das Vorderdeck	fôr'dərdek
– main deck	das Hauptdeck	houpt'dek
– poop deck	das Achterdeck	*äh*'tərdek
– promenade deck	das Promenadendeck	prō'mənä'dəndek'
– saloon deck	das Salondeck	sälôN'dek
– steerage	das Zwischendeck	tsvish'əndek
– sun deck	das Sonnendeck	zôn'əndek
– upper deck	das Oberdeck	ō'bərdek
deck chair	der Liegestuhl	lē'gəshtōōl
disembark	ausbooten	ous'bōtən
dock *(noun)*	das Dock	dôk
dock *(verb)*	anlegen	*ä*n'lāgən
excursion	der Landausflug	länt'ousflōōk
excursion program	das Ausflugsprogramm	ous'flōōksprōgräm'
farewell dinner	das Abschiedsessen	*ä*p'shētses'ən
ferry	die Fähre	fär'ə
– car ferry	die Autofähre	ou'tōfärə
– train ferry	die Eisenbahnfähre	ī'zənbänfär'ə
first officer	der erste Offizier	ers'tə ôfitsēr'
gangway	die Gangway	geng'vā
harbor	der Hafen	hä'fən
harbor police	die Hafenpolizei	hä'fənpôlitsī'
helm	das Steuer	shtoi'ər
helmsman	der Steuermann	shtoi'ərm*ä*n
island	die Insel	in'zəl
jetty	die Mole	mōl'ə
knot	der Knoten	knō'tən
lake	der See	zā
land *(noun)*	das Land	länt
land *(verb)*	anlegen	*ä*n'lāgən
landing place	der Anlegeplatz	*ä*n'lāgəpl*ä*ts
landing stage	der Anlegesteg,	*ä*n'lāgəshtāk',
	die Landungsbrücke	län'dōōngsbr*i*kə
lap rug	die Wolldecke	vôl'dekə
life belt	der Rettungsring	ret'ōōngsring'
life jacket	die Schwimmweste	shvim'vestə
lighthouse	der Leuchtturm	loi*sh*t'tōōrm
mast	der Mast	m*ä*st
mole	die Mole	mōl'ə

ocean	der Ozean	ō′tsä·än
passenger	der Passagier	päsäzhēr′
pier	die Mole	mōl′ə
place on deck	der Deckplatz	dek′pläts
playroom	das Kinderspielzimmer	kin′dərshpēltsim′ər
port *(land)*	der Hafen	hä′fən
port *(side)*	Backbord	bäk′bôrt
port fees	die Hafengebühr	hä′fəngəbēr
quai	der Kai	kī
railing	die Reling	rā′ling
river	der Fluß	floos
rope	das *Seil (Tau)*	zīl (tou)
rough seas	der Seegang	zā′gäng
rudder	das Ruder	roo′dər
sail	das Segel	zā′gəl
sailor	der Matrose	mätrō′zə
sea	die See	zā
– on the high seas . . .	auf hoher See	ouf hō′ər zā
seasickness	die Seekrankheit	zā′kränk·hīt
ship	das Schiff	shif
– freighter	das Frachtschiff	fräht′shif
– passenger ship	das Passagierschiff	päsäzhēr′shif
– warship	das Kriegsschiff	krēks′shif
ship's doctor	der Schiffsarzt	shifs′ärtst
shipboard party	das Bordfest	bôrt′fest
shipping agency	die Schiffsagentur	shifs′ägentoor′
shipping company . . .	die Reederei	rādərī′
shore	das Ufer	oo′fər
starboard	Steuerbord	shtoi′ərbôrt
steamer	das Dampfschiff	dämpf′shif
stern	das Heck	hek
steward	der Steward	styoo′ərt
strait	die Straße	shträ′sə
tourist class	die Touristenklasse	tooris′tənkläs′ə
tug	der Schlepper	shlep′ər
voyage	die *Schiffsreise (Seereise)*	shifs′rīzə (zā′rīzə)
wave	die Welle	vel′ə
yacht	die Jacht	yäht

AT THE BORDER

Passport Control

When do we get to the border?
Wann sind wir an der Grenze?
vän zint vēr än dār gren′tsə

*Your papers, please.
Ihre Papiere, bitte.
ē′rə päpē′rə, bit′ə

*Your passport, please.
Ihren Paß, bitte!
ē′rən päs, bit′ə

Here they are.
Hier, bitte.
hēr, bit′ə

I'll be staying *a week (two weeks, until the . . .).*
Ich bleibe *eine Woche (zwei Wochen, bis zum . . .).*
ish blī′bə ī′nə vô′hə (tsvī vō′hən, bis tsōōm . . .)

I'm here *on business (on vacation).*
Ich bin auf *Geschäftsreise (Urlaubsreise)* hier.
ish bin ouf gəshefts′rīzə (ōōr′loupsrī′zə) hēr

I'm (We're) visiting . . .
Ich besuche (Wir besuchen) . . .
ish bəzōō′hə (vēr bəzōō′hən) . . .

Do I have to fill in this form?
Muß ich das Formular ausfüllen?
mōōs ish däs fôrmōōlär′ ous′filən

I haven't got a vaccination certificate.
Ich habe keinen Impfschein.
ish hä′bə kī′nən impf′shīn

What should I do?
Was soll ich tun?
väs zôl ish tōōn

I *have (haven't)* **had a** *smallpox (cholera)* **vaccination.**
Ich bin (nicht) gegen *Pocken (Cholera)* geimpft.
ish bin (nisht) gā′gən pôk′ən (kō′lərä) gə·impft′

I'm traveling with the . . . group.
Ich gehöre zu der Reisegruppe von . . .
ish gəhā′rə tsōō dār rī′zəgrōōpə fôn . . .

The children are entered in my passport.
Die Kinder sind in meinem Paß eingetragen.
dē kin′dər zint in mī′nəm päs īn′gəträgən

Can I get my visa here?
Kann ich das Visum hier bekommen?
kän ish däs vē′zōōm hēr bəkôm′ən

May I please phone my consulate?
Kann ich bitte mit meinem Konsulat telefonieren?
kän ish bit′ə mit mī′nəm kônzōōlät′ tā′läfōnēr′ən

border	die Grenze	gren′tsə
color of eyes	die Augenfarbe	ou′gənfärbə
color of hair	die Haarfarbe	här′färbə
date of birth	das Geburtsdatum	gəboorts′dätoom
departure	die Ausreise	ous′rīzə
distinguishing	besondere	bəzôn′dərə
marks	Kennzeichen	ken′tsīshən
driver's license	der Führerschein	fē′rərshīn
entry	die Einreise	īn′rīzə
entry visa	das Einreisevisum	īn′rīzəvē′zoom
exit visa	das Ausreisevisum	ous′rīzəvē′zoom
extend	verlängern	ferleng′ərn
height	die Größe	grä′sə
identity card	der Ausweis	ous′vīs
insurance certificate	die Versicherungskarte	ferzish′əroongs- kär′tə
international vaccin- ation certificate	der Impfpaß	impf′päs
maiden name	der Geburtsname	gəboorts′nämə
marital status	der Familienstand	fämē′lē-ənshtänt′
– single	ledig	lā′dish
– married	verheiratet	ferhī′rätət
– widowed	verwitwet	fervit′vət
– divorced	geschieden	gəshē′dən
name	der Name	nä′mə
– first name	der Vorname	fōr′nämə
– last name	der Familienname	fämē′lē-ən·nämə
nationality	die Nationalität	näts′yōnälität′
nationality plate	das Nationalitäts- kennzeichen	näts′yōnälitäts′- kentsī′shən
number	die Nummer	noom′ər
occupation	der Beruf	bəroof′
passport	der Paß	päs
passport control	die Paßkontrolle	päs′kôntrôlə
place of birth	der Geburtsort	gəboorts′ôrt
place of residence	der Wohnort	vōn′ôrt
renew	verlängern	ferleng′ərn
signature	die Unterschrift	oon′tərshrift′
valid	gültig	gil′tish

Customs Control

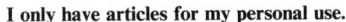

*Do you have anything to declare?
Haben Sie etwas zu verzollen?
hä'bən zē et'väs tsōō fertsôl'ən

I only have articles for my personal use.
Ich habe nur Sachen für den persönlichen Gebrauch.
ish hä'bə nōōr zä'hən fēr dän perzän'lishən gəbrouh'

That's my suitcase.
Das ist mein Koffer.
däs ist mīn kôf'ər

That isn't mine.
Das gehört mir nicht.
däs gəhärt' mēr nisht

*Please open ...
Öffnen Sie bitte ...
ef'nən zē bit'ə ...

This is a *present (souvenir)*.
Das ist ein *Geschenk (Reiseandenken)*.
däs ist īn gəshengk' (rī'zə-ändeng'kən)

I have ... *cigarettes (a bottle of perfume)*.
Ich habe ... *Zigaretten (eine Flasche Parfum)*.
ish hä'bə ... tsig'äret'ən (ī'nə fläsh'ə pärfēm')

*What's in here?
Was ist da drin?
väs ist dä drin

That's all.
Das ist alles.
däs ist äl'əs

*All right!
In Ordnung!
in ôrd'nōong

I'd like to declare this.
Ich möchte das verzollen.
ish mesh'tə däs fertsôl'ən

Do I have to pay duty on this?
Muß ich das verzollen?
mōōs ish däs fertsôl'ən

How much can I bring in duty free?
Wieviel ist zollfrei?
vē'fēl ist tsôl'frī

What do I have to pay for it?
Was muß ich dafür zahlen?
väs mōōs ish däfēr' tsä'lən

border	die Grenze	gren'tsə
border crossing	der Grenzübergang ...	grents'ēbərgäng'
customs	der Zoll.............	tsôl
customs control ...	die Zollkontrolle	tsôl'kôntrôl'ə
customs declaration .	die Zollerklärung	tsôl'erklär'ōong
customs examination .	die Zollabfertigung....	tsôl'äpfer'tigōong
customs office	das Zollamt	tsôl'ämt
customs officer	der Zollbeamte	tsôl'bə-ämtə
duty	der Zoll.............	tsôl
– **export duty**	der Ausfuhrzoll.......	ous'fōōrtsôl'
– **import duty**	der Einfuhrzoll	īn'fōōrtsôl'

ACCOMMODATIONS

Checking it out

Where is the ... *hotel (pension)*?
Wo ist *das Hotel (die Pension)* ...?
vō ist d*ä*s hōtel' (dē päNsyōn') ...

Can you recommend a good hotel?
Können Sie mir ein gutes Hotel empfehlen?
ken'ən zē mēr īn gōō'təs hōtel' empfā'lən

Is (Are) there ... near here?
Gibt es in der Nähe ...?
gēpt es in dār nā'ə ...

accommodations	eine Unterkunft	ī'nə ōōn'tərkōōnft'
apartments	Appartements	*ä*pärtəmäNs'
a boarding house	einen Gasthof	ī'nən gäst'hōf
bungalows	Bungalows	bōōng'gälōs
a camping site	einen Campingplatz	ī'nən kem'pingpläts'
a hotel	ein Hotel	īn hōtel'
an inn	einen Gasthof	ī'nən gäst'hōf
a motel	ein Motel	īn mōtel'
a pension	eine Pension	ī'nə päNsyōn'
rooms in private homes	Privatzimmer	privät'tsimər
a youth hostel	eine Jugendherberge	ī'nə yōō'gənt·her'-bergə

– **near the beach.**
– in Strandnähe.
– in shtr*ä*nt'nā·ə

– *in a quiet place (centrally located)*.
– in *ruhiger (zentraler)* Lage.
– in rōō'igər (tsenträ'lər) lä'gə

How *are the prices (is the food)* there?
Wie *sind die Preise (ist die Verpflegung)* dort?
vē zint dē prī'zə (ist dē ferpflā'gōōng) dôrt

Only the most modern European hotels have bathrooms attached to every room, and most rooming houses and pensions will require guests to share a bathroom down the hall with others. That's the difference.

Checking in

I reserved a room here.   **. . . six weeks ago.**
Ich habe bei Ihnen ein Zimmer bestellt.   . . . vor sechs Wochen.
i*sh* hä'bə bī ē'nən īn tsim'ər bəshtelt'   . . . fōr zeks vô'hən

The . . . travel agency reserved a room for *me (us)*.
Das Reisebüro . . . hat für *mich (uns)* ein Zimmer reservieren lassen.
däs rī'zəbērō' . . . hät fēr mi*sh* (ōōns) īn tsim'ər räzervēr'ən läs'ən

Have you got a *single (double)* room available?
Haben Sie ein *Einzelzimmer (Doppelzimmer)* frei?
hä'bən zē īn īn'tsəltsimər (dôp'əltsimər) frī

I'd like to have . . .
Ich hätte gern . . .
i*sh* het'ə gern . . .

– an apartment	ein Appartement	īn *ä*pärtəmäN'
– a bungalow	einen Bungalow	ī'nən bōōng'*ä*lō'
– a double room	ein Doppelzimmer	īn dôp'əltsimər
– an efficiency apartment	ein Appartement	īn *ä*pärtəmäN'
– a quiet room	ein ruhiges Zimmer . . .	īn rōō'igəs tsim'ər
– a room	ein Zimmer	īn tsim'ər
– – for . . . persons . .	für . . . Personen	fēr . . . perzō'nən
– – on the second floor	im ersten Stock	im ers'tən shtôk
– – with balcony	mit Balkon	mit b*ä*lkōn'
– – with bath	mit Bad	mit bät
– – with hot and cold running water . . .	mit fließend Kalt- und Warmwasser	mit flē'sənt kält-ōōnt värm'väsər
– – with shower	mit Dusche	mit dōōsh'ə
– – with terrace	mit Terrasse	mit ter*ä*s'ə
– – with toilet	mit Toilette	mit tô·älet'ə

. . . for *one night (two nights, one week, four weeks)*.
. . . für *eine Nacht (zwei Nächte, eine Woche, vier Wochen)*.
. . . fēr ī'nə n*ä*ht (tsvī ne*sh*'tə, ī'nə vô'hə, fēr vô'hən)

Can I have a look at the room?
Kann ich mir das Zimmer ansehen?
k*ä*n i*sh* mēr däs tsim'ər *ä*n'zā·ən

I like it.
Es gefällt mir.
es gəfelt′ mēr

I'll (We'll) take it.
Ich nehme (Wir nehmen) es.
ish nā′mə (vēr nā′mən) es

Could you show me another room?
Können Sie mir noch ein anderes Zimmer zeigen?
ken′ən zē mēr nô*h* īn än′dərəs tsim′ər tsī′gən

Could you put in *an extra bed (a crib)*?
Können Sie *noch ein Bett (ein Kinderbett)* hereinstellen?
ken′ən zē nô*h* īn bet (īn kin′dərbet) herīn′shtelən

> *Careful! Buildings in all European countries – including Britain – use*
> *a different numbering system for the floors. The bottom floor is called*
> *the ground floor (in German „das Erdgeschoß" [ārt′gəshôs]), the*
> *second (American) floor is called the first floor („der erste Stock"*
> *[ers′tə shtôk]), the third floor, the second floor, and so on.*

Price

How much is the room per *day (week)*?
Wieviel kostet das Zimmer pro *Tag (Woche)*?
vē′fēl kôs′tət däs tsim′ər prō täk (vô′*h*ə)

– with breakfast.	– with two meals a day.	– American plan.
– mit Frühstück.	– mit Halbpension.	– mit Vollpension.
– mit frē′sht*i*k	– mit hälp′päNsyōn‵	– mit fôl′päNsyōn‵

Is *everything (service)* included?
Ist *alles (Bedienung)* inbegriffen?
ist äl′əs (bədē′nŏong) in′bəgrif‵ən

What's the *single room surcharge (seasonal surcharge)*?
Wie hoch ist der *Einzelzimmer-Zuschlag (Saisonzuschlag)*?
vē hô*h* ist dār īn′tsəltsimərtsōō‵shläk (zezôN′tsōō‵shläk)

Are there reduced rates for children?
Gibt es für Kinder eine Ermäßigung?
gēpt es fĕr kin′dər ī′nə ermä′sigŏong

How much deposit do I have to pay?
Wieviel muß ich anzahlen?
vē′fēl mōōs ish än′tsälən

How much is that all together?
Wieviel macht es insgesamt?
vē′fēl mä*h*t es insgəzämt′

Registration, Luggage

I'd like to *register (check in)*.
Ich möchte mich anmelden.
ish mesh'tə mish än'meldən

Do you need our passports?
Brauchen Sie unsere Pässe?
brou'hən zē ōōn'zərə pes'ə

When do you want back the registration form?
Wann wollen Sie das Anmeldeformular zurückhaben?
vän vôl'ən zē däs än'meldəfôrmōōlär' tsōōrĭk'häbən

What do I have to fill out here?
Was muß ich hier ausfüllen?
väs mōōs ish hēr ous'fĭlən

*I just need your signature.
Ihre Unterschrift genügt.
ē'rə ōōn'tərshrift gənēkt'

Would you have my luggage picked up?
Können Sie das Gepäck holen lassen?
ken'ən zē däs gəpek' hō'lən läs'ən

It's still at the *station (airport)*.
Es ist noch am *Bahnhof (Flughafen)*.
es ist nôh äm bän'hōf (flōōk'häfən)

Here's the baggage check.
Hier ist der Gepäckschein.
hēr ist dār gəpek'shīn

Where's my luggage?
Wo ist mein Gepäck?
vō ist mīn gəpek'

Is my baggage already up in the room?
Ist mein Gepäck schon auf dem Zimmer?
ist mīn gəpek' shōn ouf dām tsim'ər

Can I leave my luggage here?
Kann ich mein Gepäck hierlassen?
kän ish mīn gəpek' hēr'läsən

Would you put these valuables in the safe?
Können Sie diese Wertsachen aufbewahren?
ken'ən zē dē'zə värt'zähən ouf'bəvärən

Do you have a *garage (parking lot)*?
Haben Sie *eine Garage (einen Parkplatz)*?
hä'bən zē ī'nə gärä'zhə (īn'ən pärk'pläts)

Reception, Desk Clerk

Where is room 308?
Wo ist Zimmer dreihundertacht?
vō ist tsim'ər drī'hōōndərt·äht'

The key, please.
Den Schlüssel, bitte.
dān shl*i*s'əl, bit'ə

Number . . ., please.
Nummer . . ., bitte.
nōōm'ər . . ., bit'ə

Has anyone asked for me?
Hat jemand nach mir gefragt?
hät yā'mänt nä*h* mēr gəfräkt'

Is there any mail for me?
Ist Post für mich da?
ist pôst fēr mi*sh* dä

What time does the mail come?
Wann kommt die Post?
vän kômt dē pôst

Do you have any *stamps (picture postcards)*?
Haben Sie *Briefmarken (Ansichtskarten)*?
hä'bən zē brēf'märkən (än'zi*sh*tskär'tən)

What's the postage on a *letter (postcard)* to the United States?
Was kostet *ein Brief (eine Postkarte)* nach den U.S.A.?
väs kôs'tət īn brēf (ī'nə pôst'kärtə) nä*h* dän ōō'esä'

Where can I *get (rent)* . . .?
Wo kann ich . . . *bekommen (mieten)*?
vō kän i*sh* . . . bəkôm'ən (mē'tən)

Where do I sign up for the excursion to . . .?
Wo kann ich mich für den Ausflug nach . . . anmelden?
vō kän i*sh* mi*sh* fēr dän ous'flōōk nä*h* . . . än'meldən

Where can I *make a phone call (change some money)*?
Wo kann ich *telefonieren (Geld wechseln)*?
vō kän i*sh* tā'lāfōnēr'ən (gelt vek'səln)

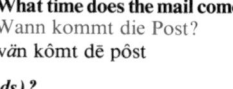

I'd like to place a long distance call to . . .
Ich möchte ein Ferngespräch nach . . . anmelden.
i*sh* mesh'tə īn fern'gəshprä*sh* nä*h* . . . än'meldən

I'm expecting a long distance call from the United States.
Ich erwarte ein Ferngespräch aus den U.S.A.
i*sh* ervär'tə īn fern'gəshprä*sh* ous dän ōō'esä'

Where can I get an American newspaper?
Wo gibt es amerikanische Zeitungen?
võ gēpt es ämärikä'nishə tsī'tōōngən

Where is (are) ...?
Wo ist (sind) ...?
võ ist (zint) ...

Could you get me ...?
Können Sie mir ... besorgen?
ken'ən zē mēr ... bəzôr'gən

What's the voltage here?
Wie hoch ist hier die Stromspannung?
vē hōh ist hēr dē shtrōm'shpän'ōōng

I'll be back in ten minutes (a couple of hours).
Ich bin in zehn Minuten (ein paar Stunden) zurück.
ish bin in tsān minōō'tən (īn pär shtōōn'dən) tsōōrik'

We're going down to the beach (into town).
Wir gehen zum Strand (in die Stadt).
vēr gā'ən tsōōm shtränt (in dē shtät)

I'll be in the lounge (bar).
Ich bin im Aufenthaltsraum (an der Bar).
ish bin im ouf'ent·hältsroum' (än dār bär)

I lost my key (left my key in the room).
Ich habe den Schlüssel verloren (im Zimmer gelassen).
ish hä'bə dān shlis'əl ferlōr'ən (im tsim'ər gəläs'ən)

What time are meals served?
Wann sind die Essenszeiten?
vän zint dē es'əns·tsī'tən

Where's the dining room?
Wo ist der Speisesaal?
võ ist dār shpī'zəzäl'

Can we have breakfast in the room?
Können wir auf dem Zimmer frühstücken?
ken'ən vēr ouf dām tsim'ər frē'shtikən

Could we have breakfast at seven tomorrow morning, please?
Können wir morgen schon um sieben Uhr frühstücken, bitte?
ken'ən vēr môr'gən shōn ōōm zē'bən ōōr frē'shtikən, bit'ə

I'd like a box lunch tomorrow morning, please.
Für morgen früh bitte ein Lunchpaket.
fēr môr'gən frē bit'ə īn länsh'päkät'

Please wake me at 7 : 30 tomorrow.
Wecken Sie mich bitte morgen um halb acht.
vek'ən zē mish bit'ə môr'gən ōōm hälp äht

Maid

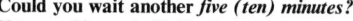

Come in!	**Just a moment, please!**
Herein!	Einen Moment, bitte!
herīn′	ī′nən mōment′, bit′ə

Could you wait another *five (ten)* minutes?
Können Sie noch *fünf (zehn)* Minuten warten?
ken′ən zē nôh fīnf (tsān) minoo′tən vär′tən

We'll be going out in another *quarter hour (half hour)*.
Wir gehen in einer *Viertelstunde (halben Stunde)*.
vēr gā′ən in ī′nər fīr′təlshtoon′də (häl′bən shtoon′də)

Please bring *me (us)* ...
Bringen Sie *mir (uns)* bitte ...
bring′ən zē mēr (oons) bit′ə ...

another blanket	noch eine Decke	nôh ī′nə dek′ə
another pillow	noch ein Kopfkissen ..	nôh īn kôpf′kisən
another towel	noch ein Handtuch	nôh īn hän′tooh
an ash tray	einen Aschenbecher ...	ī′nən äsh′ənbeshər
a blanket	eine Wolldecke	ī′nə vôl′dekə
breakfast	das Frühstück	däs frē′shtĭk
a cake of soap	ein Stück Seife	īn shtĭk zī′fə
a couple of clothes hangers	ein paar Kleiderbügel .	īn pär klī′dərbēgəl

How does this thing work?	**Is our room ready?**
Wie funktioniert das?	Ist unser Zimmer schon fertig?
vē foongk′tsyōnērt′ däs	ist oon′zər tsim′ər shōn fer′tĭsh

Would you have these things laundered for me?
Können Sie die Wäsche waschen lassen?
ken′ən zē dē vesh′ə väsh′ən läs′ən

Thanks very much!	**This is for you.**
Vielen Dank!	Das ist für Sie!
fē′lən dängk	däs ist fēr zē

Complaints

I'd like to speak to the manager, please.
Ich möchte bitte den Geschäftsführer sprechen.
i*sh* me*sh*'tə bit'ə dän gəshefts'fērər shpre*sh*'ən

There's no ...	**There are no ...**	**... doesn't work.**
Es fehlt ...	Es fehlen ...	... funktioniert nicht.
es fält ...	es fäl'ən ...	... fōōngk'tsyōnērt' ni*sh*t

There's no light in my room.
In meinem Zimmer brennt kein Licht.
in mī'nəm tsim'ər brent kīn li*sh*t

This bulb has burned out.
Diese Birne ist durchgebrannt.
dē'zə bir'nə ist dōōr*sh*'gəbränt'

The socket is broken.
Die Steckdose ist kaputt.
dē shtek'dōzə ist käpōōt'

The fuse has blown.
Die Sicherung ist durchgebrannt.
dē zi*sh*'ərōōng ist dōōr*sh*'gəbränt'

The bell (heating) doesn't work.
Die *Klingel (Heizung)* funktioniert nicht.
dē kling'əl (hī'tsōōng) fōōngk'tsyōnērt' ni*sh*t

The key doesn't fit.
Der Schlüssel paßt nicht.
där shli*s*'əl päst ni*sh*t

The rain comes in.
Es regnet durch.
es räg'nət dōōr*sh*

This window *won't shut properly (won't open).*
Das Fenster *schließt schlecht (geht nicht auf).*
d*ä*s fens'tər shlēst shle*sh*t (gät ni*sh*t ouf)

There's no (hot) water.
Es kommt kein (heißes) Wasser.
es kômt kīn (hī'səs) väs'ər

The faucet drips.
Der Hahn tropft.
där hän trôpft

The toilet won't flush.
Die Spülung geht nicht.
dē shpē'lōōng gät ni*sh*t

There's a leak in this pipe.
Die Leitung ist undicht.
dē lī'tōōng ist ōōn'di*sh*t

The drain is stopped up.
Der Abfluß ist verstopft.
där *ä*p'flōōs ist fershtôpft'

Checking out

I'll be leaving tomorrow.
Ich reise morgen ab.
i*sh* rī′zə môr′gən äp

We're continuing on tomorrow.
Wir fahren morgen weiter.
vēr fä′rən môr′gən vī′tər

Would you please make up my bill?
Machen Sie bitte die Rechnung fertig.
mä′hən zē bit′ə dē re*sh*′noong fer′ti*sh*

Could I please have *my (our)* bill?
Kann ich bitte *meine (unsere)* Rechnung haben?
kän i*sh* bit′ə mī′nə (oon′zərə) re*sh*′noong hä′bən

Please wake me tomorrow morning.
Wecken Sie mich bitte morgen früh.
vek′ən zē mi*sh* bit′ə môr′gən frē

Please order a taxi for me tomorrow morning at 8.
Bestellen Sie mir bitte für morgen acht Uhr ein Taxi.
bəshtel′ən zē mēr bit′ə fēr môr′gən äht oor īn täk′sē

Would you have my luggage taken to the *station (airport)*?
Können Sie mein Gepäck zum *Bahnhof (Flughafen)* bringen lassen?
ken′ən zē mīn gəpek′ tsoom bän′hôf (flook′häfən) bring′ən läs′ən

When does the *bus (train)* to ... leave?
Wann geht der *Bus (Zug)* nach ...?
vän gāt dār boos (tsook) nä*h* ...

Please forward my mail.
Bitte senden Sie mir meine Post nach.
bit′ə zen′dən zē mēr mī′nə pôst nä*h*

Thanks for everything!
Herzlichen Dank für alles!
herts′li*sh*ən dängk fēr äl′əs

We had a very good *time (rest)* here.
Wir haben uns hier sehr *wohlgefühlt (gut erholt)*.
vēr hä′bən oons hēr zār vōl′gəfēlt′ (goot erhōlt′)

accommodations	die Unterkunft	oͦon'tərkoͦonft
adapter plug	der Zwischenstecker...	tsvish'ənshtekər
air conditioning	die Klima-Anlage	klē'mä·änlä'gə
alternating current ..	der Wechselstrom	vek'səlshtrōm
American plan	Vollpension	fôl'päNsyōn'
apartment	die Wohnung, ...	vō'noͦong
	das Appartement	äpärtəmäN'
apartment building ..	das Mietshaus	mēts'hous
armchair	der Sessel	zes'əl
arrival	die Ankunft	än'koͦonft
ash tray	der Aschenbecher	äsh'ənbeshər
balcony	der Balkon	bälkōn'
basement	der Keller	kel'ər
bathroom	das Badezimmer	bä'dətsimər
bed	das Bett	bet
– bedspread	die Bettdecke	bet'dekə
– blanket	die Wolldecke	vôl'dekə
– crib	das Kinderbett	kin'dərbet
– mattress	die Matratze	mäträts'ə
– pillow	das Kopfkissen	kôpf'kisən
bed and two meals ...	Halbpension	hälp'päNsyōn'
bed linen	die Bettwäsche........	bet'veshə
– cover	der Bezug	bətsoͦok'
– pillowcase	der Kopfkissenbezug ..	kôpf'kisənbətsoͦok'
– sheet	das Laken	lä'kən
bed rug	der Bettvorleger	bet'fôrlāgər
bedside table	der Nachttisch	näht't'tish
bell	die Klingel	kling'əl
bill	die Rechnung	resh'noͦong
breakfast	das Frühstück	frē'shtik
– eat breakfast	frühstücken	frē'shtikən
breakfast room	der Frühstücksraum ..	frē'shtiksroum
bucket	der Eimer	ī'mər
carpet	der Teppich	tep'ish
category	die Kategorie	kät'əgōrē'
ceiling	die Zimmerdecke ...	tsim'ərdekə
cellar	der Keller	kel'ər
central heating	die Zentralheizung	tsenträl'hītsoͦong
chair	der Stuhl	shtoͦol
check in	sich anmelden	zish än'meldən
check-in	die Anmeldung	än'meldoͦong

chimney	der Kamin	kämēn′
closet	der Schrank	shrängk
clothes hanger	der Kleiderbügel	klī′dərbēgəl
complaint	die Beanstandung	bə·än′shtändo͞ong
concierge	der *Portier (Pförtner)*	pôrtyā′ (pfert′nər)
corridor	der Korridor	kôr′idōr
curtain	der Vorhang	fōr′häng
day bed	die Bettcouch	bet′koutsh
deck chair	der Liegestuhl	lē′gəshto͞ol
departure	die Abreise	äp′rīzə
deposit	die Anzahlung	än′tsälo͞ong
dining room	der Speisesaal	shpī′zəzäl′
dinner	das Abendessen	ä′bənt·esən
door	die Tür	tēr
door handle	die Türklinke	tēr′klingkə
drapery	der Vorhang	fōr′häng
drawer	die Schublade	sho͞op′lädə
elevator	der Fahrstuhl	fär′shto͞ol
entrance	der Eingang	īn′gäng
exit	der Ausgang	ous′gäng
extension cord	die Verlängerungs- schnur	ferleng′əro͞ongs- shno͞or
extra week	die Verlängerungs- woche	ferleng′əro͞ongs- vô′hə
fan	der Ventilator	ven′tilä′tôr
faucet	der Wasserhahn	väs′ərhän
fireplace	der Kamin	kämēn′
floor	der Fußboden	fo͞os′bōdən
front desk	der Empfang	empfäng′
front door	die Haustür	hous′tēr
fuse	die Sicherung	zish′əro͞ong
garden umbrella	der Sonnenschirm	zôn′ənshirm
grill room	das Grillrestaurant	gril′restôräN′
guest house	die Hotelpension	hōtel′päNsyōn′
hall	der Gang	gäng
head clerk	der Chefportier	shef′pôrtyā′
heating	die Heizung	hī′tso͞ong
hotel	das Hotel	hōtel′
– beach hotel	das Strandhotel	shtränt′hōtel
hotel restaurant	das Hotelrestaurant	hōtel′restôräN′
house	das Haus	hous

house key	der Hausschlüssel	hous′shl*i*səl
inquiry	die Erkundigung	erko͞on′dig o͞ong
key	der Schlüssel	shl*i*s′əl
kitchen	die Küche	k*i*sh′ə
kitchenette	die Kochnische	kôh′nēshə
lamp	die Lampe	läm′pə
laundry	die Wäsche	vesh′ə
– **do laundry**	Wäsche waschen	vesh′ə väsh′ən
– **dry**	trocknen	trôk′nən
– **iron**	bügeln	bē′gəln
light bulb	die Glühbirne	glē′birnə
lights	die Beleuchtung	bəloi*sh*′to͞ong
lobby	die Halle	häl′ə
lock	das Türschloß	tēr′shlôs
– **lock up**	abschließen	*ä*p′shlēsən
– **unlock**	aufschließen	ouf′shlēsən
lunch	das Mittagessen	mit′*ä*k·esən
maid	das Zimmermädchen ..	tsim′ərmäd*sh*ən
mirror	der Spiegel	shpē′gəl
move	umziehen	o͞om′tsē·ən
move in	einziehen	īn′tsē·ən
move out	ausziehen	ous′tsē·ən
night's lodging	die Übernachtung	*ē*bərnäh′to͞ong
pail	der Eimer	ī′mər
patio	die Terrasse	ter*ä*s′ə
pension	die Pension	päNsyôn′
plug	der Stecker	shtek′ər
pot	der Topf	tôpf
price	der Preis	prīs
private beach	der Privatstrand	privät′shtränt
radiator	der Heizkörper	hīts′k*ä*rpər
reading lamp	die Nachttischlampe ..	n*ä*ht′tishlämp′ə
reception desk	der Empfang,	empfäng′,
	die Rezeption	rätseptsyôn′
refrigerator	der Kühlschrank	k*ē*l′shrängk
registration	die Anmeldung	*ä*n′meldo͞ong
rent *(noun)*	die Miete	mē′tə
rent *(verb)*	mieten	mē′tən
rest room	die Toilette	tô·älet′ə
– **ladies' room**	die Damentoilette	dä′məntô·älet′ə
– **men's room**	die Herrentoilette	her′əntô·älet′ə

room	das Zimmer	tsim′ər
– bedroom	das Schlafzimmer	shläf′tsimər
– living room	das Wohnzimmer	vōn′tsimər
– nursery	das Kinderzimmer	kin′dərtsimər
season	die Saison	zezôN′
service	die Bedienung	bədē′nŏong
service charge	der Bedienungszuschlag	bədē′nŏongs·tsŏo′-shläk
shower	die Dusche	dŏosh′ə
sink	das Waschbecken	väsh′bekən
socket	die Steckdose	shtek′dōzə
staircase	die Treppe	trep′ə
stairwell	das Treppenhaus	trep′ənhous
stove	der Ofen	ō′fən
swimming pool	der Swimmingpool	svim′ingpŏol′
switch	der Lichtschalter	lisht′shältər
table	der Tisch	tish
tablecloth	die Tischdecke	tish′dekə
telephone	das Telefon	tālāfōn′
terrace	die Terrasse	teräs′ə
toilet paper	das Toilettenpapier	tô·älet′ənpäpēr′
tour guide	der Reiseleiter	rī′zəlītər
travel agency	das Reisebüro	rī′zəbērō′
vacate the room	ausziehen	ous′tsē·ən
ventilation	die Lüftung	lif′tŏong
voltage	die Stromspannung	shtrōm′shpänŏong
wall	die Wand	vänt
water	das Wasser	väs′ər
– cold water	kaltes Wasser	käl′təs väs′ər
– hot water	warmes Wasser	vär′məs väs′ər
water glass	das Wasserglas	väs′ərgläs
window	das Fenster	fens′tər
windowpane	die Fensterscheibe	fens′tərshībə

220 V ~

Camping, Youth Hostels

Is there a *camping site (youth hostel)* near here?
Gibt es hier *einen Campingplatz (eine Jugendherberge)?*
gēpt es hēr ī'nən kem'pingpläts' (ī'nə yōō'gənt·hār'bärgə)

Can we camp here?
Können wir hier zelten?
ken'ən vēr hēr tsel'tən

Is the site guarded at night?
Ist der Platz nachts bewacht?
ist dār pläts nähts bəväht'

Do you have room (for another tent)?
Haben Sie noch Platz (für ein Zelt)?
hä'bən zē nôh pläts (fēr īn tselt)

How much does it cost to stay overnight?
Wieviel kostet eine Übernachtung?
vē'fēl kôstət ī'nə ē'bərnäh'tōong

How much is it for the *car (trailer)?*
Wie hoch ist die Gebühr für *das Auto (den Wohnwagen)?*
vē hōh ist dē gəbēr' fēr däs ou'tō (dān vōn'vägən)

I'll be staying ... *days (weeks).*
Ich bleibe ... *Tage (Wochen).*
ish blī'bə ... tä'gə (vô'hən)

Can we ... here?
Kann man hier ...?
kän män hēr ...

Is there a grocery store near here?
Gibt es in der Nähe ein Lebensmittelgeschäft?
gēpt es in dār nä'ə īn lā'bənsmitəlgəsheft'

Can I *rent bottled gas (exchange gas bottles)* here?
Kann ich hier Gasflaschen *ausleihen (tauschen)?*
kän ish hēr gäs'fläshən ous'lī·ən (tou'shən)

Where are the *rest rooms (wash rooms)?*
Wo sind die *Toiletten (Waschräume)?*
vō zint dē tô·älet'ən (väsh'roimə)

Are there any electrical connections here?
Gibt es hier Stromanschluß?
gēpt es hēr shtrōm'änshlōōs

Can I rent ...?
Kann ich ... ausleihen?
kän ish ... ous'lī·ən

Can we drink the water?
Kann man das Wasser trinken?
kän män däs väs'ər tring'kən

Where can I ...?
Wo kann ich ...?
vō kän ish ...

advance reservation .	die Voranmeldung	fōr'*än*meldŏong
camp bed	die Campingliege	kem'pinglē'gə
camping	Camping	kem'ping
camping ID	der Campingausweis ..	kem'pingous'wīs
camp out	zelten	tsel'tən
camp site	der Campingplatz	kem'ping*plä*ts'
check-in	die Anmeldung	*än*'meldŏong
check-out	die Abmeldung	*äp*'meldŏong
cook	kochen	kô'*h*ən
cooking utensils	das Kochgeschirr	kô*h*'gəshir
day room	der Tagesraum	tä'gəsroum
dishes	das Eßgeschirr	es'gəshir
dormitory	der Schlafraum	shläf'roum
drinking water	das Trinkwasser	tringk'väsər
get	bekommen	bəkôm'ən
go swimming	baden, schwimmen	bä'dən, shvim'ən
hostel parents	die Herbergseltern	här'bärksel'tərn
– hostel mother	die Herbergsmutter ...	här'bärksmŏot'ər
– hostel father	der Herbergsvater	här'bärksfä'tər
iron	bügeln	bē'gəln
membership card	die Mitgliedskarte	mit'glētskär'tə
park	parken	pär'kən
playground	der Spielplatz	shpēl'pläts
recreation room	der Tagesraum	tä'gəsroum
rent	mieten	mē'tən
rental fee	die Leihgebühr	lī'gəbēr
sleeping bag	der Schlafsack	shläf'zäk
take a bath	baden	bä'dən
tent	das Zelt	tselt
trailer	der Wohnwagen	vōn'vägən
usage fee	die Benutzungsgebühr .	bənŏots'ŏongs-gəbēr'
wash	waschen	väsh'ən
youth group	die Jugendgruppe	yŏo'gəntgrŏopə
youth hostel	die Jugendherberge ...	yŏo'gənt·här'bärgə
youth hostel card	der Herbergsausweis ..	här'bärksous'vīs

FOOD AND DRINK

Ordering

Is there a *good (Chinese, seafood)* restaurant here?

Gibt es hier ein *gutes (chinesisches, Fisch-)*Restaurant?
gēpt es hēr īn gōō'təs (shinā'zishəs, fish')restôräN'

Would you please reserve a table for four at eight P.M.?

Bitte reservieren Sie für zwanzig Uhr einen Tisch für vier Personen.
bit'ə rezervēr'ən zē fēr tsvän'tsish ōōr ī'nən tish fēr fēr perzō'nən

Is this *table (seat)* taken?

Ist dieser *Tisch (Platz)* besetzt?
ist dē'zər tish (pläts) bəzetst'

Waiter!	**Waitress!**	**Is this your table?**
Herr Ober!	Fräulein!	Bedienen Sie hier?
her ō'bər	froi'līn	bədē'nən zē hēr

I'd like a meal.

Ich möchte etwas essen.
ish mesh'tə et'väs es'ən

We'd like a drink.

Wir möchten etwas trinken.
vēr mesh'tən et'väs tring'kən

Could I see the *menu (wine list)*, please?

Die *Speisekarte (Getränkekarte)*, bitte.
dē shpī'zəkärtə (gətreng'kəkärtə), bit'ə

What can we have right away?

Was können Sie uns sofort bringen?
väs ken'ən zē ōōns zōfôrt' bring'ən

Do you have . . . ?

Haben Sie . . . ?
hä'bən zē . . .

Do you have *vegetarian (diet)* food too?

Haben Sie auch *vegetarische Kost (Diätkost)?*
hä'bən zē ouh vāgātär'ishə kôst (dē-ät'kôst)

Please bring us *one portion (two portions)* of . . .

Bitte bringen Sie uns *eine Portion (zwei Portionen)* . . .
bit'ə bring'ən zē ōōns ī'nə pôrtsyōn' (tsvī pôrtsyō'nən) . . .

A *cup (pot, glass, bottle)* of . . ., please.

Bitte *eine Tasse (ein Kännchen, ein Glas, eine Flasche)* . . .
bit'ə ī'nə täs'ə (īn ken'shən, īn gläs, ī'ne fläsh'ə) . . .

Table Service

English	German	Pronunciation
ash tray	der Aschenbecher	äsh'ənbeshər
bottle	die Flasche	fläsh'ə
bowl	die Schüssel	shis'əl
bread basket	der Brotkorb	brōt'kôrp
carafe	die Karaffe	käräf'ə
cruet stand	der Essig- und Ölständer	es'ish ŏont āl'shten·dər
cup	die Tasse	täs'ə
– saucer	die Untertasse	ŏon'tərtäsə
cutlery	das Besteck	bəshtek'
decanter	die Karaffe	käräf'ə
egg cup	der Eierbecher	ī'ərbeshər
fork	die Gabel	gä'bəl
glass	das Glas	gläs
– water glass	das Wasserglas	väs'ərgläs
– wine glass	das Weinglas	vīn'gläs
knife	das Messer	mes'ər
mustard jar	das Senfglas	zenf'gläs
napkin	die Serviette	zervē·et'ə
pepper mill	die Pfeffermühle	pfef'ərmēlə
pepper shaker	der Pfefferstreuer	pfef'ərshtroi'ər
pitcher	das Kännchen	ken'shən
– cream pitcher	das Milchkännchen	milsh'kenshən
plate	der Teller	tel'ər
– bread plate	der kleine Teller	klī'nə tel'ər
– soup plate	der Suppenteller	zŏop'əntelər
pot	die Kanne	kän'ə
– coffee pot	die Kaffeekanne	käf'äkän'ə
– tea pot	die Teekanne	tā'känə
salt shaker	der Salzstreuer	zälts'shtroi'ər
serving dish	die Platte	plät'ə
silverware	das Besteck	bəshtek'
spoon	der Löffel	lef'əl
– soup spoon	der Suppenlöffel	zŏop'ənlefəl
– teaspoon	der Teelöffel	tā'lefəl
sugar bowl	die Zuckerdose	tsŏok'ərdōzə
tablecloth	das Tischtuch	tish'tŏoh
toothpick	der Zahnstocher	tsän'shtôhər
tray	das Tablett	täblet'

Breakfast

bread	das Brot	brōt
– dark bread	dunkles Brot	dōōngk'ləs brōt
– white bread	Weißbrot	vīs'brōt
– whole wheat bread	Vollkornbrot	fôl'kôrnbrōt'
breakfast	das Frühstück	frē'shtĭk
– eat breakfast	frühstücken	frē'shtĭkən
butter	die Butter	bōōt'ər
cereal	die Getreideflocken	gətrī'dəflôk'ən
coffee	der Kaffee	käf'ā
– black	schwarzer Kaffee	shvärts'ər käf'ā
– decaffeinated	koffeinfreier Kaffee	kôfā·ēn'frī·ər käf'ā
– with cream	Kaffee mit Sahne	käf'ā mit zä'nə
– with sugar	Kaffee mit Zucker	käf'ā mit tsōōk'ər
cold cuts	der Aufschnitt	ouf'shnit
croissant	das Hörnchen	hern'shən
egg	das Ei	ī
– hard-boiled	hartgekocht	härt'gəkôht
– soft-boiled	weichgekocht	vīsh'gəkôht
– bacon & eggs	Ei mit Speck	ī mit shpek
– ham & eggs	Ei mit Schinken	ī mit shing'kən
– fried eggs	Spiegeleier	shpē'gəl·ī'ər
– scrambled eggs	Rührei	rēr'·ī
fruit juice	der Fruchtsaft	frōōht'zäft
– orange juice	Orangensaft	ōräN'zhənzäft'
honey	der Honig	hō'nish
hot chocolate	die heiße Schokolade	hī'sə shōkōlä'də
jam	die Marmelade	märməlä'də
milk	die Milch	milsh
– condensed milk	die Kondensmilch	kôndens'milsh
roll	(North Germany) das Brötchen, (South Germany) die Semmel	brāt'shən, zem'əl
sausage	die Wurst	vōŏrst
slice	die Scheibe	shī'bə
sugar	der Zucker	tsōōk'ər
tea	der Tee	tā
– with lemon	Tee mit Zitrone	tā mit tsitrō'nə
– with milk	Tee mit Milch	tā mit milsh
toast	der Toast	tōst

Lunch and Dinner

I'd (We'd) like to have ...
Ich möchte (Wir möchten) ...
i*sh* me*sh*'tə (vēr me*sh*'tən) ...

Would you bring us ...?
Können Sie uns ... bringen?
ken'ən zē o͞ons ... bring'ən

Please pass ...
Würden Sie mir bitte ... reichen?
vir'dən zē mēr bit'ə ... rī'*sh*ən

What's the name of this dish?
Wie heißt dieses Gericht?
vē hīst dē'zəs gəri*sh*t'

*Would you like seconds on anything?
Möchten Sie noch etwas?
me*sh*'tən zē nôh et'väs

Yes, please.
Ja, bitte.
yä, bit'ə

Yes, indeed!
Gern!
gern

Just a little.
Nur ein wenig.
no͞or īn vā'ni*sh*

Thanks, that's enough.
Danke, das genügt.
däng'kə, däs gəno͞okt'

No, thanks.
Nein, danke!
nīn, däng'kə

I've had enough.
Ich bin satt.
i*sh* bin zät

Nothing more, thanks.
Nichts mehr, danke.
ni*sh*ts mār, däng'kə

*Did you like it?
Hat es Ihnen geschmeckt?
hät es ē'nən gə*sh*mekt'

Delicious!
Ausgezeichnet!
ousgətsī*sh*'nət

*Empty your glass!
Trinken Sie Ihr Glas aus!
tring'kən zē ēr gläs ous

Cheers!
Zum Wohl! (Prost!)
tso͞om vōl (prōst)

This dish (The wine) is delicious!
Dieses Gericht (Der Wein) ist vorzüglich!
dē'zəs gəri*sh*t' (där vīn) ist fōrtsēk'li*sh*

I'm not allowed to have any alcohol (I don't care for alcohol).
Ich *darf (möchte)* keinen Alkohol trinken.
i*sh* därf (me*sh*'tə) kī'nən äl'kōhōl tring'kən

Germans and Austrians will generally start the meal with either
,,Guten Appetit!" [go͞o'tən äpətēt'] *or* ,,Mahlzeit!" [mäl'tsīt]
(short for ,,gesegnete Mahlzeit" [gəzäg'nətə mäl'tsīt] = *Bless this*
food). Before the first drink is taken, someone (usually the host or
hostess) will propose a toast or drink to the health of the company:
,,Prost!" [prōst] *or* ,,Zum Wohl!" [tso͞om vōl].

Cooking

baked	(im Ofen) gebacken	(im ō'fən) gəbäk'ən
boiled	gekocht	gəkôht'
cold	kalt	kält
deep fried	(in Fett) gebacken	(in fet) gəbäk'ən
fat	das Fett	fet
fresh	frisch	frish
fried	(in der Pfanne) gebraten	(in dār pfän'ə) gə-brä'tən
grilled	gegrillt, vom Grill	gəgrilt', fôm gril
hard	hart	härt
hot	heiß	hīs
hot (spicy)	scharf	shärf
juicy	saftig	zäf'tish
lean	mager	mä'gər
medium (done)	halbdurch, medium	hälp'dōorsh', mē'dē·ōom
pickled (meat)	gepökelt	gəpā'kəlt
rare	englisch	eng'lish
raw	roh	rō
roasted	(im Ofen) gebraten, geröstet	(im ō'fən) gəbrä'tən, gərōs'tət
salted	gesalzen	gəzäl'tsən
seasoned	gewürzt	gəvirtst'
smoked	geräuchert	gəroi'shərt
soft	weich	vīsh
steamed	gedämpft, gedünstet	gədempft', gədins'tət
stewed	geschmort	gəshmōrt'
stuffed	gefüllt	gəfilt'
stuffing	die Füllung	fil'ōong
tender	zart	tsärt
tough	zäh	tsā
well done	durchgebraten	dōorsh'gəbrä'tən

Ingredients

bacon	der Speck	shpek
butter	die Butter	bŏŏt'ər
capers	Kapern	kä'pərn
caraway	der Kümmel	kim'əl

chives	der Schnittlauch	shnit′lou*h*
cinnamon	der Zimt	tsimt
cloves	Nelken	nel′kən
dill	der Dill	dil
fat	das Fett, das Schmalz	fet, shmälts
fatty	fett	fet
garlic	der Knoblauch	knōp′lou*h*
ginger	der Ingwer	ing′vər
herbs	Kräuter	kroi′tər
horseradish	der Meerrettich	mä′reti*sh*
jelly *(aspic)*	das Gelee	zhelā′
jelly *(fruit)*	die Konfitüre	kônfitē′rə
ketchup	*das (der)* Ketchup	ketsh′äp
lard	das Schweineschmalz	shvī′nəshmälts
lemon	die Zitrone	tsitrō′nə
margarine	die Margarine	märgärē′nə
mayonnaise	die Mayonnaise	mäyōnā′zə
mayonnaise sauce	die Remouladensoße	remoōlä′dənzōs′ə
mushrooms	Pilze,	pil′tsə,
	Champignons	shäm′pinyôNs′
mustard	der Senf	zenf
nutmeg *(powder)*	der Muskat	moōskät′
oil	das Öl	äl
olives	Oliven	ōlē′vən
onion	die Zwiebel	tsvē′bəl
paprika	die Paprika	päp′rikä
parsley	die Petersilie	pä′tərzēl′yə
pepper	der Pfeffer	pfef′ər
pickles	saure Gurken,	zou′rə goōr′kən,
	Gewürzgurken	gəvirts′goōr′kən
raisins	Rosinen,	rōzē′nən,
	Sultaninen	zoōltänē′nən
rosemary	der Rosmarin	rōs′märēn
salt	das Salz	zälts
sauce	die Soße	zō′sə
– cream sauce	die Rahmsoße	räm′zōsə
– gravy	die Bratensoße	brä′tənzōsə
seasoning, spices	Gewürze	gəvirts′ə
thyme	der Thymian	tēm′i·än
vanilla	die Vanille	vänil′yə
vinegar	der Essig	es′i*sh*

THE MENU

Appetizers

Ananassaft	än'änäs·zäft'	pineapple juice
Artischocken	är'tishôk'ən	artichokes
Aufschnitt	ouf'shnit	cold cuts
Austern	ou'stərn	oysters
Avocado	ävōkä'dō	avocado
Fischsalat	fish'zälät'	fish salad
Fleischsülze	flīsh'zīltsə	meat aspic
Gänseleberpastete	gen'zəlābərpästä'tə	goose liver pâté
Garnelen	gärnä'lən	shrimps
Grapefruitsaft	gräp'frōot·zäft'	grapefruit juice
Heringssalat	hār'ings·zälät'	herring salad
Hummercocktail	hōōm'ərkôk'tāl	lobster cocktail
Königinpastetchen	kā'niginpästāt'shən	creamed chicken or veal in a puff pastry shell
Kaviar	kä'viär	caviar
Krabben	kräb'ən	tiny shrimp
Krebse	kräp'sə	crab, crawfish
Lachs	läks	salmon
– Räucherlachs	roi'shərläks'	smoked salmon
Mayonnaise	mäyōnā'zə	mayonnaise
Melone	melō'nə	melon
Oliven	ōlē'vən	olives
Ölsardinen	äl'zärdē'nən	sardines in oil
Orangensaft	ōräN'zhənzäft'	orange juice
Räucheraal	roi'shəräl'	smoked eel
Russische Eier	rōōs'ishə ī'ər	deviled eggs on a vegetable salad bed
Sardellen	zärdel'ən	anchovies
Schinken	shing'kən	ham
Tomatensaft	tōmä'tənzäft	tomato juice
Vorspeise	fōr'shpīzə	appetizer
Weinbergschnecken	vīn'berkshnek'ən	snails
Wurstsalat	vōorst'zälät'	sausage salad

Soups

Bohnensuppe	bō'nənzo͞opə	bean soup
Champignoncreme-	sh*ä*m'pinyôNkräm-	cream of mushroom
suppe	zo͞op'ə	soup
Erbsensuppe	erp'sənzo͞opə	pea soup
Fischsuppe	fish'zo͞opə	fish soup
Fleischbrühe	flīsh'br*ē*·ə	meat broth
– mit Ei	mit ī	with egg
– mit Fleischeinlage .	mit flīsh'īnlägə	with chunks of meat
– mit Nudeln	mit no͞o'dəln	with noodles
– mit Reis	mit rīs	with rice
Gemüsesuppe	gəm*ē*'zəzo͞opə	vegetable soup
Grießnockerlsuppe ..	grēs'nôkərlzo͞op'ə ...	clear broth with fluffy
		dumplings
Hühnerbrühe	h*ē*'nərbr*ē*·ə	chicken broth
Hühnercremesuppe ..	h*ē*'nərkrämzo͞op'ə ..	cream of chicken soup
Hummersuppe	ho͞om'ərzo͞opə	lobster bisque
Kartoffelsuppe	kärtôf'əlzo͞opə	potato soup
klare Suppe	klä'rə zo͞op'ə	clear soup
Lauchsuppe	lou*h*'zo͞opə	leek soup
Leberknödelsuppe ...	lā'bərkn*ä*dəlzo͞op'ə ..	clear broth with liver
		dumplings
legierte Suppe	lāgēr'tə zo͞op'ə	thick soup
Linsensuppe	lin'zənzo͞opə	lentil soup
Ochsenschwanzsuppe	ôk'sənshv*ä*nts·zo͞op'ə	oxtail soup
Schildkrötensuppe ...	shilt'kr*ä*tənzo͞op'ə ...	turtle soup
Spargelcremesuppe ..	shp*ä*r'gəlkrämzo͞op'ə	cream of asparagus
		soup
Suppe	zo͞op'ə	soup
Tomatensuppe	tōm*ä*'tənzo͞opə	tomato soup
Zwiebelsuppe	tsv*ē*'bəlzo͞opə	onion soup

Noodles and Dumplings

Bandnudeln	bänt'no͞odəln	flat noodles
Fadennudeln	fä'dən·no͞odəln	vermicelli
Kartoffelklöße	kärtôf'əlkl*ä*sə	potato dumplings
Makkaroni	m*ä*kärō'nē	macaroni

Maultaschen	moul'tä*sh*ən	chopped spicy meat wrapped in noodle dough
Nudeln	nōo'dəln	noodles
Semmelknödel	zem'əlknä*d*əl	bread dumplings
Spätzle	shpets'lə	"little sparrows", home-made South German noodles
Spaghetti	shp*ä*get'ē	spaghetti
Teigwaren	tīk'värən	noodles, pasta

Fish

Aal	äl	eel
Barsch	b*ä*rsch	perch
Dorsch	dôrsh	cod
Fisch	fish	fish
Flunder	flōōn'dər	flounder
Forelle	fōrel'ə	trout
Hecht	he*sh*t	pike
Heilbutt	hīl'bōot	halibut
Hering	hār'ing	herring
Kabeljau	kä'bəlyou'	cod
Karpfen	k*är*'pfən	carp
Lachs	läks	salmon
Makrele	m*ä*krā'lə	mackerel
Salm	zälm	salmon
Schellfisch	shel'fish	haddock
Scholle	shôl'ə	plaice
Seelachs	zā'läks	coalfish
Seezunge	zā'tsōongə	sole
Steinbutt	shtīn'bōot	turbot
Thunfisch	tōon'fish	tuna fish
Zander	ts*än*'dər	pike-perch

Sea Food

Austern	ous'tərn	oysters
Garnelen	g*är*nā'lən	shrimps, prawns
Hummer	hōōm'ər	lobster
Krebs	krāps	crab

Languste	läng·gōōs'tə	*spiny (rock)* lobster
Miesmuscheln	mēs'mōoshəln	mussels
Muscheln	mōosh'əln	mussels
Schalentiere	shä'ləntērə	shellfish
Venusmuscheln	vā'nōosmōoshəln	clams

Poultry

Backhendl	bäk'hendəl	*(Austrian)* breaded deep-fried chicken
Brathuhn	brät'hōon	broiled chicken
Ente	en'tə	duck
Fasan	fäzän'	pheasant
Flugente	flōok'entə	wild duck
Gans	gäns	goose
– Gänsebraten	gen'zəbrätən	roast goose
Geflügel	gəflē'gəl	poultry
Hähnchen	hān'shən	*(North German)* broiler, fryer
Hühnerbrust	hē'nərbrŏost	chicken breast
Hühnerkeule	hē'nərkoilə	chicken drumstick
Hendl	hen'dəl	*(South German, Austrian)* broiler, fryer
Huhn	hōon	chicken
Kapaun	käpoun'	capon
Perlhuhn	perl'hōon	guinea hen
Pute	pōo'tə	(hen) turkey
Rebhuhn	rāp'hōon	partridge
Taube	tou'bə	squab
Truthahn	trōot'hän	(tom) turkey
Wachtel	väh'təl	quail
Wildente	vilt'entə	wild duck
Wildgans	vilt'gäns	wild goose

Meat

Braten	brä'tən	roast
Brust	brōost	brisket
Deutsches Beefsteak	doit'shəs bēf'stäk	meat loaf
Eintopf	īn'tôpf	meat and vegetable stew

Faschiertes	fäshēr'təs	*(Austrian)* **ground meat**
Filet	filā'	**filet**
Fleisch	flīsh	**meat**
Fleischbouletten *(Berlin)*	flīsh'boolet'ən	**meat balls**
Fleischfrikadellen *(Rhine, Ruhr)*	flīsh'frikädel'ən	
Fleischklößchen *(North Germany)*	flīsh'klās·shən	
Fleischlaiberl *(Austria)*	flīsh'lībərl	
Fleischpflanzerl *(South Germany)*	flīsh'pfläntsərl	
gedämpft	gədempft'	**steamed**
Gulasch	goo'läsh	**goulash**
Hackfleisch	häk'flīsh	*(German)* **ground meat**
Hammelfleisch	häm'əlflīsh	**mutton**
Hase	hä'zə	**hare**
Hirsch	hirsh	**venison**
Kalbfleisch	kälp'flīsh	**veal**
Kalbshaxe	kälps'häksə	**veal knuckle**
Kaninchen	känēn'shən	**rabbit**
Kasseler Ripperl	käs'lər rip'ərl	**smoked pork chop**
Keule	koi'lə	**leg**
Kotelett	kôtlet'	**chop**
Kutteln	koot'əln	**tripe**
Lammfleisch	läm'flīsh	**lamb**
Leber	lā'bər	**liver**
Lende	len'də	**tenderloin**
Lunge	loong'ə	**lung**
Nieren	nē'rən	**kidneys**
Rücken	rík'ən	**saddle**
Ragout	rägoo'	**ragout, delicate stew**
Reh	rā	**venison**
Rindfleisch	rint'flīsh	**beef**
Rindsrouladen	rints'roolä'dən	**spicy vegetables rolled in thin slices of beef**
Rumpsteak	roomp'stäk	**rump steak**
Sauerbraten	zou'ərbrätən	**pickled pot roast**

Schinken	shing'kən	ham
– gekochter	gəkôh'tər	boiled
– roher	rō'ər	raw
Schnitzel	shnits'əl	cutlet
Schulter	shōōl'tər	shoulder
Schweinefleisch	shvī'nəflīsh	pork
Schweinshaxe	shvīns'häksə	pork hock
Steak	stāk	steak
Tatar	tätär'	beefsteak tartar
Würstchen	virst'shən	sausages
Wiener Schnitzel	vē'nər shnits'əl	breaded veal cutlet
Wild	vilt	game
Wildschwein	vilt'shvīn	boar
Zunge	tsōōng'ə	tongue
gebacken, fritiert	gəbäk'ən, fritērt'	deep fried
gebraten	gəbrät'ən	roasted
gekocht	gəkôht'	boiled
gepökelt	gəpā'kəlt	pickled, marinated
geräuchert	gəroi'shərt	smoked
geschmort	gəshmōrt'	stewed
(in der Pfanne)	(in dār pfän'ə)	
gebraten	gəbrä'tən	fried

Vegetables

Artischocken	ärtēshôk'ən	artichokes
Blumenkohl	blōō'mənkōl	(German) cauliflower
Bohnen	bō'nən	beans
Brechbohnen	bresh'bōnən	string beans
Broccoli	brôk'ōlē	broccoli
Chicorée	shik'ōrā	endive
Eissalat	īs'zälät'	iceberg lettuce
Endivie	endē'vē·ə	escarole
Erbsen	er'psən	peas
Gemüse	gəmē'zə	vegetables
Grünkohl	grēn'kōl	kale
Gurke	gōōr'kə	cucumber
Kürbis	kir'bis	pumpkin, squash
Karfiol	kärfē·ōl'	(Austrian) cauliflower
Karotten	kärôt'ən	(South German) carrots

Kartoffeln	kärtôf′əln	potatoes
– Bratkartoffeln	brät′kärtôfəln	home-fried potatoes
– gebackene Kartoffeln	gəbäk′ənə kärtôf′əln	baked potatoes
– Kartoffelbrei, Kartoffelpürée	kärtôf′əlbrī, kärtôf′əlpirā′	mashed potatoes
– Pellkartoffeln	pel′kärtôfəln	baked potatoes
– Pommes frites	pômfrit′	French-fried potatoes
– Salzkartoffeln	zälts′kärtôfəln	boiled potatoes
Kohl	kōl	cabbage
Kopfsalat	kôpf′zälät′	Boston lettuce
Mais	mīs	corn
Möhren, Mohrrüben	mä′rən, mōr′rēbən	*(North German)* carrots
Paprikaschoten	päp′rikäshō′tən	peppers
Paradeiser	pärädī′zər	*(Austrian)* tomatoes
Pilze	pilts′ə	mushrooms
Rosenkohl	rō′zənkōl	Brussels sprouts
rote *Bete (Rüben)*	rō′tə bā′tə (rē′bən)	beets
Rotkohl	rōt′kōl	red cabbage
Salat	zälät′	salad
Salzgurke	zälts′gŏŏrkə	pickle
Sauerkraut	zou′ərkrout	sauerkraut *(pickled cabbage)*
Sellerie	zel′ərē	celery root
Selleriestauden	zel′ərēshtoudən	(stalk) celery
Spargel	shpär′gəl	asparagus
Spinat	shpinät′	spinach
weiße Rüben	vī′sə rē′bən	turnips
Wirsingkohl	vir′zing·kōl′	Savoy cabbage

Cheese

Camembert	käm′əmbār	camembert
Edamer	ā′dämər	edam
Edelpilzkäse	ā′dəlpiltskä′zə	blue cheese
Emmentaler	em′əntälər	Swiss cheese
Hüttenkäse	hit′ənkäzə	cottage cheese
Quark	kvärk	farmer cheese, ricotta
Rahmkäse	räm′käzə	cream cheese
Schmelzkäse	shmelts′käzə	cheese spread

Desserts

Eis, Eiscreme	īs, īs´krām	**ice cream**
Halbgefrorenes	hälp´gəfrōrənəs	**frozen dessert**
Käsekuchen	kā´zəkōōhən	**cheese cake**
Kompott	kômpôt´	**fruit cup**
Krapfen	kräpf´ən	**jelly doughnuts**
Lebkuchen	lāp´kōōhən	**gingerbread**
Mehlspeisen	māl´shpīzən	**hot baked goods**
Mohnkuchen	mōn´kōōhən	**poppy seed cake**
Mousse	mōōs	**mousse**
Nußzopf	nōōs´tsôpf	**nut braid**
Obstsalat	ōpst´sälät´	**fruit salad**
Palatschinken	pälätshing´kən	**filled pancakes**
Prinzregententorte ..	prints´rägent´antôr´tə	**chocolate layer cake**
rote Grütze	rō´tə grits´ə	**berry pudding**
Streuselkuchen	shtroi´zəlkōōhən	**crumb cake**
Strudel	shtrōō´dəl	**strudel**
– Apfelstrudel	äp´fəlshtrōōdəl	**apple strudel**
– Käsestrudel,	kā´zəshtrōōdəl,	
Topfenstrudel	tôpf´ənshtrōōdəl	**cheese strudel**
Süßspeisen	zēs´shpīzən	**desserts**
Sachertorte	zäh´ərtôrtə	**black chocolate cake**
Schwarzwälder	shvärts´veldər	**Black Forest cherry**
Kirschtorte	kirsh´tôrtə	**cake**
Stollen	shtôl´ən	**East German raisin and nut bread**
Strauben	shtrou´bən	**raised doughnuts**
Zitronencreme	tsitrō´nənkräm`	**lemon cream**

Fruit

Ananas	än´änäs`	**pineapple**
Apfel	äp´fəl	**apple**
Apfelsine	äpfəlzē´nə	*(North German)* **orange**
Aprikose	äprikō´zə	**apricot**
Banane	bänä´nə	**banana**
Birne	bir´nə	**pear**
Brombeeren	brôm´bärən	**blackberries**

Erdbeeren	ārt'bārən	**strawberries**
Erdnüsse	ārt'nisə	**peanuts**
Feigen	fī'gən	**figs**
Grapefruit	grāp'frōōt	(*South German*) **grapefruit**
Haselnüsse	hä'zəlnisə	**hazel nuts**
Heidelbeeren	hī'dəlbārən	**blueberries**
Himbeeren	him'bārən	**raspberries**
Kirschen	kir'shən	**cherries**
Kokosnuß	kō'kôsnōōs	**coconut**
Mandarine	mändärē'nə	**tangerine**
Mandeln	män'dəln	**almonds**
Maroni	märō'nē	**roast chestnuts**
Melone	melō'nə	**melon**
– Honigmelone	hō'nishmelō'nə	**honeydew melon**
– Wassermelone	väs'ərmelō'nə	**watermelon**
Nüsse	nis'ə	**nuts**
Obst	ōpst	**fruit**
Orange	ōräN'zhə	(*South German*) **orange**
Pampelmuse	päm'pəlmōōzə	(*North German*) **grapefruit**
Pfirsich	pfir'zish	**peach**
Pflaume	pflou'mə	**plum**
Preiselbeeren	prī'zəlbārən	**cranberries**
Rhabarber	räbär'bər	**rhubarb**
rote Johannisbeeren	rō'tə yōhän'isbā'rən	**red currants**
schwarze Johannis- beeren	shvär'tsə yōhän'is- bā'rən	**black currants**
Stachelbeeren	shtäh'əlbārən	**gooseberries**
Walnüsse	väl'nisə	**walnuts**
Weintrauben	vīn'troubən	**grapes**
Zitrone	tsitrō'nə	**lemon**
Zwetschge	tsvetsh'gə	(*South German*) **plum**

At best, this is just a sketch of the many good things you can look forward to eating in the German-speaking countries. As you can see, there is no such thing as "German cuisine", but rather a set of regional foods, which vary – like many of their names – from place to place.

BEVERAGES

Wine

Baden wine	badischer Wein	bä′dishər vīn
Bordeaux	Bordeauxwein	bôrdō′vīn
Burgundy	Burgunderwein	bŏŏrgŏŏn′dərvīn
cider *(hard)*	Apfelwein	äpf′əlvīn
dessert wine	Dessertwein	desärt′vīn
Franconian wine	Frankenwein	fräng′kənvīn
Moselle wine	Moselwein	mō′zəlvīn
mulled wine	Glühwein	glē′vīn
Muscatel	Muskatellerwein	mŏŏs′kätel′ərvīn
red wine	Rotwein	rōt′vīn
Rhine wine	Rheinwein	rīn′vīn
sherry	Sherry	sher′ē
vermouth	Wermut	vär′mŏŏt
vintage	der Jahrgang	yär′gäng
white wine	Weißwein	vīs′vīn
wine	der Wein	vīn
– dry wine	*trockener (herber)* Wein	trôk′ənər (här′bər) vīn
– fruity wine	fruchtiger Wein	frŏŏh′tigər vīn
– sweet wine	süßer Wein	zē′sər vīn

Beer

beer	das Bier	bēr
beer mug	der Bierkrug	bēr′krŏŏk
bock beer	Bockbier	bôk′bēr
dark beer	dunkles Bier	dŏŏng′kləs bēr
a glass of beer	ein Glas Bier	īn gläs bēr
lager beer	Lagerbier	lä′gərbēr
light beer	helles Bier	hel′əs bēr
malt liquor	Starkbier	shtärk′bēr
Pilsener beer	Pilsenerbier, Pils	pilz′nərbēr, pils
white beer	Weißbier, Weizenbier	vīs′bēr, vī′tsənbēr

Other Alcoholic Beverages

alcoholic beverage ...	alkoholisches Getränk	älkōhō'lishəs gətrengk
bitters	der Magenbitter	mä'gənbitər
brandy	der Branntwein	bränt'vīn
cognac	der Kognak	kôn'yäk
gin	der Gin	jin
grog	der Grog	grôk
liqueur	der Likör	likār'
– apricot brandy	Aprikosenlikör	äprikō'zənlikār'
– cherry brandy	Kirschlikör	kirsh'likār
punch	der Punsch	pŏŏnsh
rum	der Rum	rŏŏm
vodka	der Wodka	vôt'kä
whiskey	der Whisky	vis'kē

In virtually all European countries, when you order a whiskey, you are ordering Scotch whisky. If you would prefer rye, bourbon, or some other beverage, you should say this when placing your order.

Non-Alcoholic Beverages

For coffee, tea, chocolate and milk, please see pp. 113–114.

fruit juice	der Fruchtsaft	frōōht'zäft
– apple juice	Apfelsaft	äpf'əlzäft
– grapefruit juice	Grapefruitsaft	grāp'frōōt·zäft'
– orange juice	Orangensaft	ōräN'zhənzäft
juice	der Saft	zäft
lemonade	die Zitronenlimonade	tsitrō'nənlimōnä'də
milk shake	das Milchmixgetränk	milsh'miksgətrengk'
orangeade	die Orangeade	ōräNzhä'də
soda water	das Sodawasser	zō'däväsər
soft drink	die Limonade	limōnä'də
tonic	das Tonicwasser	tô'nikväsər
water	das Wasser	väs'ər
– mineral water	das Mineralwasser ..	minerāl'väsər
– carbonated	mit Kohlensäure	mit kō'lənzoirə
– non-carbonated ...	ohne Kohlensäure ...	ō'nə kō'lənzoirə

In the Café

In German-speaking countries, „Kaffee" [käf'ā, käfā'] is considered a regular meal of the day. Most restaurants will only serve simple desserts, knowing that their customers will generally be moving on to a combination café-bakery for their after-dinner treats. In Vienna, for example, there is a whole long list of coffee and cocoa preparation methods, and other parts of the area have their coffee and cake specialties as well.

I'd like ...
Ich möchte ...
i*sh* mesh'tə

a piece of cake	ein Stück Kuchen	ĭn sht*i*k kōō'*h*ən
a cup of *coffee (tea)* .	einen *Kaffee (Tee)*	ĭ'nən käfā' (tā)
a (two cup) pot of *coffee (tea)*	eine Portion *Kaffee* *(Tee)*	ĭ'nə pôrtsyōn' käfā' (tā)
a dish of ice cream ..	eine Portion Eis	ĭ'nə pôrtsyōn' īs
– with (without) **whipped cream**	*mit (ohne)* Sahne	mit (ō'nə) zä'nə
cake	der Kuchen	kōō'*h*ən
candy	Süßigkeiten	zē'si*sh*kī'tən
chocolate	die Schokolade	shōkōlä'də
chocolate with ice **cream**	die Eisschokolade	īs'shōkōlä'də
confectionery	die Konditorei	kônditōrī'
cookies	Plätzchen	plets'*sh*ən
cream	der Rahm, die Sahne, *(Austria)* das Obers ...	räm, zä'nə, ō'bərs
ice cream	das Eis, die Eiskrem ..	īs, īs'krām
– chocolate ice cream	Schokoladeneis	shōkōlä'dən·īs
– strawberry ice **cream**	Erdbeereis	ārt'bār·īs'
– vanilla ice cream ..	Vanilleeis	vänil'yə·īs'
– assorted ice cream .	gemischtes Eis	gəmish'təs īs
ice cream parlor	die Eisdiele	īs'dēlə
macaroon	Makrone.............	m*a*krō'nə
meringue	der Sahnebaiser	zä'nəbāzā'

milk	die Milch	mil*sh*
– *cold (warm)* milk	*kalte (warme)* Milch	kăl'tə (vär'mə) mil*sh*
– evaporated milk	Kondensmilch	kôndens'mil*sh*
peach melba	Pfirsich Melba	pfir'zi*sh* mel'bä
sherbet	das Wassereis	väs'ər·īs'
– lemon sherbet	Zitroneneis	tsitrō'nən·īs'
– orange sherbet	Orangeneis	ōräN'zhən·īs'
sugar	der Zucker	tsōٜok'ər
– cube sugar	Würfelzucker	vēr'fəl·tsōٜokər
sundae	der Eisbecher	īs'be*sh*ər
sweets	Süßigkeiten	zē'si*sh*kī'tən
tart	die Torte	tôr'tə
– fruit tart	Obsttorte	ōpst'tôrtə
tea	der Tee	tā
wafers	Eiswaffeln	īs'väfəln
whipped cream	die Schlagsahne,	shläk'zänə,
	der Schlagobers	shläk'ōbərs

> *Incidentally, nobody will expect you to know all the names of the different cakes, pies, pastries, tarts, cookies, candies and other tempting sweets available in this part of the world. Things are always on display in any café or bakery, which means all you have to do is walk up to the counter and use the universal language, in other words, point! Your cake or pastry will be delivered to your table.*

Vienna coffee house coffee varieties:

Cappucino	käpōٜootshē'nō	coffee with whipped cream and chocolate sprinkles
Einspänner	īn'shpenər	black coffee and cream
kleiner (großer) Brauner	klī'nər (grō'sər) brou'nər	coffee with milk
Mokka	môk'ä	black coffee, mocha
Schale Gold	shä'lə gôlt	coffee with light cream
Schale Melange	shä'lə meläNzh'	half and half – coffee and milk
Verkehrter	ferkär'tər	more milk than coffee

Complaints, Paying the Check

We need another *portion (set of silverware, glass)*.
Hier fehlt *eine Portion (ein Besteck, ein Glas)*.
hēr fālt ī'nə pôrtsyōn' (īn bəshtek', īn gläs)

This isn't what I ordered.
Das habe ich nicht bestellt.
däs hä'bə ish nisht bəshtelt'

I wanted ...
Ich wollte ...
ish vôl'tə ...

This is ...
Das ist ...
däs ist ...

not fresh any more	nicht mehr frisch	nisht mār frish
too fatty	zu fett	tsoo fet
too hard	zu hart	tsoo härt
too hot *(temperature)*	zu heiß	tsoo hīs
too hot *(spicy)*	zu scharf	tsoo shärf
too cold	zu kalt	tsoo kält
too salty	zu salzig	tsoo zäl'tsish
too sour	zu sauer	tsoo zou'ər
too tough	zu zäh	tsoo tsä

I'd like to pay.
Ich möchte zahlen!
ish mesh'tə tsä'lən

The check, please!
Die Rechnung, bitte!
dē resh'noong, bit'ə

All together, please.
Ich zahle alles zusammen.
ish tsä'lə äl'əs tsoozäm'ən

Separate checks, please.
Wir zahlen getrennt.
vēr tsä'lən gətrent'

I don't think this is correct.
Das scheint nicht zu stimmen.
däs shīnt nisht tsoo shtim'ən

We didn't have that.
Das haben wir nicht gehabt.
däs hä'bən vēr nisht gəhäpt'

Thanks very much.
Vielen Dank!
fē'lən dängk

Keep the change.
Der Rest ist für Sie.
dār rest ist fēr zē

DOWNTOWN

On the Street

Where is ...?
Wo ist ...?
vō ist ...

the bus stop	die Bushaltestelle	bŏŏs′hältəstel′ə
the Catholic church	die katholische Kirche .	kätō′lishə kēr′shə
city hall	das Rathaus	rät′hous
the harbor	der Hafen	hä′fən
the ... Hotel	das ...-Hotel	-hōtel′
the museum	das Museum	mŏŏzā′ŏŏm
the police station	das Polizeirevier	pôlitsī′revēr
the post office	das Postamt	pôst′ämt
the Protestant church	die evangelische Kirche	ā′vän·gā′lishə kēr′shə
... Square	der ...-Platz	-pläts
St. Paul's Church ...	die Paulskirche	pouls′kērshə
... Street	die ...-Straße	-shträ′sə
the station	der Bahnhof	bän′hōf
the synagogue	die Synagoge	zin′ägō′gə
a taxi stand	ein Taxistand	täk′sēshtänt′

Is it far from here?
Ist es weit?
ist es vīt

How far is it to the ...?
Wie weit ist es *zum (zur)* ...?
vē vīt ist es tsŏŏm (tsŏŏr) ...

How many minutes on foot?
Wie viele Minuten zu Fuß?
vē fē′lə minŏŏ′tən tsŏŏ fŏŏs

A good distance (Not far).
Ziemlich (Nicht) weit.
tsēm′lish (nisht) vīt

Which direction is ...?
In welcher Richtung liegt ...?
in vel′shər rish′tŏŏng lēkt ...

What street is ... on?
In welcher Straße ist ...?
in vel′shər shträ′sə ist ...

There.	**Straight ahead.**	**To the right.**	**To the left.**
Dort.	Geradeaus.	Nach rechts.	Nach links.
dôrt	gərä′də·ous′	näh rehts	näh lingks

Bus, Taxi

Can I get there by bus?
Kann ich mit dem Bus fahren?
kän ish mit dām boos fä'rən

Which bus goes to (the) . . .?
Welcher Bus fährt *nach (zum, zur)* . . .?
vel'shər boos färt näh (tsoom, tsoor) . . .

How many stops is it from here?
Wie viele Haltestellen sind es?
vē fē'lə häl'təshtelən zint es

Do I have to change?
Muß ich umsteigen?
moos ish oom'shtīgən

Where do I have to get off (change)?
Wo muß ich *aussteigen (umsteigen)?*
vō moos ish ous'shtīgən (oom'shtīgən)

Would you please tell me when we get there?
Sagen Sie es mir bitte, wenn wir dort sind?
zä'gən zē es mēr bit'ə, ven vēr dôrt zint

A *one-way (transfer)* ticket to . . .
Einen *einfachen (Umsteige-)*Fahrschein nach . . .
ī'nən īn'fähən (oom'shtīgə-)fär'shīn näh . . .

Where can I get a taxi?
Wo bekomme ich ein Taxi?
vō bəkôm'ə ish īn täk'sē

Take me to . . .
Fahren Sie mich *zum (zur)* . . .
fä'rən zē mish tsoom (tsoor) . . .

To the station, please.
Zum Bahnhof, bitte.
tsoom bän'hôf, bit'ə

How much is the fare to . . .?
Wieviel kostet es *nach (zum, zur)* . . .?
vē'fēl kôs'tət es näh (tsoom, tsoor) . . .

Could you show us some of the sights?
Können Sie uns einige Sehenswürdigkeiten zeigen?
ken'ən zē oons ī'nigə zā'ənsvirdishkī'tən tsī'gən

Please *wait (stop)* here for a minute.
Warten (Halten) Sie bitte hier einen Augenblick.
vär'tən (häl'tən) zē bit'ə hēr ī'nən ou'gənblik

Most German cities now have universal public transportation tickets, valid on all subways, buses and regional suburban trains (S-Bahn). They are also valid for unlimited transfers in the same direction within a given time period (usually 2 hours).

Sight-seeing and Excursions

Two tickets to ... for tomorrow, please.
Für morgen bitte zwei Plätze nach ...
fēr môr′gən bit′ə tsvī plets′ə näh ...

Is lunch included?
Ist das Mittagessen im Preis inbegriffen?
ist däs mit′äk·es′ən im prīs in′bəgrifən

When (Where) do we meet?
Wann (Wo) treffen wir uns?
vän (vō) tref′ən vēr o͞ons

We'll be meeting ...
Wir treffen uns ...
vēr tref′ən o͞ons ...

When do we get going?
Wann geht es los?
vän gāt es lōs

Will we be seeing the ... too?
Besichtigen wir auch ...?
bəzish′tigən vēr ouh ...

Will we have some free time?
Haben wir Zeit zur freien Verfügung?
hä′bən vēr tsīt tso͞or frī′ən ferfē′go͞ong

How much?
Wieviel?
vēfēl′

Will we be able to do some shopping?
Können wir Einkäufe machen?
ken′ən vēr īn′koifə mä′hən

When do we get back?
Wann kommen wir zurück?
vän kôm′ən vēr tso͞orĭk′

How long will we stay in ...?
Wie lange bleiben wir in ...?
vē läng′ə blī′bən vēr in ...

Will we be going to ... too?
Kommen wir auch nach ...?
kôm′ən vēr ouh näh ...

What's worth seeing in ...?
Welche Sehenswürdigkeiten gibt es in ...?
vel′shə zā′ənsvĭrdishkī′tən gēpt es in ...

When does ... *open (close)*?
Wann wird ... *geöffnet (geschlossen)*?
vän virt ... gə·ef′nət (gəshlôs′ən)

How much does the *admission (guided tour)* cost?
Wieviel kostet *der Eintritt (die Führung)*?
vē′fēl kôs′tət dār īn′trit (dē fē′ro͞ong)

Is there an English-speaking guide?
Gibt es einen Fremdenführer, der Englisch spricht?
gēpt es ī′nən frem′dənfērər, dār eng′lish shprisht

I'd like to see the ...
Ich würde mir gern ... ansehen.
ish vir'də mēr gern ... än'zä·ən

Can we take a look at ... today?
Kann man heute ... besichtigen?
kän män hoi'tə ... bəzish'tigən

the castle	das Schloß	shlôs
the cathedral	den Dom	dän dōm
the church	die Kirche	kēr'shə
the fortress	die Burg	bŏŏrk
the exhibition	die Ausstellung	ous'shtel'ŏŏng
the gallery	die Galerie	gälərē'
the memorial	die Gedenkstätte	gədenk'shtetə
the museum	das Museum	mōŏzā'ŏŏm
the palace	den Palast	dän päläst'
the zoo	den Zoo	dän tsō

When does the tour start?
Wann fängt die Führung an?
vän fengt dē fē'rŏŏng än

Can we take pictures?
Darf man photographieren?
därf män fō'tōgräfē'rən

What is that *building (monument)*?
Was für ein *Gebäude (Denkmal)* ist das?
väs fēr īn gəboi'də (dengk'mäl) ist däs

Who *painted this picture (sculpted this statue)*?
Von wem stammt *dieses Bild (diese Statue)*?
fôn väm shtämt dē'zəs bilt (dē'zə shtä'tōŏ·ə)

What period does this ... date from?
Aus welcher Epoche stammt ...?
ous vel'shər epô'hə shtämt ...

When was ... built?
Wann wurde ... gebaut?
vän vŏŏr'də ... gəbout'

Who built ...?
Wer hat ... gebaut?
vär hät ... gəbout'

Where can I find ...?
Wo befindet sich ...?
vō bəfin'dət zish ...

Is this ...?
Ist das ...?
ist däs ...

*This is where ... *lived (was born, died)*.
Hier *lebte* ... *(wurde ... geboren, starb ...)*.
hēr läp'tə ... (vŏŏr'də ... gəbōr'ən, shtärp ...)

airport	der Flughafen	floōk'häfən
alley	die Gasse	gäs'ə
amusement park	der Vergnügungspark .	fergne͞'go͞ongspärk`
area	das Gebiet	gəbēt'
avenue	die Allee	älā'
boat trip	die Bootsfahrt	bōts'färt
botanical gardens . . .	der botanische Garten .	bōtä'nishə gär'tən
bridge	die Brücke	brĭk'ə
building	das Gebäude	gəboi'də
bus	der Bus	bo͞os
capital	die Hauptstadt	houpt'shtät
– **national capital** . . .	die Bundeshauptstadt .	bo͞on'dəs·houpt'-shtät
– **state capital**	die Landeshauptstadt .	län'dəs·houpt'shtät
castle	das Schloß, die Burg . .	shlôs, bo͞ork
cathedral	der Dom	dōm
cave	die Höhle	hä'lə
cemetery	der Friedhof	frēt'hōf
church	die Kirche	kēr'shə
churchyard	der Friedhof	frēt'hōf
city	die Stadt	shtät
city hall	das Rathaus	rät'hous

Almost every „Rathaus" in the German-speaking countries boasts a „Rathauskeller" [rät'houskel'ər], a restaurant used by the city fathers for official entertaining and featuring whatever are the local food and beverage specialties. The „Rathauskeller" (or „Ratskeller" [räts'kelər]) is a good place for a get-acquainted meal.

consulate	das Konsulat	kônzo͞olät'
corner	die Ecke	ek'ə
countryside	die Landschaft	länt'shäft
courthouse	das Gerichtsgebäude . .	gərishts'gəboidə
covered market	die Markthalle	märkt'hälə
dead-end street	die Sackgasse	zäk'gäsə
district	der Stadtteil	shtät'tīl
ditch	der Graben	grä'bən
downtown area	die Stadtmitte	shtät'mit'ə
embassy	die Botschaft	bōt'shäft
environs	die Umgebung	o͞omgā'bo͞ong
excavations	die Ausgrabungen	ous'gräbo͞ongən

excursion	der Ausflug	ous'flook
exhibition	die Ausstellung	ous'shteloong
factory	die Fabrik	fäbrēk'
farmhouse	das Bauernhaus	bou'ərnhous
fire department	die Feuerwehr	foi'ərvār
first-aid station	die Rettungsstation ...	ret'oongs-shtätsyōn'
fountain	der Brunnen	broon'ən
gallery	die Galerie	gälərē'
garden	der Garten	gär'tən
gate	das Tor	tōr
government office ...	das Amt	ämt
grave	das Grab	gräp
guide	der Fremdenführer	frem'dənfērər
harbor	der Hafen	hä'fən
high-rise building	das Hochhaus	hōh'hous
hiking path	der Fußweg	foos'vāk
hill	der Berg	bärk
hospital	das Krankenhaus	kräng'kənhous
house	das Haus	hous
house number	die Hausnummer	hous'noomər
landscape	die Landschaft	länt'shäft
lane	die Gasse	gäs'ə
last stop	die Endhaltestelle	ent'hältəshtel'ə
library	die *Bibliothek (Bücherei)*	bi'blē-ōtāk' (bēshərī')
lost and found office .	das Fundbüro	foont'bērō'
main street	die Hauptstraße	houpt'shträsə
memorial	das Denkmal,	dengk'mäl,
	die Gedenkstätte	gədengk'shtetə
military base	die Kaserne	käzer'nə
ministry	das Ministerium	min'istär'ē-oom
motion picture theatre	das Kino	kē'nō
mountain	der Berg	bärk
mountain range	das Gebirge	gəbir'gə
museum	das Museum	moozā'oom
national park	das Naturschutz-	nätoor'shoots-
	gebiet	gəbēt'
observatory	das Observatorium	ōp'zervätōr'ē-oom
old town	die Altstadt	ält'shtät
open market	der Markt	märkt
palace	der Palast	päläst'

park	der Park, ...	pärk,
	die Grünanlage	grēn'änläg'ə
part of town	der Stadtteil	shtät'tīl
path	der Weg	vāk
pavilion	der Pavillon	pä'vilyôN'
pedestrian	der Fußgänger	foos'gengər
– pedestrian crossing	der Fußgängerübergang	foos'gengər-ē'bərgäng
police	die Polizei	pôlitsī'
police station	das Polizeirevier	pôlitsī'revēr'
policeman	der Polizist	pôlitsist'
port	der Hafen	hä'fən
post office	die Post, das Postamt .	pôst, pôst'ämt
power station	das Kraftwerk	kräft'värk
public garden	die Grünanlage	grēn'änläg'ə
public rest room	die Bedürfnisanstalt . . .	bədirf'nisänshtält
river	der Fluß	floos
road	die Straße	shträ'sə
road sign	das Verkehrsschild	ferkärs'shilt
ruin	die Ruine	roo-ē'nə
school	die Schule	shoo'lə
sidewalk	der *Gehsteig (Bürgersteig)*	gä'shtīk (bir'gərshtīk)
shop	das Geschäft, ...	gəsheft',
	der Laden	lä'dən
shopping mall	das Einkaufszentrum . .	īn'koufs·tsen'troom
side road	die Nebenstraße	nä'bənshträsə
sightseeing	die Besichtigung	bəzish'tigoong
square	der Platz	pläts
stadium	das Stadion	shtä'dē·ôn
station	der Bahnhof	bän'hôf
stop	die Haltestelle	häl'təshtelə
store	der Laden	lä'dən
street	die Straße	shträ'sə
suburb	der Vorort	fōr'ôrt
suburban express train	die *Schnellbahn (S-Bahn)*	shnel'bän (es'bän)
subway	die *Untergrundbahn (U-Bahn)*	oon'tərgroontbän' (oo'bän)
surroundings	die Umgebung	oomgā'boong
swimming area	die Badegelegenheit . . .	bä'dəgəlā'gənhīt

synagogue	die Synagoge	zin'ägō'gə
taxi	das Taxi	täk'sē
taxi stand	der Taxistand	täk'sēshtänt'
temple	der Tempel	tem'pəl
throughway	der Durchgang	dŏŏrsh'gäng
tomb	das Grab	gräp
tower	der Turm	tŏŏrm
town	die Stadt	shtät
traffic	der Verkehr	ferkār'
traffic light	die Verkehrsampel	ferkārs'ämpəl
travel agency	das Reisebüro	rī'zəbērō'
university	die Universität	ōō'niverzität'
valley	das Tal	täl
village	das Dorf	dôrf
wall	die Mauer	mou'ər
waterfall	der Wasserfall	väs'ərfäl
zebra crossing	der Zebrastreifen	tsā'brāshtrī'fən
zoo	der Zoo (Tiergarten)	tsō (tēr'gärtən)

Religion, Churches

Where is the Catholic church?
Wo ist die katholische Kirche?
vō ist dē kätō'lishə kēr'shə

... St. Mary's Church?
... die Marienkirche?
... dē märē'ənkērshə

What time *are services (is high mass)*?
Wann findet *der Gottesdienst (das Hochamt)* statt?
vän fin'dət där gôt'əsdēnst (däs hōh'ämt) shtät

Is there a *wedding (christening)* today?
Findet heute eine *Trauung (Taufe)* statt?
fin'dət hoi'tə ī'nə trou'ŏong (tou'fə) shtät

Who's preaching the sermon?
Wer hält die Predigt?
vār helt dē prä'disht

Do they have church concerts?
Werden Kirchenkonzerte veranstaltet?
vār'dən kēr'shənkôntser'tə ferän'shtältət

Please call a *clergyman (priest)*!
Rufen Sie bitte einen *Geistlichen (Priester)*!
rōō'fən zē bit'ə ī'nən gīst'lishən (prēs'tər)

I am a ...	Ich bin ...	i*sh* bin ...
Christian	Christ	krist
Jew	Jude	yōō'də
Catholic	Katholik	k*ä*'tōlēk'
Methodist	Methodist	met'ōdist'
Moslem	Moslem, Muslim	môs'ləm, mōōs'lim
Protestant	Protestant	prō'test*ä*nt'

I don't belong to any religious denomination.
Ich bin konfessionslos.
i*sh* bin kôn'fesyōns'lōs

abbey	die Abtei	*ä*ptī'
altar	der Altar	*ä*l'tär
arch	der Bogen	bō'gən
baptism	die Taufe	tou'fə
Baroque	barock	b*ä*rôk'
bell	die Glocke	glôk'ə
candlestick	der Leuchter	loi*sh*'tər
cathedral	der Dom	dōm
(Roman) Catholic	(römisch-)katholisch	(r*ä*'mish-)k*ä*tō'lish
cemetery	der Friedhof	frēt'hōf
chapel	die Kapelle	k*ä*pel'ə
choir	der Chor	kōr
Christ	Christus	kris'tōōs
christening	die Taufe	tou'fə
Christian	der Christ	krist
Christianity	das Christentum	kris'təntōōm
church	die Kirche	kēr'shə
church concert	das Kirchenkonzert	kēr'*sh*ənkôntsert'
churchyard	der Friedhof	frēt'hōf
clergyman	der Geistliche	gīst'li*sh*ə
communion	das Abendmahl	ä'bəntmäl
confess	beichten	bī*sh*'tən
confession	die Beichte	bī*sh*'tə
convent	das (Nonnen)Kloster	(nôn'ən)klōs'tər
creed	das Glaubensbekenntnis	glou'bənsbəkent'nis
cross	das Kreuz	kroits
crucifix	das Kruzifix	krōōtsēfiks'
denomination	die Konfession	kôn'fesyōn'
dome	die Kuppel	kōōp'əl
font	das Taufbecken	touf'bekən

fresco	das Fresko	fres'kō
God	Gott	gôt
Gospel	das Evangelium	ä'väng·gā'lē·oo͡m
Gothic	gotisch	gō'tish
grave	das Grab	gräp
High Mass	das Hochamt	hōh'ämt
Islam	der Islam	is'läm, isläm'
Jew	der Jude,	yoo͞'də,
	die Jüdin	yē'din
Jewish	jüdisch	yē'dish
Judaism	das Judentum	yoo͞'dəntoo͞m
mass	die Messe	mes'ə
meditation	die Andacht	än'däht
monastery	das Kloster	klōs'tər
mosaic	das Mosaik	mōzä·ēk'
Moslem	der *Moslem (Muslim)*	môs'lem (moo͞s'lim)
mosque	die Moschee	môshā'
nave	das Schiff	shif
organ	die Orgel	ôr'gəl
pastor	der Pastor	päs'tôr
pillar	die Säule	zoi'lə
portal	das Portal	pôrtäl'
priest	der Priester	prēs'tər
procession	die Prozession	prō'tsesyōn'
Protestant	der Protestant	prō'testänt'
pulpit	die Kanzel	kän'tsəl
rabbi	der Rabbiner	räbē'nər
religion	die Religion	rel'igyōn'
religious	religiös	rel'igyös'
Romanesque	romanisch	rōmä'nish
sacristan	der *Mesner*	mes'nər
	(Kirchendiener)	(kēr'shəndēnər)
sacristy	die Sakristei	zäkristī'
sermon	die Predigt	prā'disht
service	der Gottesdienst	gôt'əsdēnst
Stations of the Cross	der Kreuzweg	kroits'vāg
Star of David	der Davidsstern	dä'vitshtern'
statue	die Statue	shtä'too͞·ə
synagogue	die Synagoge	zin'ägō'gə
tomb	das Grab	gräp
tower	der Turm	too͞rm

GOING SHOPPING

General Words and Phrases

Where can I *get (buy)* ...?
Wo kann ich ... *bekommen (kaufen)?*
vō kän ish ... bəkôm′ən (kou′fən)

Is there a *leather (china)* shop here?
Gibt es hier ein Fachgeschäft für *Leder (Porzellan)?*
gēpt es hēr īn *fäh′*gəsheft fēr lā′dər (pôrtselän′)

Have you got ...?	***I'd (We'd)* like ...**
Haben Sie ...?	*Ich möchte (Wir möchten)* ...
hä′bən zē ...	ish mesh′tə (vēr mesh′tən) ...
Please show me ...	**I need...**
Zeigen Sie mir bitte ...	Ich brauche ...
tsī′gən zē mēr bit′ə ...	ish brou′hə ...
Please give me ...	
Geben Sie mir bitte ...	
gä′bən zē mēr bit′ə ...	

a bag	eine Tüte	ī′nə tē′tə
a bottle	eine Flasche	ī′nə fläsh′ə
a box	einen Karton	ī′nən kärtông′
a few	ein paar	īn pär
a jar	ein Glas	īn gläs
a pound	*(approx.)* ein Pfund,	īn pfoont,
	fünfhundert Gramm	fīnf′hoondərt gräm
a *pack (packet)*	ein Päckchen	īn pek′shən
a pair	ein Paar	īn pär
a piece	ein Stück	īn shtik
a quart	*(approx.)* einen Liter	īn′ən lē′tər
a quarter pound	*(approx.)* hundert Gramm	hoon′dərt gräm
a roll	eine Rolle	ī′nə rôl′ə
a tube	eine Tube	ī′nə too′bə
two pounds	*(approx.)* ein Kilo	īn kē′lō
a yard	*(approx.)* einen Meter	ī′nən mā′tər

That's plenty.
Genug (Das reicht).
gənook' (däs rīsht)

A little more.
Noch etwas.
nôh et'väs

Even more.
Noch mehr.
nôh mār

Can you order it for me?
Können Sie es bestellen?
ken'ən zē es bəshtel'ən

When will you get it in?
Wann bekommen Sie es?
vän bəkôm'ən zē es

Can I exchange it?
Kann ich es umtauschen?
kän ish es oom'toushən

I don't like the *shape (color)*.
Die *Form (Farbe)* gefällt mir nicht.
dē fôrm (fär'bə) gəfelt' mēr nisht

This is ...
Das ist ...
däs ist ...

too big	zu groß	tsoo grōs
too dark	zu dunkel	tsoo doong'kəl
too expensive	zu teuer	tsoo toi'ər
too *light (pale)*	zu hell	tsoo hel
too narrow	zu schmal	tsoo shmäl
too small	zu klein	tsoo klīn
too wide	zu breit	tsoo brīt
too much	zuviel	tsoofēl'
not enough	zuwenig	tsoovā'nish

Have you got something a little *nicer (less expensive)*?
Haben Sie etwas *Besseres (Billigeres)*?
hä'bən zē et'väs bes'ərəs (bil'igərəs)

I like that.
Das gefällt mir.
däs gəfelt' mēr

I'll take *it (them)*.
Ich nehme *es (sie)*.
ish nā'mə es (zē)

How much is that?
Wieviel kostet das?
vē'fēl kôs'tət däs

Thanks, that'll be all.
Danke, das wär's.
däng'kə, däs värs

Can you send my stuff to the ... hotel please?
Können Sie mir bitte die Ware ins Hotel ... schicken?
ken'ən zē mēr bit'ə dē vä'rə ins hōtel' ... shik'ən

Do you take *credit cards (traveler's cheques)*?
Nehmen Sie *Kreditkarten (Reiseschecks)*?
nä'mən zē krādēt'kärtən (rī'zəsheks)

Stores

antique shop	Antiquitätenhändler ...	än'tikvitä'tən-hend'lər
art gallery	Kunsthändler	koonst'hendlər
bakery	Bäckerei	bekərī'
barber shop	(Herren)Friseur	(her'ən)frizär'
beauty parlor	(Damen)Friseur	(dä'mən)frizär'
bookshop	Buchhandlung	booh'händloong
butcher shop	Metzgerei,	metsgərī',
	Fleischerei	flīshərī'
candy store	Süßwarengeschäft	zēs'värəngəsheft'
china shop	Porzellangeschäft	pôr'tselän'gəsheft'
cigar store	*(Germany)* Tabakladen,	täb'äklädən,
	(Austria) Trafik	träfik'
cobbler shop	Schuhmacherei	shoo'mähərī'
cosmetic salon	Kosmetiksalon	kôsmā'tikzälôN'
dairy	Milchgeschäft, ...	milsh'gəsheft,
	Molkerei	môlkərī'
department store	Kaufhaus,	kouf'hous,
	Warenhaus	vä'rənhous
dressmaker's shop ...	(Damen)Schneiderei ...	(dä'mən)shnīdərī'
drug store *(cosmetics & sundries)*	Drogerie	drōgərē'
drug store *(prescription pharmacy)*	Apotheke	äpōtā'kə
dry cleaner's	Reinigung	rī'nigoong
electrical shop	Elektrohandlung	älek'trōhänd'loong
fashion boutique	Boutique	bootēk'
fish market	Fischhandlung	fish'händloong
flower shop	Blumenhandlung	bloo'mən-händ'loong
fruit market	Obstgeschäft	ōpst'gəsheft
furrier	Pelzhandlung	pelts'händloong
furniture store	Möbelgeschäft	mä'bəlgəsheft
grocery store	Lebensmittelgeschäft ..	lā'bənsmitəlgəsheft'
haberdashery	Kurzwarengeschäft	koorts'värəngəsheft'

hardware store	Eisenwarengeschäft ...	ī'zənvärəngəsheft'
hat shop	Hutgeschäft	hōot'gəsheft
jewelry store	Juwelier	yōovelēr'
laundromat	Waschsalon	väsh'zälôN'
laundry	Wäscherei	veshərī'
leather goods store ..	Lederwarengeschäft ...	lā'dərvärəngəsheft'
lingerie shop	Wäschegeschäft	vesh'əgəsheft
liquor store	Spirituosengeschäft ...	shpir'itōo·ō'zən- gəsheft'
music store	Musikalienhandlung ...	mōozikä'lē·ən- händ'lōong
newsdealer	Zeitungshändler	tsī'tōongs·hend'lər
optician	Optiker	ôp'tikər
perfume shop	Parfümerie	pärfēmərē'
pet shop	Tierhandlung	tēr'händlōong
photo shop	Fotogeschäft	fō'tōgəsheft'
photographer's studio	Fotograf	fōtōgräf'
real estate agency ...	Immobilienhändler	imōbēl'ē·ənhend'lər
record store	Schallplattengeschäft ..	shäl'plätəngəsheft'
second-hand bookshop	Buchantiquariat	bōoh'äntikvärē·ät'
self-service	Selbstbedienung	selpst'bədēnōong
shoemaker's shop ...	Schuhmacher	shōo'mähər
shoe store	Schuhgeschäft	shōo'gəsheft
souvenir shop	Souvenirladen	zōovənēr'lädən
sporting goods store	Sportwarengeschäft ...	shpôrt'värən- gəsheft'
stationery store	Schreibwarengeschäft .	shrīp'värən- gəsheft'
supermarket	Supermarkt	zōo'pərmärkt
tailor shop	(Herren)Schneiderei ...	(her'ən)shnīdərī'
textile shop	Textilwarengeschäft ...	tekstēl'värən- gəsheft'
toy store	Spielwarengeschäft	shpēl'värən- gəsheft'
travel agency	Reisebüro	rī'zəbērō'
vegetable market	Gemüsehandlung	gəmē'zəhänd'lōong
watchmaker's shop ..	Uhrmacher..........	ōor'mähər
wine shop	Weinhandlung	vīn'händlōong

Flowers

bouquet	Blumenstrauß	bloo′mənshtrous
flower pot	Blumentopf	bloo′məntôpf
flowers	Blumen	bloo′mən
gladioli	Gladiolen	glädē-ō′lən
lilacs	Flieder	flē′dər
orchids	Orchideen	ôr′shidä′ən
roses	Rosen	rō′zən
tulips	Tulpen	tool′pən
vase	Vase	vä′zə
violets	Veilchen	fīl′shən

Bookshop

autobiography	die Autobiographie	ou`tōbē-ōgräfē′
biography	die Biographie	bē-ōgräfē′
book	das Buch	booh
brochure	die Broschüre	brōshē′rə
catalogue	der Katalog	kätälōk′
children's book	das Kinderbuch	kin′dərbooh
city map	der Stadtplan	shtät′plän
detective novel	der Kriminalroman	krim′inäl′rōmän′
dictionary	das Wörterbuch	ver′tərbooh
guide book	der Reiseführer	rī′zəfērər
map	die Landkarte	länt′kärtə
novel	der Roman	rōmän′
paperback	das Taschenbuch	täsh′ənbooh
phrase book	der Sprachführer	shpräh′fērər
poetry book	der Gedichtband	gədisht′bänt
record	die Schallplatte	shäl′plätə
reference book	das *Sachbuch*	zäh′booh
	(*Nachschlagewerk*)	(näh′shlägəvärk′)
road map	die Straßenkarte	shträ′sənkärtə
story book	das Märchenbuch	mär′shənbooh
street map	der Stadtplan	shtät′plän
text book	das Lehrbuch	lär′booh
thriller	der Kriminalroman	krim′inäl′rōmän′
translation	die Übersetzung	ē′bərzets′oong
travel reading	die Reiselektüre	rī′zəlektē′rə
volume	der Band	bänt

Photo Shop

Would you please develop this film?
Entwickeln Sie mir bitte diesen Film.
entvik′əln zē mēr bit′ə dē′zən film

One *print (enlargement)* of each negative, please.
Von jedem Negativ bitte *einen Abzug (eine Vergrößerung)*.
fôn yā′dəm nā′gätēf bit′ə ī′nən äp′tsōōk (ī′nə fergrā′sərōōng)

– **three by four (inches).** – sieben mal zehn (cm.). – zē′bən mäl tsän (tsen′timätər)	– **three and a half by three and a half (inches).** – neun mal neun (cm.). – noin mäl noin (tsen′timatər)

– **three and a half by five (inches).**
– neun mal dreizehn (cm.).
– noin mäl drī′tsän (tsen′timätər)

I'd like . . . Ich möchte . . . ish mesh′tə . . .	– **a cartridge film.** – einen Kassettenfilm. – ī′nən käset′ənfilm
– **a super eight color film.** – einen Super-8- Farbfilm. – ī′nən zōō′pər-*äht*′- färp′film	– **a sixteen millimeter color film.** – einen Sechzehn-Millimeter- Farbfilm. – ī′nən zes*h*′tsän-milimä′tər färp′film

– **a film for color slides.**
– einen Farbfilm für Dias.
– ī′nən färp′film fēr dē′äs

– **a thirty-five millimeter film.**
– einen Fünfunddreißig-Millimeter-Film.
– ī′nən finf′ōōnt·drī′si*sh*-milimä′tər film

– **a *twenty (thirty-six)* exposure film.**
– einen *zwanziger (sechsunddreißiger)* Film.
– ī′nən tsvän′tsigər (zeks′ōōnt·drī′sigər) film

Would you please put the film in the camera for me?
Würden Sie mir den Film bitte einlegen?
vir′dən zē mēr dän film bit′ə īn′lāgən

camera	der Fotoapparat	fō'tō·äpärät'
color film	der Farbfilm	färp'film
color negative film	der Negativ-Farbfilm	nā'gätēf-färp'film
daylight color film	der Tageslichtfilm	tä'gəslisht film'
develop	entwickeln	entvik'əln
development	die Entwicklung	entvik'loong
diaphragm	die Blende	blen'də
8-mm film	der Schmalfilm	shmäl'film
enlargement	die Vergrößerung	fergrā'sərōong
exposure	die Belichtung	bəlish'tōong
exposure meter	der Belichtungs-messer	bəlish'tōongs-mes'ər
film	der Film	film
film (*take moving pictures*)	filmen	fil'mən
flash bulb	die Blitzlichtbirne	blits'lisht bir'nə
flash cube	der Blitzlichtwürfel	blits'lisht vēr'fəl
lens	das Objektiv	ôp'yektēf'
movie camera	die Filmkamera	film'kämerä
negative	das Negativ	nā'gätēf
paper	das Papier	päpēr'
– glossy	glänzend	glen'tsənt
– matte	matt	mät
photo	das Foto	fō'tō
photograph (*verb*)	fotografieren	fō'tōgräfēr'ən
picture	das Bild, die Aufnahme	bilt, ouf'nämə
print	der Abzug	äp'tsōok
– color print	der Farbabzug	färp'äptsōok
reversal film	der Umkehrfilm	ōōm'kärfilm
roll film	der Rollfilm	rôl'film
shutter	der Verschluß	fershlōōs'
shutter (release)	der Auslöser	ous'lāzər
– automatic shutter	der Selbstauslöser	selpst'ouslāzər
slide	das Dia	dē'ä
slide frame	der Diarahmen	dē'ärä'mən
snapshot	der Schnappschuß	shnäp'shōōs
take a picture	ein Foto machen	īn fō'tō mä'hən
tripod	das Stativ	shtätēf'
viewfinder	der Sucher	zōō'hər
yellow filter	das Gelbfilter	gelp'filtər

Jeweler

amber	der Bernstein	bern'shtīn
bracelet	das Armband	ärm'bänt
brooch	die Brosche	brôsh'ə
costume jewelry	der Modeschmuck	mō'dəshmo͞ok
cufflinks	Manschettenknöpfe	mänshet'ənkne͝pfə
diamond	der *Diamant (Brillant)*	dē·ämänt' (brilyänt')
ear clips	Ohrklipps	ōr'klips
earrings	Ohrringe	ōr'ringə
emerald	der Smaragd	smäräkt'
gold	das Gold	gôlt
gold plated	vergoldet	fergôl'dət
jewelry	der Schmuck	shmo͞ok
necklace	die Halskette	häls'ketə
pearls	Perlen	per'lən
pendant	der Anhänger	än'hengər
ring	der Ring	ring
ruby	der Rubin	ro͞obēn'
sapphire	der Saphir	zäfēr'
silver	das Silber	zil'bər
silver plated	versilbert	ferzil'bərt
wedding ring	der *Ehering (Trauring)*	ā'əring (trou'ring)

Clothing

May I try it on?	**I take a size . . .**	**This is . . .**
Darf ich es anprobieren?	Ich habe Größe . . .	Das ist . . .
därf ish es än'prōbēr'ən	ish hä'bə grä'sə . . .	däs ist . . .

too long	zu lang	tso͞o läng
too short	zu kurz	tso͞o ko͞orts
too tight	zu knapp	tso͞o knäp
too wide	zu breit	tso͞o brīt

Can it be altered?   *. . . fits just fine (doesn't fit).*
Kann es geändert werden?   . . . paßt *gut (nicht)*.
kän es gə·en'dərt ver'dən   . . . päst go͞ot (nisht)

apron	die Schürze	shir'tsə
bathing cap	die Bademütze	bä'dəmitsə
bathing trunks	die Badehose	bä'dəhōzə
bathrobe	der Bademantel	bä'dəmäntəl
belt	der Gürtel	gir'təl
bikini	der Bikini	bikē'nē
blouse	die Bluse	bloo'zə
blue jeans	Bluejeans	bloo'jēns
bra, brassière	der *Büstenhalter (BH)*	bis'tənhältər (bā'hä')
cap	die Mütze	mits'ə
cardigan	die Strickjacke	shtrik'yäkə
coat	der Mantel	män'təl
corset	das Mieder	mē'dər
dress	das Kleid	klīt
dressing gown	der Morgenmantel	môr'gənmäntəl
fur coat	der Pelzmantel	pelts'mäntəl
fur jacket	die Pelzjacke	pelts'yäkə
garter belt	der *Hüfthalter (Hüft-haltergürtel)*	hift'hältər (hift'-hältərgir'təl)
girdle	das Mieder	mē'dər
gloves	Handschuhe	hänt'shoo·ə
handkerchief	das Taschentuch	täsh'əntooh
hat	der Hut	hoot
– straw hat	der Strohhut	shtrō'hoot
jacket *(lady's)*	das Jackett	zhäket'
jacket *(man's)*	die Jacke, das Sakko	yäk'ə, zäk'ō
knee socks	Kniestrümpfe	knē'shtrimpfə
leather coat	der Ledermantel	lā'dərmäntəl
leather jacket	die Lederjacke	lā'dəryäkə
lingerie	die Damenunterwäsche	dä'mənoon'tərveshə
night shirt	das Herrennachthemd	her'ən·näht'hemt
nightie	das Nachthemd	näht'hemt
pajamas	der Pyjama	pijä'mä
panties	der *Schlüpfer (Slip)*, das Höschen	shlipf'ər (slip), häs'shən
pants	die Hose	hō'zə
pants suit	der Hosenanzug	hō'zənän'tsook
parka	der Anorak	än'ōräk
petticoat	der Unterrock	oon'tərôk

raincoat	der Regenmantel	rā'gənmäntəl
scarf	der Schal, das Halstuch	shäl, häls'tōōh
shirt	das Hemd *(Oberhemd)*	hemt (ō'bərhemt)
– drip-dry	bügelfrei	bē'gəlfrī
– short-sleeved	mit kurzen Ärmeln	mit kōōr'tsən er'məln
shorts	Shorts,	shôrts,
	die kurze Hose	kōōr'tsə hō'zə
ski pants	die Skihose	shē'hōzə
skirt	der Rock	rôk
slacks	die Hose	hō'zə
slip	der Unterrock	ōōn'tərôk
socks	Socken, Strümpfe	zôk'ən, shtrim'pfə
sport shirt	das *Freizeithemd*	frī'tsīt·hemt'
	(Sporthemd)	(shpôrt'hemt)
sportswear	die Sportkleidung	shpôrt'klīdōōng
stockings	Strümpfe	strim'pfə
stole	die Stola	shtō'lä
suède coat	der Wildledermantel	vilt'lädərmän'təl
suède jacket	die Wildlederjacke	vilt'lädəryäk'ə
suit *(lady's)*	das Kostüm	kôstēm'
suit *(man's)*	der Anzug	än'tsōōk
summer dress	das Sommerkleid	zôm'ərklīt
suspenders	Hosenträger	hō'zəntrāgər
sweater	der Pullover	pōōlō'vər
sweatshirt	das Sweatshirt	svet'shärt
swimsuit	der Badeanzug	bä'də·än'tsōōk
tie	die Krawatte	krävät'ə
tights	die Strumpfhose	shtrōōmpf'hōzə
track suit	der Trainingsanzug	trā'ningsän'tsōōk
trousers	die Hose	hō'zə
two-piece	das Jackenkleid	yäk'ənklīt
underpants	die Unterhose	ōōn'tərhōzə
undershirt	das Unterhemd	ōōn'tərhemt
underwear	die Unterwäsche	ōōn'tərveshə
vest	die Weste	ves'tə
windbreaker	die Windjacke	vint'yäkə

Dry Goods

accessories	das Zubehör	tsoo'bəhār
belt	der Gürtel	gir'təl
braces	Sockenhalter	zôk'ənhältər
buckle	die Schnalle	shnäl'ə
button	der Knopf	knôpf
buttonhole thread	die Knopflochseide	knôpf'lōhzīdə
darning cotton	das Stopfgarn	shtôpf'gärn
darning wool	die Stopfwolle	shtôpf'vôlə
dress-shield	das Schweißblatt	shvīs'blät
dry goods	Kurzwaren	koorts'värən
elastic	das Gummiband	goom'ēbänt
garters	Sockenhalter	zôk'ənhältər
hooks and eyes	Haken und Ösen	hä'kən oont ā'zən
lining	das Futter	foot'ər
needle	die Nadel	nä'dəl
– sewing needle	die Nähnadel	nä'nädəl
pin	die Stecknadel	shtek'nädəl
press-stud	der Druckknopf	drook'knôpf
ribbon	das Band	bänt
safety pin	die Sicherheitsnadel	zish'ərhītsnä'dəl
scissors	die Schere	shā'rə
silk thread	die Nähseide	nä'zīdə
suspenders	Hosenträger	hō'zəntrāgər
synthetic thread	synthetisches	zintā'tishəs
	Nähgarn	nä'gärn
tape	das Band	bänt
tape measure	das Zentimetermaß	tsentimä'tərmäs
thimble	der Fingerhut	fing'ərhoot
thread	das Garn,	gärn,
	der *Faden (Zwirn)*	fä'dən (tsvirn)
wool	die Wolle	vôl'ə
zipper	der Reißverschluß	rīs'fershloos'

Fabrics

cloth	das Tuch	tooh
corduroy	der Kord(samt)	kôrt'(zämt)
cotton	die Baumwolle	boum'vôlə

fabric	der Stoff	shtôf
– checked	kariert	kärērt'
– patterned	gemustert	gəmoos'tərt
– printed	bunt	boont
– solid color	einfarbig	īn'färbish
flannel	der Flanell	flänel'
jersey	der Jersey	jär'zē
linen	das Leinen	lī'nən
material	der Stoff	shtôf
nylon	das Nylon	nī'lôn
silk	die Seide	zī'də
– artificial silk	die Kunstseide	koonst'zīdə
synthetic fibre	die Kunstfaser	koonst'fäzər
velvet	der Samt	zämt
wool	die Wolle	vôl'ə
– pure wool	reine Wolle	rī'nə vôl'ə
– pure virgin wool	reine Schurwolle	rī'nə shoor'vôlə
worsted	das Kammgarn	käm'gärn

Cleaning, Alterations, Repairs

I'd like to have this *dress (suit)* cleaned.
Ich möchte *dieses Kleid (diesen Anzug)* reinigen lassen.
ish meh'tə dē'zəs klīt (dē'zən än'tsook) rī'nigən läs'ən

I'd like to have these things laundered.
Ich möchte diese Wäsche waschen lassen.
ish meh'tə dē'zə vesh'ə väsh'ən läs'ən

Would you please *press this (take out this stain)*?
Können Sie *das aufbügeln (diesen Fleck entfernen)*?
ken'ən zē däs ouf'bēgəln (dē'zən flek entfer'nən)

Could you *darn this (sew on this button)*?
Können Sie *das stopfen (diesen Knopf annähen)*?
ken'en zē däs shtôpf'ən (dē'zən knôpf än·nä'ən)

Could you *lengthen (shorten)* this?
Können Sie das etwas *länger (kürzer)* machen?
ken'ən zē däs et'väs leng'ər (kir'tsər) mä'hən

Where can I find a laundromat?
Wo gibt es hier einen Waschsalon?
vō gēpt es hēr ī'nən väsh'zälôN'

Optician

Can you fix these glasses?
Können Sie diese Brille reparieren?
ken'ən zē dē'zə bril'ə repärēr'ən

Can you replace these lenses?   **I'm *near-sighted (far-sighted)*.**
Können Sie diese Gläser ersetzen? Ich bin *kurzsichtig (weitsichtig)*.
ken'ən zē dē'zə glā'zər erzets'ən   ish bin kŏorts'zishtish (vīt'zishtish)

binoculars	das Fernglas	fern'gläs
compass	der Kompaß	kôm'päs
contact lenses	Kontaktlinsen,	kôntäkt'linzən,
	Haftschalen	häft'shälən
eyeglass case	das Brillenetui	bril'ənetvē'
frame	die Brillenfassung	bril'ənfäs'ŏong
glasses	die Brille	bril'ə
spectacles	die Brille	bril'ə
sunglasses	die Sonnenbrille	zôn'ənbrilə

Stationery

ball point pen	der Kugelschreiber	kōo'gəlshrībər
– ball point cartridge	die Mine	mē'nə
crayons	Buntstifte	bŏont'shtiftə
envelope	der Briefumschlag,	brēf'ŏomshläk',
	das Kuvert	kŏovär'
eraser	der Radiergummi	rädēr'gŏom'ē
fountain pen	der Füllfederhalter	fîl'fädərhäl'tər
glue	der Klebstoff	kläp'shtôf
ink	die Tinte	tin'tə
pad	der Block	blôk
– scratch pad	der Notizblock	nōtēts'blôk
– sketch pad	der Zeichenblock	tsī'shənblôk
paper	das Papier	päpēr'
– typewriter paper	das Schreib-	shrīp'-
	maschinenpapier	mäshē'nənpäpēr'
– wrapping paper	das Packpapier	päk'päpēr'
– writing paper	das Briefpapier	brēf'päpēr'
pencil	der Bleistift	blī'shtift
photocopies	Fotokopien	fō'tōkōpē'ən

Shoes

I take a size ...	**I'd like a pair of ...**
Ich habe Größe...	Ich möchte ein Paar ...
i*sh* hä′bə grä′sə ...	i*sh* m*e*sh′tə īn pär ...

beach sandals	Badeschuhe, ...	bä′dəshōō·ə,
	Strandschuhe	shtränt′shōō·ə
bedroom slippers	Hausschuhe	hous′shōō·ə
boots	Stiefel	shtē′fəl
ladies' shoes	Damenschuhe	dä′mənshōō·ə
loafers	Slipper	slip′ər
rubber boots	Gummistiefel	gōōm′ēshtē′fəl
sandals	Sandalen	zändä′lən
sneakers, gym shoes .	Turnschuhe	tōōrn′shōō·ə
walking shoes	Halbschuhe	hälp′shōō·ə

They're too *tight (wide)*.	**They pinch here.**
Sie sind zu *eng (weit)*.	Hier drücken sie.
zē zint tsōō eng (vīt)	hēr dr*i*k′ən zē

Could you fix these shoes for me?
Können Sie mir diese Schuhe reparieren?
k*e*n′ən zē mēr dē′zə shōō′ə repärēr′ən

crepe sole	die Kreppsohle	krep′zōlə
heel	der Absatz	äp′zäts
– **flat**	flacher	flä′hər
– **high**	hoher	hō′ər
in-sole	die Einlegesohle	īn′lāgəzō′lə
leather	das Leder	lā′dər
leather sole	die Ledersohle	lā′dərzōlə
rubber sole	die Gummisohle	gōōm′ēzōl′ə
shoe horn	der *Schuhlöffel*	shōō′lefəl
	(Schuhanzieher)	(shōō′äntsē·ər)
shoe laces	Schnürsenkel	shn*e*r′zengkəl
shoe polish	die Schuhkrem	shōō′krām
sole *(noun)*	die Sohle............	zō′lə
sole *(verb)*	besohlen	bəzō′lən
suede	das Wildleder........	vilt′lādər

Cigar Store

A pack of ... *cigarettes (tobacco)*, please.
Ein Päckchen ... *Zigaretten (Tabak)*, bitte.
īn pek'sh*ə*n ... tsig*ä*ret'en (t*ä*b'*ä*k), bit'*ə*

Do you have American cigarettes?
Haben Sie amerikanische Zigaretten?
hä'b*ə*n zē *ä*märik*ä*'nish*ə* tsig*ä*ret'*ə*n

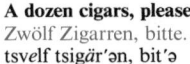

A dozen cigars, please.
Zwölf Zigarren, bitte.
tsv*e*lf tsig*ä*r'*ə*n, bit'*ə*

Would you please refill my lighter?
Würden Sie mir bitte das Feuerzeug füllen?
v*i*r'd*ə*n zē mēr bit'*ə* d*ä*s foi'*ə*rtsoik fil'*ə*n

A box of matches, please.
Eine Schachtel Streichhölzer, bitte.
ī'n*ə* sh*ä*h'tǝl shtrīsh'heltsǝr, bit'*ə*

Could I please have a light?
Haben Sie bitte Feuer?
hä'b*ə*n zē bit'*ə* foi'*ə*r

cigar	die Zigarre	tsig*ä*r'*ə*
cigarette	die Zigarette	tsig*ä*ret'*ə*
– filtered	die Filterzigarette	fil'tǝrtsig*ä*ret'*ə*
– unfiltered	Zigarette ohne Filter	tsig*ä*ret'*ə* ō'n*ə* fil'tǝr
cigarillo	der Zigarillo	tsig*ä*ril'ō
flint	der Feuerstein	foi'*ə*rshtīn
lighter	das Feuerzeug	foi'ertsoik
– gas lighter	das Gasfeuerzeug	gäs'foi·*ə*rtsoik
lighter fluid	das Feuerzeugbenzin	foi'*ə*rtsoik-bentsēn'
matches	Streichhölzer, Zündhölzer	shtrīsh'heltsǝr, tsint'heltsǝr
pipe	die Pfeife	pfī'f*ə*
pipe cleaner	der Pfeifenreiniger	pfī'fǝnrī'nigǝr
tobacco	der Tabak	t*ä*b'*ä*k

Toiletries

after shave	das Rasierwasser	räzēr'väsǝr
barette	die Spange	shp*ä*ng'*ə*
bath salts	das Badesalz	bä'dǝz*ä*lts
bobby pins	Haarklemmen	här'klem*ə*n
brush	die Bürste	b*i*rs't*ə*

clothes brush	die Kleiderbürste	klī'dərbirstə
cologne	das Kölnisch Wasser ..	kel'nish väs'ər
comb	der Kamm	käm
compact	die Puderdose	pōō'dərdōzə
cream	die *Krem (Creme)* ...	krām (krām)
curler	der Lockenwickler ...	lôk'ənviklər
deodorant	das Deodorant	dā-ōdōränt'
dye	das Haarfärbemittel ...	här'färbəmitəl
eye liner	der *Lidstrich*	lēt'shtrish
	(Eyeliner)	(ī'līnər)
eye shadow	der Lidschatten	lēt'shätən
eyebrow pencil	der Augenbrauenstift ..	ou'gənbrou·ən- shtift'
face cream	die Gesichtscreme	gəzishts'krām
hair conditioner	die Haarspülung	här'shpēlŏŏng
hair net	das Haarnetz	här'nets
hair spray	das Haarspray	här'shprā
hair tonic	das Haarwasser	här'väsər
hairbrush	die Haarbürste	här'birstə
hairpins	Haarnadeln	här'nädəln
lipstick	der Lippenstift	lip'ənshtift
mascara	die Wimperntusche, ...	vim'pərntŏŏshə,
	das Mascara	mäskä'rä
mirror	der Spiegel	shpē'gəl
mouthwash	das Mundwasser	mŏŏnt'väsər
nail file	die Nagelfeile	nä'gəlfīlə
nail polish	der Nagellack	nä'gəläk
nail polish remover ..	der Nagellackentferner	nä'gəläkentfer'nər
nail scissors	die Nagelschere	nä'gəlshārə
orange stick	der Nagelreiniger	nä'gəlrī'nigər
perfume	das Parfüm	pärfēm'
powder	der Puder	pōō'dər
powder puff	die Puderquaste	pōō'dərkvästə
prophylactics	Präservative	prā`zervätē'və
razor	der Rasierapparat	räzēr'äpärät'
– electric shaver	der Trockenrasierer ...	trôk'ənräzēr'ər
– safety razor	der Naßrasierer	näs'räzēr'ər
– straight razor	das Rasiermesser	räzēr'mesər
razor blades	Rasierklingen	räzēr'klingən

rouge	das Rouge	rōozh
sanitary napkins	Damenbinden	dä'mənbindən
scissors	die Schere	shä'rə
shampoo	*das Haarwaschmittel (Shampoo)*	här'väshmitəl (shämpōō')
shaving brush	der Rasierpinsel	räzēr'pinzəl
shaving cream	die Rasiercreme	räzēr'kräm
shaving foam	der Rasierschaum	räzēr'shoum
shaving soap	die Rasierseife	räzēr'zīfə
soap	die Seife	zī'fə
sponge	der Schwamm	shväm
sun tan cream	die Sonnencreme	zôn'ənkräm
– sun tan lotion	die Sonnenmilch	zôn'ənmil*sh*
– sun tan oil	das Sonnenöl	zôn'ənäl'
tampons	Tampons	täm'pôns
tissues	Papierhandtücher	päper'häntē'hər
toilet articles, toiletries	Toilettenartikel	tō·älet'ən- ärtik'əl
toilet kit	das Reisenecessaire	rī'zə·nesesär'
toilet paper	das Toilettenpapier	tō·älet'ənpäpēr'
wash cloth	der Waschlappen	väsh'läpən
tooth brush	die Zahnbürste	tsän'birstə
tooth paste	die Zahnpasta	tsän'pästä
tooth powder	das Zahnpulver	tsän'pōolfər
towel	das Handtuch	hän'tōo*h*
– bath towel	das Badetuch	bä'dətōo*h*
tweezers	die Pinzette	pin'tsetə

Watchmaker

Can you fix this *watch (clock)*?
Können Sie diese Uhr reparieren?
ken'ən zē dē'zə ōor repärēr'ən

It's *running fast (slow)*.
Sie geht *vor (nach)*.
zē gāt fōr (nä*h*)

How much will the repair cost?
Wieviel wird die Reparatur kosten?
vē'fēl virt dē repärätōōr' kôs'tən

alarm clock	der Wecker	vek'ər
crystal	das Glas	gläs
clock	die Uhr	o͞or
face	das Zifferblatt	tsif'ərblät
hand	der Zeiger	tsī'gər
pocket watch	die Taschenuhr	täsh'əno͞or'
spring	die Feder	fā'dər
stop watch	die Stoppuhr	shtôp'o͞or'
watch	die Uhr	o͞or
watch band	das (Uhren)Armband	(o͞or'ən)ärm'bänt
wrist watch	die Armbanduhr	ärm'bänto͞or'

Sundries

ash tray	der Aschenbecher	äsh'ənbeshər
bag	die *Tasche (Tüte)*	täsh'ə (tē'tə)
ball	der Ball	bäl
basket	der Korb	kôrp
battery	die Batterie	bätərē'
beach bag	der Campingbeutel	kem'pingboi'təl
bottle opener	der Flaschenöffner	fläsh'ənefnər
briefcase	die Aktentasche	äk'təntäshə
camp stove	der Spirituskocher	shpē'rito͞oskô'hər
can opener	der Dosenöffner	dō'zənefnər
candle	die Kerze	ker'tsə
– beeswax	aus Bienenwachs	ous bē'nənväks
candlestick	der Kerzenständer	ker'tsənshtendər
candy	Bonbons,	bôNbôNs',
	Süßigkeiten	zē'sishkī'tən
canned goods	Konserven	kônzär'vən
cassette	die Kassette	käset'ə
ceramics	Keramik	kerä'mik
china	Porzellan	pôr'tselän'
corkscrew	der Korkenzieher	kôr'kəntsē·ər
detergent	das Waschmittel	väsh'mitəl
– dishwashing		
detergent	das Spülmittel	shpēl'mitəl
doll	die Puppe	po͞o'pə

figurine	die Figur	figo͞or′
flashlight	die Taschenlampe	täsh′ənlämpə
flight bag	die Schultertasche	sho͞ol′tərtäshə
hammock	die Hängematte	heng′əmätə
handbag	die Handtasche	hänt′täshə
handicrafts	Handarbeiten	hänt′ärbī′tən
kerchief	das Kopftuch	kôpf′to͞oh
jackknife	das Taschenmesser	täsh′ənmesər
leash	die Leine	lī′nə
mat	der Untersetzer	o͞on′tərzetsər
paper napkins	Papierservietten	päpēr′zärvē·et′ən
phonograph record	die Schallplatte	shäl′plätə
picture	das Bild	bilt
plastic bags	Plastiktüten	pläs′tiktē′tən
playing cards	Spielkarten	shpēl′kärtən
pocket knife	das Taschenmesser	täsh′ənmesər
purse	die Handtasche	hänt′täshə
recording tape	das Tonband	tōn′bänt
rucksack	der Rucksack	ro͞ok′zäk
Scotch tape	das Klebeband	klä′bəbänt
sled	der Schlitten	shlit′ən
spot remover	das Fleckenwasser,	flek′ənväsər,
	der Fleckenentferner	flek′ənentfer′nər
string	der Bindfaden	bint′fädən
stuffed animal	das Stofftier	shtôf′tēr
suitcase	der Koffer	kôf′ər
tape recorder	das Tonbandgerät	tōn′bäntgərät′
thermometer	das Thermometer	ter′mōmä′tər
thermos bottle	die Thermosflasche	ter′môsfläsh′ə
toy	das Spielzeug	shpēl′tsoik
umbrella	der Regenschirm	rä′gənshirm
vase	die Vase	vä′zə
video cassette	die Videokassette	vē′dä·ōkäset′ə
wallet	die Brieftasche,	brēf′täshə,
	das Portemonnaie	pôrt′mônä′
washing line	die Wäscheleine	vesh′əlīnə
wood carving	Holzschnitzerei	hôlts′shnitsərī′

AT THE POST OFFICE

The activities of European post offices are far broader in scope than they are in the United States. In addition to all the usual mail services, the post office is also the telegraph and telephone company, and provides full banking services, including checking and savings accounts. They will also hold mail for travelers. Simply tell your correspondents to write you ,,Postlagernd" [pōst'lägərnt] in the city of your destination.

Post Office

Where is the post office?
Wo ist das Postamt?
vō ist däs pôst'ämt

Where is there a mail box?
Wo ist ein Briefkasten?
vō ist īn brēf'kästən

How much does this *letter (card)* cost?
Was kostet *dieser Brief (diese Karte)?*
väs kôstət dē'zər brēf (dē'zə kär'tə)

– to Canada.
– nach Kanada.
– näh kän'ädä

– to the United States.
–nach den Vereinigten Staaten.
– näh dān ferī'nishtən shtä'tən

What's the postage on ...
Wieviel beträgt das Porto für ...
vē'fēl bəträkt' däs pôr'tō fēr ...

this air mail letter ...	diesen Luftpostbrief ...	dē'zən lōoft'-pôstbrēf
this greeting card ...	diese Grußkarte	dē'zə grōos'kärtə
this letter abroad	diesen Auslandsbrief ..	dē'zə ous'läntsbrēf
this local letter	diesen Inlandsbrief	dē'zən in'läntsbrēf
this parcel	dieses Paket	dē'zəs päkät'
this picture post card	diese Ansichtskarte	dē'zə än'zishtskär'tə
this post card	diese Postkarte	dē'zə pôst'kärtə
this printed matter ..	diese Drucksache	dē'zə drōok'zähə
this registered letter .	diesen Einschreibebrief	dē'zən īn'shrībəbrēf
this small parcel	dieses Päckchen	dē'zəs pek'shən
this special delivery letter	diesen Eilbrief	dē'zən īl'brēf

Two eighty pfennig stamps, please.
Bitte zwei Briefmarken zu achtzig Pfennig.
bit'ə tsvī brēf'märkən tsoo äh'tsish pfen'ish

Two of each, please.
Je zwei Stück, bitte.
yā tsvī shtĭk, bit'ə

Do you have any special issues?
Haben Sie auch Sondermarken?
hä'bən zē ouh zôn'dərmärkən

This set of stamps, please.
Diesen Briefmarkensatz, bitte.
dē'zən brēf'märkənzäts', bit'ə

I'd like to send this letter *by registered mail (special delivery)*.
Diesen Brief *per Einschreiben (als Eilbrief)*.
dē'zən brēf per īn'shrībən (äls īl'brēf)

A *postal transfer (money order)*, please.
Eine *Postanweisung (Zahlkarte)*, bitte.
ī'nə pôst'änvī'zoong (tsäl'kärtə), bit'ə

How long does it take for a *letter (package)* to get to . . .?
Wie lange braucht ein *Brief (Paket)* nach . . .?
vē läng'ə brouht īn brēf (päkāt') näh . . .

Is there any mail here for me?
Ist Post für mich da?
ist pôst fēr mish dä

My name is . . .
Ich heiße . . .
ish hī'sə . . .

Where can I *mail (pick up)* a package?
Wo ist die *Paketannahme (Paketausgabe)*?
vō ist dē päkāt'än·nä'mə (päkāt'ousgä'bə)

Do I need a customs declaration?
Brauche ich eine Zollerklärung?
brou'hə ish ī'nə tsôl'erklär'oong

I'd like to have my mail forwarded.
Ich möchte meine Post nachsenden lassen.
ish meh'tə mī'nə pôst näh'zendən läs'ən

This is my new address.
Hier ist meine neue Adresse.
hēr ist mī'nə noi'ə ädres'ə

***Sign here, please.**
Bitte hier unterschreiben.
bit'ə hēr oontərshrī'bən

> *You can pay bills at the post office simply by transferring the money to your creditor's postal account or having a money order delivered to him by mail. The German, Austrian, or Swiss Post Offices can help you send money to almost any country in the world.*

Telegrams

A telegram form, please.
Ein Telegrammformular, bitte.
īn tālāgräm'fôrmoōlär', bit'ə

I'd like to send . . .
Ich möchte . . . aufgeben.
ish mesh'tə . . . ouf'gäbən

a telegram	ein Telegramm	īn tālāgräm'
– with prepaid reply .	mit vorbezahlter Rückantwort	mit fōr'bətsältər rik'äntvôrt
an urgent telegram . .	ein dringendes Telegramm	īn dring'əndəs tālāgräm'
a night letter	ein Brieftelegramm	īn brēf'tälāgräm'
a greeting card telegram	ein Glückwunsch-telegramm	īn glik'voōnsh-tālāgräm'

How much do ten words to . . . cost?
Wieviel kosten zehn Worte nach . . . ?
vē'fēl kôs'tən tsān vôr'tə näh . . .

When will it arrive at . . . ?
Wann ist es in . . . ?
vän ist es in . . .

Will the wire get to . . . today?
Ist das Telegramm heute noch in . . . ?
ist däs tālāgräm' hoi'tə noh in . . .

Telephone

> In most European countries it is wise to place long distance calls at the post office, as many hotels make sizable surcharges for use of the phone.

Where is the nearest phone booth?
Wo ist die nächste Telefonzelle?
vō ist dē näsh'stə tālāfōn'tselə

May I use your phone?
Darf ich bei Ihnen telefonieren?
därf ish bī ē'nən tālāfōnēr'ən

Where can I make a phone call?
Wo kann ich telefonieren?
vō kän ish tālāfōnēr'ən

Can I direct dial to . . . ?
Kann ich nach . . . durchwählen?
kän ish näh . . . doōrsh'välən

The phone book, please.
Das Telefonbuch, bitte.
däs tālāfōn'boōh, bit'ə

How much does a call to . . . cost?
Wieviel kostet ein Gespräch nach . . . ?
vē'fēl kôs'tət īn gəshprä sh' näh . . .

What's the area code for ...?	**5**	**6**	**0**	**5**
Wie ist die Vorwahlnummer nach ...?	fünf	sechs	null	fünf
vē ist dē fōr'välnoom'ər näh ...	fĭnf	zeks	nool	fĭnf

> *You can direct-dial North America from almost any telephone in Europe. The country code for the U.S. and Canada is 001, followed, of course, by the area code and the subscriber's number. You will need operator assistance for person-to-person or collect calls.*

A long distance call to ..., please.
Bitte ein Ferngespräch nach ...
bit'ə īn fern'gəshpräsh näh ...

How long will that take?
Wie lange wird es dauern?
vē läng'ə virt es dou'ərn

Can I have some coins for the pay phone?
Haben Sie Münzen für den Münzfernsprecher?
hä'bən zē min'tsən fēr dān mints'fernshpresh'ər

What time does the night rate begin?
Ab wieviel Uhr gilt der Nachttarif?
äp vē'fēl ōor gilt dār näht'tärēf

*Your call is ready in booth four.
Ihr Gespräch ist in Kabine vier.
ēr gəshpräsh' ist in käbē'nə fēr

*What's your number?
Welche Nummer haben Sie?
vel'shə noom'ər hä'bən zē

Please connect me with...
Bitte verbinden Sie mich mit ...
bit'ə ferbin'dən zē mish mit ...

There's no answer at that number.
Der Teilnehmer meldet sich nicht.
dār tīl'nämər mel'dət zish nisht

The line is *busy (out of order)*.
Die Leitung ist *besetzt (gestört)*.
dē lī'toong ist bəzetst' (gəshtärt')

Wrong number!
Falsch verbunden!
fälsh ferboon'dən

May I speak to *Mr. (Mrs., Miss)* ...?
Kann ich bitte *Herrn (Frau, Fräulein)* ... sprechen?
kän ish bit'ə hern (frou, froi'līn) ... shpresh'ən

Speaking!	**This is ... speaking.**	**Who is this?**
Am Apparat!	Hier spricht ...	Wer spricht?
äm äpärät'	hēr shprisht ...	vār shprisht

Please hold the line.
Bitte bleiben Sie am Apparat.
bit'ə blī'bən zē äm äpärät'

Would you please cancel that call.
Bitte streichen Sie das Gespräch.
bit'ə shtrī'shən zē däs gəshpräsh'

Code Alphabet

A Anton [än'tōn]
B Berta [ber'tä]
C Cäsar [tsä'zär]
D Dora [dō'rä]
E Emil [ā'mēl]
F Friedrich [frēd'rish]
G Georg (gā'ôrk)
H Heinrich (hīn'rish)
I Ida [ē'dä]
J Johann [yō'hän]

K Kaufmann [kouf'män]
L Ludwig [lōōt'vish]
M Martha [mär'tä]
N Nordpol [nôrt'pōl]
O Otto [ôt'ō]
P Paula [pou'lä]
Q Quelle [kvel'ə]
R Richard [rish'ärt]
S Samuel [zä'mōō·äl]

T Theodor [tā'ōdōr]
U Ulrich [ōōl'rish]
V Viktor [vik'tôr]
W Wilhelm [vil'helm]
X Xaver [ksä'vər]
Y Ypsilon [ip'silôn]
Z Zeppelin [tsep'əlēn]
Ä Ärger [är'gər]
Ö Ökonom [ākōnōm']
Ü Übermut [ē'bərmōōt]

address	die Adresse	ädres'ə
addressee	der Empfänger	empfeng'ər
air mail	Luftpost	lōōft'pôst
area code	die Vorwahlnummer	fōr'välnōōm'ər
c.o.d.	die Nachnahme	näh'nämə
coin changer	der Münzwechsler	mints'vekslər
collect call	das R-Gespräch	er'gəshpräsh
counter	der Schalter	shäl'tər
customs declaration	die Zollerklärung	tsôl'erklär'ōōng
destination	der Bestimmungsort	bəshtim'ōōngsôrt'
dial *(noun)*	die Wählscheibe	väl'shībə
dial *(verb)*	wählen	väl'ən
direct dialing	die Durchwahl	dōōrsh'väl
general delivery	postlagernd	pôst'lägərnt
information	die Fernsprech-auskunft	fern'shpresh-ous'kōōnft
insured mail	versicherte Sendung	ferzish'ərtə zen'dōōng
letter	der Brief	brēf
local call	das Ortsgespräch	ôrts'gəshpräsh
long distance call	das Ferngespräch	fern'gəshpräsh

mail box	der Briefkasten	brēf'kästən
mail man	der Briefträger	brēf'trāgər
night letter	das Brieftelegramm	brēf'tālāgram'
operator	die Telefonistin	tā'lāfōnis'tin
package	das Paket	päkāt'
package card	die Paketkarte	päkāt'kärtə
parcel	das Paket	päkāt'
person to person call	das Gespräch mit Voranmeldung	gəshprāsh' mit fōr'änmel'dōong
picture post card	die Ansichtskarte	än'zishtskär'tə
post card	die Postkarte	pôst'kärtə
post office box	das Postfach	pôst'fäh
postage	das Porto	pôr'tō
postal clerk	der Postbeamte	pôst'bə-ämtə
postal savings book	das Postsparbuch	pôst'shpärbōoh
postman	der Briefträger	brēf'trāgər
printed matter	die Drucksache	drōok'zähə
pushbutton telephone	das Tastentelefon	täs'təntālāfōn'
receipt	die Quittung	kvit'ōong
register	einschreiben	īn'shrībən
registered letter	der Einschreibebrief	īn'shrībəbrēf
registered parcel with declared value	das Wertpaket	värt'päkāt'
return postage	das Rückporto	rĭk'pôrtō
sender	der Absender	äp'zendər
small parcel	das Päckchen	pek'shən
special delivery	durch Eilboten	dōorsh īl'bōtən
special delivery letter	der Eilbrief	īl'brēf
special issue stamp	die Sondermarke	zôn'dərmärkə
stamp *(noun)*	die Briefmarke	brēf'märkə
stamp *(verb)*	frankieren	frängkēr'ən
stamp machine	der Briefmarken- automat	brēf'märkən- outōmāt'
telegram	das Telegramm	tālāgräm'
telephone	das Telefon, der Fernsprech- apparat	tālāfōn', fern'shpresh- äpärät'
unstamped	unfrankiert	ōon'frängkērt'
value declaration	die Wertangabe	värt'ängä'bə

BANK, CURRENCY EXCHANGE

Where can I change some money?
Wo kann ich Geld umtauschen?
vō kän ish gelt ōōm'toushən

Where is the bank?
Wo ist die Bank?
vō ist dē bängk

I need a hundred dollars in . . .
Ich möchte hundert Dollar in . . . umwechseln.
ish mesh'tə hōōn'dərt dôl'är in . . . ōōm'veksəln

How much will I get for . . . ?
Wieviel bekomme ich für . . . ?
vē'fēl bəkôm'ə ish fēr . . .

What's the rate of exchange?
Wie ist der Wechselkurs?
vē ist dār veks'əlkōōrs

Can you change . . . into German marks for me?
Können Sie mir . . . in Deutsche Mark umtauschen?
ken'ən zē mēr . . . in doitsh'ə märk ōōm'toushən

Could I have some change please?
Bitte auch etwas Kleingeld.
bit'ə ouh et'väs klīn'gelt

Can you change this?
Können Sie mir das wechseln?
ken'ən zē mēr däs veks'əln

I'd like to cash this *check (traveler's cheque)*.
Ich möchte diesen *Scheck (Reisescheck)* einlösen.
ish meh'tə dē'zən shek (rī'zəshek) īn'lāzən

Has some money arrived for me?
Ist Geld für mich eingegangen?
ist gelt fēr mish īn'gəgängən

amount	der Betrag	bəträk'
bank	die Bank	bängk
bank account	das Bankkonto	bängk'kôntō
bank charges	Bankgebühren	bängk'gəbērən
bank note	der Geldschein	gelt'shīn
bank transfer	die Banküberweisung . .	bängk'ēbərvī'zōōng
bill	der Geldschein	gelt'shīn
branch manager . . .	der Filialleiter	fil'ē·äl'lītər
cash *(adj.)*	bar	bär
cash *(noun)*	das Bargeld	bär'gelt
check	der Scheck	shek
coin	die Münze	min'tsə
credit	der Kredit	krādēt'
– take out a loan . .	einen Kredit	ī'nən krādēt'
	aufnehmen	ouf'nāmən

credit card	die Kreditkarte	krädēt′kärtə
currency	die Währung	vär′ooong
Austrian Schillings	Österreichische	ä′stərī′shishə
	Schilling	shil′ing
Canadian dollars	Kanadische Dollar	känä′dishə dôl′är
German marks	Deutsche Mark,	doitsh′ə märk,
	D-Mark	dā′märk
Swiss Francs	Schweizer Franken	shvī′tsər fräng′kən
American dollars	US-Dollar	oo′es′ dôl′är
daily rate	der Tageskurs	tä′gəskoors
deposit	einzahlen	īn′tsälən
foreign currency	Devisen	dəvē′zən
form	das Formular	fôrmoolär′
letter of credit	der Kreditbrief	krädēt′brēf
money	das Geld	gelt
money exchange	der Geldwechsel	gelt′veksəl
mortgage	die Hypothek	hēpōtāk′
pay out	auszahlen	ous′tsälən
payment	die Zahlung	tsä′loong
rate of exchange	der (Wechsel)Kurs	(vek′səl)koors
receipt	die Quittung	kvit′oong
savings bank	die Sparkasse	shpär′käsə
savings book	das Sparbuch	shpär′booh
security	das Wertpapier	värt′päpēr′
share of stock	die Aktie	äk′tsyə
signature	die Unterschrift	oon′tərshrift
stock	die Aktie	äk′tsyə
telegraphic	telegraphisch	tālägrä′fish
teller	der Schalterbeamte	shäl′tərbə·ämtə
transfer	die Überweisung	ēbərvī′zoong
traveler's cheque	der Reisescheck	rī′zəshek
withdraw	abheben	äp′hābən

West German Marks (DM) – DM 1 = 100 Pf (Pfennig [pfen′ig]),

Austrian Schillings (ÖS) – ÖS 1 = 100 g (Groschen [grôsh′ən]),

Swiss Francs (SFR) – SFR 1 = 100 Ct./Rp. (Centimes [säNtēm′]/
Rappen [räp′ən]).

AT THE POLICE STATION

STOP

Reporting

POLICE

I'd like to report ...
Ich möchte ... anzeigen.
i*sh* mesh'tə ... än'tsīgən

an accident	einen Unfall	ī'nən ŏŏn'fäl
a blackmail attempt .	eine Erpressung	ī'nə erpres'ŏŏng
a hold up	einen Überfall	ī'nən ē'bərfäl
a kidnapping	eine Entführung	ī'nə entfē'rŏŏng
a loss	einen Verlust	ī'nən ferlŏŏst'
a murder	einen Mord	ī'nən môrt
a theft	einen Diebstahl	ī'nən dēp'shtäl

My ... has been stolen.
Man hat mir ... gestohlen.
män hät mēr ... gəshtō'lən

I lost my ...
Ich habe *mein(e, -en)* ... verloren.
i*sh* hä'bə mīn(ə, -ən) ... ferlō'rən

bag	die Tasche	täsh'ə
billfold	das Portemonnaie	pôrt'mônā'
bracelet	das Armband	ärm'bänt
briefcase	die Aktentasche	äk'təntäshə
camera	den Fotoapparat	fō'tō·äpärät'
car key	den Autoschlüssel	ou'tōshlis'əl
handbag	die Handtasche	hänt'täshə
jewelry	den Schmuck	shmŏŏk
key	den Schlüssel	shlis'əl
money	das Geld	gelt
necklace	die Kette	ket'ə
purse	die Handtasche, ...	hänt'täshə,
	das Portemonnaie	pôrt'mônā'
ring	den Ring	ring
suitcase	den Koffer	kôf'ər
umbrella	den Regenschirm	rā'gənshirm
wallet	die Brieftasche, ...	brēf'täshə,
	das Portemonnaie	pôrt'mônā'
watch	die Uhr	ŏŏr
– wrist watch	die Armbanduhr	ärm'bäntŏŏr'

I have nothing to do with *it (this business)*.
Ich habe *damit (mit dieser Sache)* nichts zu tun.
i*sh* hä′bə dä′mit (mit dē′zər zä′hə) ni*sh*ts tso͞o to͞on

I'm innocent.
Ich bin unschuldig.
i*sh* bin o͞on′sho͞oldi*sh*

I didn't do it.
Das habe ich nicht getan.
däs hä′bə i*sh* ni*sh*t gətän′

How long do I have to stay here?
Wie lange muß ich hierbleiben?
vē läng′ə mo͞os i*sh* hēr′blībən

This man is *bothering (following)* me.
Dieser Mann *belästigt (verfolgt)* mich.
dē′zər män bəles′ti*sh*t (ferfôlkt′) mi*sh*

arrest	die Verhaftung	ferhäf′to͞ong
attorney	der (Rechts)Anwalt	(re*sh*ts′)än′vält
confiscate	beschlagnahmen	bəshläk′nämən
court	das Gericht	gəri*sh*t′
crime	das Verbrechen	ferbre*sh*′ən
criminal	der Verbrecher	ferbre*sh*′ər
criminal investigation division	die Kriminalpolizei	kriminäl′pôlitsī′
custody	die Haft	häft
– pre-trial custody	die Untersuchungshaft	o͞on′tər-zo͞o′ho͞ongs·häft′
drugs	Drogen,	drō′gən,
	das Rauschgift	roush′gift
guilt	die Schuld	sho͞olt
hold-up	der Überfall	ē′bərfäl
judge	der Richter	ri*sh*′tər
lawyer	der Rechtsanwalt	re*sh*ts′änvält
narcotics	das Rauschgift	roush′gift
police	die Polizei	pôlitsī′
police car	der *Polizeiwagen* *(Funkstreifenwagen)*	pôlitsī′vägən (fo͞ongk′shtrīfən-vä′gən)
police station	das Polizeirevier	pôlitsī′revēr′
prison	das Gefängnis	gəfeng′nis
smuggling	der Schmuggel	shmo͞og′əl
thief	der Dieb	dēp
verdict	das Urteil	o͞or′tīl

BEAUTY SHOP, BARBER SHOP

At the Beauty Shop

May I make an appointment for Saturday?
Kann ich mich für *Sonnabend (Samstag)* anmelden?
kän i*sh* mi*sh* fēr zôn'äbənt (zäms'täk) än'meldən

Would you put me down for a permanent wave?
Können Sie mich zur Dauerwelle vormerken?
ken'ən zē mi*sh* tso͞or dou'ərvelə fōr'merkən

For tomorrow?
Für morgen?
fēr môr'gən

Will I have to wait?
Muß ich warten?
mo͞os i*sh* vär'tən

Will it take long?
Wird es lange dauern?
virt es läng'ə dou'ərn

Wash and set, please.
Waschen und legen, bitte.
vä*sh*'ən o͞ont lā'gən, bit'ə

I'd like a *permanent (set)*, please.
Ich möchte eine *Dauerwelle (Wasserwelle)*, bitte.
i*sh* me*h*'tə ī'nə dou'ərvelə (väs'ərvelə), bit'ə

Please set my hair for the evening.
Ich brauche eine Abendfrisur.
i*sh* brou'*h*ə ī'nə ä'bəntfrizo͞or'

Please *dye (rinse)* my hair ...
Die Haare bitte ... *färben (tönen)*.
dē hä'rə bit'ə ... fär'bən (tä'nən)

Please cut my hair a little shorter.
Schneiden Sie bitte die Haare etwas kürzer.
shnī'dən zē bit'ə dē hä'rə et'väs kir'tsər

Just trim it, please.
Schneiden Sie bitte nur die Spitzen ab.
shnī'dən zē bit'ə no͞or dē shpits'ən äp

Please cut it wet.
Naß schneiden, bitte.
näs shnī'dən, bit'ə

Please pin it up.
Die Haare aufstecken, bitte.
dē hä'rə ouf'shtekən, bit'ə

Please tease it a little on the *top (sides)*.
Bitte *oben (seitlich)* etwas toupieren.
bit'ə ō'bən (zīt'lish) et'väs tōōpēr'ən

It's a little too hot under the drier.
Es ist etwas zu heiß unter der Haube.
es ist et'väs tsōō hīs ōōn'tər dār hou'bə

No *setting lotion (hair spray)*, please.
Bitte *keinen Festiger (kein Haarspray)*.
bit'ə kī'nən fes'tigər (kīn här'shprā)

Could you give me a *manicure (pedicure)*?
Können Sie mir *Maniküre (Pediküre)* machen?
ken'ən zē mēr mänikēr'ə (pedikēr'ə) mä'hən

Please file my nails *round (to a point)*.
Feilen Sie bitte die Nägel *rund (spitz)*.
fī'lən zē bit'ə dē nä'gəl rōōnt (shpits)

Just polish them, please.
Bitte nur polieren.
bit'ə nōōr pōlēr'ən

With (Without) nail polish.
Mit (Ohne) Nagellack.
mit (ō'nə) nä'gəläk'

Please *tweeze (shave)* my eyebrows.
Die Augenbrauen bitte *nachziehen (ausrasieren)*.
dē ou'gənbrou·ən bit'ə näh'tsē·ən (ous'räzēr'ən)

A *facial mask (face massage)*, please.
Bitte eine *Gesichtsmaske (Gesichtsmassage)*.
bit'ə ī'nə gəzishts'mäskə (gəzishts'mäsä'zhə)

Would you please put this *hairpiece (wig)* on for me?
Setzen Sie mir bitte *dieses Haarteil (diese Perücke)* auf.
zets'ən zē mēr bit'ə dē'zəs här'tīl (dē'zə perík'ə) ouf

Yes, thank you, that's just fine.
Ja, danke, so ist es recht.
yä, däng'kə, zō ist es resht

Very nice!
Sehr gut!
zār gōōt

At the Barber Shop

(Shave and) A haircut, please.
(Rasieren und) Haarschneiden, bitte!
(räzēr'ən ŏont) här'shnīdən, bit'ə

Not too short, please.
Bitte nicht zu kurz.
bit'ə nisht tsŏo kŏorts

(Very) Short, please.
(Ganz) Kurz, bitte.
(gänts) kŏorts, bit'ə

– at the back.
– hinten.
– hin'tən

– on top.
– oben.
– ō'bən

– in front.
– vorne.
– fôr'nə

– on the sides.
– an den Seiten.
– än dān zī'tən

A razor cut, please.
Einen Messerformschnitt, bitte.
īn'ən mes'ərfôrm'shnit, bit'ə

With (Without) part, please.
Mit (Ohne) Scheitel, bitte.
mit (ō'nə) shī'təl, bit'ə

Part on the *left (right)*, please.
Den Scheitel bitte *links (rechts).*
dān shī'təl bit'ə lingks (reshts)

A shampoo too, please!
Die Haare bitte auch waschen.
dē hä'rə bit'ə ouh väsh'ən

Scalp massage, please.
Eine Kopfmassage, bitte.
ī'nə kôpf'mäsä'zhə, bit'ə

Would you trim my *beard (moustache)*, please?
Den *Bart (Schnurrbart)* bitte etwas stutzen.
dān bärt (shnŏor'bärt) bit'ə et'väs shtŏots'ən

Just a shave, please.
Bitte nur rasieren.
bit'ə nŏor räzēr'ən

Please don't shave against the grain.
Rasieren Sie bitte nicht gegen den Strich.
räzēr'ən zē bit'ə nisht gā'gən dān shtrish

***Some hair tonic (A little brilliantine)*, please.**
Mit Haarwasser (Etwas Brillantine), bitte.
mit här'väsər (et'väs bril'yäntē'nə), bit'ə

Please leave it dry.
Bitte trocken lassen.
bit'ə trô'kən läs'ən

Yes, thank you, that's just great.
Ja, danke, so ist es recht.
yä, däng'kə, zō ist es resht

barber	der (Herren)Friseur	(her'ən)frizār'
beard	der Bart	bärt
beauty parlor	der Schönheitssalon	shān'hīts·zälôN'
brilliantine	die Brillantine	bril'yäntē'nə
cold wave	die Kaltwelle	kält'velə
comb *(noun)*	der Kamm	käm
comb *(verb)*	kämmen	kem'ən
curls	Locken	lôk'ən
cut	schneiden	shnī'dən
dandruff	Schuppen	shoop'ən
do s.o.'s hair	jemanden frisieren	yā'mändən frizēr'ən
dye	färben	fär'bən
hair	das Haar, die Haare	här, hä'rə
– dry hair	trockenes Haar	trôk'ənəs här
– greasy hair	fettiges Haar	fet'igəs här
haircut	der Haarschnitt	här'shnit
hair-do	die Frisur	frizoor'
hairdresser	der Damenfriseur, die Damenfriseuse	dä'mənfrizār', dä'mənfrizā'zə
hair drier	die Trockenhaube	trôk'ənhoubə
hair loss	der Haarausfall	här'ousfäl
hair style	die Frisur	frizoor'
hairpiece	das Haarteil	här'tīl
manicure	die Maniküre	mänikēr'ə
moustache	der Schnurrbart	shnoor'bärt
part	der Scheitel	shī'təl
pedicure	die Pediküre	pedikēr'ə
permanent wave	die Dauerwelle	dou'ərvelə
scalp massage	die Kopfmassage	kôpf'mäsäzhə
set	legen	lā'gən
shave	rasieren	räzēr'ən
sideburns	die Koteletten	kôtlet'ən
strand	die Strähne	shtrā'nə
tease	toupieren	toopēr'ən
tint	tönen	tā'nən
toupé	das Toupet	toopā'
wash	waschen	väsh'ən
wig	die Perücke	perik'ə
wisp	die Strähne	shtrā'nə

HEALTH

Pharmacy

Where is the next pharmacy?
Wo ist die nächste Apotheke?
vō ist dē näsh'stə äpōtā'kə

Which pharmacy has night duty?
Welche Apotheke hat Nachtdienst?
vel'shə äpōtā'kə hät näht'dēnst

I'd like this medicine, please.
Ich möchte dieses Medikament, bitte.
ish mesh'tə dē'zəs med'ikäment', bit'ə

Please give me something for ...
Geben Sie mir bitte etwas gegen ...
gā'bən zē mēr bit'ə et'väs gā'gən ...

I'd like ...
Ich möchte ...
ish mesh'tə ...

Do I need a prescription for this medicine?
Ist diese Arznei rezeptpflichtig?
ist dē'zə ärtsnī' retsept'pflishtish

Can you order this medicine for me?
Können Sie mir dieses Medikament besorgen?
ken'ən zē mēr dē'zəs med'ikäment' bəzôr'gən

Where can I pick it up?
Wo kann ich es bekommen?
vō kän ish es bəkôm'ən

Can I wait for it?
Kann ich warten?
kän ish vär'tən

for external use ...	nur zur äußerlichen Anwendung	nōōr tsōōr oi'sərlishən än'vendōōng
for internal use	nur zur innerlichen Anwendung	nōōr tsōōr in'ərlishən än'vendōōng
before meals	vor dem Essen	fōr dām es'ən
after meals	nach dem Essen ...	näh dām es'ən
three times a day ..	dreimal täglich	drī'mäl tāk'lish
as prescribed	nach Anweisung des Arztes	näh än'vīzōōng des ärts'təs
on an empty stomach	auf nüchternen Magen	ouf nish'tərnən mä'gən

Medication and Bandages

absorbent cotton	die Watte	vät′ə
ace bandage	die Elastikbinde	eläs′tikbin′də
adhesive bandage	das Heftpflaster	heft′pflästər
alcohol	der Alkohol	äl′kōhōl
ampule	die Ampulle	ämpŏŏl′ə
antidote	das Gegengift	gā′gəngift
aspirin	das Aspirin	äspirēn′
bandage	das Pflaster	pfläs′tər
bicarbonate of soda ..	doppeltkohlensaures Natron	dôp′əltkō′lən- zou′rəs nä′trôn
boric acid ointment ..	die Borsalbe	bōr′zälbə
burn ointment	die Brandsalbe	bränt′zälbə
camomile tea	der Kamillentee	kämil′əntā
cardiovascular drug .	das Kreislaufmittel	krīs′loufmit′əl
castor oil	das Rizinusöl	rē′tsinōosäl′
charcoal pills	Kohletabletten	kō′lətäblet′ən
contraceptive pills ...	Antibabypillen	än′tēbā′bēpil′ən
corn plaster	das Hühneraugen- pflaster	hē′nərougən- pfläs′tər
cotton swabs	Wattestäbchen	vät′əshtäpshən
cough medicine	das Hustenmittel	hŏŏs′tənmitəl
cough syrup	der Hustensaft	hŏŏs′tənzäft
dextrose	der Traubenzucker	trou′bəntsookər
diaphoretic	schweißtreibendes Mittel	shvīs′trībəndəs mit′əl
digestive tablets	Magentabletten	mä′gəntäblet′ən
digestive tonic	Magentropfen	mä′gəntrôpfən
disinfectant	das Desinfektions- mittel	des′infektsyōns′- mit′əl
diuretic	das Diuretikum	dē′ōorä′tikŏŏm
drops	Tropfen	trôpf′ən
ear drops	Ohrentropfen	ōr′əntrôpfən
elastic bandage	die Elastikbinde :.....	eläs′tikbin′də
elastic stocking	der Gummistrumpf ...	gŏŏm′əshtrŏŏmpf
emetic	das Brechmittel	bresh′mitəl
enema	der Einlauf, ...	īn′louf,
	das Klistier	klistēr′
eye drops	Augentropfen	ou′gəntrôpfən
eye ointment	die Augensalbe	ou′gənzälbə

fever cure	fiebersenkendes Mittel .	fē´bərzeng`kəndəs mit´əl
first-aid kit	das Verbandszeug	ferbänts´tsoik
gargle	das Gurgelwasser	gōor´gəlväsər
gauze bandage	die Mullbinde	mōōl´bində
glycerine	das Glyzerin	glitsərēn´
hydrogen peroxide ...	das Wasserstoff-superoxyd	väs´ərshtôf-zōō´pərôksēt´
injection	die Spritze	shprits´ə
insect repellent	das Insektenmittel ...	inzek´tənmitəl
iodine	die Jodtinktur	yōt´tingktōor´
laxative	das Abführmittel	äp´fērmit`əl
liniment	das Einreibemittel ...	īn´rībəmit`əl
medicine	das *Medikament (Mittel)*	med´ikäment´ (mit´əl)
mouthwash	das Mundwasser	mōont´väsər
ointment	die Salbe	zäl´bə
pain pills	Schmerztabletten ...	shmerts´täblet`ən
peppermint	die Pfefferminze	pfef´ərmintsə
pill	die *Pille (Tablette)* ..	pil´ə (täblet´ə)
powder	der Puder, das Pulver .	pōō´dər (pōōl´fər)
prophylactics	Präservative	prä´zervätē´və
quinine	das Chinin	*shi*nēn´
remedy	das Mittel	mit´əl
salve	die Salbe	zäl´bə
sanitary napkins	Damenbinden	dä´mənbindən
sleeping pills	Schlaftabletten	shläf´täblet`ən
styptic pencil	der Blutstillstift	blōot´shtilshtift`
suppository	das Zäpfchen	tsepf´*sh*ən
tablet	die Tablette	täblet´ə
talcum powder	der Talkumpuder	täl´kōompōo´dər
thermometer	das Thermometer	ter´mōmā´tər
tincture	die Tinktur	tingktōor´
tonic	das Stärkungsmittel ...	shter´kōongsmit`əl
tranquilizer	das Beruhigungsmittel .	bərōō´igōongs-mit`əl
valerian drops	Baldriantropfen	bäl´drē-äntrôpf`ən
vaseline	die Vaseline	väzəlē´nə
vitamin pills	Vitamintabletten	vit*ä*mēn´täblet`ən
wound salve	die Wundsalbe	vōont´zälbə

The doctor is in

Quick, call a doctor!
Rufen Sie bitte schnell einen Arzt!
rōō′fən zē bit′ə shnel ī′nən ärtst

Is there a doctor in the house?
Ist ein Arzt im Hause?
ist īn ärtst im hou′zə

Please get a doctor!
Holen Sie bitte einen Arzt!
hō′lən zē bit′ə ī′nən ärtst

Where is there a doctor?
Wo gibt es hier einen Arzt?
vō gēpt es hēr ī′nən ärtst

Can he come here?
Kann er herkommen?
kän är här′kômən

Where is there a hospital?
Wo ist *ein Krankenhaus (eine Klinik)?*
vō ist īn kräng′kənhous (ī′nə klē′nik)

When does the doctor have office hours?
Wann hat der Arzt Sprechstunde?
vän hät där ärtst shpresh′shtōōndə

Would you please come to the ...
Kommen Sie bitte *zum (zur)* ...
kôm′ən zē bit′ə tsōōm (tsōōr) ...

I'm sick.
Ich bin krank.
ish bin krängk

My husband (My wife, Our child) is sick.
Mein Mann (Meine Frau, Unser Kind) ist krank.
mīn män (mī′nə frou, ōōn′zər kint) ist krängk

doctor	der Arzt	ärtst
dermatologist	der Hautarzt	hout′ärtst
ear, nose and throat specialist	der *Hals-, Nasen- und Ohrenarzt (HNO-Arzt)*	häls-, nä′zən ōōnt ōr′ənärtst (hä′enō′ ärtst)
eye doctor	der Augenarzt	ou′gənärtst
general practitioner	der praktische Arzt ...	präk′tishə ärtst
gynecologist	der *Frauenarzt (Gynäkologe)*	frou′ənärtst (gi′nekōlō′gə)
internist	der Internist	intərnist′
neurologist	der *Nervenarzt (Neurologe)*	ner′fənärtst (noi′rōlō′gə)
ophthalmologist	der Augenarzt	ou′gənärtst

orthopedist	der Orthopäde	ôr'tōpā'də
otolaryngologist	der Hals-, Nasen-	häls-, nä'zən-
	und Ohrenarzt	ōōnt ōr'ənärtst
pediatrician	der Kinderarzt	kin'dərärtst
psychiatrist	der Psychiater	psē'shē·ät'ər
psychologist	der Psychologe	psē'shōlō'gə
surgeon	der Chirurg	shirōork'
– plastic surgeon	der plastische Chirurg .	pläs'tishə shirōork'
urologist	der Urologe	ōōrōlō'gə
doctor's office	das Sprechzimmer	shpresh'tsimər
office hours	die Sprechstunde......	shpresh'shtōōndə
waiting room	das Wartezimmer	vär'tətsimər

I haven't felt well the last few days.

Seit einigen Tagen fühle ich mich nicht wohl.
zīt ī'nigən tä'gən fē'lə ish mish nisht vōl

My *head (throat, stomach)* hurts.

Der *Kopf (Hals, Bauch)* tut mir weh.
där kôpf (häls, bouh) tōot mēr vä

It hurts here.	**I've got a (high) fever.**	**I've caught a cold.**
Hier tut es weh.	Ich habe (hohes) Fieber.	Ich habe mich erkältet.
hēr tōot es vä	ish hä'bə (hō'əs) fē'bər	ish hä'bə mish erkel'tət

I've got a *(severe, sharp, dull)* pain here.

Ich habe hier *(starke, stechende, dumpfe)* Schmerzen.
ish hä'bə hēr (shtär'kə, shtesh'əndə, dōom'pfə) shmer'tsən

I can't handle the *heat (food)* here.

Ich vertrage *die Hitze (das Essen)* nicht.
ish fertrā'gə dē hits'ə (däs es'ən) nisht

I must have done something to my stomach.	**I ate ...**
Ich habe mir den Magen verdorben.	Ich habe ... gegessen.
ish hä'bə mēr dān mä'gən ferdôr'bən	ish hä'bə ... gəges'ən

I threw up.	**I feel sick.**
Ich habe mich übergeben.	Mir ist schlecht.
ish hä'bə mish ē'bərgā'bən	mēr ist shlesht

I have *no appetite (diarrhea)*.	**I'm constipated.**
Ich habe *keinen Appetit (Durchfall)*.	Ich habe Verstopfung.
ish hä'bə kī'nən äpātēt' (dōorsh'fäl)	ish hä'bə fershtôpf'ōong

My eyes hurt.
Meine Augen schmerzen.
mī'nə ou'gən shmer'tsən

I have an earache.
Meine Ohren schmerzen.
mī'nə ō'rən shmer'tsən

I can't sleep.
Ich kann nicht schlafen.
i*sh* kän ni*sh*t shlä'fən

I feel nauseated.
Mir wird ständig übel.
mēr virt shten'di*sh* ē'bəl

I've got chills.
Ich habe Schüttelfrost.
i*sh* hä'bə shi't'əlfrôst

I can't move . . .
Ich kann . . . nicht bewegen.
i*sh* kän . . . ni*sh*t bəvā'gən

I'm diabetic.
Ich bin Diabetiker.
i*sh* bin dē'äbā'tikər

I'm expecting a baby.
Ich erwarte ein Baby.
i*sh* ervär'tə īn bā'bē

I fell.
Ich bin gestürzt.
i*sh* bin gəshtirtst'

I sprained my ankle.
Ich habe mir den Fuß verstaucht.
i*sh* hä'bə mēr dän fo͞os fershtou*h*t'

. . . is (are) swollen.
. . . ist (sind) geschwollen.
. . . ist (zint) gəshvôl'en

Is it serious?
Ist es schlimm?
ist es shlim

I'm feeling *a little (much)* better.
Ich fühle mich *etwas (bedeutend)* besser.
i*sh* fē'lə mi*sh* et'väs (bədoi'tənt) bes'ər

Could you give me a prescription for . . .?
Können Sie mir . . . verschreiben?
ken'ən zē mēr . . . fershrī'bən

I'd like to be vaccinated against . . .
Ich möchte mich gegen . . . impfen lassen.
i*sh* me*sh*'tə mi*sh* gā'gən . . . impf'ən läs'ən

The doctor will tell you:

Take your clothes off, please.
Machen Sie sich bitte frei.
mä'hən zē zish bit'ə frī

Breathe deeply!
Atmen Sie tief!
ät'mən zē tēf

Does this hurt?
Tut es hier weh?
tōōt es hēr vā

Open your mouth.
Öffnen Sie den Mund.
ef'nən zē dän mōōnt

Let me see your tongue.
Zeigen Sie die Zunge.
tsī'gən zē dē tsōōng'ə

Cough.
Husten Sie.
hōōs'tən zē

What have you been eating?
Was haben Sie gegessen?
väs hä'bən zē gəges'ən

How long have you been ill?
Seit wann sind Sie schon krank?
zīt vän zint zē shōn krängk

We'll have to do a *blood test (urinalysis)*.
Wir müssen *das Blut (den Urin)* untersuchen.
vēr mis'ən däs blōōt (dän ōōrēn') ōōntərzōō'hən

You're going to need an operation.
Sie müssen operiert werden.
zē mis'ən ôpərērt' vär'dən

I'll have to refer you to . . .
Ich muß Sie an . . . überweisen.
ish mōōs zē än . . . ēbərvī'zən

You must stop *drinking (smoking)*.
Sie dürfen nicht *trinken (rauchen)*.
zē dir'fən nisht tring'kən (rou'hən)

You'll have to stay *in bed (on a strict diet)*.
Ich muß Ihnen *Bettruhe (strenge Diät)* verordnen.
ish mōōs ē'nən bet'rōō·ə (shtreng'ə dē·ät') ferôrd'nən

Spend the next few days in bed.
Bleiben Sie einige Tage im Bett!
blī'bən zē ī'nigə tä'gə im bet

Take *two tablets (ten drops)* three times a day.
Nehmen Sie davon dreimal täglich *zwei Tabletten (zehn Tropfen)*.
nā'mən zē däfôn' drī'mäl tāk'lish tsvī täblet'ən (tsän trôpf'ən)

It's nothing serious.
Es ist nichts Ernstes.
es ist nishts erns'təs

Come back and see me a week from now.
Kommen Sie in acht Tagen wieder.
kôm'ən zē in äht tä'gən vē'dər

Parts of the Body and their Functions

abdomen	der *Bauch (Unterleib)*	bouh (o͞on'tərlīp)
ankle	der Knöchel	kne'shəl
appendix	der Blinddarm	blint'därm
arm	der Arm	*ä*rm
armpit	die Achselhöhle	*ä*k'səlhälə
artery	die *Arterie (Schlagader)*	ärtär'ē·ə (shläk'ädər)
back	der Rücken	r*i*k'ən
bile	die Galle	gäl'ə
bladder	die Blase	blä'zə
blood	das Blut	blo͞ot
blood pressure	der Blutdruck	blo͞ot'dro͞ok
body	der Körper	ker'pər
bone	der Knochen	knô'hən
bowel movement	der Stuhlgang	shto͞ol'gäng
brain	das Gehirn	gəhirn'
breast	die Brust	bro͞ost
breathing	die Atmung	ät'mo͞ong
buttocks	das Gesäß	gəzäs'
calf	die Wade	vä'də
cheek	die *Backe (Wange)*	bäk'ə (väng'ə)
chest	die Brust	bro͞ost
chin	das Kinn	kin
circulation	der Kreislauf	krīs'louf
collarbone	das Schlüsselbein	shl*i*s'əlbīn
digestion	die Verdauung	ferdou'o͞ong
disc	die Bandscheibe	bänt'shībə
ear	das Ohr	ōr
eardrum	das Trommelfell	trôm'əlfel
elbow	der Ellbogen	el'bōgən
eye	das Auge	ou'gə
– eyeball	der Augapfel	ouk'*ä*pfəl
– eyelid	das Augenlid	ou'gənlēt
face	das Gesicht	gəz*i*sht'

finger	der Finger	fing'ər
– thumb	der Daumen	dou'mən
– index finger	der Zeigefinger	tsī'gəfingər
– middle finger	der Mittelfinger	mit'əlfingər
– ring finger	der Ringfinger	ring'fingər
– pinkie	der kleine Finger	klī'nə fing'ər
foot	der Fuß	fōos
forehead	die Stirn	shtirn
frontal sinus	die Stirnhöhle	shtirn'hälə
gall bladder	die Gallenblase	gäl'ənbläzə
genital organs	die Geschlechtsorgane	gəshlechts'ôrgä'nə
gland	die Drüse	drē'zə
hair	das Haar, die Haare	här, hä'rə
hand	die Hand	hänt
head	der Kopf	kôpf
heart	das Herz	herts
heel	die Ferse	fer'zə
hip	die Hüfte	hif'tə
intestine	der Darm	därm
jaw	der Kiefer	kē'fər
– upper jaw	der Oberkiefer	ō'bərkēfər
– lower jaw	der Unterkiefer	ōon'tərkēfər
joint	das Gelenk	gəlengk'
kidney	die Niere	nēr'ə
knee	das Knie	knē
kneecap	die Kniescheibe	knē'shībə
larynx	der Kehlkopf	kāl'kôpf
leg	das Bein,	bīn,
	der Schenkel	sheng'kəl
– thigh	der Oberschenkel	ō'bərshengkəl
– lower leg	der Unterschenkel	ōon'tərshengkəl
limbs	Glieder	glē'dər
lip	die Lippe	lip'ə
liver	die Leber	lā'bər
lung	die Lunge	lōong'ə
male organ	das Glied	glēt
maxillary sinus	die Kieferhöhle	kē'fərhälə
menstruation	die *Menstruation*	men'strōo·ätsyōn'
	(Monatsregel)	(mō'nätsrā'gəl)
metabolism	der Stoffwechsel	shtôf'veksəl
mouth	der Mund	mōont

mucous membrane	die Schleimhaut	shlīm'hout
muscle	der Muskel	moos'kəl
nail	der Nagel	nä'gəl
neck	der Hals	häls
– back of the neck	das Genick	gənik'
– nape of the neck	der Nacken	näk'ən
nerve	der Nerv	nerf
nerves	die Nerven	ner'fən
nose	die Nase	nä'zə
palate	der Gaumen	gou'mən
pancreas	die Bauchspeichel-drüse	bouh'shpīshəl-drē'zə
pelvis	der Unterleib	oon'tərlīp
penis	der Penis	pā'nis
pregnancy	die Schwangerschaft	shväng'ərshäft
respiration	die Atmung	ät'moong
rib	die Rippe	rip'ə
shin	das Schienbein	shēn'bīn
shoulder	die Schulter	shool'tər
sinew	die Sehne	zä'nə
skin	die Haut	hout
skull	der Schädel	shā'dəl
sole	die Fußsohle	foos'zōlə
spinal cord	das Rückenmark	rĭk'ənmärk
spine	das Rückgrat, die Wirbelsäule	rĭk'grät, vir'bəlzoilə
spleen	die Milz	milts
stomach	der Magen	mä'gən
temple	die Schläfe	shlā'fə
tendon	die Sehne	zä'nə
thorax	der Brustkorb	broost'kôrp
throat	der *Hals (Rachen)*	häls (räh'ən)
toe	die Zehe, der Zeh	tsā'ə, tsā
tongue	die Zunge	tsoong'ə
tonsils	Mandeln	män'dəln
tooth	der Zahn	tsän
urin	der *Urin (Harn)*	oorēn' (härn)
uterus	die Gebärmutter	gəbär'mootər
vagina	die *Vagina (Scheide)*	vägē'nä (shīdə)
vein	die *Ader (Vene)*	ä'dər (vā'nə)
wrist	das Handgelenk	hänt'gəlengk

What's wrong?

abscess	der Abszeß	äps·tses'
air sickness	die Luftkrankheit	loöft'krängk'hīt
allergy	die Allergie	äl'ergē'
anemia	die Anämie	änämē'
appendicitis	die Blinddarm-entzündung	blint'därm-entsin'doong
arthritis	der Gelenkrheuma-tismus	gəlengk'roimä-tis'moos
asthma	das Asthma	äst'mä
attack	der Anfall	än'fäl
backache	Rückenschmerzen	rik'ənshmertsən
bleeding	die Blutung	bloo'toong
blood poisoning	die Blutvergiftung	bloot'fergif'toong
blood pressure	der Blutdruck	bloot'drook
– high blood pressure	hoher Blutdruck	hō'ər bloot'drook
– low blood pressure	niedriger Blutdruck	nē'drigər bloot'-drook
breathing problem	Atembeschwerden	ä'təmbəshvär'dən
bronchitis	die Bronchitis	brônshē'tis
bruise	die Quetschung	kvetsh'oong
burn	die Verbrennung	ferbren'oong
cancer	der Krebs	kräps
cardiac infarction	der Herzinfarkt	herts'infärkt'
chicken pox	die Windpocken	vint'pókən
chills	der Schüttelfrost	shit'əlfrôst
cholera	die Cholera	kō'lərä
circulatory problem	die Kreislaufstörung	krīs'loufshtä'roong
cold	die Erkältung	erkel'toong
colic	die Kolik	kō'lik
concussion	die Gehirn-erschütterung	gəhirn'-ershit'əroong
conjunctivitis	die Bindehaut-entzündung	bin'dəhout-entsin'doong
constipation	die Verstopfung	fershtôpf'oong
cough	der Husten	hoos'tən
cramp	der Krampf	krämpf
cut	die Schnittwunde	shnit'voondə

diabetes	die Zuckerkrankheit	tsŏok´ərkrängk´hīt
diarrhea	der Durchfall	dōorsh´fäl
diphtheria	die Diphtherie	diftərē´
disease	die Krankheit	krängk´hīt
– **contagious disease**	ansteckende Krankheit	än´shtekəndə krängk´hīt
dislocation	die Verrenkung	fereng´kŏong
dizziness	der Schwindel,	shvin´dəl,
	das Schwindelgefühl	shvin´dəlgəfēl
dysentery	die Ruhr	rōor
eye inflammation	die Augenentzündung	ou´gənentsin´dŏong
fever	das Fieber	fē´bər
fit	der Anfall	än´fäl
flatulence	Blähungen	blä´ŏongən
flu	die Grippe	grip´ə
food poisoning	die Lebensmittel-	lä´bənsmitəl-
	vergiftung	fergif´tŏong
fracture	der Knochenbruch	knô´hənbrooh
frostbite	die Erfrierung	erfrēr´ŏong
gall stones	Gallensteine	gäl´ənshtīnə
German measles	Röteln	rā´təln
hay fever	der Heuschnupfen	hoi´shnŏopfən
heart attack	der Herzanfall	herts´änfäl
heart problems	Herzbeschwerden	herts´bəshvärdən
heartburn	das Sodbrennen	zōt´brenən
hemorrhage	die Blutung	blŏo´tŏong
hemorrhoids	Hämorrhoiden	hem´ôrō-ē´dən
hoarseness	die Heiserkeit	hī´zərkīt
hypertension	die Hypertonie	hēpərtōnē´
illness	die Krankheit	krängk´hīt
indigestion	die Verdauungs-	ferdou´ŏongs-
	störung	shtā´rŏong
inflammation	die Entzündung	entsin´dŏong
influenza	die Grippe	grip´ə
injury	die Verletzung	ferlets´ŏong
insomnia	die Schlaflosigkeit	shläf´lōzishkīt´
intestinal catarrh	der Darmkatarrh	därm´kätär´
jaundice	die Gelbsucht	gelp´zŏoht
kidney stones	Nierensteine	nē´rənshtīnə
leukemia	die Leukämie	loikämē´
liver problem	das Leberleiden	lä´bərlīdən

lockjaw	der Tetanus	tet′änō̆os
lumbago	der Hexenschuß	hek′sənshō̆os
measles	Masern	mä′zərn
middle ear	die Mittelohr-	mit′əlōr-
inflammation	entzündung	entsin′dōong
mumps	der Mumps	mō̆omps
nausea	die Übelkeit	ē′bəlkīt
nephritis	die Nierenentzündung .	nē′rənentsin′dōong
neuralgia	die Neuralgie	noirälgē′
nosebleed	das Nasenbluten	nä′zənblōōtən
pain	der Schmerz	shmerts
paralysis	die Lähmung	lä′mōong
passing out	die Ohnmacht	ōn′mäht
peptic ulcer	das Magengeschwür	mä′gəngəshvēr
piles	Hämorrhoiden	hem′ōrō·ē′dən
pleurisy	die Rippenfell-	rip′ənfel-
	entzündung	entsin′dōong
pneumonia	die Lungenentzündung	lōong′ən-
		entsin′dōong
poisoning	die Vergiftung	fergif′tōong
pulled tendon	die Sehnenzerrung	zā′nəntser′ōong
rash	der Ausschlag	ous′shläk
rheumatism	das Rheuma	roi′mä
scarlet fever	der Scharlach	shär′läh
sciatica	der Ischias	ish′ē·äs
seasickness	die Seekrankheit	zā′krängk′hīt
shock	der Nervenschock	ner′fənshôk
skin disease	die Hauterkrankung ..	hout′erkräng′kōong
skin lesion	die Hautabschürfung .	hout′äpshir′fōong
smallpox	Pocken	pôk′ən
sore throat	Halsschmerzen	häls′shmertsən
sprain	die Verstauchung	fershtou′hōong
stitches in the side ...	das Seitenstechen	zī′tənshteshən
stomach pains	Magenschmerzen	mä′gənshmertsən
stroke	der *Gehirnschlag*	gəhirn′shläk
	(Schlaganfall)	(shläk′änfäl)
sunburn	der Sonnenbrand	zôn′ənbränt
sunstroke	der Sonnenstich	zôn′ənshtish
suppuration	die Vereiterung	fer·ī′tərōong
swelling	die Schwellung	shvel′ōong

tetanus	der Tetanus	tet'änoͮos
tonsilitis	die Mandelentzündung	män'dəlents*i*n'dooͮng
tuberculosis	die Tuberkulose	tooͮ'berkooͮlō'zə
tumor	die Geschwulst	gəshvooͮlst'
typhoid fever	der Typhus	tē'fooͮs
ulcer	das Geschwür	gəshvēr'
venereal disease	die Geschlechts-	gəshle*sh*ts'-
	krankheit	krängk'hīt
vomiting	das Erbrechen	erbre*sh*'ən
wound	die Wunde	vooͮn'də

In the Hospital

anesthetic	die Narkose	närkō'zə
bed	das Bett	bet
blood count	das Blutbild	blooͮt'bilt
blood test	die Blutprobe	blooͮt'prōbə
blood transfusion	die Bluttransfusion	blooͮt'tränsfooͮzyōn'
diagnosis	die Diagnose	dē'*ä*gnō'zə
discharge	die Entlassung	entl*ä*s'ooͮng
doctor	der Arzt	ärtst
examination	die Untersuchung	ooͮntərzooͮ'hooͮng
examine	untersuchen	ooͮntərzooͮ'hən
head nurse	die Oberschwester	ō'bərshvestər
hospital	das Krankenhaus	kräng'kənhous
infusion	die Infusion	infooͮzyōn'
injection	die Spritze	shprits'ə
intensive care unit	die Intensivstation	intenzēf'shtätsyōn'
medical director	der Chefarzt	shef'ärtst
night nurse	die Nachtschwester	n*ä*ht'shvestər
nurse	die (Kranken-)	(kräng'kən-)
	Schwester	shves'tər
operate (on)	operieren	ôpərēr'ən
operating room	der Operationssaal	ôp'ərätsyōns'zäl
operation	die Operation	ôp'ərätsyōn'
patient	der Patient,	pätsyent',
	die Patientin	pätsyen'tin
surgeon	der Chirurg	*sh*irooͮrk'
temperature	das Fieber	fē'bər
temperature chart	die Fieberkurve	fē'bərkooͮrfə
visiting hours	die Besuchszeit	bəzooͮhs'tsīt

ward . . . . die Station . . . . shtätsyōn′
x-ray *(noun)* . . . . die Röntgenaufnahme . rent′gənoufnä′mə
x-ray *(verb)* . . . . durchleuchten . . . . dōōrshloish′tən

Nurse, could you give me a *pain killer (sleeping pill).*
Schwester, geben Sie mir etwas *gegen Schmerzen (zum Einschlafen).*
shves′tər, gā′bən zē mēr et′väs gā′gən shmer′tsən (tsōōm īn′shlä′fən)

When can I get out of bed?
Wann kann ich aufstehen?
vän kän ish ouf′shtā·ən

What's the diagnosis?
Wie lautet die Diagnose?
vē lou′tət dē dē′ägnō′zə

At the Dentist's

Where is there a dentist here?
Wo gibt es hier einen Zahnarzt?
vō gēpt es hēr ī′nən tsän′ärtst

I've got a toothache.
Ich habe Zahnschmerzen.
ish hä′bə tsän′shmertsən

I'd like to make an appointment.
Ich möchte mich zur Behandlung anmelden.
ish mesh′tə mish tsōōr bəhänd′lōōng än′meldən

This tooth hurts.
Dieser Zahn tut weh.
dē′zər tsän tōōt vä

– up here.
– oben.
– ō′bən

– down here.
– unten.
– ōōn′tən

I've lost a filling.
Eine Plombe ist herausgefallen.
ī′nə plôm′bə ist herous′gəfälən

This tooth is loose.
Der Zahn wackelt.
dār tsän väk′əlt

Does this tooth have to be pulled?
Muß der Zahn gezogen werden?
mōōs dār tsän gətsō′gən vār′dən

. . . broke off.
. . . ist abgebrochen.
. . . ist äp′gəbrôhən

Can you do a temporary repair on this tooth?
Können Sie den Zahn provisorisch behandeln?
ken′ən zē dān tsän prōvēzōr′ish bəhän′dəln

Can you fix these dentures?
Können Sie diese Prothese reparieren?
ken′ən zē dē′zə prōtā′zə repärēr′ən

*Please don't *eat anything (smoke)* for two hours.
Bitte zwei Stunden *nichts essen (nicht rauchen).*
bit′ə tsvī shtōōn′dən nishts es′ən (nisht rou′hən)

When do you want me to come back?
Wann soll ich wiederkommen?
vän zôl ish vê'dərkômən

abscess	der Abszeß	äps·tses'
anesthesia	die Betäubung	bətoi'bo̅o̅ng
– local anesthesia ...	die örtliche Betäubung	ert'lishə bətoi'bo̅o̅ng
– general anesthesia .	die Vollnarkose	fôl'närkō'zə
bicuspid	der *Backenzahn (Prämolar)*	bäk'əntsän (prä'-mōlär')
braces	die Zahnspange	tsän'shpängə
bridge	die Brücke	brĭk'ə
cap *(artificial)*	die Krone	krō'nə
cavities	die Karies	kär'ē·es
crown *(natural)*	die Krone	krō'nə
cuspid	der Eckzahn..........	ek'tsän
dental clinic	die Zahnklinik	tsän'klē'nik
dentist	der Zahnarzt	tsän'ärtst
denture	das Gebiß, die Prothese	gəbis', prōtā'zə
extract	ziehen	tsē'ən
false tooth	der Zahnersatz	tsän'erzäts
fill	füllen	fĭl'ən
filling	die Füllung	fĭl'o̅o̅ng
gums	das Zahnfleisch	tsän'flīsh
incisor	der Schneidezahn	shnī'dətsän
injection	die Spritze	shprits'ə
jaw	der Kiefer	kē'fər
molar	der *Mahlzahn (Molar)* .	mäl'tsän (mōlär')
nerve	der Nerv	nerf
oral surgeon	der Kieferchirurg	kē'fərshiro̅o̅rk'
orthodontist	der Kieferorthopäde ..	kē'fərôrtōpä'də
plate	die Platte	plät'ə
root	die Zahnwurzel	tsän'vo̅o̅rtsəl
root canal work	die Wurzelbehandlung .	vo̅o̅r'tsəl-bəhänd'lo̅o̅ng
tartar	der Zahnstein	tsän'shtīn
temporary filling	die Einlage	īn'lägə
tooth	der Zahn...........	tsän
tooth cervix	der Zahnhals	tsän'häls
toothache	Zahnschmerzen	tsän'shmertsən
wisdom tooth	der Weisheitszahn	vīs'hītstsän'

Taking a Cure

bath	das Bad	bät
bath attendant	der Bademeister	bä′dəmīstər
convalescent home	das Erholungsheim	erhō′lōongs·hīm′
cure	die Kur	kōor
cure tax	die Kurtaxe	kōor′täksə
cure vacation	der Kuraufenthalt	kōor′oufent·hält′
diet	die Diät	dē·ät′
gymnastics	die Gymnastik	gimnäs′tik
health resort	der Luftkurort	lōoft′kōorôrt
hot spring	die Thermalquelle	termäl′kvelə
inhale	inhalieren	inhälēr′ən
massage (noun)	die Massage	mäsä′zhə
massage (verb)	massieren	mäsēr′ən
masseur	der Masseur	mäsär′
masseuse	die Masseuse	mäsä′zə
medicinal spring	die Heilquelle	hīl′kvelə
mineral bath	das Mineralbad	min′eräl′bät
mineral spring	der Brunnen	brōon′ən
minerals	Mineralien	min′erä′lē·ən
mud	der Schlamm	shläm
mud bath	das Moorbad	mōr′bät
mud pack	die Packung	päk′ōong
pump room	die Trinkhalle	tringk′hälə
radiation therapy	die Bestrahlung	bəshträ′lōong
rest cure	die Liegekur	lē′gəkōor
sanatorium	das Sanatorium	zän′ätōr′ē·ōom
sauna	die Sauna	zou′nä
sea water	das Meerwasser	mär′väsər
short wave	die Kurzwelle	kōorts′velə
spa	der Badeort	bä′də·ôrt′
steam bath	das Dampfbad	dämpf′bät
sunlamp	die Höhensonne	hä′ənzônə
ultrasonics	der Ultraschall	ōol′träshäl

CONCERT, THEATRE, MOVIES

> *Most Central European theatres are repertory theatres, featuring a
> permanent company performing a different play, opera or operetta
> each evening. Many theatres and concert halls provide discount
> tickets for the disabled, for students and for senior citizens.*

At the Box Office

What's on tonight?
Was wird heute abend *gegeben (gespielt)?*
väs virt hoi′tə ä′bənt gəgā′bən (gəshpēlt′)

When does *the performance (the concert)* start?
Wann beginnt *die Vorstellung (das Konzert)?*
vän bəgint′ dē fōr′shtelo͞ong (däs kôntsert′)

Where can we get tickets?   **Are there any discounts for …?**
Wo bekommt man Karten?   Gibt es Ermäßigung für …?
vō bəkômt′ män kär′tən   gēpt es ermä′sigo͞ong fēr …

Are there still tickets available for *this (tomorrow)* evening?
Gibt es noch Karten für *heute (morgen)* abend?
gēpt es nôh kär′tən fēr hoi′tə (môr′gən) ä′bənt

Two seats in the third row, first balcony, please.   **– in the middle.**
Bitte zwei Plätze im ersten Rang, dritte Reihe.   – in der Mitte.
bit′ə tsvī plets′ə im er′stən räng, drit′ə rī′ə   – in där mit′ə

– on the side.   **One ticket in the *third (tenth)* row, please.**
– an der Seite.   Bitte einmal *dritte (zehnte)* Reihe.
– än där zī′tə   bit′ə īn′mäl drit′ə (tsān′tə) rī′ə

Concert, Theatre

accompanist	der Begleiter	bəglī′tər
act	der *Akt (Aufzug)*	äkt (ouf′tso͞ok)
actor	der Schauspieler	shou′shpēlər
actress	die Schauspielerin	shou′shpēlərin

advance ticket sales	der Vorverkauf	fōr'ferkouf
alto	der Alt, die Altistin	ält, ältis'tin
applause	der Beifall	bī'fäl
aria	die Arie	ä'rē·ə
ballet	das Ballett	bälet'
balcony	der Rang	räng
band	die Kapelle	käpel'ə
baritone	der Bariton	bär'itōn
bass	der Baß	bäs
box office	die Kasse	käs'ə
chamber music	die Kammermusik	käm'ərmōozēk'
check room	die Garderobe	gärdərō'bə
chorus	der Chor	kōr
coat check	die Garderobenmarke	gär'dərōʻbənmärkə
comedy	die Komödie	kōmö'dē·ə
composer	der Komponist	kômpōnist'
concert	das Konzert	kôntsert'
concert hall	der Konzertsaal	kôntsert'zäl`
conductor	der Dirigent	dirigent'
costumes	Kostüme	kôstē'mə
costume designer	der Kostümbildner	kôstēm'bildnər
curtain	der Vorhang	fōr'häng
curtain time	der Beginn	bəgin'
dancer	der Tänzer,	ten'tsər,
	die Tänzerin	ten'tsərin
director	der Regisseur	rezhisär'
drama	das Drama	drä'mä
duet	das Duett	dōō·et'
final curtain	das Ende	en'də
grand piano	der Flügel	flē'gəl
intermission	die Pause	pou'zə
legitimate theatre	das Schauspiel	shou'shpēl
libretto	der Text	tekst
lobby	das Foyer	fō·äyä'
music	die Musik	mōozēk'
musical	das Musical	myōō'zikəl
note	die Note	nō'tə
opera	die Oper	ō'pər
opera glasses	das Opernglas	ō'pərngläs
operetta	die Operette	ōpəret'ə
orchestra	das Orchester	ôrkes'tər

orchestra seats	das Parkett	pärket'
overture	die Ouvertüre	ōōvertēr'ə
part/rôle	die Rolle *(drama)*, ...	rôl'ə
	die Partie *(opera, operetta)*	pärtē'
– leading role	die *Hauptrolle (Hauptpartie)*	houpt'rôlə (houpt'pärtē')
performance	die *Aufführung (Vorstellung)*	ouf'fērōong (fōr'shtelōong)
pianist	der Pianist, ...	pē'änist'
	die Pianistin	pē'änis'tin
piano recital	der Klavierabend	klävēr'äbənt
piece of music	das Musikstück	mōōzēk'shtik
play	das Theaterstück	tä-ä'tərshtik
producer	der Produzent	prōdōōtsent'
production	die Inszenierung	instsänēr'ōong
program	das Programmheft	prōgräm'heft
scenery/settings	das Bühnenbild	bē'nənbilt
set designer	der Bühnenbildner	bē'nənbildnər
singer	der Sänger, ...	zeng'ər,
	die Sängerin	zeng'ərin
singing	der Gesang	gəzäng'
soloist	der Solist, ...	zōlist',
	die Solistin	zōlis'tin
song	das Lied	lēt
– folk song	das Volkslied	fōlks'lēt
song recital	der Liederabend	lē'dəräbənt
soprano	der Sopran, ...	zōprän',
	die Sopranistin	zōpränis'tin
stage	die Bühne	bē'nə
stage director	der Regisseur	rezhisär'
symphony concert . . .	das Symphoniekonzert	zimfōnē'kôntsert'
tenor	der Tenor	tenōr'
theatre	das Theater	tä-ä'tər
theatre schedule	der Spielplan	shpēl'plän
ticket	die Karte	kär'tə
ticket sales	der Kartenverkauf	kär'tənferkouf
tragedy	die Tragödie	trägä'dē·ə
violin recital	der Violinabend	vē·ōlēn'äbənt
work	das Werk	verk

At the Movies

What's on tonight at the movies?
Was gibt es heute abend im Kino?
väs gēpt es hoi'tə ä'bənt im kē'nō

What time does *the box office open (the film start)*?
Wann beginnt *der Vorverkauf (der Film)*?
vän bəgint' dār fōr'ferkouf (dār film)

How long is the picture?
Wie lange dauert die Vorführung?
vē läng'ə dou'ərt dē fōr'fēröong

audience	das Publikum,	pōob'likōom,
	die Zuschauer	tsōo'shou·ər
auditorium	der Zuschauerraum	tsōo'shou·əroum`
cartoon	der Zeichentrickfilm	tsī'shəntrikfilm`
cinema	das Kino	kē'nō
color film	der Farbfilm	färp'film
documentary	der Dokumentarfilm	dōk'ōomentär'film
drive-in movie	das Autokino	ou'tōkē'nō
dubbed	synchronisiert	zin'krōnizērt'
dubbing	die Synchronisation	zin'krōnizätsyōn'
educational film	der Kulturfilm	kōoltōor'film
feature film	der Spielfilm	shpēl'film
film	der Film	film
film actor	der Filmschauspieler	film'shoushpē'lər
film festival	Filmfestspiele	film'festshpē'lə
film screening	die Filmvorführung	film'fōr'fēröong
motion picture theatre	das Kino	kē'nō
movie	der Film	film
movie house	das Kino	kē'nō
preview	der Trailer,	trā'lər,
	die Programmvorschau	prōgräm'fōrshou
screen	die Leinwand	līn'vänt
screenplay	das Drehbuch	drā'bōoh
short subject	der Kurzfilm	kōorts'film
subtitled	mit Untertiteln	mit ōon'tərtētəln
usher	der Platzanweiser	pläts'änvī'zər

PASTIMES

Fun and Games

Where is there ...?
Wo ist hier ...?
vō ist hēr...

a bar	eine Bar	ī′nə bär
a discotheque	eine Diskothek	īnə diskōtāk′
an ice skating rink ..	eine Eisbahn	ī′nə īs′bän
a miniature golf course	eine Minigolf-anlage	ī′nə min′ēgôlf-än′lägə
a night club	ein Nachtklub	īn näht′klōōp
a pool hall	ein Billardraum	īn bil′yärtroum
a riding stable	eine Reitschule	ī′nə rīt′shōōlə
a sailing school	eine Segelschule	ī′nə zā′gəlshōōlə
a tennis court	ein Tennisplatz	īn ten′ispläts

I'd like to ...
Ich möchte ...
ish mesh′tə ...

play badminton	Federball spielen	fā′dərbäl shpē′lən
play miniature golf ..	Minigolf spielen	min′ēgôlf shpē′lən
play ping pong	Tischtennis spielen	tish′tenis shpē′lən
watch the fashion show	die Modenschau anschauen	dē mō′dənshou än′shou·ən

Do you have television?
Haben Sie Fernsehen?
hä′bən zē fern′zā·ən

Can I listen to the radio here?
Kann ich hier Radio hören?
kän ish hēr rä′dē·ō hā′rən

What station is that?
Welcher Sender ist das?
vel′shər zen′dər ist däs

What's on today?
Was wird heute gegeben?
väs virt hoi′tə gəgā′bən

Do you play *chess (ping pong)*?
Spielen Sie *Schach (Tischtennis)*?
shpē′lən zē *shäh* (tish′tenis)

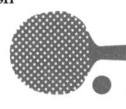

amusement	die Unterhaltung	o͞ontərhäl´to͞ong
beauty contest	der Schönheits-	shān´hīts-
	wettbewerb	vet´bəverp
bowling alley	die Bowlingbahn	bō´lingbän´
card game	das Kartenspiel	kär´tənshpēl
– cut	abheben	äp´hābən
– deal	geben	gā´bən
– shuffle	mischen	mish´ən
– ace	das As	äs
– jack	der Bube	bo͞o´bə
– queen	die Dame	dä´mə
– king	der König	kā´nish
– clubs	Kreuz	kroits
– diamonds	Karo	kä´rō
– hearts	Herz	herts
– spades	Pik	pēk
– joker	der Joker	yō´kər
– trick	der Stich	shtish
– trump	der Trumpf	tro͞ompf
checkers	Dame	dä´mə
chess	Schach	shäh
– board	das Brett	bret
– chessman	die Figur	figo͞or´
– square	das Feld	felt
– bishop	der Läufer	loi´fər
– castle	der Turm	to͞orm
– king	der König	kā´nish
– knight	der Springer	shpring´ər
– pawn	der Bauer	bou´ər
– queen	die Dame	dä´mə
– rook	der Turm	to͞orm
chip	die Spielmarke	shpēl´märkə
circus	der Zirkus	tsir´ko͞os
club	der Klub	klo͞op
country fair	das Volksfest	fólks´fest
dice	der Würfel	vēr´fəl
– shoot dice	würfeln	vēr´fəln
gambling casino	das Spielkasino	shpēl´käzē´nō
gambling game	das Spiel	shpēl
– banker	der Bankhalter	bängk´hältər
– bet	setzen	zets´ən

English	German	Pronunciation
– **draw**	ziehen	tsē′ən
– **move**	der Zug	tsōōk
– **piece**	der Stein	shtīn
– **play**	spielen	shpē′lən
– **stake**	der Einsatz	īn′zäts
magazine	die Zeitschrift	tsīt′shrift
– **fashion magazine**	die Modezeitschrift	mō′dətsītshrift
– **glossy**	die Illustrierte	il′ōōstrēr′tə
newspaper	die Zeitung	tsī′tōong
party games	Gesellschaftsspiele	gəzel′shäfts·shpē′lə
pastime	der Zeitvertreib	tsīt′fertrīp
ping pong	Tischtennis	tish′tenis
radio	der Rundfunk,	rōont′fōongk,
	das Radio	rä′dē·ō
– **FM**	UKW	ōō′kä′vä′
– **long wave**	Langwelle	läng′velə
– **medium wave**	Mittelwelle	mit′əlvelə
– **short wave**	Kurzwelle	kōōrts′velə
– **radio play**	das Hörspiel	hằr′shpēl
record	die Schallplatte	shäl′plätə
record player	der Plattenspieler	plät′ənshpēlər
recording tape	das Tonband	tōn′bänt
table tennis	Tischtennis	tish′tenis
tape recorder	das Tonbandgerät	tōn′bäntgərät′
television	das Fernsehen	fern′zā·ən
– **announcer**	der Ansager,	än′zägər,
	die Ansagerin	än′zägərin
– **breakdown**	die Störung	shtằ′rōong
– **news**	Nachrichten	näh′rishtən
– **program**	die Sendung	zen′dōong
– **program schedule**	das Programm	prōgräm′
– **turn off**	ausschalten	ous′shältən
– **turn on**	anschalten	än′shältən
– **television play**	das Fernsehspiel	fern′zāshpēl

Getting acquainted

Hope you don't mind if I talk to you.
Verzeihen Sie, daß ich Sie anspreche.
fertsī'ən zē, däs ish zē än'shpreshə

Mind if I join you?
Darf ich mich zu Ihnen setzen?
därf ish mish tsoo ē'nən zets'ən

May I treat you to a *drink (coffee, tea)*?
Darf ich Sie zu einem *Drink (Kaffee, Tee)* einladen?
därf ish zē tsoo ī'nəm dringk (käfā', tā) īn'lädən

You got something on for this evening?
Haben Sie heute abend etwas vor?
hä'bən zē hoi'tə ä'bənt et'väs fōr

Shall we dance?   **Is there a *discotheque (dance hall)* here?**
Wollen wir tanzen?   Gibt es hier *eine Diskothek (ein Tanzlokal)*?
vôl'en vēr tän'tsən   gēpt es hēr ī'nə diskōtāk' (īn tänts'lōkäl')

May I have the next dance?
Darf ich um den nächsten Tanz bitten?
därf ish oom dän näsh'stən tänts bit'ən

We can chat undisturbed here.
Hier können wir uns ungestört unterhalten.
hēr ken'ən vēr oons oon'gəshtärt oontərhäl'tən

May I invite you to a party?
Darf ich Sie zu einer Party einladen?
därf ish zē tsoo ī'nər pär'tē īn'lädən

I'll be expecting you at . . .
Ich erwarte Sie *bei (am, in)* . . .
ish ervär'tə zē bī (äm, in) . . .

You look good in that dress.
Dieses Kleid steht Ihnen sehr gut.
dē'zəs klīt shtāt ē'nən zār gōot

When can you come visit me?
Wann kommen Sie mich besuchen?
vän kôm'ən zē mish bəzoo'hən

When can we meet again?
Wann können wir uns wiedersehen?
vän ken'ən vēr ōōns vē'dərzā·ən

May I give you a lift home?
Darf ich Sie nach Hause fahren?
därf ish zē näh hou'zə fä'rən

Where do you live?
Wo wohnen Sie?
vō vō'nən zē

Won't you come in for a minute?
Wollen Sie nicht kurz reinkommen?
vôl'ən zē nisht kōōrts rīn'kômən

May I walk part of the way with you?
Darf ich Sie noch ein Stück begleiten?
därf ish zē nôh īn shtük bəglī'tən

Thanks very much for a nice evening.
Vielen Dank für den netten Abend.
fē'lən dängk fēr dān net'ən ä'bənt

accompany	begleiten	bəglī'tən
dance (*noun*)	der Tanz	tänts
dance (*verb*)	tanzen	tän'tsən
dance hall	das Tanzlokal	tänts'lōkäl'
discotheque	die Diskothek	diskōtāk'
enjoy oneself	sich amüsieren	zish ämēzēr'ən
expect somebody	jemanden erwarten	yā'mändən ervär'tən
flirting	der Flirt	flert
invite	einladen	īn'lädən
kiss (*noun*)	der Kuß	kōōs
kiss (*verb*)	küssen	kis'ən
live	wohnen	vō'nən
love (*noun*)	die Liebe	lē'bə
love (*verb*)	lieben	lē'bən
meet	sich treffen	zish tref'ən
meet again	sich wiedersehen	zish vē'dərzā·ən
party	die Party	pär'tē
take a walk	spazierengehen	shpätsēr'əngā·ən
visit	besuchen	bəzōō'hən
visit (*chat*)	sich unterhalten	zish ōōntərhäl'tən

On the Beach

Where can we go swimming here?
Wo kann man hier baden?
vō kän män hēr bä'dən

Can we go swimming here?
Darf man hier baden?
därf män hēr bä'dən

Two tickets, (with cabaña,) please.
Bitte zwei Eintrittskarten (mit Kabine).
bit'ə tsvī īn'tritskär'tən (mit käbē'nə)

Can we swim topless (nude) here?
Kann man hier *oben ohne (nackt)* baden?
kän män hēr ō'bən ō'nə (näkt) bä'dən

How *deep (warm)* is the water?
Wie *tief (warm)* ist das Wasser?
vē tēf (värm) ist däs väs'ər

Is there an undertow here?
Gibt es hier Strömungen?
gēpt es hēr shtrā'mōōngən

Is it dangerous for children?
Ist es für Kinder gefährlich?
ist es fēr kin'dər gəfär'lish

*No swimming!
Baden verboten!
bä'dən ferbō'tən

How far out can we swim?
Wie weit darf man hinausschwimmen?
vē vīt därf män hinous'shvimən

Where is the lifeguard?
Wo ist der Bademeister?
vō ist dār bä'dəmīstər

A *deck chair (umbrella)*, please.
Bitte einen *Liegestuhl (Sonnenschirm)*.
bit'ə ī'nən lē'gəshtool (zōn'ənshirm)

How much does ... cost?
Was kostet ...?
väs kôs'tət ...

I'd like to rent a *cabaña (boat)*.
Ich möchte *eine Kabine (ein Boot)* mieten.
ish mesh'tə ī'nə käbē'nə (īn bōt) mē'tən

Where *is (are)*...?
Wo gibt es ...?
vō gēpt es ...

I'd like to go water skiing.
Ich möchte Wasserski fahren.
ish mesh'tə väs'ərshē` fä'rən

Where can I go fishing?
Wo kann man angeln?
vō kän män äng'əln

Would you be good enough to keep an eye on my gear.
Würden Sie bitte auf meine Sachen aufpassen?
vir'dən zē bit'ə ouf mī'nə zä'hən ouf'päsən

air mattress	die Luftmatratze	looft'mäträts'ə
air temperature	die Lufttemperatur	looft'tempərätoor`
bathing cap	die Badekappe	bä'dəkäpə

bathing suit	der Badeanzug	bä'də·än'tsōōk
– trunks	die Badehose	bä'dəhōzə
bathrobe	der Bademantel	bä'dəmäntəl
bay	die Bucht	bōōht
boat	das Boot	bōt
– dinghy	das Schlauchboot	shlouh'bōt
– motorboat	das Motorboot	mō'tôrbōt
– pedal boat	das Pedalboot	pedäl'bōt
– sailboat	das Segelboot	zā'gəlbōt
cabaña	die Kabine	käbē'nə
dive	springen	shpring'ən
diving board	das Sprungbrett	shprōōng'bret
dune	die Düne	dē'nə
locker room	der Umkleideraum	ōōm'klīdəroum'
non-swimmer	der Nichtschwimmer . .	nisht'shvimər
nude beach	der FKK-Strand	ef'kä'kä' shtränt
saline content	der Salzgehalt	zälts'gəhält
sandy beach	der Sandstrand	zänt'shtränt
scuba diving	das Tauchen	tou'hən
scuba equipment	die Taucherausrüstung	tou'hərous'ristōōng
shells	Muscheln	mōōsh'əln
shower	die Dusche	dōōsh'ə
swim	baden, schwimmen	bä'dən, shvim'ən
swimmer	der Schwimmer	shvim'ər
swimming pier	der Badesteg	bä'dəshtāk
take a sunbath	ein Sonnenbad	īn zôn'ənbät
	nehmen	nā'mən
water	das Wasser	väs'ər
water temperature . . .	die Wassertemperatur .	väs'ərtempərätōōr'
wave	die Welle	vel'ə

Sports

What sports events do they have here?
Welche Sportveranstaltungen gibt es hier?
vel'shə shpôrt'ferän'shtältōōngən gēpt es hēr

Where's the *stadium (soccer field)*?
Wo ist *das Stadion (der Fußballplatz)*?
vō ist däs shtä'dē·ôn (där fōōs'bälpläts')

*. . . is playing . . . today.
Heute spielt . . . gegen . . .
hoi'tə shpēlt . . . gā'gən . . .

I'd love to see the *game (race, fight).*
Ich würde mir gern *das Spiel (das Rennen, den Kampf)* anschauen.
i*sh* vir'də mēr gern d*äs* shpēl (d*äs* ren'ən, dän kämpf) än'shou·ən

When (Where) is the soccer game?
Wann (Wo) findet das Fußballspiel statt?
vän (vō) fin'dət d*äs* fōōs'bälshpēl' shtät

Can you get us tickets for it?	**Goal!**
Können Sie uns Karten dafür besorgen?	Tor!
ken'ən zē ōōns kär'tən däfēr' bəzôr'gən	tōr

What's the score?	***The score is three to two for . . .**
Wie steht das Spiel?	Das Spiel steht drei zu zwei für . . .
vē shtāt d*äs* shpēl	d*äs* shpēl shtāt drī tsōō tsvī fēr . . .

Is there an *outdoor (indoor)* swimming pool here?
Gibt es hier ein *Freibad (Hallenbad)?*
gēpt es hēr īn frī'bät (häl'ənbät)

What sports do you like to play?
Welchen Sport treiben Sie?
vel'*sh*ən shpôrt trī'bən zē

I'm . . .	**I play . . .**	**I'm fond of . . .**
Ich bin . . .	Ich spiele . . .	Ich begeistere mich für . . .
i*sh* bin . . .	i*sh* shpē'lə . . .	i*sh* bəgīs'tərə mi*sh* fēr . . .

athlete	der *Athlet (Sportler)* . . .	ätlāt' (shpôrt'lər)
auto racing	das Autorennen	ou'tōren'ən
– race	das Rennen	ren'ən
– race car driver	der Rennfahrer	ren'färər
– racing car	der Rennwagen	ren'vägən
bicycling	der Radsport	rät'shpôrt
– bicycle	das Fahrrad	fä'rät
– bicycle race	das Radrennen	rät'renən
– bicycle rider	der Radfahrer	rät'färər
– ride a bike	radfahren	rät'färən
boat racing	das Bootsrennen	bōts'renən
– racing boat	das Rennboot	ren'bōt

bowling	das Bowling	bō'ling
– **bowling alley**	die Bowlingbahn	bō'lingbän'
boxing	der Boxsport	bôks'shpôrt
– **box**	boxen	bôk'sən
– **boxer**	der Boxer	bôk'sər
competition	der Wettkampf	vet'kämpf
– **championship**	die Meisterschaft	mīs'tərshäft
– **defeat**	die Niederlage	nē'dərlägə
– **draw**	das Unentschieden	ōōn'ent·shē'dən
– **free style**	die Kür	kēr
– **game**	das Spiel	shpēl
– **goal**	das Tor	tōr
– **half time**	die Halbzeit	hälp'tsīt
– **match**	das Spiel	shpēl
– **play**	spielen	shpē'lən
– **point**	der Punkt	pōōngkt
– **practice**	das Training	trä'ning
– **result**	das Ergebnis	ergäp'nis
– **start**	der Start	shtärt
– **victory**	der Sieg	zēk
– **win**	gewinnen	gəvin'ən
fencing	das Fechten	fesh'tən
figure skating	der Eiskunstlauf	īs'kōōnstlouf
– **skate**	eislaufen	īs'loufən
– **skates**	Schlittschuhe	shlit'shōō·ə
– **skater**	der Schlittschuhläufer	shlit'shōōloi'fər
fishing	der Angelsport	äng'əlshpôrt
– **fishing rod**	die Angel	äng'əl
– **go fishing**	angeln	äng'əln
– **fishing license**	der Angelschein	äng'əlshīn
golf	das Golf	gôlf
gymnastics	die Gymnastik,	gimnäs'tik,
	das Turnen	tōōr'nən
– **gymnast**	der Turner	tōōr'nər
– **gymnastics with apparatus**	das Geräteturnen	gərä'tətōōrnən
– **balance beam**	der Schwebebalken	shvā'bəbälkən
– **horizontal bar**	das Reck	rek
– **parallel bars**	der Barren	bär'ən
– **rings**	Ringe	ring'ə

handball	der Handball	hänt'bäl
hockey	das Eishockey	īs'hôkē
hunting	die Jagd	yäkt
– hunting license	der Jagdschein	yäkt'shīn
judo	das Judo	yōō'dō
marksmanship	der Schießsport	shēs'shpôrt
– clay pigeon shooting	das Tontauben- schießen	tōn'toubən- shē'sən
– rifle range	der Schießstand	shēs'shtänt
– shoot	schießen	shē'sən
– target	die Zielscheibe	tsēl'shībə
mountain climbing	das Bergsteigen	bärk'shtīgən
– mountain climber	der Bergsteiger	bärk'shtīgər
ninepins	das Kegeln	kā'gəln
player	der Spieler	shpē'lər
referee	der Schiedsrichter	shēts'rishtər
riding	der Reitsport	rīt'shpôrt
– horse	das Pferd	pfärt
– horse race	das *Pferderennen (Galopprennen)*	pfär'dərenən (gälôp'renen)
– jumping	das Springen	shpring'ən
– ride	reiten	rī'tən
– rider	der Reiter	rī'tər
– trotting race	das Trabrennen	träp'renən
rowing	das Rudern	rōō'dərn
– scull	das Ruderboot	rōō'dərbōt
– oarsman	der Ruderer	rōō'dərər
– coxswain	der Steuermann	shtoi'ərmän
sailing	der Segelsport	zā'gəlshpôrt
– sail *(noun)*	das Segel	zā'gəl
– sail *(verb)*	segeln	zā'gəln
– sailboat	das Segelboot	zā'gəlbōt
skiing	der Skisport	shē'shpôrt
– ski *(noun)*	der Ski	shē
– ski *(verb)*	skilaufen	shē'loufən
– ski binding	die Bindung	bin'dōōng
– ski jump	die Sprungschanze	shprōōng'shäntsə
– ski lift	der Skilift	shē'lift
soccer	der Fußball	fōōs'bäl
– ball	der Ball	bäl
– corner	der Eckball	ek'bäl

– **forward**	der Stürmer	shtir'mər
– **free kick**	der Freistoß	frī'shtōs
– **fullback**	der Verteidiger	fertī'digər
– **kick a goal**	ein Tor schießen	īn tōr shē'sən
– **goal**	das Tor	tōr
– **goalie**	der Torwart	tōr'värt
– **midfield man**	der Mittelfeldspieler	mi'təlfeltshpē'lər
– **off-side**	abseits	äp'zīts
– **penalty kick**	der Strafstoß	shträf'shtōs
– **play soccer**	Fußball spielen	fōōs'bäl shpē'lən
– **player**	der Spieler	shpē'lər
– **throw-in**	der Einwurf	īn'vōorf
sports	der Sport	shpôrt
– **athletic club**	der Sportverein	shpôrt'ferīn'
– **sports fan**	der Sportsfreund	shpôrts'froint
swimming	das Schwimmen	shvim'ən
– **dive**	springen	shpring'ən
– **diving board**	das Sprungbrett	shprōōng'bret
– **swimmer**	der Schwimmer	shvim'ər
team	die Mannschaft	män'shäft
tennis	das Tennis	ten'is
– **singles/doubles**	Einzel/Doppel	īn'tsəl/dôp'əl
– **play tennis**	Tennis spielen	ten'is shpē'lən
– **tennis ball**	der Tennisball	ten'isbäl'
– **tennis court**	der Tennisplatz	ten'ispläts'
– **badminton**	der Federball	fā'dərbäl
– **ping pong**	das Tischtennis	tish'tenis
toboganing	das Rodeln	rō'dəln
– **toboggan**	der Schlitten	shlit'ən
track and field	die Leichtathletik	līsht'ätlā'tik
umpire	der Schiedsrichter	shēts'rishtər
volleyball	der Volleyball	vôl'ēbäl
wrestling	der Ringkampf	ring'kämpf
– **wrestle**	ringen	ring'ən
– **wrestler**	der Ringer	ring'ər

Baseball and American football are virtually unknown sports in Europe. Think of them as something nice to look forward to when you get home.

APPENDIX

Signs

ABFAHRT	departures
ANKLEBEN VERBOTEN	post no bills
ANKUNFT	arrivals
(NOT)AUSGANG	(emergency) exit
BADEN VERBOTEN	no swimming allowed
BISSIGER HUND	beware of the dog
BITTE TÜR SCHLIESSEN	please close the door
DAMEN	ladies
DRÜCKEN, STOSSEN	push
DURCHGANG VERBOTEN (PRIVAT-STRASSE)	private (road)
EINGANG	entrance
EINTRITT FREI	admission free
ERDGESCHOSS	first floor
ERFRISCHUNGEN	refreshments
1. STOCK	second floor
FEUERLÖSCHER	fire extinguisher
FRISCH GESTRICHEN	wet paint
GEFAHR	danger
GESCHLOSSEN	closed
HALTESTELLE	stop
HERREN	gentlemen
KEIN EINTRITT	no admittance
LEBENSGEFAHR	mortal danger
NICHT BERÜHREN	do not touch
NICHT HINAUSLEHNEN	do not lean out the window
NICHT ÖFFNEN	do not open
ÖFFENTLICHE BEKANNT-MACHUNGEN	public notices
RASEN NICHT BETRETEN	keep off the grass
RAUCHEN VERBOTEN	no smoking
ROLLTREPPE	escalator
TAXISTAND	taxi stand
VORSICHT!	caution!
ZIEHEN	pull
ZU VERKAUFEN	for sale
ZU VERMIETEN	to let

Abbreviations

ADAC ..	Allgemeiner Deutscher Automobilclub [*äl'gəmīnər doitsh'ər ou'tōmōbēl'klōop*]	**Automobile Association**
AG	Aktiengesellschaft .... [*äk'tsyəngəzel'shäft*]	**Co., Inc.**
ARD	Arbeitsgemeinschaft der öffentlich-rechtlichen Rundfunkanstalten der Bundesrepublik Deutschland .... [*är'bītsgəmīn'shäft där ef'ənt-li*sh*-resht'li*sh*ən roont'foongk-änshtäl'tən där boon'dəs-repooblik' doitsh'länt*]	**German Broadcasting Corporation**
bzgl.	bezüglich [*bətsēk'li*sh*]	**with reference to**
C.	Celsius [*tsel'zi·oos*]	**Celsius**
d.h.	das heißt [*däs hīst*]	**i.e.**
DB	Deutsche Bundesbahn [*doitsh'ə boon'dəsbän*]	**German Federal Railroad**
DM	Deutsche Mark .... [*doitsh'ə märk*]	**West German Mark**
g	Gramm [*gräm*]	**grams**
GmbH...	Gesellschaft mit beschränkter Haftung [*gəzel'shäft mit bə-shrengk'tər häf'toong*]	**limited liability corporation**
MEZ	Mitteleuropäische Zeit .... [*mit'əloiröpä'ishə tsīt*]	**Central European Time**
ÖBB	Österreichische Bundesbahn ... [*äs'tərī*sh*ishə boon'dəsbän*]	**Austrian Federal Railroad**
p.Adr. ..	per Adresse [*per ädres'ə*]	**c/o**
Pl.	Platz [*pläts*]	**Square**
qm	Quadratmeter [*kvädrät'mätər*] .	**square meter**
Str.	Straße [*shträ'sə*]	**Street**
u.a.	unter anderem .... [*oon'tər än'dərəm*]	**among other things**
usw.	und so weiter [*oont zō vī'tər*] ..	**etc.**
z.B.	zum Beispiel [*tsoom bī'shpēl*] .	**for example**
ZDF	Zweites Deutsches Fernsehen .. [*tsvī'təs doitsh'əs fern'zä·ən*]	**Second Program – German Television**

Weights and Measures

1 millimeter	1 Millimeter (mm)	milēmā′tər
1 centimeter	1 Zentimeter (cm)	tsentēmā′tər
1 decimeter	1 Dezimeter (dm)	dātsēmā′tər
1 meter	1 Meter (m) *(= 1.0936 yards)*	mā′tər
1 kilometer	1 Kilometer (km) *(= 0.6214 miles)*	kēlōmā′tər
I inch	2.54 cm	
1 foot	30.48 cm	
1 yard	0.914 m	
1 (statute) mile	1.609 km	
1 nautical mile	1 Seemeile *(= 1.853 km)*	zā′mīlə
1 square foot	0.0929 m²	
1 square yard	0.836 m²	
1 square meter	1 Quadratmeter (m²) *(= 1.196 square yards)* ..	kvädrät′mātər
1 square mile	2.59 km²	
1 cubic foot	0.028 m³	
1 cubic yard	0.765 m³	
1 cubic meter	1 Kubikmeter (m³) *(= 1.307 cubic yards)* ...	kōōbēk′mātər
1 liter	1 Liter (l) *(= 2.113 pints)*	lē′tər
1 pint	0.473 l	
1 quart	0.946 l	
1 gallon	3.785 l	
1 kilogram	1 Kilogramm (kg) *(= 2.2046 pounds)*	kē′lōgräm
1 gram	1 Gramm (g) *(= 0.035 ounces)*	gräm
1 ounce	1 Unze *(= 28.349 g)*	ōon′tsə
1 pound *(453.59 g)* ..	≈ 1 Pfund *(500 g)*	pfōont
1 hundredweight *(45.359 kg)*	≈ 1 Zentner *(50 kg)*	tsent′nər
1 ton *(907.185 kg)* ...	≈ 1 Tonne *(1000 kg)* ...	tôn′ə
a piece (of . . .)	ein Stück	īn shti̇k
a pair (of . . .)	ein Paar	īn pär
a dozen	ein Dutzend	īn dōōts′ənt
a pack(et) (of . . .) ...	eine Packung	ī′nə päk′ōong

Colors

beige	beige	bāsh
black	schwarz	shvärts
blonde	blond	blônt
blue	blau	blou
– light blue	hellblau	hel'blou
– navy blue	dunkelblau	dŏong'kəlblou
brown	braun	broun
– chestnut brown	kastanienbraun	kästä'nē·ənbroun'
color	die Farbe	fär'bə
– colored	farbig	fär'bish
– colorful	bunt	bŏont
– solid-colored	einfarbig	īn'färbish
gold	golden	gôl'dən
green	grün	grēn
– dark green	dunkelgrün	dŏong'kəlgrēn
– light green	hellgrün	hel'grēn
gray	grau	grou
– ash gray	aschgrau	äsh'grou
– dark gray	dunkelgrau	dŏong'kəlgrou
– pale gray	hellgrau	hel'grou
lavender/mauve	lila	lē'lä
orange	orangefarben	ōräN'zhəfär'bən
pink	rosarot	rō'zärōt'
purple	purpur	pŏor'pŏor
red	rot	rōt
– bright red	hellrot	hel'rōt
– fire engine red	knallrot	knäl'rōt
– dark red/maroon	dunkelrot	dŏong'kəlrōt
silver	silbern	zil'bərn
violet	violett	vē'ōlet'
white	weiß	vīs
yellow	gelb	gelp

BASIC GERMAN GRAMMAR

I. Gender

In German there are 3 **genders:** masculine, feminine and neuter. The
definite articles are *der* (masculine), *die* (feminine), und *das* (neuter):

   der Mann the man   *die Katze* the cat   *das Kind* the child

The plural form of the definite article is *die*:

   die Männer the men   *die Katzen* the cats   *die Kinder* the children

The **indefinite articles** are *ein* (masculine and neuter) and *eine*
(feminine):

   ein Mann a man   *eine Katze* a cat   *ein Kind* a child

For the use of the articles see section II.

II. Nouns

German nouns and articles are declined according to their function in a
sentence. There are four cases: nominative (subject case), accusative
(direct object case), genitive (possessive case), and dative (indirect object
case).

Singular

Nominative	*der Mann*	*die Katze*	*das Kind*
Accusative	*den Mann*	*die Katze*	*das Kind*
Genitive	*des Mann(e)s*	*der Katze*	*des Kind(e)s*
Dative	*dem Mann*	*der Katze*	*dem Kind*
Nominative	*ein Mann*	*eine Katze*	*ein Kind*
Accusative	*einen Mann*	*eine Katze*	*ein Kind*
Genitive	*eines Mann(e)s*	*einer Katze*	*eines Kind(e)s*
Dative	*einem Mann*	*einer Katze*	*einem Kind*

Plural

Nominative	*die Männer*	*die Katzen*	*die Kinder*
Accusative	*die Männer*	*die Katzen*	*die Kinder*
Genitive	*der Männer*	*der Katzen*	*der Kinder*
Dative	*den Männern*	*den Katzen*	*den Kindern*

Examples: Nominative   *Der Mann (Eine Katze, Das Kind) sitzt auf
                          dem Bett.*
                           The man (A cat, The child) is sitting on the
                           bed.

           Accusative   *Ich kann den Mann (die Katze, die Kinder)
                          nicht sehen.*
                           I can't see the man (the cat, the children).

Genitive	*Ich kenne den Namen des Mannes (der Katze) nicht.*
	I don't know the man's (the cat's) name.
Dative	*Sie gab der Katze (den Kindern) Milch.*
	She gave the cat (the children) some milk.

The **plural** of nouns is usually formed by adding a suffix; often the stem vowel becomes an umlaut *(a > ä, o > ö, u > ü)*. Occasionally the singular and plural forms are the same.

III. Pronouns

The **personal pronouns** are:

	Nominative		Accusative		Dative	
			Singular			
1st person	*ich*	I	*mich*	me	*mir*	(to) me
2nd person	*du*	you (familiar)	*dich*	you	*dir*	(to) you
	Sie	you (polite)	*Sie*		Ihnen	
3rd person	*er*	he	*ihn*	him	*ihm*	(to) him
	sie	she	*sie*	her	*ihr*	(to) her
	es	it	*es*	it	*ihm*	(to) it
			Plural			
1st person	*wir*	we	*uns*	us	*uns*	(to) us
2nd person	*ihr*	you (familiar)	*euch*	you	*euch*	(to) you
	Sie	you (polite)	*Sie*		*Ihnen*	
3rd person	*sie*	they	*sie*	them	*ihnen*	(to) them

The **interrogative personal pronouns** are:

Singular and Plural

N	*wer?*	who?	*was?*	what?
A	*wen?*	who(m)?	*was?*	
G	*wessen?*	whose?		
D	*wem?*	(to) whom?		

Reflexive pronouns are used with reflexive verbs, i.e. those verbs preceded in the infinitive by an accusative *sich*. The pronouns are conjugated as follows:

	Singular		Plural	
1st person	*mich*		*uns*	
2nd person	*dich*	(familiar)	*euch*	(familiar)
	sich	(polite)	*sich*	(polite)
3rd person	*sich*		*sich*	

Er wäscht sich gerade. — He's just getting washed.
Wir haben uns sehr amüsiert. — We had a great time.
Ich muß mich hinlegen. — I must lie down.

Some infinitives preceded by *sich* take the dative form of the pronoun, which only varies from the scheme above in the 1st and 2nd person singular *(mir, dir)*:

sich (etwas) überlegen consider, think about
Ich werde es mir überlegen. / Er wird es sich überlegen.
I'll/He'll think about it.

sich vorstellen — imagine
Stell dir vor ... — Just imagine ...

IV. Verbs

The verbs *haben* to have, *sein* to be, and *werden* to become, are verbs in their own right but are also used to form the compound tenses of other verbs. *Haben* and *sein* are used to form the perfect, pluperfect, future perfect and conditional perfect, while *werden* is used to form the future, future perfect and conditional (see below). They are conjugated as follows:

Present

ich habe	*ich bin*	*ich werde*
du hast	*du bist*	*du wirst*
Sie haben	*Sie sind*	*Sie werden*
er, sie, es hat	*er, sie, es ist*	*er, sie, es wird*
wir haben	*wir sind*	*wir werden*
ihr habt	*ihr seid*	*ihr werdet*
Sie haben	*Sie sind*	*Sie werden*
sie haben	*sie sind*	*sie werden*

Imperfect

ich hatte	*ich war*	*ich wurde*
du hattest	*du warst*	*du wurdest*
Sie hatten	*Sie waren*	*Sie wurden*
er, sie, es hatte	*er, sie, es war*	*er, sie, es wurde*
wir hatten	*wir waren*	*wir wurden*
ihr hattet	*ihr wart*	*ihr wurdet*
Sie hatten	*Sie waren*	*Sie wurden*
sie hatten	*sie waren*	*sie wurden*

Perfect

ich habe . . . gehabt I have had/
  I had
du hast . . . gehabt etc.

ich bin . . . gewesen I have been/
  I was
du bist . . . gewesen etc.

Pluperfect

ich hatte . . . gehabt I had had
du hattest . . . gehabt etc.

ich war . . . gewesen I had been
du warst . . . gewesen etc.

Future

ich werde . . . haben I will have
du wirst . . . haben etc.

ich werde . . . sein I will be
du wirst . . . sein etc.

Future Perfect

ich werde . . . gehabt haben I will
  have had
du wirst . . . gehabt haben etc.

ich werde . . . gewesen sein I will
  have been
du wirst . . . gewesen sein etc.

Conditional

ich würde . . . haben I would have
du würdest . . . haben
Sie würden . . . haben
er, sie, es würde . . . haben

wir würden . . . haben
ihr würdet . . . haben
Sie würden . . . haben
sie würden . . . haben

ich würde . . . sein I would be
du würdest . . . sein
Sie würden . . . sein
er, sie, es würde . . . sein

wir würden . . . sein
ihr würdet . . . sein
Sie würden . . . sein
sie würden . . . sein

Conditional Perfect

ich hätte . . . gehabt I would have
  had
du hättest . . . gehabt
Sie hätten . . . gehabt
er, sie, es hätte . . . gehabt

wir hätten . . . gehabt
ihr hättet . . . gehabt
Sie hätten . . . gehabt
sie hätten . . . gehabt

ich wäre . . . gewesen I would have
  been
du wärst . . . gewesen
Sie wären . . . gewesen
er, sie, es wäre . . . gewesen

wir wären . . . gewesen
ihr wärt . . . gewesen
Sie wären . . . gewesen
sie wären . . . gewesen

German verbs are either "strong" or "weak". The **strong verbs** (like irregular English verbs) change their stem vowel in the past tenses, while the **weak verbs** retain their stem vowel and form the past tenses by means of prefixes and/or suffixes. For the use of the tenses, see p. 200.

Strong conjugation	**Weak conjugation**	
	Present	
lesen to read	*reden* to talk	*kaufen* to buy
ich lese	*ich rede*	*ich kaufe*
du liest	*du redest*	*du kaufst*
Sie lesen	*Sie reden*	*Sie kaufen*
er, sie, es liest	*er, sie, es redet*	*er, sie, es kauft*
wir lesen	*wir reden*	*wir kaufen*
ihr lest	*ihr redet*	*ihr kauft*
Sie lesen	*Sie reden*	*Sie kaufen*
sie lesen	*sie reden*	*sie kaufen*
	Imperfect	
ich las	*ich redete*	*ich kaufte*
du last	*du redetest*	*du kauftest*
Sie lasen	*Sie redeten*	*Sie kauften*
er, sie, es las	*er, sie, es redete*	*er, sie, es kaufte*
wir lasen	*wir redeten*	*wir kauften*
ihr last	*ihr redetet*	*ihr kauftet*
Sie lasen	*Sie redeten*	*Sie kauften*
sie lasen	*sie redeten*	*sie kauften*

(For the following tenses, compare the conjugations of *haben*, *sein* and *werden* above.)

	Perfect	
ich habe gelesen	*ich habe geredet*	*ich habe gekauft*
du hast gelesen etc.	*du hast geredet* etc.	*du hast gekauft* etc.
	Pluperfect	
ich hatte gelesen	*ich hatte geredet*	*ich hatte gekauft*
du hattest gelesen etc.	*du hattest geredet* etc.	*du hattest gekauft* etc.
	Future	
ich werde lesen	*ich werde reden*	*ich werde kaufen*
du wirst lesen etc.	*du wirst reden* etc.	*du wirst kaufen* etc.

Future Perfect

ich werde gelesen haben	*ich werde geredet haben*	*ich werde gekauft haben*
du wirst gelesen haben etc.	*du wirst geredet haben* etc.	*du wirst gekauft haben* etc.

Conditional

ich würde lesen	*ich würde reden*	*ich würde kaufen*
du würdest lesen etc.	*du würdest reden* etc.	*du würdest kaufen* etc.

Conditional Perfect

ich hätte gelesen	*ich hätte geredet*	*ich hätte gekauft*
du hättest gelesen etc.	*du hättest geredet* etc.	*du hättest gekauft* etc.

The Use of the Tenses

Present
ich fahre

> I drive
> I am driving

Imperfect
ich fuhr

> I drove
> I was driving

Perfect
ich bin gefahren

> I drove
> I have driven
> I have been driving

Pluperfect
ich war gefahren

> I had driven
> I had been driving

Future
ich werde fahren

> I will drive
> I will be driving

Future Perfect
ich werde gefahren sein

> I will have driven
> I will have been driving

Conditional
ich würde fahren

> I would drive
> I would be driving

Conditional Perfect
ich wäre gefahren

> I would have driven
> I would have been driving

V. Adjectives

Adjectives are declined differently according to whether they are used with the definite or indefinite article:

	Masculine	Feminine	Neuter
		Singular	
N	*der kleine Mann*	*die schwarze Katze*	*das kranke Kind*
	the little man	the black cat	the sick child
A	*den kleinen Mann*	*die schwarze Katze*	*das kranke Kind*
G	*des kleinen Mannes*	*der schwarzen Katze*	*des kranken Kindes*
D	*dem kleinen Mann*	*der schwarzen Katze*	*dem kranken Kind*
		Plural	
N	*die kleinen Männer*	*die schwarzen Katzen*	*die kranken Kinder*
A	*die kleinen Männer*	*die schwarzen Katzen*	*die kranken Kinder*
G	*der kleinen Männer*	*der schwarzen Katzen*	*der kranken Kinder*
D	*den kleinen Männern*	*den schwarzen Katzen*	*den kranken Kindern*
N	*ein kleiner Mann*	*eine schwarze Katze*	*ein krankes Kind*
	a little man	a black cat	a sick child
A	*einen kleinen Mann*	*eine schwarze Katze*	*ein krankes Kind*
G	*eines kleinen Mannes*	*einer schwarzen Katze*	*eines kranken Kindes*
D	*einem kleinen Mann*	*einer schwarzen Katze*	*einem kranken Kind*

The **possessive adjectives** are:

	Masculine		Feminine	Neuter
		Singular		
1st person	*mein*	my	*meine*	*mein*
2nd person	*dein*	your (familiar)	*deine*	*dein*
	Ihr	your (polite)	*Ihre*	*Ihr*
3rd person	*sein*	his, its	*seine*	*sein*
	ihr	her	*ihre*	*ihr*
		Plural		
1st person	*unser*	our	*unsere*	*unser*
2nd person	*euer*	your (familiar)	*eure*	*euer*
	Ihr	your (polite)	*Ihre*	*Ihr*
3rd person	*ihr*	their	*ihre*	*ihr*

They are declined like the indefinite article *ein(e)* (see above).

The **comparative** and **superlative** are generally formed by adding -*er* and
-*(e)st* respectively to the simple form of the adjective, followed by the
adjective endings (see above) if used with a noun.

| *schnell* | fast | *schneller* | faster | *der/die/das schnellste* | the fastest |
| *klein* | small | *kleiner* | smaller | *der/die/das kleinste* | the smallest |

VI. Adverbs

Adverbs generally do not differ from their corresponding adjectives.

The **comparative** of the adverb is also the same as that of the adjective;
the **superlative** is generally formed by adding -*(e)sten* to the simple
form of the adverb and inserting *am* before it:

Peter läuft langsamer als ich, aber du läufst am langsamsten.
Peter walks more slowly than me, but you're the slowest of all.

VII. Prepositions

In German, prepositions determine the case of the noun following or
preceding them. In some cases, the preposition and the accusative or
dative article can be contracted (*an dem > am, auf das > aufs, zu der >
zur* etc.). Prepositions taking the **dative** case are:

aus from, out of *bei* at; near *mit* with *nach* to; after *seit* since
von from *zu* to *außer* except; besides *gegenüber* opposite

Prepositions taking the **accusative** case are:

bis till, until; as far as *durch* through; by means of *für* for
gegen against *ohne* without *um* around, round

The following prepositions take either the dative or the accusative:

an on, at; onto, to *auf* on; onto *hinter* behind; after; beyond *in* in;
into *neben* beside, next to *über* over, above; across *unter* under,
below; among *vor* in front of; before *zwischen* between; among

They take the accusative when they express movement towards
something and the dative when they denote either rest or movement
within an area.

ENGLISH-GERMAN DICTIONARY

The translations are followed by phonetic transcriptions and page references, so that this dictionary serves as an index as well.

A

abbey Abtei [äptī′] 124

abdomen Bauch [bouh], Unterleib [ōōn′tərlīp] 166

about über [ē′bər] 23; ungefähr [ōōn′gəfär] 30

above über [ē′bər] 25

abscess Abszeß [äps·tses′] 169, 174

absorbent cotton Watte [vät′ə] 160

accelerate Gas geben [gäs gā′bən] 51

accelerator Gaspedal [gäs′pədäl] 51

access road Einfahrt [īn′färt] 42

accessories Zubehör [tsōō′bəhör] 136

accident Unfall [ōōn′fäl] 48, 153

accommodations Unterkunft [ōōn′-tərkōōnft] 81, 90

accompanist Begleiter [bəglī′tər] 176

accompany begleiten [bəglī′tən] 184

ace As [äs] 181

acquaintance Bekanntschaft [bə-känt′shäft] 183

act Akt [äkt], Aufzug [ouf′tsōōk] 176

actor Schauspieler [shou′shpēlər] 176

actress Schauspielerin [shou′shpē-lərin] 176

adapter plug Zwischenstecker [tsvish′ənshtekər] 90

address Adresse [ädres′ə] 48, 146, 149

addressee Empfänger [empfeng′ər] 149

admission Eintritt [īn′trit] 118; ~ **free** Eintritt frei [īn′trit frī] 191

advance reservation Voranmeldung [fōr′änmeldōōng] 95

advance ticket sales Vorverkauf [fōr′-ferkouf] 177

afraid: I'm ~ leider [lī′dər] 16, 22, 23

after nach [näh] 159; ~ **shave** Rasierwasser [räzēr′väsər] 140

afternoon Nachmittag [näh′mitäk] 31; **Good ~!** Guten Tag! [gōō′tən täk] 12; **in the ~** nachmittags [näh′mi-täks] 31; **this ~** heute nachmittag [hoi′tə näh′mitäk] 31

again noch einmal [nōh īn′mäl] 15; wieder [vē′dər] 26, 184

against gegen [gā′gən] 164

age Alter [äl′tər] 35; **under ~** minderjährig [min′dəryā′rish] 35

ago: a month ~ vor einem Monat [fōr ī′nəm mō′nät] 32

air Luft [lōōft] 26; ~ **filter** Luftfilter [lōōft′filtər] 51; ~ **pump** Luftpumpe [lōōft′pōōmpə] 57; ~ **sickness** Luftkrankheit [lōōft′krängk·hīt] 70, 169; ~ **temperature** Lufttemperatur [lōōft′tempərätōōr′] 185; ~ **mattress** Luftmatratze [lōōft′mäträtsə] 185; ~ **jet** Frischluftdüse [frish′lōōft-dē′zə] 70; ~ **conditioning** Klimaanlage [klē′mä·änlä′gə] 75, 90; ~ **mail** Luftpost [lōōft′pōst] 145, 149

aircraft Flugzeug [flōōk′tsoik] 70

airline Fluggesellschaft [flōōk′gə-zelshäft] 70; ~ **passenger** Fluggast [flōōk′gäst] 70

airport Flughafen [flōōk′häfən] 68, 70, 84, 89, 120; ~ **service charge** Flughafengebühr [flōōk′häfəngəbēr′] 68, 70

alcohol Alkohol [äl′kōhōl] 99, 160

all alles [äl′əs] 80

allergy Allergie [äl′ergē′] 169

alley Gasse [gäs′ə] 120

allow gestatten [gəshtät′ən] 20, 65; **is ... allowed here?** Darf man hier ...? [därf män hēr ...] 18

almonds Mandeln [män′dəln] 110

alone allein [älīn′] 14

already schon [shōn] 69, 84

altar Altar [ältär′] 124

alter ändern [en´dərn] 133
alto Alt [ält], Altistin [ältis´tin] 177
A.M.: nine ~ neun Uhr morgens [noin ōōr môr´gəns] 30
amber Bernstein [bern´shtīn] 133
ambulance Krankenwagen [kräng´-kənvä´gən] 48
American amerikanisch [ämärikä´-nish] 152; **~ dollars** US-Dollar [ōō´es´ dôl´är] 152; **~ plan** Vollpension [fôl´päNsyōn´] 83, 90; **~ studies** Amerikanistik [ämär´ikänis´tik] 39
among zwischen [tsvish´ən] 192; **~ other things** unter anderem [ōōn´tər än´dərəm] 192
amount Betrag [bəträk´] 151
ampule Ampulle [ämpool´ə] 160
amusement Unterhaltung [ōōn`tər-häl´tōōng] 181; **~ park** Vergnügungspark [fergnē´gōōngspärk´] 120
anchor Anker [äng´kər] 75
anchovies Sardellen [zärdel´ən] 102
anemia Anämie [änämē´] 169
anesthesia Betäubung [bətoi´-bōōng] 174; **local ~** örtliche Betäubung [ert´lishə bətoi´bōōng] 174; **general ~** Vollnarkose [fôl´närkō´-zə] 174
anesthetic Narkose [närkō´zə] 172
angry: Please don't be ~ Nehmen Sie es bitte nicht übel! [nä´mən zē es bit´ə nisht ē´bəl] 22
ankle Knöchel [kne´shəl] 164, 166
announcer Ansager [än´zägər], Ansagerin [än´zägərin] 182
annually jedes Jahr [yä´dəs yär] 32
another ein anderer [īn än´dərər] 83
answer Antwort [änt´vôrt] 148
antidote Gegengift [gä´gəngift] 160
anti-freeze Frostschutzmittel [frôst´shōōtsmit´əl] 45, 51
anyone jemand [yä´mänt] 85
anything etwas [et´väs] 80
apartment Appartement [äpärtə-mäN´] 81, Wohnung [vō´nōōng] 90; **efficiency ~** Appartement [äpärtə-mäN´] 82; **~ building** Mietshaus [mēts´hous] 90
apologize sich entschuldigen [zish entshōōl´digən] 22

appendicitis Blinddarmentzündung [blint´därmentsin´dōōng] 169
appendix Blinddarm [blint´därm] 166
appetite Appetit [äpätēt´] 163
appetizer Vorspeise [fōr´shpīzə] 102
applause Beifall [bī´fäl] 177
apple Apfel [äp´fəl] 109
appointment Verabredung [feräp´rä-dōōng] 155, 173
apprentice Lehrling [lär´ling] 36
approach (plane) Anflug [än´flōōk] 70
apricot Aprikose [äprikō´zə] 109
April April [äpril´] 33
apron Schürze [shir´tsə] 134
arch Bogen [bō´gən] 124
archaeology Archäologie [är`shä·ōlō-gē´] 39
architecture Architektur [är´shētek-tōōr´] 39
area Gebiet [gəbēt´] 120; **~ code** Vorwahlnummer [fōr´välnōōm`ər] 149
aria Arie [ä´rē·ə] 177
arm Arm [ärm] 166
armchair Sessel [zes´əl] 90
armpit Achselhöhle [äk´səlhölə] 166
around (time) gegen [gä´gən] 31
arrest Verhaftung [ferhäf´tōōng] 154
arrival Ankunft [än´kōōnft] 60, 66, 70, 90, 191
arrive ankommen [än´kômən] 34, 66, 147
art Kunst [kōōnst]; **~ history** Kunstge-schichte [kōōnst´gəshishtə] 39; **~ gallery** Kunsthändler [kōōnst´-hend`lər] 128
artery Arterie [ärtär´ē·ə] 166
arthritis Gelenkrheumatismus [gə-lengk´roimätis`mōōs] 169
artichokes Artischocken [är´ti-shōk`ən] 102, 107
articles Sachen [zä´hən] 80
artist Künstler [kinst´lər] 36
ash tray Aschenbecher [äsh´ən-beshər] 87, 90, 97, 143
ashore: to go ~ an Land gehen [än länt gä´ən] 72
asparagus Spargel [shpär´gəl] 108
aspirin Aspirin [äspirēn´] 160
asthma Asthma [äst´mä] 169

at *(time)* um [ŏŏm] 30; ~ **night** nachts [nähts] 94

athlete Athlet [ätlāt´], Sportler [shpôrt´lǝr] 187

athletic club Sportverein [shpôrt´ferīn´] 190

atmospheric pressure Luftdruck [lŏŏft´drŏŏk] 26

attack Anfall [än´fäl] 169

attend: ~ **college** studieren [shtŏŏdē´rǝn] 38; ~ **university** studieren [shtŏŏdē´rǝn] 38; ~ **school** Schule besuchen [shŏŏ´lǝ bǝzŏŏ´hǝn] 38

attorney (Rechts)Anwalt [(reshts´)-än´vält] 154

audience Publikum [pŏŏb´likŏŏm], Zuschauer [tsŏŏ´shouǝr] 179

auditorium Zuschauerraum [tsŏŏ´-shou·ǝroum´] 179

August August [ougŏŏst´] 33

aunt Tante [tän´tǝ] 35

Austrian österreichisch [ǟ´stǝrī´shish] 152, 192; ~ **Schillings** Österreichische Schilling [ǟ´stǝrī´shishǝ shil´ing] 152

auto racing Autorennen [ou´tŏrenǝn] 187

autobiography Autobiographie [ou`-tŏbē·ŏgräfē´] 130

automatic transmission Automatik [ou´tŏmä´tik] 51

automobile club Automobilklub [ou`-tŏmŏbēl´klŏŏp] 42

available erhältlich [erhelt´lish] 176; *(seat)* frei [frī] 68

avenue Allee [älā´] 120

avocado Avocado [ävŏkä´dŏ] 102

axle Achse [äk´sǝ] 51

B

baby Baby [bā´bē] 164

back *(adv)* zurück [tsŏŏrik´] 40, 73, 86; **from ... to ... and** ~ von ... nach ... und zurück [vôn ... näh ... ŏŏnt tsŏŏrik´] 73

back *(noun)* Rücken [rik´ǝn] 166; ~ **seat** Rücksitz [rik´zits], Fond [fôN] 55; ~ **wheel** Hinterrad [hin´tǝrät´] 47

backache Rückenschmerzen [rik´ǝnshmertsǝn] 169

backfire Fehlzündung [fāl´tsindŏŏng] 51

backwards rückwärts [rik´verts] 66

bacon Speck [shpek] 100

bad schlecht [shlesht]; **too** ~! (wie) schade! [(vē) shä´dǝ] 22

badminton Federball [fā´dǝrbäl] 180, 190

bag Tüte [tē´tǝ] 126, 143, 153; **beach** ~ Campingbeutel [kem´pingboitǝl] 143; **plastic** ~ Plastiktüte [pläs´tiktē´tǝ] 144; **flight** ~ Schultertasche [shŏŏl´tǝrtäshǝ] 144; **traveling** ~ Reisetasche [rī´zǝtäshǝ] 65

baggage Gepäck [gǝpek´] 63, 66, 74, 84; ~ **check area** Gepäckaufbewahrung [gǝpek´oufbǝvä´rŏŏng] 63, 64; ~ **claim area** Gepäckausgabe [gǝpek´ousgä´bǝ] 64; ~ **check** Gepäckschein [gǝpek´shīn] 84; ~ **allowance** freies Gepäck [frī´ǝs gǝpek´] 68; ~ **car** Gepäckwagen [gǝpek´vägǝn] 67; ~ **deposit area** Gepäckannahme [gǝpek´än·nä´-mǝ] 63; ~ **checking** Gepäckannahme [gǝpek´än·nä´mǝ] 65

baked gebacken [gǝbäk´ǝn] 100

baker Bäcker [bek´ǝr] 36

bakery Bäckerei [bekǝrī´] 128

balcony Balkon [bälkōng´] 82, 90; Rang [räng] 176

ball Ball [bäl] 143, 189; ~ **point cartridge** Mine [mē´nǝ] 138

ballet Ballett [bälet´] 177

banana Banane [bänä´nǝ] 109

band Kapelle [käpel´ǝ] 177

bandage Pflaster [pfläs´tǝr] 160; **ace** ~ Elastikbinde [eläs´tikbin´dǝ] 160; **adhesive** ~ Heftpflaster [heft´-pfläs´tǝr] 160

bandages Verbandszeug [ferbänts´-tsoik] 48

bank Bank [bängk] 151; **savings** ~ Sparkasse [shpär´käsǝ] 152; ~ **transfer** Banküberweisung [bängk´-ēbǝrvī´zŏŏng] 151; ~ **charges** Bankgebühren [bängk´gǝbērǝn] 151; ~ **account** Bankkonto [bängk´-kôntŏ] 151; ~ **note** Geldschein [gelt´shīn] 151; ~ **teller** Bankbeamte(r) [bängk´bǝ·ämtǝ(r)] 36

bank Ufer [ōō'fər] 75
baptism Taufe [tou'fə] 124
bar Bar [bär] 74, 86, 180
barber Friseur [frizär'] 74, 155, 157; ~ **shop** Friseursalon [frizär'zälôN] 74, 155, 157
barette Spange [shpän'gə] 140
barge Kahn [kän] 75
baritone Bariton [bär'itōn] 177
barometer Barometer [bärōmā'tər] 25
Baroque barock [bärôk'] 124
barrier Sperre [shper'ə] 67
basement Keller [kel'ər] 90
bass Baß [bäs] 177
bath Bad [bät] 82, 175; ~ **attendant** Bademeister [bä'dəmīstər] 175; **steam** ~ Dampfbad [dämpf'bät] 175; **mineral** ~ Mineralbad [min'əräl'bät] 175; **take a** ~ baden [bä'dən] 95; ~ **salts** Badesalz [bä'dəzälts] 140
bathing cap Badekappe [bä'dəkäpə] 185; Bademütze [bä'dəmītsə] 134
bathing suit Badeanzug [bä'də·äntsōōk] 186
bathing trunks Badehose [bä'dəhōzə] 134, 186
bathrobe Bademantel [bä'dəmäntəl] 134, 186
bathroom Badezimmer [bä'dətsimər] 90
battery Batterie [bätərē'] 51, 143
bay Bucht [bōōht] 75, 186
be sein [zīn]
beach Strand [shtränt] 81, 92, 185; **sandy** ~ Sandstrand [zänt'shtränt] 186; **private** ~ Privatstrand [privät'shtränt] 186
beam Strahl [shträl]
bean Bohne [bō'nə] 107; **string** ~ Brechbohne [bresh'bōnə] 107
beard Bart [bärt] 157
beauty contest Schönheitswettbewerb [shōn'hītsvet'bəverp] 181
beauty parlor Schönheitssalon [shōn'hīts·zälôN] 158; Friseursalon [frizär'zälôN] 74; (Damen)Friseur [(dä'mən)frizär'] 128
beauty shop Schönheitssalon [shōn'hīts·zälôN] 155

bed Bett [bet] 90, 172; ~ **linen** Bettwäsche [bet'veshə] 90; ~ **and two meals** Halbpension [hälp'pāNsyôn'] 90; ~**side table** Nachttisch [näht'tish] 90; **day** ~ Bettcouch [bet'koutsh] 91; ~**spread** Bettdecke [bet'dekə] 90; ~ **rug** Bettvorleger [bet'fōrlāgər] 90
bedroom Schlafzimmer [shläf'tsimər] 93
beef Rindfleisch [rint'flīsh] 106
beefsteak Beefsteak [bēf'stäk] 107; ~ **tartar** Tatar [tätär'] 107
beer Bier [bēr] 111; ~ **mug** Bierkrug [bēr'krōōk] 111; **bock** ~ Bockbier [bôk'bēr] 111; **dark** ~ dunkles Bier [dōōng'kləs bēr] 111; **lager** ~ Lagerbier [lä'gərbēr] 111; **light** ~ helles Bier [hel'əs bēr] 111; **Pilsener** ~ Pilsenerbier [pilz'nərbēr], Pils [pilz] 111; **white** ~ Weißbier [vīs'bēr], Weizenbier [vī'tsənbēr] 111
beeswax Bienenwachs [bē'nənväks] 143
beets rote Bete [rō'tə bā'tə], rote Rüben [rō'tə rē'bən] 108
before vor [fōr] 31, 159; vorher [fōr'hār] 32; bis [bis] 66
beige beige [bäsh] 194
bell Glocke [glôk'ə] 124; Klingel [kling'əl] 88, 90
below unter [ōōn'tər] 25
belt Gürtel [gir'təl] 134, 136
berry pudding rote Grütze [rō'tə grit'sə] 109
best beste(r) [bes'tə(r)]; **All the** ~**!** Alles Gute! [äl'əs gōō'tə] 17, 20, 23; Herzlichen Glückwunsch! [herts'lishən glik'vōōnsh] 23; **Give ... my** ~**!** Grüßen Sie ...! [grē'sən zē ...] 17
beverage Getränk [gətrengk'] 111; **alcoholic** ~ alkoholisches Getränk [älkōhō'lishəs gətrengk] 112; **non-alcoholic** ~ alkoholfreies Getränk [älkōhōl'frī·əs gətrengk'] 112
bicuspid Backenzahn [bäk'əntsän] 174
bicycle Fahrrad [fä'rät] 41, 73, 187; **to go by** ~ mit dem Fahrrad fahren [mit däm fä'rät fä'rən] 42; ~ **race** Radrennen [rät'renən] 187; ~ **rider** Radfahrer [rät'färər] 187

bicycling Radsport [rät´shpôrt] 187

big groß [grös] 127

bike Fahrrad [fä´rät] 187; **ride a ~** radfahren [rät´färən] 187; **~ lane** Radfahrweg [rät´färväk] 42

bikini Bikini [bikē´ni] 134

bile Galle [gä´lə] 166

bill Rechnung [resh´noong] 89, 90; Geldschein [gelt´shīn] 151

billfold Portemonnaie [pôrt`mônä´] 153

binoculars Fernglas [fern´gläs] 138

biography Biographie [bē·ōgrəfē´] 130

biology Biologie [bē·ōlōgē´] 39

birthday Geburtstag [gəbōōrts´täk] 22; **Happy ~!** Herzlichen Glückwunsch zum Geburtstag! [herts´lishən glík´voonsh tsōōm gəbōōrts´täk] 23

bitters Magenbitter [mä´gənbitər] 112

black schwarz [shvärts] 194

black chocolate cake Sachertorte [zäh´ərtôrtə] 109

black currants schwarze Johannisbeeren [shvär´tsə yōhän´isbärən] 110

blackberries Brombeeren [brôm´bärən] 109

Black Forest cherry cake Schwarzwälder Kirschtorte [shvärts´veldər kirsh´tôrtə] 109

blackmail attempt Erpressungsversuch [erpres´oongsferzōōh`] 153

bladder Blase [blä´zə] 166

blanket Wolldecke [vôl´dekə] 75, 87, 90

bleeding Blutung [blōō´toong] 169

blinker Blinker [bling´kər] 51

blizzard Schneesturm [shnā´shtōōrm] 26

blonde blond [blônt] 194

blood Blut [blōōt] 165; **~ count** Blutbild [blōōt´bilt] 172; **~ test** Blutprobe [blōōt´prōbə] 165, 172; **~ pressure** Blutdruck [blōōt´drook] 166, 169; **~ poisoning** Blutvergiftung [blōōt´fergif`toong] 169; **~ transfusion** Bluttransfusion [blōōt´tränsfōō`zyōn`] 172

blouse Bluse [blōō´zə] 134

blow *(fuse)* durchbrennen [dŏŏrsh´brenən] 55

blow-out Reifenpanne [rī´fənpänə] 47

blue blau [blou] 194; **light ~** hellblau [hel´blou] 194; **navy ~** dunkelblau [dŏŏng´kəlblou] 194; **~ jeans** Bluejeans [blōō´jēns] 134

blueberries Heidelbeeren [hī´dəlbärən] 110

boar Wildschwein [vilt´shvīn] 107

board Bord [bôrt] 72, 74, 75; Brett [bret] 181

boarding house Gasthof [gäst´hôf] 81

boarding school Internat [in´tərnät`] 38

boat Boot [bōt] 75, 186; **pedal ~** Pedalboot [pedäl´bōt] 186; **~ racing** Bootsrennen [bōts´renən] 187; **~ trip** Bootsfahrt [bōts´färt] 120

body Körper [ker´pər] 166; *(car)* Karosserie [kärŏsərē´] 51; **~ and fender damage** Blechschaden [blesh´shä`dən] 49

boiled gekocht [gəkôht´] 100, 107

bolt Schraube [shrou´bə] 51, 57; **~ nut** Schraubenmutter [shrou´bənmōōtər] 51, 57

bone Knochen [knô´hən] 166

book Buch [bōōh] 130; **~shop** Buchhandlung [bōōh´händlōong] 128, 130; **second-hand ~shop** Buchantiquariat [bōōh´äntikvärē·ät`] 129; **children's ~** Kinderbuch [kin´dərbōōh] 130; **guide ~** Reiseführer [rī´zəfērər] 130; **phrase ~** Sprachführer [shpräsh´fērər] 130; **poetry ~** Gedichtband [gədisht´bänt] 130; **reference ~** Sachbuch [zäh´bōōh], Nachschlagewerk [näh´shlägəvärk`] 130; **story ~** Märchenbuch [mär´shənbōōh] 130; **text ~** Lehrbuch [lär´bōōh] 130

bookkeeper Buchhalter [bōōh´hältər] 36

bookseller Buchhändler [bōōh´hendlər] 36

booth Kabine [käbē´nə] 148

boots Stiefel [shtē´fəl] 139

Bordeaux Bordeauxwein [bôrdō´vīn] 111

border Grenze [grent'sə] 78, 80; ~
  crossing Grenzübergang [grents'-
  ēbərgäng'] 80
born geboren [gəbō'rən] 34, 119
Boston lettuce Kopfsalat [köpf'zälät]
  108
botanical gardens botanischer Garten
  [bōtä'nishər gär'tən] 120
bother stören [shtä'rən] 16; belästi-
  gen [bəles'tigən] 154
bottle Flasche [fläsh'ə] 96, 126; ~
  opener Flaschenöffner [fläsh'ənef-
  nər] 143
bouquet Blumenstrauß [blōō'mən-
  shtrous] 130
bow Bug [bōōk] 75
bowl Schüssel [shis'əl] 97
bowling Bowling [bō'ling] 188; ~ **alley** Bowlingbahn [bō'lingbän'] 181,
  188
box (verb) boxen [bôk'sən] 188; ~
  (noun) Karton [kärtōng'] 126; ~
  lunch Lunchpaket [länsh'päkät] 86;
  ~ **office** Kasse [käs'ə] 176
boxer Boxer [bôk'sər] 188
boxing Boxsport [bôks'shpôrt] 188
boy Junge [yōōng'ə] 35
bra Büstenhalter [bis'tənhältər], BH
  [bā'hä'] 134
bracelet Armband [ärm'bänt] 133,
  153
braces Sockenhalter [zôk'ənhältər]
  136; Zahnspange [tsän'shpängə]
  174
brain Gehirn [gəhirn'] 166
brake (verb) bremsen [brem'zən] 43;
  ~ (noun) Bremse [brem'zə] 51; ~
  fluid Bremsflüssigkeit [brems'flisishkīt'] 45, 51; ~ **drum** Bremstrommel
  [brems'trôməl] 51; ~ **lights** Brems-
  lichter [brems'lishtər] 51; ~ **lining**
  Bremsbelag [brems'bəläk] 51; ~
  pedal Bremspedal [brems'pədäl] 51
branch manager Filialleiter [fil'ēäl'-
  lītər] 151
brandy Branntwein [bränt'vīn] 112;
  apricot ~ Aprikosenlikör [äprikō'-
  zənlikȫr] 112; **cherry** ~ Kirschlikör
  [kirsh'likȫr] 112
brassière Büstenhalter [bis'tənhäl-
  tər], BH [bā'hä'] 134

bread Brot [brōt] 98; **dark** ~ dunkles
  Brot [dōōngk'ləs brōt] 98; **white** ~
  Weißbrot [vīs'brōt] 98; **whole wheat**
  ~ Vollkornbrot [fôl'kôrnbrōt'] 98;
  ~ **basket** Brotkorb [brōt'kôrp] 97
break brechen [bre'shən]; ~ **off** ab-
  brechen [äp'breshən] 55, 173
breakdown Panne [pän'ə] 48; Stö-
  rung [shtä'rōōng] 182
breakfast Frühstück [frē'shtik] 83, 86,
  87, 90, 98; ~ **room** Frühstücksraum
  [frē'shtiksroum] 90; **eat** ~ frühstük-
  ken [frē'shtikən] 90, 98
breast Brust [brōōst] 166
breathe atmen [ät'mən] 165
breathing Atmung [ät'mōōng] 166;
  ~ **problem** Atembeschwerden
  [ä'təmbəshvär'dən] 169
breeze Brise [brē'zə] 75
bricklayer Maurer [mou'rər] 36
bridge Brücke [brik'ə] 42, 120, 174;
  Kommandobrücke   [kômän'dō-
  brik'ə] 75
briefcase Aktentasche [äk'təntä-
  shə] 143, 153
brillantine Brillantine [bril'yäntē'-
  nə] 157
bring bringen [bring'ən] 20, 87, 99;
  ~ **back** zurückbringen [tsōōrik'-
  bringən] 41
brisket (meat) Brust [brōōst] 105
broadcast senden [zen'dən] 192
broccoli Brokkoli [brôk'ōlē] 107
brochure Broschüre [brôshē'rə] 130
broiler Hähnchen [hän'shən], Hendl
  [hen'dəl] 105
broken kaputt [käpōōt'] 23
bronchitis Bronchitis [brônshē'tis]
  169
brooch Brosche [brô'shə] 133
broth Brühe [brē'ə] 103; **meat** ~
  Fleischbrühe [flīsh'brē'ə] 103; **chick-
  en** ~ Hühnerbrühe [hē'nərbrē'ə]
  103; **clear** ~ klare Brühe [klär'ə
  brē'-ə] 103
brother Bruder [brōō'dər] 35; ~**-in-
  law** Schwager [shvä'gər] 35
brown braun [broun] 194; **chestnut** ~
  kastanienbraun   [kästä'nē·ən-
  broun'] 194

bruise Quetschung [kvetsh´ŏŏng] 169

brush Bürste [birs´tə] 140; **clothes ~** Kleiderbürste [klī´dərbirstə] 141

Brussels sprouts Rosenkohl [rō´zənkōl] 108

bucket Eimer [ī´mər] 90

buckle Schnalle [shnäl´ə] 136

building Gebäude [gəboi´də] 119

bulb Birne [bir´nə] 51, 88; **light ~** Glühbirne [glē´birnə] 92

bumper Stoßstange [shtōs´shtängə] 51, 56

bungalow Bungalow [bŏŏng´gälō] 81

buoy Boje [bō´yə] 75

Burgundy Burgunderwein [bŏŏrgŏŏn´dərvīn] 111

burn (verb) brennen [bren´ən] 26; **~** (noun) Verbrennung [ferbren´ŏŏng] 169

burned out durchgebrannt [dŏŏrsh´gəbränt] 88

bus Bus [bŏŏs] 59, 64, 89, 117; **~ stop** Bushaltestelle [bŏŏs´hältəshtelə] 59; **~ terminal** Busbahnhof [bŏŏs´bänhōf] 59; **~ stop** Bushaltestelle [bŏŏs´hältəshtel´ə] 116

business Geschäft [gəsheft´]; **~ administration** Betriebswirtschaft [bətrēps´virtshäft] 39; **~ class** Business-Klasse [biz´nis·kläs´ə] 69; **~ school** Handelsschule [hän´dəls·shŏŏ´lə] 38

busted defekt [däfekt´] 48

busy besetzt [bəzetst´] 148

butcher Fleischer [flī´shər], Metzger [mets´gər] 36

butter Butter [bŏŏt´ər] 98, 100

buttocks Gesäß [gəzäs´] 166

button Knopf [knopf] 136

buttonhole thread Knopflochseide [knopf´lôhzīdə] 136

buy kaufen [kou´fən] 126

C

cabaña Kabine [käbē´nə] 185

cabbage Kohl [kōl] 108

cabin Kabine [käbē´nə] 73, 75; **double ~** Zweibettkabine [tsvī´betkäbē´nə] 73; **inside ~** Innenkabine [in´ənkäbē´nə] 73; **outside ~** Außenkabine [ou´sənkäbē´nē] 73; **single ~** Einzelkabine [īn´tsəlkäbē´nə] 73

cabinetmaker Schreiner [shrī´nər] 36

cable Kabel [kä´bəl] 52, 57, 75

café Café [käfä´] 113

cake Kuchen [kŏŏ´hən] 113

calf Wade [vä´də] 166

call (verb) rufen [rŏŏ´fən] 48, 123, 162, anrufen [än´rŏŏfən] 147; (police) verständigen [fershten´digən] 48; (at port) anlaufen [än´loufən] 75; **What do you ~ ...?** Was heißt ...? [väs hīst ...] 24; **give someone a ~** jemanden anrufen [yā´mändən än´rŏŏfən] 17; **~** (noun) Anruf [än´rŏŏf] 148; **long distance ~** Ferngespräch [fern´gəshpräsh] 148; **person to person ~** Gespräch mit Voranmeldung [gəshpräsh´ mit fōr´änmel`dŏŏng] 150

camembert Camembert [käm´əmbär] 108

camera Kamera [kä´mərä], Fotoapparat [fō´tō·äpärät`] 131, 153; **movie ~** Filmkamera [film´kämərä] 132

camomile tea Kamillentee [kämil´əntā] 160

camp: ~ out zelten [tsel´tən] 94; **~ site** Campingplatz [kem´pingpláts´] 95; **~ bed** Campingliege [kem´pinglē`gə] 95; **~ stove** Spirituskocher [shpē´ritŏŏskôhər] 143

camping Camping [kem´ping] 94; **~ site** Campingplatz [kem´pingpláts´] 81, 94; **~ ID** Campingausweis [kem´pingous`vis] 95; **~ trailer** Wohnwagen [vōn´vägən], Campingwagen [kem´pingvä`gən] 40

can können [ken´ən] 17, 18, 44, etc.

can opener Dosenöffner [dō´zənefnər] 143

canal Kanal [känäl´] 75

cancel annullieren [änŏŏlēr´ən] 69, streichen [shtrī´shən] 148

cancellation Annullierung [änōō-lēr´ōong]; ~ **fee** Annullierungsgebühr [änōōlēr´ōongsgəbēr´] 69
cancer Krebs [krāps] 169
candle Kerze [ker´tsə] 143
candlestick Leuchter [loish´tər] 124, 143
candy Bonbons [bôNbôNs´] 143; Süßigkeiten [zē´sishkī´tən] 113
canned goods Konserven [kônzer´-vən] 143
cap Mütze [mits´ə] 134
capers Kapern [kä´pərn] 100
capital Hauptstadt [houpt´shtät] 120; **national ~** Bundeshauptstadt [bōōn´dəs-houpt´shtät] 120; **state ~** Landeshauptstadt [län´dəs-houpt´shtät] 120
capon Kapaun [käpoun´] 105
captain Kapitän [käpitän´] 74, 75; **~'s table** Kapitänstisch [käp´itäns´tish] 75
car Auto [ou´tō] 40, 48, 73, 94, 153, Wagen [vä´gən] 40, 48; (railroad) Wagen [vä´gən], Waggon [vägôN´] 67; **~ key** Autoschlüssel [ou´tō-shlis´əl] 52, 153; **~ door** Wagentür [vä´gəntēr´] 52, 67; **~ ferry** Autofähre [ou´tōfä´rə] 72; **~ repair service** Kundendienst [kōōn´dəndēnst´] 45; **go by ~** mit dem Auto fahren [mit däm ou´tō fä´rən] 42
carafe Karaffe [käräf´ə] 97
caraway Kümmel [kim´əl] 100
carburetor Vergaser [fergä´zər] 52, 56; **~ jet** Vergaserdüse [fergä´zərdē-zə] 52
card Karte [kär´tə] 145; **greeting ~** Grußkarte [grōōs´kärtə] 145; **greeting ~ telegram** Glückwunschtelegramm [glik´vōōnshtälägräm´] 147; **post ~** Postkarte [pôst´kärtə] 145; **picture post ~** Ansichtskarte [än´-zishtskärtə] 145; **~ game** Kartenspiel [kär´tənshpēl] 181
cardiac infarction Herzinfarkt [herts´-infärkt] 169
cardigan Strickjacke [shtrik´yäkə] 134
cardiovascular drug Kreislaufmittel [krīs´loufmit´əl] 160

careful! Vorsicht! [fōr´zisht] 49
carp Karpfen [kär´pfən] 104
carpenter Tischler [tish´lər], Zimmermann [tsim´ərmän] 36
carpet Teppich [tep´ish] 90
carrot Karotte [kärôt´ə], Möhre [mä´rə] 107
cartoon Zeichentrickfilm [tsī´shən-trikfilm] 179
cash (adj.) bar [bär] 151
cassette Kassette [käset´ə] 143
castle Schloß [shlôs] 119, Turm [tōōrm] 181
castor oil Rizinusöl [rē´tsinōōsäl] 160
catalogue Katalog [kätälōk´] 130
category Kategorie [kät´əgōrē´] 90
cathedral Dom [dōm] 119, 124
cauliflower (German) Blumenkohl [blōō´mənkōl], (Austrian) Karfiol [kärfē·ōl´] 107
caution! Vorsicht! [fōr´zisht] 191
cave Höhle [hä´lə] 120
caviar Kaviar [kä´viär] 102
cavities Karies [kär´ē·es] 174
ceiling Zimmerdecke [tsim´ərdekə] 90
celery Sellerie [zel´ərē] 108; **~ root** Sellerie [zel´ərē] 108; **stalk ~** Selleriestauden [zel´ərēshtou´dən] 108
cellar Keller [kel´ər] 90
cemetery Friedhof [frēt´hôf] 120, 124
center strip Mittelstreifen [mit´əl-shtrī´fən] 42
centimeter Zentimeter [tsentēmä´-tər] 193
ceramics Keramik [kerä´mik] 143
cereal Getreideflocken [gətrī´də-flôk´ən] 98
certainly gewiß [gəvis´] 21; **~!** Bitte sehr [bit´ə zär] 20; **~ not** auf keinen Fall [ouf kī´nən fäl] 21
chain Kette [ket´ə] 52
chair Stuhl [shtōōl] 90; **deck ~** Liegestuhl [lē´gəshtōōl] 91
chamber music Kammermusik [käm´-ərmōōzēk´] 177
championship Meisterschaft [mīs´-tərshäft] 188

change *(noun)* Wechselgeld [vek´-zəlgelt], Rest [rest] 115, Kleingeld [klīn´gelt] 151; ~ *(verb)* wechseln [vek´səln] 46, 85, 151, umsteigen [ŏŏm´shtīgən] 117, sich ändern [zish en´dərn] 26, auswechseln [ous´veksəln] 51, 56; tauschen [tou´shən] 66; umbuchen [ŏŏm´bŏŏhən] 69; *(wind)* sich drehen [zish drā´ən] 26

chapel Kapelle [käpel´ə] 124

charcoal pills Kohletabletten [kō´lətäblet´ən] 160

charge *(noun)* Gebühr [gəbér´]; ~ *(verb)* laden [lä´dən] 51; *(dynamo)* Strom geben [shtrōm gā´bən] 52

charter plane Chartermaschine [tshär´tərmäshē`nə] 70

chassis Fahrgestell [fär´gəshtel] 52

chat unterhalten [ŏŏntərhäl´tən] 183

chauffeur Fahrer [fä´rər] 41

check *(noun)* Rechnung [resh´-nŏŏng] 115, Scheck [shek] 127, 151; ~ *(verb)* (über)prüfen [(é´bər)pré´fən] 45, 50, 56; ~ **(over)** nachsehen [näh´zā·ən] 52; ~ **in** sich anmelden [zish än´meldən] 90; ~ **room** Garderobe [gärdərō´-bə] 177

checked kariert kärērt´] 137

checkers Dame [dä´mə] 181

check-in Anmeldung [än´meldŏŏng] 90, 95

check-out Abmeldung [äp´mel-dŏŏng] 95

cheek Backe [bäk´ə], Wange [väng´ə] 166

cheers! zum Wohl! [tsŏŏm vōl], Prost! [prōst] 99

cheese Käse [kā´zə] 108; **blue ~** Edelpilzkäse [ā´dəlpiltskä`zə] 108; **Swiss ~** Emmentaler [em´əntä-lər] 108; **cottage ~** Hüttenkäse [hit´-ənkāzə] 108; **farmer ~** Quark [kvärk] 108; **cream ~** Rahmkäse [räm´kāzə] 108; ~ **spread** Schmelzkäse [shmelts´kāzə] 108; ~ **cake** Käseku-chen [kā´zəkŏŏhən] 109

chef Koch [kōh] 36

chemistry Chemie [shāmē´] 39

cherries Kirschen [kir´shən] 110

chess Schach [shäh] 180

chessman Schachfigur [shäh´fi-gŏŏr`] 181

chest Brust [brŏŏst] 166

chicken Huhn [hŏŏn] 105; **breaded deep-fried ~** Backhendl [bäk´-hendəl] 105; **broiled ~** Brathuhn [brät´hŏŏn] 105; ~ **breast** Hühner-brust [hé´nərbrŏŏst] 105; ~ **drum-stick** Hühnerkeule [hé´nərkoilə] 105; ~ **pox** Windpocken [vint´pō-kən] 169

child Kind [kint] 34, 78, 162, 185

chills Schüttelfrost [shit´əlfrôst] 164, 169

chimney Kamin [kämēn´] 91

chin Kinn [kin] 166

china Porzellan [pôr´tselän´] 126, 143

chip Spielmarke [shpēl´märkə] 181

chisel Meißel [mī´səl] 57

chives Schnittlauch [shnit´louh] 101

chocolate Schokolade [shōkōlä´də] 113; ~ **layer cake** Prinzregententorte [prints´rāgent`əntôr`tə] 109

choir Chor [kōr] 124

cholera Cholera [kō´lərä] 78, 169

chop Kotelett [kôtlet´] 106

chorus Chor [kōr] 177

christening Taufe [tou´fə] 123

church Kirche [kir´shə] 116, 124; **Catholic ~** katholische Kirche [kätō´-lishə kir´shə] 116, 123; **Protestant ~** evangelische Kirche [ā´vängā`lishə kir´shə] 116; ~ **concert** Kirchenkon-zert [kir´shənkônt`sert`] 124

churchyard Friedhof [frēt´hôf] 120, 124

cider Apfelwein [äpf´əlvīn] 111

cigar Zigarre [tsigär´ə] 140

cigarette Zigarette [tsigäret´ə] 80, 140; **filtered ~** Filterzigarette [fil´tərtsigäret`ə] 140; **unfiltered ~** Zigarette ohne Filter [tsigäret´ə ō´nə fil´tər] 140

cigarillo Zigarillo [tsigäril´ō] 140

cinema Kino [kē´nō] 179

cinnamon Zimt [tsimt] 101

circle traffic Kreisverkehr [krīs´fer-kär`] 43

circulation Kreislauf [krīs´louf] 166

circulatory problem Kreislaufstörung [krīs´loufshtố´rōong] 169

circus Zirkus [tsir´kōōs] 181

city Stadt [shtät] 120; **~ hall** Rathaus [rät´hous] 116, 120

civil servant Beamte(r) [bə·äm´-tə(r)] 36

claim *(luggage)* abholen [äp´hōlən] 63; **~ check** Gepäckschein [gəpek´-shīn] 63

class Klasse [kläs´ə] 73; **first ~** Erste Klasse [ers´tə kläs´ə] 73; **tourist ~** Touristenklasse [tōōris´tənkläs´ə] 73, 77

clay pigeon shooting Tontaubenschießen [tōn´toubənshēsən] 189

clean (out) reinigen [rī´nigən] 47, 56, 137

clear *(adj.)* klar [klär] 26

clergyman Pfarrer [pfär´ər] 36, Geistlicher [gīst´lishər] 36, 123

climate Klima [klē´mä] 26

climb aufsteigen [ouf´shtīgən] 70

clock Uhr [ōōr] 31, 142; **alarm ~** Wecker [vek´ər] 143; **It's ... o'clock** Es ist ... Uhr [es ist ... ōōr] 30

close schließen [shlē´sən] 18, 44, 65, 118

closed geschlossen [gəshlôs´ən] 191

closet Schrank [shrängk] 91

cloth Tuch [tōōh] 57, 136

clothes Kleider [klī´dər] 87; **~ hanger** Kleiderbügel [klī´dərbēgəl] 87, 91

clothing Kleidung [klī´dōōng] 133

cloud Wolke [vôl´kə] 26; **~ cover** Bewölkung [bəvel´kōōng] 26

cloudburst Wolkenbruch [vôl´kənbrōōh] 26

cloudy bewölkt [bəvelkt´] 26; **~ skies** Bewölkung [bəvel´kōōng] 26

cloves Nelken [nel´kən] 101

club Klub [klōōp] 181

clubs *(cards)* Kreuz [kroits] 181

clutch Kupplung [kōōp´lōōng] 52; **~ pedal** Kupplungspedal [kōōp´-lōōngspədäl´] 52

coalfish Seelachs [zā´läks] 104

coast Küste [kis´tə] 75

coastal road Küstenstraße [kis´tən-shträ`sə] 43

coat Mantel [män´təl] 134; **~ check** Garderobenmarke [gärdərō´-bənmärkə] 177

cobbler Schuster [shōō´stər] 36

coconut Kokosnuß [kō´kôsnōōs] 110

cod Dorsch [dôrsh], Kabeljau [kä´-bəlyou`] 104

c.o.d. Nachnahme [näh´nämə] 149

code Code [kōd] 148; **area ~** Vorwahlnummer [fōr´välnōōmər] 148; **~ alphabet** Buchstabieralphabet [bōōh-shtäbēr´älfäbät`] 149

coffee Kaffee [käf´ä] 98, 113, 183; **black ~** schwarzer Kaffee [shvärts´-ər käf´ä] 98; **decaffeinated ~** koffeinfreier Kaffee [kôfä·ēn´frī·ər käf´ä] 98; **~ with cream** Kaffee mit Sahne [käf´ä mit zä´nə] 98; **~ with sugar** Kaffee mit Zucker [käf´ä mit tsōōk´-ər] 98

cognac Kognak [kôn´yäk] 112

coin Münze [min´tsə] 148, 151; **~ changer** Münzwechsler [mints´veks-lər] 149

cold *(noun)* Erkältung [erkel´tōōng] 163, 169; **~** *(adj.)* kalt [kält] 25, 67, 93, 100; **I'm ~** Mir ist kalt [mēr ist kält] 25; **~ cuts** Aufschnitt [ouf´shnit] 98, 102; **~ wave** Kaltwelle [kält´velə] 158

colic Kolik [kō´lik] 169

collarbone Schlüsselbein [shlis´əl-bīn] 166

collect call R-Gespräch [er´gə-shpräsh] 149

college College [kôl´ij] 38; **I'm at ...** Ich studiere am ... College [ish shtōō-dē´rə äm ... kôl´ij] 38

collision Zusammenstoß [tsōōzäm´-ənshtōs] 49

cologne Kölnisch Wasser [kel´nish väs´ər] 141

color Farbe [fär´bə] 127, 194; **~ of eyes** Augenfarbe [ou´gənfärbə] 79; **~ of hair** Haarfarbe [här´färbə] 79

colored farbig [fär´bish] 194

colorful bunt [bōōnt] 194

comb *(noun)* Kamm [käm] 141, 158; **~** *(verb)* kämmen [kem´ən] 158

come kommen [kôm´ən] 15; **~ in
(train)** ankommen [än´kômən] 61; **~
in!** Herein! [herīn´] 16, 87; **~ right in!**
Treten Sie näher! [trā´tən zē nā´ər]
16; **Thanks so much for coming** Vielen Dank für Ihren Besuch [fē´lən
dängk fēr ē´rən bəzōōh´] 16; **how
~** weshalb [ves·hälp´] 18

comedy Komödie [kômẽ´dē·ə] 177

communion Abendmahl [ä´bəntmäl]
124

compact Puderdose [pŏŏ´dərdōzə]
141

compartment Abteil [äptīl´] 67

compass Kompaß [kôm´päs] 138

competition Wettkampf [vet´kämpf]
188

complaint Beanstandung [bə·än´-
shtändōong] 88, 91, Beschwerde
[bəshver´də] 115; **register a ~** sich
beschweren [zish bəshvā´rən] 23;
make a ~ sich beschweren [zish bə-
shvā´rən] 23

composer Komponist [kômpōnist´]
177

compression Kompression [kômpre-
syõn´] 52

concert Konzert [kôntsert´] 123, 176;
~ hall Konzertsaal [kôntsert´zäl] 177

concierge Portier [pôrtyā´], Pförtner
[pfert´nər] 91

concussion Gehirnerschütterung [gə-
hirn´ershit˙ərōong] 169

condenser Kondensator [kôndenzä´-
tôr] 52

condolences Beileid [bī´līt] 23

conductor Schaffner [shäf´nər] 59,
67; Dirigent [dirigent´] 177

confectioner Konditor [kôndē´tôr] 36

confectionery Konditorei [kônditôrī´]
113

confess beichten [bīsh´tən] 124

confession Beichte [bīsh´tə] 124

confiscate beschlagnahmen [bə-
shläk´nämən] 154

congratulate beglückwünschen [bə-
glik´vinshən] 22

congratulations! Ich gratuliere Ihnen
(dir) [ish grä´tŏŏlē´rə ē´nən (dēr)] 22

conjunctivitis Bindehautentzündung
[bin´dəhoutents˙in˙dōōng] 169

connect verbinden [ferbin´dən] 148

connection Anschluß [än´shlŏŏs] 61,
67, 72; Anschlußzug [än´-
shlŏŏs·tsŏōk´] 61

constipate verstopfen [fershtôpf´ən]
163

constipation Verstopfung [fershtôpf´-
ōōng] 169

consulate Konsulat [kônzŏōlät´] 78,
120

contact Kontakt [kôntäkt´] 52; **~
lenses** Kontaktlinsen [kôntäkt´lin-
zən], Haftschalen [häft´shälən] 138

contraceptive pills Antibabypillen
[än´tēbä´bēpil˙ən] 160

convalescent home Erholungsheim
[erhō´lōōngs·hīm´] 175

convent (Nonnen)Kloster [(nôn´ən)-
klōs´tər] 124

cook (verb) kochen [kô´hən] 95; **~
(noun)** Koch [kôh], Köchin [ke´shin]
36

cookies Plätzchen [plets´shən] 113

cooking Kochen [kô´hən] 100; **~
utensils** Kochgeschirr [kôh´gəshir]
95

coolant Kühlflüssigkeit [kēl´flisish-
kīt´] 45

cordial herzlich [herts´lish] 12; **Cor-
dially yours** Mit freundlichen Grüßen
[mit froint´lishən grē´sən] 13

corduroy Kord(samt) [kôrt´(zämt)]
136

corkscrew Korkenzieher [kôr´kən-
tsē·ər] 143

corn Mais [mīs] 108; **~ plaster** Hühner-
augenpflaster [hē´nərougən-
pfläs´tər] 160

corner Ecke [ek´ə] 120; (sports) Eck-
ball [ek´bäl] 189

correct richtig [rish´tish] 115

corridor Korridor [kôr´idôr] 91

corset Mieder [mē´dər] 134

cosmetic salon Kosmetiksalon [kôs-
mā´tikzälôN´] 128

cost kosten [kôs´tən] 18, 44, 50, 64,
68, 69

costume Kostüm [kôstēm´] 177; **~
designer** Kostümbildner [kôstēm´-
bildnər] 177

cotton Baumwolle [boum′vôlə] 136;
~ **swabs** Wattestäbchen [vät′ə-shtäpshən] 160

couchette car Liegewagen [lē′gə-vä′gən] 64

couchette sleeper Liegewagen [lē′-gəvä′gən] 60

cough husten [hōōs′tən] 165, 169; ~ **medicine** Hustenmittel [hōōs′tənmit-təl] 160; ~ **syrup** Hustensaft [hōōs′-tənzáft] 160

counter Schalter [shäl′tər] 149

country Land [länt]; ~ **fair** Volksfest [fôlks′fest] 181; ~ **road** Landstraße [länt′shträ′sə] 43

countryside Landschaft [länt′shäft] 120

course Kurs [kōōrs] 75; **of** ~ selbst-verständlich [zelpst′fershtent′lish] 21

court Gericht [gərisht′] 154

courthouse Gerichtsgebäude [gə-rishts′gəboidə] 120

cousin *(female)* Cousine, Kusine [kōō-zē′nə] 35; *(male)* Cousin [kōō-zeN′], Vetter [fet′ər] 35

cover Bezug [bətsōōk′] 90

covered market Markthalle [märkt′-hälə] 120

coxswain Steuermann [shtoi′ərmän] 189

crab Krebs [krāps] 102, 104

cramp Krampf [krämpf] 169

cranberries Preiselbeeren [prī′zəl-bärən] 110

crawfish Krebs [krāps] 102

crayon Buntstift [bōōnt′shtift] 138

cream Krem [krām], Creme [krām] 141; Sahne [zä′nə] 113; **whipped** ~ Schlagsahne [shläk′zänə], Schlag-obers [shläk′ōbərs] 114; **face** ~ Gesichtscreme [gəzishts′krām] 141

credit Kredit [krādēt′] 151; ~ **card** Kreditkarte [krādēt′kärtə] 127, 152; **letter of** ~ Kreditbrief [krādēt′brēf] 152

creed Glaubensbekenntnis [glou′-bənsbəkent′nis] 124

crew Besatzung [bəzäts′ōōng] 70, Mannschaft [män′shäft] 75

crib Kinderbett [kin′dərbet] 83, 90

crime Verbrechen [ferbresh′ən] 154

criminal Verbrecher [ferbresh′ər] 154; ~ **investigation division** Kriminalpolizei [kriminäl′pôlitsī′] 154

croissant Hörnchen [hern′shən] 98

cross Kreuz [kroits] 124; ~ **road** Querstraße [kvār′shträ′sə] 43

crossing Überfahrt [ē′bərfärt] 72, 75

crown Krone [krō′nə] 174

crucifix Kruzifix [krōōtsēfiks′] 124

cruet stand Essig- und Ölständer [es′ish ōōnt öl′shten′dər] 97

cruise Kreuzfahrt [kroits′färt] 75

crumb cake Streuselkuchen [shtroi′-zəlkōōhən] 109

crystal (Uhren)Glas [(ōōr′ən)gläs] 143

cubic Kubik... [kōōbēk′...] 193

cucumber Gurke [gōōr′kə] 107

cufflinks Manschettenknöpfe [män-shet′ənknepfə] 133

cup Tasse [täs′ə] 96

cure Kur [kōōr] 175; ~ **tax** Kurtaxe [kōōr′täksə] 175; ~ **vacation** Kuraufenthalt [kōōr′oufent·hält′] 175; **rest** ~ Liegekur [lē′gəkōōr] 175

curler Lockenwickler [lôk′ənviklər] 141

curls Locken [lôk′ən] 158

currency Währung [vār′ōōng] 151; **foreign** ~ Devisen [dəvē′zən] 152

current Strom [shtrōm] 90; **alternating** ~ Wechselstrom [vek′səlshtrōm] 90

curtain Vorhang [fōr′häng] 91, 177; ~ **time** Beginn [bəgin′] 177; **final** ~ Ende [en′də] 177

curve Kurve [kōōr′və] 42

cuspid Eckzahn [ek′tsän] 174

custody Haft [häft] 154; **pre-trial** ~ Untersuchungshaft [ōōn′tərzōō′-hōōngs·häft′] 154

customs Zoll [tsôl] 58, 73, 80; ~ **control** Zollkontrolle [tsôl′kôntrôlə] 80; ~ **declaration** Zollerklärung [tsôl′erklär′ōōng] 80, 146; ~ **examination** Zollabfertigung [tsôl′äpfer′ti-gōōng] 80; ~ **office** Zollamt [tsôl′-ämt] 80; ~ **officer** Zollbeamte [tsôl′-bə·ämtə] 80

cut *(verb)* schneiden [shnī′dən] 155, 158; *(cards)* abheben [äp′hābən] 181; ~ *(noun)* Schnittwunde [shnit′-vōōndə] 169

cutlery Besteck [bəshtek′] 97
cutlet Schnitzel [shnit′səl] 107
cylinder Zylinder [tsı̈lin′dər] 52
Canadian kanadisch [känä′dish] 152; **~ dollars** Kanadische Dollar [känä′dishə dôl′är] 152
Catholic Katholik [kä′tôlēk′] 124; **Roman ~** römisch-katholisch [rō′mish-kätō′lish] 124
Celsius Celsius [tsel′zi-ōōs] 192
Christ Christus [kris′tōōs] 124
Christian Christ [krist] 124
Christianity Christentum [kris′təntōōm] 124
Christmas Weihnachten [vı̈′nähtən] 33; **Merry ~!** Frohe Weihnachten! [frō′ə vı̈′nähtən], Frohes Fest! [frō′əs fest] 23

D

daily täglich [täk′lish] 31; **~ rate** Tageskurs [tä′gəskōōrs] 152
dairy Milchgeschäft [milsh′gəsheft], Molkerei [môlkərı̈′] 128
damage (verb) beschädigen [bəshä′digən] 48; **~** (noun) Unfallschaden [ōōn′fälshä`dən] 49
dance (noun) Tanz [tänts] 183; **~** (verb) tanzen [tän′tsən] 183; **~ hall** Tanzlokal [tänts′lōkäl`] 183
dancer Tänzer [ten′tsər], Tänzerin [ten′tsərin] 177
dandruff Schuppen [shōōp′ən] 158
danger Gefahr [gəfär′] 191; **~!** Vorsicht! [fōr′zisht] 49; (sign) Gefahrenstelle [gəfä′rənshtelə] 58
dangerous gefährlich [gəfär′lish] 185
dark dunkel [dōōng′kəl] 127
darn stopfen [shtôp′fən] 137
darning cotton Stopfgarn [shtôpf′gärn] 136
darning-wool Stopfwolle [shtôpf′vôlə] 136
date Datum [dä′tōōm]; **What's the ~?** Den wievielten haben wir? [dän vēfēl′tən hä′bən vēr] 34; **~ of birth** Geburtsdatum [gebōōrts′dätōōm] 79
daughter Tochter [tôh′tər] 14, 35

dawn (Morgen)Dämmerung [(môr′gən)dem′ərōōng] 26
day Tag [täk] 31; **New Year's Day** Neujahr [noi′yär] 33; **~ room** Tagesraum [tä′gəsroum] 95
dead-end street Sackgasse [zäk′gäsə] 120
deal geben [gā′bən] 181
dealership garage Vertragswerkstatt [ferträks′verk`shtät] 49
decanter Karaffe [käräf′ə] 97
December Dezember [dātsem′bər] 33
decimeter Dezimeter [dätsēmā′tər] 193
deck Deck [dek] 76; **boat ~** Bootsdeck [bōts′dek] 76; **fore ~** Vorderdeck [fōr′dərdek] 76; **main ~** Hauptdeck [houpt′dek] 76; **poop ~** Achterdeck [äh′tərdek] 76; **promenade ~** Promenadendeck [prō`mənä′dəndek`] 76; **saloon ~** Salondeck [sälōN′dek] 76; **sun ~** Sonnendeck [zôn′əndek] 76; **upper ~** Oberdeck [ō′bərdek] 76; **~ chair** Liegestuhl [lē′gəshtōōl] 76, 185
declare deklarieren [däkläre′rən] 80
deep tief [tēf] 165, 185
defeat Niederlage [nē′dərlägə] 188
delicate stew Ragout [rägōō′] 106
delicious ausgezeichnet [ousgətsı̈sh′nət], vorzüglich [fōrtsēk′lish] 99
delighted: I'm ~ Es freut mich [es froit mish] 12
delivery truck Lieferwagen [lē′fərvä`gən] 41
denomination: religious ~ Konfession [kôn′fesyōn′] 124
dental clinic Zahnklinik [tsän′klē`nik] 174
dentist Zahnarzt [tsän′ärtst], Zahnärztin [tsän′ärts`tin] 36, 173
dentistry Zahnmedizin [tsän′mädi`tsēn] 39
denture (Zahn)Prothese [(tsän)prōtä′zə] 173
deodorant Deodorant [dä·ōdōränt′] 141
depart abfahren [äp′färən] 67
departure Abfahrt [äp′färt] 60, 67, 191, Abreise [äp′rı̈zə] 91, Ausreise [ous′rı̈zə] 79

deposit *(noun)* Anzahlung [än´tsäloõng] 83, 91; ~ *(verb)* einzahlen [īn´tsälən] 152, hinterlegen [hintərlā´gən] 41

dermatologist Hautarzt [hout´ärtst] 162

dessert Süßspeise [zēs´shpīzə] 109

destination Bestimmungsort [bəshtim´oõngsôrt´] 149; *(planes)* Ziel (-flughafen) [tsēl´ (floõk´häfən)] 70

detergent Waschmittel [väsh´mitəl] 143; **dishwashing** ~ Spülmittel [shpēl´mitəl] 143

detour Umleitung [oõm´lītoõng] 42, 58

develop entwickeln [entvik´əln] 131

development Entwicklung [entvik´loõng] 132

dew Tau [tou] 26

dextrose Traubenzucker [trou´bəntsoõkər] 160

diabetes Zuckerkrankheit [tsoõk´ərkrängk´hīt] 170

diabetic Diabetiker [dē`äbä´tikər] 164

diagnosis Diagnose [dē`ägnō´zə] 172

dial *(noun)* Wählscheibe [väl´shībə] 149; ~ *(verb)* wählen [vä´lən] 149

diamond Diamant [dē`ämänt´], Brillant [brilyänt´] 133

diamonds *(cards)* Karo [kä´rō] 181

diaphoretic schweißtreibendes Mittel [shvīs´trībəndəs mit´əl] 160

diaphragm Blende [blen´də] 132

diarrhea Durchfall [doõrsh´fál] 163, 170

dice Würfel [vēr´fəl] 181; **shoot** ~ würfeln [vēr´fəln] 181

dictionary Wörterbuch [ver´tərboõh] 130

die sterben [shtär´bən] 119

diesel Diesel [dē´zəl] 45; ~ **motor** Dieselmotor [dē´zəlmōtôr] 54

diet Diät [dē-ät´] 165, 175

differential Differential [difərentsyäl´] 52

digestion Verdauung [ferdou´oõng] 166

digestive tablets Magentabletten [mä´gəntäblet´ən] 160

digestive tonic Magentropfen [mä´gəntrôpfən] 160

dill Dill [dil] 101

dinghy Schlauchboot [shlouh´bōt] 186

dining car Speisewagen [shpī´zəvä´gən] 60, 61, 64, 66

dining room Speisesaal [shpī´zəzäl´] 74, 86, 91

dinner Abendessen [ä´bənt-esən] 91, 99

dip stick Ölmeßstab [äl´mes-shtäp] 52

diphtheria Diphtherie [diftərē´] 170

dipped headlights Abblendlicht [äp´blentlisht] 53

direct direkt [direkt´] 68; ~ **dialing** Durchwahl [doõrsh´väl] 149

direct dial durchwählen [doõrsh´vä-lən] 147

direction Richtung [rish´toõng] 59, 116; ~ **sign** Wegweiser [vāk´vīzər] 42

director Regisseur [rezhisär´] 177

disc Bandscheibe [bänt´shība] 166; ~ **brake** Scheibenbremse [shī´bənbremzə] 51

discharge Entlassung [entläs´oõng] 172

discotheque Diskothek [diskōtäk´] 180, 182

discount Ermäßigung [ermä´sigoõng] 176

disease Krankheit [krängk´hīt] 170; **contagious** ~ ansteckende Krankheit [än´shtekəndə krängk´hīt] 170

disembark ausbooten [ous´bōtən] 76

disengage trennen [tren´ən] 53

dish Gericht [gərisht´] 99

dishes Eßgeschirr [es´gəshir] 95

disinfectant Desinfektionsmittel [des´infektsyōns´mit´əl] 160

dislocation Verrenkung [fereng´koõng] 170

distilled water destilliertes Wasser [destilēr´təs väs´ər] 45

distributor Verteiler [fertī´lər] 52

district Stadtteil [shtät´tīl] 120

ditch Graben [grä´bən] 120

dive springen [shpring´ən] 186, 190

diving board Sprungbrett [shproõng´bret] 186, 190

divorced geschieden [gəshē´dən] 79

dizziness Schwindel [shvin´dəl], Schwindelgefühl [shvin´dəlgəfēl] 170

do tun [tōōn] 18, 20, 22

dock *(noun)* Dock [dôk] 76; ~ *(verb)* anlegen [än´lāgən] 72, 76

doctor Arzt [ärtst] 36, 48, 162, 172, Ärztin [ärts´tin] 36, 48; *(in names)* Herr (Frau) Doktor [her (frou) dôk´tôr] 13; ~'s **office** Sprechzimmer [shpresh´tsimər] 163

documentary Dokumentarfilm [dôk`ōōmentär´film] 179

dog Hund [hŏŏnt] 191; **beware of the ~** Bissiger Hund [bis´igər hŏŏnt] 191

doll Puppe [pŏŏ´pə] 143

dome Kuppel [kŏŏp´əl] 124

door Tür [tēr] 91, 191; ~ **handle** Türklinke [tēr´klingkə] 91, 191; ~ **lock** Türschloß [tēr´shlôs] 52

dormitory Schlafraum [shläf´roum] 95

doubles Doppel [dôp´əl] 190

downtown Innenstadt [in´ənshtät] 116; ~ **area** Stadtmitte [shtät´mit´ə] 120

dozen dutzend [dŏŏts´ənt] 193

draft Luftzug [lŏŏf´tsōōk] 26

drain Abfluß [äp´flōōs] 88

drama Drama [drä´mä] 177

drapery Vorhang [fōr´häng] 91

draw *(verb)* ziehen [tsē´ən] 182; ~ *(noun)* Unentschieden [ŏŏn´ent·shē´dən] 188

drawer Schublade [shōōp´lädə] 91

dress Kleid [klīt] 134, 137, 183

dressing gown Morgenmantel [môr´gənmäntəl] 134

dressmaker Schneiderin [shnī´dərin] 36

dress-shield Schweißblatt [shvīs´blät] 136

drier Haube [hou´bə] 156

drill Bohrer [bō´rər] 57

drink *(verb)* trinken [tring´kən] 94, 165; ~ *(noun)* Getränk [gətrengk´] 96, Drink [dringk] 183

drinking water Trinkwasser [tringk´väsər] 65

drip tropfen [trôpf´ən] 88

drip-dry bügelfrei [bē´gəlfrī] 135

drive fahren [fä´rən] 42, 50

drive-in movie Autokino [ou´tōkē`nō] 179

driver (Kraft)Fahrer [(kräft´)fä´rər] 36, 59

driver's license Führerschein [fē´rərshīn] 42, 79

driver's seat Fahrersitz [fä´rərzits] 55

driveway Einfahrt [īn´färt] 42

driving instructor Fahrlehrer [fär´lārər] 36

drop: *(wind)* sich legen [zish lā´gən] 26; ~ **by** wiederkommen [vē´dərkôm`ən] 15

drops Tropfen [trôpf´ən] 160; **ear ~** Ohrentropfen [ōr´əntrôpfən] 160; **eye ~** Augentropfen [ou´gəntrôpf´ən] 160

druggist *(pharmacist)* Apotheker [äpōtā´kər] 36; *(drugstore owner)* Drogist [drōgist´] 36

drugs Drogen [drō´gən], Rauschgift [roush´gift] 154

dry trocknen [trôk´nən] 92; ~ **cleaner's** Reinigung [rī´nigŏŏng] 128; ~ **goods** Kurzwaren [kŏŏrts´värən] 136

dubbed synchronisiert [zin`krōnizērt´] 179

dubbing Synchronisation [zin`krōnizätsyōn´] 179

duck Ente [en´tə] 105; **wild ~** Wildente [vilt´entə], Flugente [flōōk´entə] 105

duet Duett [dŏŏ·et´] 177

dull dumpf [dŏŏmpf] 163

dumpling Knödel [knȫ´dəl] 103; **liver ~** Leberknödel [lā´bərknȫdəl] 103; **potato ~s** Kartoffelklöße [kärtôf´əlklȫsə] 103; **bread ~s** Semmelknödel [zem´əlknȫdəl] 104

dune Düne [dē´nə] 186

during während [vā´rənt]; ~ **the day** am Tage [äm tä´gə] 31; ~ **the morning** vormittags [fōr´mitäks] 31

dusk (Abend)Dämmerung [(ä´bənt)dem´ərŏŏng] 26

duty Zoll [tsôl] 80; **pay ~** verzollen [fertsôl´ən] 80; ~ **free** zollfrei [tsôl´-

frī] 69, 80; **export** ~ Ausfuhrzoll [ous'-fŏŏrtsôl'] 80; **import** ~ Einfuhrzoll [īn'fŏŏrtsôl'] 80

dye Haarfärbemittel [här'färbə-mitəl] 141, 155

dynamo Lichtmaschine [lisht'mä-shē'nə] 52

dysentery Ruhr [rōōr] 170

E

ear Ohr [ōr] 162; ~ **clips** Ohrklipps [ōr'klips] 133

earache Ohrenschmerzen [ō'rən-shmer'tsən] 164

eardrum Trommelfell [trôm'əlfel] 166

earlier früher [frē'ər] 32

early früh [frē] 31

earrings Ohrringe [ōr'ringə] 133

Easter Ostern [ōs'tərn] 33

economics Wirtschaftswissenschaft [virt'shäftsvis'ənshäft] 39

economy Wirtschaft [virt'shäft]; ~ **class** Economy-Klasse [ikôn'əmi kläs'ə] 69

edam Edamer [ā'dämər] 108

eel Aal [äl] 102, 104; **smoked** ~ Räu-cheraal [roi'shəräl'] 102

egg Ei [ī] 98; **soft boiled** ~ weichge-kochtes Ei [vīsh'gəkôhtəs ī'] 98; **hard-boiled** ~ hartgekochtes Ei [härt'gəkôhtəs ī] 98; **bacon and eggs** Ei mit Speck [ī mit shpek] 98; **ham and eggs** Ei mit Schinken [ī mit shing'kən] 98; **fried eggs** Spiegelei-er [shpē'gəl·Тər] 98; **scrambled eggs** Rührei [rēr'-ī] 98; ~ **cup** Eier-becher [ī'ərbeshər] 97

eight acht [äht] 28, 89

eighty achtzig [äh'tsish] 146

elastic Gummiband [gōo'mēbänt] 136; ~ **bandage** Elastikbinde [eläs'-tikbin`də] 160; ~ **stocking** Gummi-strumpf [gōōm'eshtrōōmpf'] 160

elbow Ellbogen [el'bōgən] 140

electric shaver Trockenrasierer [trôk'ənräzērər] 141

electrical connection Stromanschluß [shtrōm'änshlōōs] 94

electrician Elektriker [älek'trikər] 36

elevator Fahrstuhl [fär'shtōōl] 91

embassy Botschaft [bōt'shäft] 120

emerald Smaragd [smäräkt'] 133

emergency Notfall [nōt'fál]; ~ **ward** Notstation [nōt'shtätsyōn'] 49; ~ **chute** Notrutsche [nōt'rōōtshə] 70; ~ **exit** Notausgang [nōt'ousgäng] 70; ~ **brake** Notbremse [nōt'bremzə] 66; ~ **landing** Notlandung [nōt'län-dōōng] 70

empty leer [lār] 159

endive Chicorée [shik'ōrä] 107

engine Triebwerk [trēp'verk] 71; *(rail-road)* Lokomotive [lôkômōtē'və] 67

engineer *(scientific)* Ingenieur [in`-zhenyär'] 36; *(railroad)* Lokführer [lôk'fērər] 36, 67

English Englisch [eng'lish] 24

enjoy genießen [gənē'sən] 17; ~ **oneself** sich amüsieren [zish ämēzē'-rən] 184

enlargement Vergrößerung [fergrœ'-sərōōng] 131

enough genug [gənōōk'] 46, 127; **not** ~ zuwenig [tsōōvā'nish] 127

enter betreten [bətrā'tən]; **do not** ~ Einfahrt verboten [īn'färt ferbō'tən] 58

entered eingetragen [īn'gəträgən] 78

entrance Eingang [īn'gäng] 67, 91, 191

entry Einreise [īn'rīzə] 79; ~ **visa** Einreisevisum [īn'rīzəvē'zōōm] 79

envelope Briefumschlag [brēf'ōōm-shläk`] 138

environs Umgebung [ōōmgä'-bōōng] 120

eraser Radiergummi [rädēr'-gōōm'ē] 138

escalator Aufzug [ouf'tsōōk] 191

escarole Endivie [endē'vē·ə] 107

European europäisch [oirōpä'ish] 192

eve: New Year's Eve Silvester [zil-ves'tər] 33

evening Abend [ä'bənt] 16, 155, 176, 183; **Good** ~! Guten Abend! [gōō'tən ä'bənt] 12; **in the** ~ abends [ä'bənts] 31; **this** ~ heute abend [hoi'tə ä'bənt] 31, 44

every jede(r) [yā′də(r)] 32; **~ day** täglich [täk′lish] 31

everything alles [ál′əs] 83, 89

exact(ly) genau [gənou′] 30

examination Untersuchung [ŏŏntərzōō′hŏŏng] 172

examine untersuchen [ŏŏntərzōō′hən] 172

example Beispiel [bī′shpēl] 192

excavations Ausgrabungen [ous′grä-bŏŏngən] 120

excess baggage Übergepäck [ē′bər-gəpek′] 68, 71

exchange *(verb)* umtauschen [ŏŏm′-toushən] 127; **~** *(noun)* Wechsel [vek′səl] 151; **rate of ~** Wechselkurs [vek′səlkŏŏrs] 152

excursion Ausflug [ous′flŏŏk] 72, 85, 118, 121; **~ program** Ausflugsprogramm [ous′flŏŏksprōgräm′] 76; **land excursions** Landausflüge [länt′-ousflēgə] 72, 76

excuse: ~ me! Entschuldigung! [ent-shŏŏl′digŏŏng] 22; **~ me?** Gestatten Sie? [gəshtät′ən zē] 20

exhaust Auspuff [ous′pŏŏf] 52

exhibition Ausstellung [ous′-shtel′ŏŏng] 119, 121

exit Ausfahrt [ous′färt] 42; Ausgang [ous′gäng] 64, 67, 69, 71, 91, 191; **emergency ~** Notausgang [nōt′ous-gäng] 191; **~ visa** Ausreisevisum [ous′rīzəve′zŏŏm] 79

expect erwarten [ervär′tən] 85, 164, 183

expensive teuer [toi′ər] 127

exposure Belichtung [bəlish′tŏŏng] 132; **~ meter** Belichtungsmesser [bə-lish′tŏŏngsmesər] 132

express train Schnellzug [shnel′-tsŏŏk], D-Zug [dā′tsŏŏk] 60, 61

expressway Autobahn [ou′tōbän] 58

extend verlängern [ferleng′ərn] 79

extension cord Verlängerungsschnur [ferleng′ərŏŏngsshnŏŏr] 91

external äußerlich [oi′sərlish] 159

extract ziehen [tsē′ən] 174

extra week Verlängerungswoche [fer-leng′ərŏŏngsvŏ′hə] 91

eye Auge [ou′gə] 141, 166; **~ liner** Lidstrich [lēt′shtrish] 141; **~ shadow** Lidschatten [lēt′shätən] 141; **~ inflammation** Augenentzündung [ou′-gənentsin′dŏŏng] 170; **~ doctor** Augenarzt [ou′gənärtst] 162

eyeball Augapfel [ouk′äpfəl] 166

eyebrow Augenbraue [ou′gən-brou′ə] 156; **~ pencil** Augenbrauenstift [ou′gənbrou·ənshtift] 141

eyeglass case Brillenetui [bril′ən-etvē′] 138

eyelid Augenlid [ou′gənlēt] 166

F

fabric Stoff [shtōf] 136

face Gesicht [gəzisht′] 156, 166; *(clock)* Ziffernblatt [tsif′ərnblät] 143; **~ massage** Gesichtsmassage [gə-zishts′mäsä·zhə] 156

facial mask Gesichtsmaske [gə-zishts′mäskə] 156

factory Fabrik [fäbrēk′] 121

fall *(verb)* fallen [fäl′ən] 25, stürzen [shtir′tsən] 164; **~** *(noun)* Herbst [herpst] 33

falling rocks Steinschlag [shtīn′-shläk] 42

family Familie [fämē′lē·ə] 12, 35

fan Ventilator [ven′tilä′tōr] 53, 91; **~ belt** Keilriemen [kīl′rēmən] 53

far weit [vīt] 40, 59, 116; **as ~ as ...** bis zu ... [bis tsōō ...] 40; **how ~** wie weit [vē vīt] 45

fare Fahrpreis [fär′prīs] 62, 67; **pay the excess ~** zuzahlen [tsōō′tsälən] 66; **~ discount** Ermäßigung [ermä′-sigŏŏng] 67

farewell dinner Abschiedsessen [äp′shētses′ən] 76

farmer Landwirt [länt′virt], Bauer [bou′ər] 36

farmhouse Bauernhaus [bou′ərn-hous] 121

far-sighted weitsichtig [vīt′zishtish] 138

fashion Mode [mō′də]; **~ boutique** Boutique [bŏŏtēk′] 128; **~ show** Modenschau [mō′dənshou] 180

fast schnell [shnel] 42; **This clock is ~** Diese Uhr geht vor [dē′zə ōŏr gāt fōr] 31; **~ train** Eilzug [īl′tsōŏk] 60

fasten seat belts sich anschnallen [zi*sh* än´shnälən] 70

fat Fett [fet] 100

father Vater [fä´tər] 35

father-in-law Schwiegervater [shvē´-gərfä´tər] 35

fatty fett [fet] 115

faucet Wasserhahn [väs´ərhän] 88, 91

fault Fehler [fā´lər] 48

February Februar [fä´brōō-är] 33

fee Gebühr [gəbēr´] 95; **rental ~** Leihgebühr [lī´gəbēr] 95; **usage ~** Benutzungsgebühr [bənoōts´-ōōngsgəbēr] 95

feel fühlen [fē´lən] 12

fencing Fechten [fe*sh*´tən] 188

fender Kotflügel [kōt´flēgəl] 53

ferry Fähre [fār´ə] 72, 76; **car ~** Autofähre [ou´tōfārə]; **train ~** Eisenbahnfähre [ī´zənbänfär´ə] 76

fetch holen [hō´lən] 20

fever Fieber [fē´bər] 161, 170; **~ cure** fiebersenkendes Mittel [fē´bər-zeng´kəndəs mit´əl] 161

fiancé Verlobter [ferlōp´tər] 14

fiancée Verlobte [ferlōp´tə] 14

fibre Faser [fä´zər] 137; **synthetic ~** Kunstfaser [koōnst´fäzər] 137

fight Kampf [kämpf] 187

figs Feigen [fī´gən] 110

figure skating Eiskunstlauf [īs´-koōnstlouf] 188

figurine Figur [figōōr´] 144

file (verb) feilen [fī´lən] 156; **~** (noun) Feile [fī´lə] 57

filet Filet [filä´] 106

fill füllen [fi´lən] 174; **~ her up** volltanken [fōl´tängkən] 45; **~ in** ausfüllen [ous´filən] 78; **~ out** ausfüllen [ous´filən] 78

filled pancakes Palatschinken [pälät-shing´kən] 109

filling Füllung [fi´lōōng] 174; Plombe [plōm´bə] 173; **temporary ~** Einlage [īn´lägə] 174

film (noun) Film [film] 131, 179; **~** (verb) filmen [fil´mən] 132; **cartridge ~** Kassettenfilm [käset´ənfilm] 131; **color ~** Farbfilm [färp´film] 132, 179; **educational ~** Kulturfilm [koōltōōr´-film] 179; **daylight color ~** Tageslicht-

film [tä´gəsli*sh*tfilm´] 132; **reversal ~** Umkehrfilm [ōōm´kärfilm] 132; **roll ~** Rollfilm [rōl´film] 132; **feature ~** Spielfilm [shpēl´film] 179; **~ actor** Filmschauspieler [film´shouspē´-lər] 179; **~ festival** Filmfestspiele [film´festshpē´lə] 179; **super eight color ~** Super-8-Farbfilm [zōō´-pəräht´färp´film] 131; **sixteen millimeter color ~** Sechzehn-Millimeter-Farbfilm [zesh´tsän milimä´tər färp´film] 131; **thirty-five millimeter ~** Fünfunddreißig-Millimeter-Film[fünf´-ōōnt-drī´si*sh* milimä´tər film] 131; **twenty exposure ~** zwanziger Film [tsvän´tsigər film] 131; **thirty-six exposure ~** sechsunddreißiger Film [zeks´ōōnt-drī´sigər film] 131; **color negative ~** Negativ-Farbfilm [nä´gätēf färp´film] 132; **~ screening** Filmvorführung [film´fōr´fē-rōōng] 179

filter Filter [fil´tər] 132

find finden [fin´dən] 19

fine gut [gōōt] 12, 21; (weather) schön [shōn] 25

finger Finger [fing´ər] 167; **index ~** Zeigefinger [tsī´gəfingər] 167; **middle ~** Mittelfinger [mit´əl-fingər] 167; **ring ~** Ringfinger [ring´-fingər] 167

fire Feuer [foi´ər]; **~ department** Feuerwehr [foi´ərvär] 49; **~ extinguisher** Feuerlöscher [foi´ərle-shər] 53, 191; **~ department** Feuerwehr [foi´ərvär] 121

fireplace Kamin [kämēn´] 91

first erste(r) [ers´tə(r)] 29, 59; **~ class** erste Klasse [ers´tə kläs´ə] 62, 64, 69; **~ aid** Erste Hilfe [ärs´tə hil´fə]; **~-aid station** Unfallstation [ōōn´fälshtatsyōn´] 49; Sanitätsraum [zänitāts´roum] 60, 65; Rettungsstation [ret´ōōngs-shtätsyōn] 121; **~-aid kit** Verbandszeug [ferbänts´tsoik] 161

fish (noun) Fisch [fish] 104; **~** (verb) angeln [äng´əln] 185; **~ salad** Fischsalat [fish´zälät´] 102; **~ market** Fischhandlung [fish´händ´lōōng] 128

fisherman Fischer [fish´ər] 36
fishing Angelsport [äng´əlshpôrt]
188; ~ **rod** Angel [äng´əl] 188; **go** ~
angeln [äng´əln] 188; ~**license** An-
gelschein [äng´əlshīn] 188
fishing trawler Fischerboot [fish´ər-
bōt] 75
fit (verb) passen [päs´ən] 133; ~
(noun) Anfall [än´fäl] 170
five fünf [fünf] 28
fix machen [mäh´ən] 50, reparieren
[repärē´rən] 50, 138
flannel Flanell [flänel´] 137
flash Blitz [blits] 132; ~ **bulb** Blitzlicht-
birne [blits´lishtbirnə] 132; ~ **cube**
Blitzlichtwürfel [blits´lishtvēr´fəl] 132
flashing signal Lichthupe [lisht´hōō-
pə] 53
flashlight Taschenlampe [täsh´ən-
lämpə] 144
flat flach [fläh] 139
flight Flug(verbindung) [flōōk´(fer-
bin´dōong)] 68, 71; ~ **attendant** Steward [styōō´ərt], Stewardeß
[styōō´ərdes] 71
flint Feuerstein [foi´ərshtīn] 140
flirt Flirt [flert] 184
floor Fußboden [fōōs´bōdən] 91;
Stock(werk) [shtôk´(verk)] 82; **first** ~
Erdgeschoß [ārt´gəshôs] 191; **second** ~ erster Stock [ers´tər
shtôk] 82, 191; **ground** ~ Erdgeschoß
[ārt´gəshôs] 83
flounder Flunder [flōōn´dər] 104
flower Blume [blōō´mə] 130; ~ **pot**
Blumentopf [blōō´məntôpf] 130
flu Grippe [grip´ə] 170
flush spülen [shpē´lən] 88
fly fliegen [flē´gən] 70
flying time Flugzeit [flōōk´tsīt] 71
FM UKW [ōō´kä´vä´] 182
fog Nebel [nā´bəl] 26, 71
foggy neblig [nāb´lish] 25
follow folgen [fôl´gən] 154
food Kost [kôst] 96, Essen [es´ən] 96,
163, Verpflegung [ferpflā´gōōng] 81;
vegetarian ~ vegetarische Kost [vā-
gätär´ishə kôst] 96; **diet** ~ Diätkost
[dē-ät´kôst] 96; ~ **poisoning** Lebens-
mittelvergiftung [lā´bənsmitəl-
fergif´tōōng] 170

foot (also measure) Fuß [fōōs] 167,
193; **on** ~ zu Fuß [tsōō fōōs] 116; ~
brake Fußbremse [fōōs´bremzə] 51
footpath Fußweg [fōōs´vāk] 119
for für [fēr] 18, 20, 24; (time) seit [zīt]
32; (place) nach [näh] 59, 72; ~**sale** zu
verkaufen [tsōō ferkou´fən] 191
forehead Stirn [shtirn] 167
forester Förster [fers´tər] 36
forgive verzeihen [fertsī´ən] 22
fork Gabel [gä´bəl] 97
form Formular [fôrmōōlär´] 78, 152
fortress Burg [bōōrk] 119
forward (verb) nachsenden [näh´-
zen`dən] 89, 146; ~ (noun; sports)
Stürmer [shtir´mər] 190
fountain Brunnen [brōōn´ən] 121
four vier [fēr] 28
fracture Knochenbruch [knô´hən-
brōōh] 170
frame Brillenfassung [bril´ənfä-
sōōng] 138
free frei [frī] 44; ~ **kick** Freistoß [frī´-
shtōs] 190; ~ **style** Kür [kēr] 188; ~
wheel Freilauf [frī´louf] 53
freeway Autobahn [ou´tōbän] 58
freeze frieren [frē´rən]; **it's freezing**
es friert [es frērt] 27
freighter Frachtschiff [fräht´shif] 77
French Französisch [fräntsœ´zish] 24
fresco Fresko [fres´kō] 125
fresh frisch [frish] 100
Friday Freitag [frī´täk] 33; **Good** ~
Karfreitag [kärfrī´täk] 33
fried gebraten [gəbrä´tən] 100
friend (male) Freund [froint] 14; (female) Freundin [froin´din] 14
from aus [ous] 64; ~ **... to** ... von ... bis
... [fôn ... bis ...] 30
front vorderer Teil [fôr´dərər tīl] 66;
the ~ **...** (car) vorn [fôrn] 46; **up** ~ vorn
[fôrn] 65; ~ **desk** Empfang [em-
pfäng´] 91; ~ **door** Haustür [hous´-
tēr] 91; ~ **seat** Vordersitz [fôr´dər-
zits] 55; ~ **passenger seat** Beifahrer-
sitz [bī´färerzits´] 55; ~ **wheel** Vor-
derrad [fôr´dərät´] 47
frost Frost [frôst] 27
frostbite Erfrierung [erfrēr´ōōng] 170
frozen dessert Halbgefrorenes
[hälp´gəfrörənəs] 109

fruit Obst [ōpst] 109; ~ **cup** Kompott [kômpôt'] 109; ~ **market** Obstgeschäft [ōpst'gəsheft'] 128; ~ **salad** Obstsalat [ōpst'sälät] 109

fryer Hähnchen [hān'shən], Hendl [hen'dəl] 105

fuel Benzin [bentsēn'] 53

full voll [fôl], ~ **beam** Fernlicht [fern'lisht] 53; ~ **coverage insurance** Vollkaskoversicherung [fôl'käs'kōferzish'əroōõng] 41; ~ **fare** einmal [īn'mäl] 59, 62

fullback Verteidiger [fertī'digər] 190

fun Spaß [shpäs] 20, 180

funnel Trichter [trish'tər] 57

fur coat Pelzmantel [pelts'mäntəl] 134

fur jacket Pelzjacke [pelts'yäkə] 134

furrier Pelzhandlung [pelts'händ'loōõng] 128

fuse Sicherung [zish'əroōõng] 53, 88, 91

G

gall bladder Gallenblase [gäl'ənbläzə] 167

gall stones Gallensteine [gäl'ənshtīnə] 170

gallery Galerie [gälərē'] 119, 121

gallon Gallone [gälō'nə] 193

gambling casino Spielkasino [shpēl'käzē'nō] 181

gambling game Spiel [shpēl] 181

game Spiel [shpēl] 180, 187; (animals) Wild [vilt] 107

gangway Gangway [geng'vä] 76

garage Garage [gärä'zhə] 44, 84; Reparaturwerkstatt [repärätōōr'verk'shtät] 50

garden Garten [gär'tən] 121

gardener Gärtner [gert'nər] 37

gargle Gurgelwasser [goōr'gəlväsər] 161

garlic Knoblauch [knôp'louh] 101

garter belt Hüfthalter [hĭft'hältər], Hüfthaltergürtel [hĭft'hältərgĭrtəl] 134

garters Sockenhalter [zôk'ənhältər] 136

gas Benzin [bentsēn']; Gas [gäs] 53; ~ **station** Tankstelle [tängk'shtelə] 45; ~ **bottle** Gasflasche [gäs'fläshə] 94

gasket Dichtung [dish'toōõng] 53

gasoline Benzin [bentsēn'] 41, 45; ~ **can** Benzinkanister [bentsēn'känis'tər] 45

gate Tor [tōr] 121; (airport) Flugsteig [floōk'shtīk] 69, 71

gauze bandage Mullbinde [moōl'bində] 161

gear Sachen [zäh'ən] 185; (car) Gang [gäng] 52, 53; ~ **lever** Schalthebel [shält'hābəl] 53; ~ **oil** Getriebeöl [gətrē'bə-äl] 52

gear-box Getriebe [gətrē'bə] 52

gearshift Gangschaltung [gäng'shältoōõng] 52

general delivery postlagernd [pôst'lägərnt] 149

general practitioner praktischer Arzt [präk'tishər ärtst] 162

genital organs Geschlechtsorgane [gəshleshts'órgä'nə] 167

gentlemen Herren [her'ən] 65, 191; ~! Meine Herren! [mī'nə her'ən] 13

geology Geologie [gä'ōlōgē'] 39

German deutsch [doitsh] 24, 152, 192; ~ **measles** Röteln [rā'təln] 170; **West ~ Mark** Deutsche Mark [doit'shə märk] 192; ~ **marks** Deutsche Mark [doit'shə märk], D-Mark [dā'märk] 152

get bekommen [bəkôm'ən] 18, 78, 95, 126; holen [hō'lən] 20, 48; schikken [shik'ən] 48; ~ **off** aussteigen [ous'shtīgən] 67, 117; ~ **out** aussteigen [ous'shtīgən] 43; ~ **together again** sich wiedersehen [zish vē'dərzā-ən] 17; ~ **to** kommen nach [kôm'ən näh] 19, 40; ~ **in** einsteigen [īn'shtīgən] 67; ~ **aboard** einsteigen [īn'shtīgən] 67

gin Gin [jin] 112

ginger Ingwer [ing'vər] 101

gingerbread Lebkuchen [läp'koōhən] 109

girl Mädchen [mād'shən] 35

give geben [gä´bən] 20, 48, 126
glad froh [frō] 12, 14
gladiolus Gladiole [glädē·ō´lə] 130
gland Drüse [drē´zə] 167
glass Glas [gläs] 96; **water ~** Wasserglas [vä´sərgläs] 97; **wine ~** Weinglas [vīn´gläs] 97
glasses *(spectacles)* Brille [bril´ə] 138
glazier Glaser [glä´zər] 37
glossy *(adj.)* glänzend [glen´tsənt] 132; **~** *(noun)* Illustrierte [il´ŏŏstrēr´tə] 182
gloves Handschuhe [hänt´shŏŏ·ə] 134
glue Klebstoff [kläp´shtôf] 138
glycerine Glyzerin [glitsərēn´] 161
go gehen [gä´ən] 15, 19; fahren [fä´rən] 40, 42, 59
goal Tor [tōr] 187, 190
God Gott [gôt] 125
gold *(noun)* Gold [gôlt] 133; **~ plated** vergoldet [fergôl´dət] 133; **~** *(adj.)* golden [gôl´dən] 194
golf Golf [gôlf] 188
good gut [gŏŏt] 21
good-bye! Auf Wiedersehen! [ouf vē´derzā·ən] 17; **say ~** sich verabschieden [zish ferâp´shēdən] 17
goods Waren [vä´rən] 70
goose Gans [gäns] 105; **roast ~** Gänsebraten [gen´zəbrätən] 105; **wild ~** Wildgans [vilt´gäns] 105; **~ liver paté** Gänseleberpastete [gen´zələbərpästä´tə] 102
gooseberries Stachelbeeren [shtäh´əlbärən] 110
Gospel Evangelium [ā·vang·gä´lē·ŏŏm] 125
Gothic gotisch [gō´tish] 125
goulash Gulasch [gŏŏ´läsh] 106
government office Amt [ämt] 121
grain Strich [shtrish] 157
gram Gramm [gräm] 192
grammar school Volksschule [fôlks´shŏŏlə] 38
grand piano Flügel [flē´gəl] 177
grandchild Enkel(in) [eng´kəl(in)] 35
granddaughter Enkelin [eng´kəlin], Enkeltochter [eng´kəltôhtər] 35
grandfather Großvater [grōs´fätər] 35

grandmother Großmutter [grōs´mŏŏtər] 35
grandparents Großeltern [grōs´eltərn] 35
grandson Enkel [eng´kəl] 35
grapefruit *(South German)* Grapefruit [gräp´frŏŏt], *(North German)* Pampelmuse [päm´pəlmŏŏzə] 110; **~ juice** Grapefruitsaft [gräp´frŏŏt·zäft] 102
grapes Weintrauben [vīn´troubən] 110
grass Rasen [rä´zən] 191
grateful dankbar [dängk´bär] 21
grave Grab [gräp] 121, 125
gravy Bratensoße [brä´tənzōsə] 101
gray grau [grou] 194; **ash ~** aschgrau [äsh´grou] 194; **dark ~** dunkelgrau [dŏŏng´kəlgrou] 194; **pale ~** hellgrau [hel´grou] 194
grease Fett [fet] 53
greasy fettig [fet´ish] 158
great groß [grōs] 22
green grün [grēn] 194; **dark ~** dunkelgrün [dŏŏng´kəlgrēn] 194; **light ~** hellgrün [hel´grēn] 194
grilled gegrillt [gəgrilt´] 100
grill room Grillrestaurant [gril´restōräN´] 91
grocery store Lebensmittelgeschäft [lä´bənsmitəlgəsheft´] 94
grog Grog [grôk] 112
group fare ticket Sammelfahrschein [zäm´əlfär´shīn] 62
grown up erwachsen [ervāk´sən] 35
guard bewachen [bəvāh´ən] 44
guarded bewacht [bəvāht´] 94
guest house Hotelpension [hōtel´-päNsyōn] 91
guide Fremdenführer [frem´dənfērər] 121
guilt Schuld [shŏŏlt] 154
guinea hen Perlhuhn [perl´hŏŏn] 105
gums Zahnfleisch [tsän´flīsh] 174
gym shoes Turnschuhe [tŏŏrn´shŏŏ·ə] 139
gymnast Turner [tŏŏr´nər] 188
gymnastics Gymnastik [gimnäs´tik] 175
gymnastics Turnen [tŏŏr´nən] 188; **~ with apparatus** Geräteturnen [gərä´tətŏŏrnən] 188
gynecologist Frauenarzt [frou´ən-

ärtst], Gynäkologe [gînekōlōʹgə] 162

H

haberdashery Kurzwarengeschäft [koŏrts'värəngəsheft'] 128

haddock Schellfisch [shelʹfish] 104

hail Hagel [häʹgəl] 27; **it's hailing** es hagelt [es häʹgəlt] 27

hair Haar [här] 155, 156, 167; ~ **spray** Haarspray [härʹshprä] 141, 156; ~ **tonic** Haarwasser [härʹväsər] 141, 157; ~ **conditioner** Haarspülung [härʹshpēloŏng] 141; ~ **net** Haarnetz [härʹnets] 141; ~ **style** Frisur [frizōōrʹ] 158; ~ **drier** Trockenhaube [trōkʹənhoubə] 158; ~ **loss** Haarausfall [härʹousfäl] 158

hairbrush Haarbürste [härʹbirstə] 141

haircut Haarschnitt [härʹshnit] 157

hair-do Frisur [frizōōrʹ] 158; **hairdresser** Damenfriseur [däʹmənfrizär'], Damenfriseuse [däʹmənfrizäʹzə] 158

hairpiece Haarteil [härʹtīl] 156

hairpin Haarnadel [härʹnädəl] 141

half halb [hälp] 30; ~ **fare** Kinderfahrkarte [kindʹərfär'kärtə] 59, 62; ~ **time** Halbzeit [hälpʹtsīt] 188

halibut Heilbutt [hīlʹboŏt] 104

hall Gang [gäng] 91

ham Schinken [shingʹkən] 102, 107

hammer Hammer [hämʹər] 57

hammock Hängematte [hengʹəmätə] 144

hand Hand [hänt] 167; (clock) Zeiger [tsīʹgər] 143; ~ **brake** Handbremse [häntʹbremzə] 51; ~ **luggage** Handgepäck [häntʹgəpek] 63, 69, 71

handbag Handtasche [häntʹtäshə] 144, 153

handball Handball [häntʹbäl] 189

handicrafts Handarbeiten [häntʹärbītən] 144

handkerchief Taschentuch [täshʹəntōōh] 134

handle Griff [grif] 53

happen geschehen [gəshäʹən] 18

harbor Hafen [häʹfən] 72, 76, 116, 121; ~ **police (station)** Hafenpolizei [häʹfənpōlitsī] 73

hard hart [härt] 100, 115

hare Hase [häʹzə] 106

hat Hut [hoŏt] 134; **straw ~** Strohhut [shtrōʹhoŏt] 134

have haben [häʹbən] 16, 18, 20, 23, 25, 41, 44

hay fever Heuschnupfen [hoiʹshnoŏpfən] 170

hazel nuts Haselnüsse [häʹzəlnisə] 110

he er [är]

head Kopf [kôpf] 167; ~ **clerk** Chefportier [shefʹpôrtyä'] 91; ~ **conductor** Zugführer [tsoŏkʹfērər] 67; ~ **nurse** Oberschwester [ōʹbərshvestər] 172

headlight Scheinwerfer [shīnʹverfər] 53

head-on collision Frontalzusammenstoß [frôntälʹtsoŏzäm'ənshtôs] 49

health resort Luftkurort [loŏftʹkoŏrôrt] 175

heart Herz [herts] 170; ~ **attack** Herzanfall [hertsʹänfäl] 170; ~ **problems** Herzbeschwerden [hertsʹbəshvärdən] 170

heartburn Sodbrennen [zōtʹbrenən] 170

hearts (cards) Herz [herts] 181

heat Hitze [hitsʹə] 27, 163

heating (system) Heizung [hīʹtsoŏng] 53, 67, 88, 91; **central ~** Zentralheizung [tsenträlʹhītsoŏng] 90

heel Absatz [äpʹzäts] 139, Ferse [ferʹzə] 167

height Größe [grōʹsə] 79

helicopter Hubschrauber [hoŏpʹshroubər] 71

hello! Guten Tag! [goŏʹtən täk], Grüß Gott! [grēs gôt] 12

helm Steuer [shtoiʹər] 76

helmsman Steuermann [shtoiʹərmän] 76

help (verb) helfen [helʹfən] 20, 66; (noun) Hilfe [hilʹfə] 18, 20, 21, 49

hemorrhage Blutung [bloŏʹtoŏng] 170

hemorrhoids Hämorrhoiden [hem`ô-rō-ēʹdən] 170

herbs Kräuter [kroi'tər] 101

here hier [hēr] 14, 40, 75, 89

herring Hering [hār'ing] 104; ~ **salad** Heringssalat [hār'ings-zálät'] 102

Hi! Hallo! [hálō'] 12

high hoch [hōh] 70, 139, 169; ~ **mass** Hochamt [hōh'ämt] 123; ~ **pressure (system)** Hoch [hōh] 27; ~ **school** *(academic)* Gymnasium [gimnä'-zē·ōōm] 39; *(general)* Oberschule [ō'bərshōō'lə] 39; ~ **test** Super [zōō'pər] 45

high-rise building Hochhaus [hōh'-hous] 121

highway Autobahn [ou'tōbän] 42; ~ **patrol** Verkehrspolizei [ferkārs'pōli-tsī'] 42

hiking path Fußweg [fōōs'vāk] 121

hill Berg [bärk] 121

hip Hüfte [hif'tə] 167

history Geschichte [gəshish'tə] 39

hitch-hike per Anhalter (Autostopp) fahren [per än'hältər (ou'tō-shtôp') fä'rən] 43

hoarseness Heiserkeit [hī'zərkīt] 170

hockey Eishockey [īs'hôkē] 189

holdup Überfall [ē'bərfäl] 153

home nach Hause [näh hou'zə] 17; **at ~** zu Hause [tsōō hou'zə] 15

honey Honig [hō'nish] 98

hood (Motor)Haube [(mō'tôr)hou'-bə] 53

horn Hupe [hōō'pə] 53

horse Pferd [pfärt] 189; ~ **race** Pferderennen [pfär'dərenən], Galopprennen [gálôp'renən] 189; ~ **cart** Pferdewagen [pfär'dəvä'gən] 41

horseradish Meerrettich [mā'retish] 101

hospital Krankenhaus [kräng'kən-hous] 49, 121, 162, 172, Klinik [klē'-nik] 162, 172

hostel father Herbergsvater [hār'-bärksfä'tər] 95

hostel mother Herbergsmutter [hār'-bärksmōōt'ər] 95

hostel parents Herbergseltern [hār'-bärksel'tərn] 95

hot heiß [hīs], warm [värm] 25, 51, 93, 100; *(spicy)* scharf [shärf] 100; ~ **chocolate** heiße Schokolade [hī'sə

shōkōlä'də] 98; ~ **spring** Thermalquelle [termäl'kvelə] 175

hotel Hotel [hōtel'] 81, 91; **beach ~** Strandhotel [shtránt'hōtel'] 91; ~ **restaurant** Hotelrestaurant [hōtel'restō-räN'] 91

hour Stunde [shtōōn'də] 31; **every ~** stündlich [shtint'lish] 31; **quarter ~** Viertelstunde [fir'təlshtōōn'də] 87; **half ~** halbe Stunde [häl'bə shtōōn'də] 87

hourly stündlich [shtint'lish] 31

house Haus [hous] 91, 121; ~ **key** Hausschlüssel [hous'shlisəl] 92; ~ **number** Hausnummer [hous'nōō-mər] 121

how wie [vē] 12, 14, 18; ~ **much (many)?** wieviel? [vēfēl'], wie viele? [vē fē'lə] 18; ~ **far?** wie weit entfernt? [vē vīt entfernt'] 72

hub Nabe [nä'bə] 53; ~ **cap** Radkappe [rät'käpə] 53

hundred hundert [hōōn'dərt] 151

hundredweight Zentner [tsent'nər] 193

hunting Jagd [yäkt] 189; ~ **license** Jagdschein [yäkt'shīn] 189

hurt *(verb)* schmerzen [shmer'tsən] 163; ~ *(adj.)* verletzt [ferletst'] 49

husband (Ehe)Mann [(ā'ə)män], Gatte [gät'ə] 13, 14, 35, 162

hydrogen peroxide Wasserstoffsuperoxyd [väs'ərshtôfzōō'pərōksēt'] 161

hypertension Hypertonie [hēpərtō-nē'] 170

I

I ich [ish]

ice Eis [īs] 27

ice cream Eis [īs], Eiscreme [īs'krām] 109; ~ **parlor** Eisdiele [īs'dēlə] 113; **chocolate with ~** Eisschokolade [īs'-shōkōlä'də] 113; **vanilla ~** Vanilleeis [vänil'yə-īs] 113; **chocolate ~** Schokoladeneis [shōkōlä'dən·īs] 113; **strawberry ~** Erdbeereis [ārt'-bār·īs] 113; **assorted ~** gemischtes Eis [gəmish'təs īs] 113

ice skating rink Eisbahn [īs´bän] 180
iceberg lettuce Eissalat [īs´zälät`] 107
icy road Glatteis [glät´īs] 27
identity card Ausweis [ous´vīs] 79
ignition Zündung [tsín´doong] 54; ~ **key** Zündschlüssel [tsínt´shlísəl] 54; ~ **lock** Zündschloß [tsínt´shlôs] 54
illness Krankheit [krángk´hīt] 170
impact Aufprall [ouf´präl] 49
inch Zoll [tsôl] 193
incisor Schneidezahn [shnī´dətsän] 174
included inbegriffen [in´bəgrifən] 83, 118
including einschließlich [īn´shlēslish] 41
indicator light Kontrollampe [kôntrôl´lämpə] 54
indigestion Verdauungsstörung [ferdou´oongs-shtå´roong] 170
inflammation Entzündung [entsín´doong] 170
influenza Grippe [grip´ə] 170
information Auskunft [ous´koonft] 65,67,71; *(telephone)* Fernsprechauskunft [fern´shpreshous`koonft] 149; ~ **office** Auskunftsbüro [ous´koonftsbērō`] 60; ~ **counter** Informationsschalter [infôrmätsyōns´shältər] 69, 71
infusion Infusion [infōōzyōn´] 172
ingredient Zutat [tsoō´tät] 100
inhale inhalieren [inhälē´rən] 175
injection Spritze [shprits´ə] 161, 172, 174
injure verletzen [ferlets´ən] 48
injury Verletzung [ferlets´oong] 49, 170
ink Tinte [tin´tə] 138
inn Gasthof [gäst´hōf] 81
inner tube *(tire)* Schlauch [shlouh] 46
innocent unschuldig [oon´shooldish] 154
inquiry Erkundigung [erkoōn´digoong] 92
insect repellent Insektenmittel [inzek´tənmitəl] 161
inside innen [in´ən] 47
in-sole Einlegesohle [īn´lāgəzō`lə] 139

insomnia Schlaflosigkeit [shläf´lōzishkīt`] 170
inspection Überprüfung [ēbərprē´foong]; ~ **light** Prüflampe [prēf´lämpə] 57
insulation Isolierung [izōlēr´oong] 54
insurance Versicherung [ferzish´əroong] 49; ~ **certificate** Versicherungskarte [ferzish´əroōongskär`tə] 79
insure versichern [ferzish´ərn] 49, 63
insured mail versicherte Sendung [ferzish´ərtə zen´doong] 149
intensive care unit Intensivstation [intenzēf´shtätsyōn] 172
intermediate landing Zwischenlandung [tsvish´ənländoong] 71
intermission Pause [pou´zə] 177
internal innerlich [in´ərlish] 159
internist Internist [intərnist´] 162
interpreter Dolmetscher [dôl´metshər] 37
interrupt unterbrechen [oontərbresh´ən] 61, 62
interrupter Unterbrecher [oontərbresh´ər] 54
intersection Kreuzung [kroi´tsoong] 42, 58
intestine Darm [därm] 167
invitation Einladung [īn´lädoong] 16
invite einladen [īn´lädən] 183
iodine Jodtinktur [yōt´tingktōr] 161
iron bügeln [bē´gəln] 92, 95
Islam Islam [is´läm, isläm´] 125
island Insel [in´zəl] 76

J

jack *(cards)* Bube [boō´bə] 181; *(tool)* Wagenheber [vä´gənhā`bər] 47, 57
jacket *(lady's)* Jackett [zhäket´] 134; *(man's)* Jacke [yäk´ə], Sakko [zäk´ō] 134
jackknife Taschenmesser [täsh´ənmesər] 144
jam Marmelade [märmələ´də] 98
January Januar [yän´ōō-är] 33
jar Glas [gläs] 126
jaundice Gelbsucht [gelp´zoōht] 170

jaw Kiefer [kē´fər] 167, 174; **upper ~** Oberkiefer [ō´bərkēfər] 167; **lower ~** Unterkiefer [oon´tərkēfər] 167

jelly *(aspic)* Gelee [zhelā´] 101; *(fruit)* Konfitüre [kônfitē´rə] 101; **~ doughnuts** Krapfen [kräpf´ən] 109

jersey Jersey [jär´zē] 137

jet Düse [dē´zə] 71; **~ plane** Düsenflugzeug [dē´zənfl ̄ook´tsoik] 71

jetty Mole [mō´lə] 76

Jew Jude [yoo´də] 124

jeweler Juwelier [yōovəlēr´] 133

jewelry Schmuck [shmook] 133, 153; **costume ~** Modeschmuck [mō´dəshmook] 133

Jewish jüdisch [yē´dish] 125

joint Gelenk [gəlengk´] 167

joker *(cards)* Joker [yō´kər] 181

journalism Publizistik [poob`litsis´-tik] 39

journalist Journalist [zhoornälist´] 37

journey Fahrt [färt] 43

Judaism Judentum [yoo´dəntoom] 125

judge Richter [rish´tər] 37, 154

judo Judo [yoo´dō] 189

juice Saft [zäft] 98, 112; **fruit ~** Fruchtsaft [frookht´zäft] 98, 112; **orange ~** Orangensaft [ōräN´zhənzäft`] 98, 112; **grapefruit ~** Grapefruitsaft [grāp´fr ̄oot-zäft] 112; **apple ~** Apfelsaft [äp´fəlzäft] 112

juicy saftig [zäf´tish] 100

July Juli [yoo´lē] 33

jumping Springen [shpring´ən] 189

June Juni [yoo´nē] 33

K

kale Grünkohl [grēn´kōl] 107

keep behalten [bəhäl´tən] 115

kerchief Kopftuch [kôpf´tooh] 144

ketchup Ketchup [ketsh´äp] 101

key Schlüssel [shlis´əl] 85, 88, 153

kidnapping Entführung [entfē´-rōong] 153

kidney Niere [nēr´ə] 106, 167; **~ stones** Nierensteine [nē´rənshtīnə] 170

kilogram Kilogramm [kē´lōgräm] 193

kilometer Kilometer [kēlōmā´tər] 40, 193

kind: what **~ of** ... was für ... [väs fēr ...] 18

king König [kä´nish] 181

kiss *(noun)* Kuß [koos] 183; **~** *(verb)* küssen [kis´ən] 183

kitchen Küche [kish´ə] 92

kitchenette Kochnische [kôh´nēshə] 92

knee Knie [knē] 167; **~ socks** Kniestrümpfe [knē´shtrimpfə] 134

kneecap Kniescheibe [knē´shībə] 167

knife Messer [mes´ər] 97; **pocket ~** Taschenmesser [täsh´ənmesər] 144

knight *(chess)* Springer [shpring´ər] 181

knock klopfen [klôpf´ən] 54

knot Knoten [knō´tən] 76

L

ladies Damen [dä´mən] 65, 191; **~!** Meine Damen! [mī´nə dä´mən] 13

ladies' room Damentoilette [dä´məntō-älet`ə] 92

lake See [zā] 76

lamb Lamm(fleisch) [läm´(flīsh)] 106

lamp Lampe [läm´pə] 54, 92; **reading ~** Nachttischlampe [näht´tishlämp`ə] 92

land *(noun)* Land [länt] 76; **~** *(verb; ships)* anlegen [än´lāgən] 72, 76; *(planes)* landen [län´dən] 69, 70

landing Landung [län´doong] 71; **~ gear** Fahrwerk [fär´verk] 71; **~ place** Anlegeplatz [än´lāgəpläts] 76; **~ stage** Anlegesteg [än´lāgəshtāk], Landungsbrücke [län´doongsbrik`ə] 76

landscape Landschaft [länt´shäft] 121

lane Fahrspur [fär´shpoor] 42; Gasse [gäs´ə] 121; **get in ~** sich einordnen [zish īn´ôrdnən] 43

lap rug Wolldecke [vôl´dekə] 76

lard Schweineschmalz [shvī´nəshmälts] 101

larynx Kehlkopf [kāl´kôpf] 167

last letzte(r) [lets´tə(r)] 59; ~ **year** voriges Jahr [fō´rigəs yär] 32; ~ **stop** Endhaltestelle [ent´hältəshtel´ə] 59, 121

late spät [shpāt] 17, 31; **be** ~ *(trains, planes)* Verspätung haben [fershpā´tŏŏng hä´bən] 61, 69

later später [shpā´tər] 15, 32

launch Barkasse [bärkäs´ə] 75

launder waschen [väsh´ən] 87, 137

laundromat Waschsalon [väsh´zälōN´] 129, 137

laundry Wäsche [vesh´ə] 92; *(shop)* Wäscherei [vesherī´] 129

lavender lila [lē´lä] 194

law Jura [yŏŏ´rä] 39

lawyer Rechtsanwalt [reshts´änvält] 37, 154

laxative Abführmittel [äp´fērmit´əl] 161

lead *(road, path)* führen [fē´rən] 19

leak *(verb)* tropfen [trôpf´ən] 52; ~ *(noun)* Leck [lek] 53

lean mager [mä´gər] 100

leash Leine [lī´nə] 144

leather Leder [lā´dər] 126, 139; ~ **coat** Ledermantel [lā´dərmäntəl] 134; ~ **jacket** Lederjacke [lā´dəryäkə] 134

leave *(let)* lassen [läs´ən] 15, 44; *(for a trip)* abreisen [äp´rīzən] 34, 89, abfahren [äp´färən] 59, 61; *(continue a trip)* weiterfahren [vī´tərfä´rən] 44; ~ **for** abfahren [äp´färən] 72; *(a car)* unterstellen [ŏŏn´tərshtel´ən] 44; ~ **... here** hierlassen [hēr´läsən] 63

lecture Vorlesung [fōr´lāzŏŏng] 38

left links [lingks] 40, 116

leg Bein [bīn] 167; *(food)* Keule [koi´lə] 106; **lower** ~ Unterschenkel [ŏŏn´tərsheng´kəl] 167

legitimate theatre Schauspiel [shou´shpēl] 177

lemon Zitrone [tsi´trō´nə] 101, 110; ~ **cream** Zitronencreme [tsitrō´nənkräm´] 109

lemonade Zitronenlimonade [tsitrō´nənlimōnä´də] 112

lend leihen [lī´ən] 48

lengthen verlängern [ferleng´ərn] 137

lens Linse [lin´zə], Glas [gläs] 138; *(camera)* Objektiv [ôp´yektēf´] 132

letter Brief [brēf] 34, 85, 145; **local** ~ Inlandsbrief [in´läntsbrēf] 145; **registered** ~ Einschreibebrief [īn´shrībəbrēf] 145; **night** ~ Brieftelegramm [brēf´tälägräm] 147, 150; **special delivery** ~ Eilbrief [īl´brēf] 145; ~ **abroad** Auslandsbrief [ous´läntsbrēf] 145

leukemia Leukämie [loikämē´] 170

librarian Bibliothekar [bib´lē-ōtäkär´] 37

library Bibliothek [bi´blē-ōtäk´], Bücherei [bēsherī´] 121

libretto Text [tekst] 177

license plate Nummernschild [nŏŏm´ərnshilt] 54

life Leben [lā´bən]; ~ **jacket** Schwimmweste [shvim´vestə] 71; ~ **belt** Rettungsring [ret´ŏŏngsring´] 76; ~ **jacket** Schwimmweste [shvim´vestə] 76

lifeboat Rettungsboot [ret´ŏŏngsbōt] 75

lifeguard Bademeister [bä´dəmīstər] 185

lift: give someone a ~ jemanden ein Stück mitnehmen [yä´mändən īn shtïk mit´nä´mən] 17, 48

light *(adj.)* hell [hel] 127; ~ *(noun)* Licht [lisht] 88; **lighter** Feuerzeug [foi´ərtsoik] 140; **gas** ~ Gasfeuerzeug [gäs´foi-ərtsoik] 140; ~ **fluid** Feuerzeugbenzin [foi´ərtsoikbentsēn´] 140

lighthouse Leuchtturm [loisht´tŏŏrm] 76

lighting system Beleuchtung [bəloish´tŏŏng] 54

lightning Blitz [blits] 27

lights Beleuchtung [bəloish´tŏŏng] 92

like mögen [mö´gən] 16, 73; **Do you** ~ **...?** Gefällt dir ...? [gəfelt´ dēr ...] 14; **I'd like ...** Ich hätte gern ... [ish het´ə gern ...] 20; **I'd like to ...** Ich möchte ... [ish mesh´tə ...] 23, 45, 63

lilac Flieder [flē´dər] 130

limb *(Körper)*Glied [(ker´pər)glēt] 167

linen Leinen [lī'nən] 137

lingerie Damenunterwäsche [dä'-mənŏŏn'tərveshə] 134

liniment Einreibemittel [īn'rībəmit'-əl] 161

lining Futter [fŏŏt'ər] 136

lip Lippe [lip'ə] 167

lipstick Lippenstift [lip'ənshtift] 141

liqueur Likör [likär'] 112

liter Liter [lē'tər] 45, 193

little klein [klīn]; **a ~** etwas [et'väs] 24; **~ sparrows** Spätzle [shpets'lə] 104

live leben [lā'bən] 119; *(in a place)* wohnen [vō'nən] 14, 15, 19, 184

liver Leber [lā'bər] 106, 167; **~ problem** Leberleiden [lā'bərlīdən] 170

living room Wohnzimmer [vōn'tsimər] 67

loafers Slipper [slip'ər] 139

loan leihen [lī'ən] 57

lobby Foyer [fō-äyā'] 177; Halle [häl'ə] 92

lobster Hummer [hŏŏm'ər] 104; **spiny ~** Languste [läng·gŏŏs'tə] 105; **rock ~** Languste [läng·gŏŏs'tə] 105; **~ cocktail** Hummercocktail [hŏŏm'ərkôk'tāl] 102; **~ bisque** Hummersuppe [hŏŏm'ərzŏŏpə] 103

local call Ortsgespräch [ôrts'gəshpräsh] 149

located: Where is ... ~? Wo befindet sich ...? [vō bəfin'dət zish ...] 19

lock *(noun)* Türschloß [tēr'shlôs] 92; **~ up** abschließen [äp'shlēsən] 92

locker room Umkleideraum [ŏŏm'-klīdəroum] 186

lockjaw Tetanus [tet'änŏŏs] 171

locksmith Schlosser [shlôs'ər] 37

locomotive Lokomotive [lōkōmōtē'-və] 67

long *(dimension)* lang [läng] 133, 148, 155; *(time)* lange [läng'ə] 14, 18, 40, 44, 72; **~ distance express** Fernschnellzug [fern'shnel'tsŏŏk] 60; **~ wave** Langwelle [läng'velə] 182

look: ~ for suchen [zŏŏ'hən] 15, 18; **~ after** sich kümmern um [zish kim'ərn ŏŏm] 49

loose lose [lō'zə], wacklig [väk'-lish] 173

loosen lockern [lôk'ərn] 55

lose verlieren [ferlē'rən] 153

loss Verlust [ferlŏŏst'] 153

lounge Aufenthaltsraum [ouf'enthältsroum'] 74, 86

love *(noun)* Liebe [lē'bə] 183; **~** *(verb)* lieben [lē'bən] 16, 183

lovely nett [net] 16, 17

low niedrig [nē'drig] 169; **~ pressure (system)** Tief [tēf] 27

lubricant Schmierstoff [shmēr'shtôf] 54

luck Glück [glik]; **Good ~!** Viel Glück [fēl glik] 23

luggage Gepäck [gəpek'] 59, 63, 67, 73, 84, 89; **~ car** Gepäckwagen [gəpek'vägən] 64; **~ forwarding office** Gepäckabfertigung [gəpek'äpfer'-tigŏŏng] 63; **~ locker** Schließfach [shlēs'fäh] 63; **~ rack** Gepäcknetz [gəpek'nets] 67

lumbago Hexenschuß [hek'sənshŏŏs] 171

lunch Mittagessen [mit'äk·esən] 92, 99

lung Lunge [lŏŏng'ə] 106, 167

M

macaroni Makkaroni [mäkärō'nē] 103

macaroon Makrone [mäkrō'nə] 113

mackerel Makrele [mäkrā'lə] 104

Madam Madame [mädäm'], Gnädige Frau [gnä'digə frou] 13

magazine Zeitschrift [tsīt'shrift] 182; **fashion ~** Modezeitschrift [mō'dətsītshrift] 182

maid Zimmermädchen [tsim'ərmädshən] 87, 92

maiden name Geburtsname [gəbŏŏrts'nämə] 79

mail *(verb)* abschicken [äp'shikən] 34; **~** *(noun)* Post [pôst] 85, 89, 146; **~ box** Briefkasten [brēf'kästən] 145, 150; **mailman** Briefträger [brēf'trägər] 37, 150

main road Hauptstraße [houpt'-shträ`sə] 43

main station Hauptbahnhof [houpt'-bänhōf] 60

main street Hauptstraße [houpt´-
shträ´sə] 43, 121
major Studienfach [shtōō´dē-ənfäh]
38
male organ Glied [glēt] 167
malt liquor Starkbier [shtärk´bēr] 111
manager Geschäftsführer [gə-
shefts´fērər] 23, 88
manicure Maniküre [mänikē´rə] 156,
158
many viel(e) [fēl(´ə)]; **how ~** wieviel
[vēfēl´], **wie viele** [vē fēl´ə] 18, 40
map (Land)karte [(länt´)kär´tə] 40,
130; **city ~** Stadtplan [shtät´plän]
130; **road ~** Straßenkarte [shträ´sən-
kärtə] 130; **street ~** Stadtplan
[shtät´plän] 130
March März [merts] 33
margarine Margarine [märgärē´nə]
101
marinated gepökelt [gəpö´kəlt] 107
marital status Familienstand [fämē´-
lē-ənshtänt`] 79
mark Kennzeichen [ken´tsīshən] 79
marksmanship Schießsport [shēs´-
shpôrt] 189
marriage Vermählung [fermä´lōōng] 22
married verheiratet [ferhī´rätət] 79
mascara Wimperntusche [vim´pərn-
tōōshə], Mascara [mäskä´rä] 156
mass Messe [mes´ə] 125; **high ~**
Hochamt [hōh´ämt] 125
massage (noun) Massage [mä-
sä´zhə] 175; **~** (verb) massieren
[mäsē´rən] 175
masseur Masseur [mäsär´] 175
masseuse Masseuse [mäsä´zə] 175
mast Mast [mäst] 76
mat Untersetzer [ōōn´tərzetsər]
144
match (sports) Spiel [shpēl] 188
matches Streichhölzer [shtrīsh´hel-
tsər] 140
material Stoff [shtôf] 137
mathematics Mathematik [mä´tämä-
tēk`] 39
matte matt [mät] 132
mattress Matratze [mäträts´ə] 90
mauve lila [lē´lä] 194
maximum speed Höchstgeschwindigkeit [hāshst´gəshvin`dishkīt] 42
May Mai [mī] 33
maybe vielleicht [filīsht´] 21
mayonnaise Mayonnaise [mäyō-
nä´zə] 101, 102; **~ sauce** Remoula-
densoße [remōōlä´dənzōs`ə] 101
meal Essen [es´ən] 86, 96, 159
mean bedeuten [bədoi´tən] 18, 24
meanwhile während dieser Zeit [vä´-
rənt dē´zər tsīt] 92
measles Masern [mä´zərn] 171
measure Maß [mäs] 193
meat Fleisch [flīsh] 105; **~ loaf** Deut-
sches Beefsteak [doit´shəs bēf´-
stäk] 105; **ground ~** (German) Hack-
fleisch [häk´flīsh] 106, (Austrian) Fa-
schiertes [fäshēr´təs] 106
meat aspic Fleischsülze [flīsh´zíltsə]
102
mechanic Mechaniker [meshä´nikər]
37; 48
mechanical engineering Maschinen-
bau [mäshē´nənbou] 39
medical director Chefarzt [shef´ärtst]
172
medication medizinische Behandlung
[meditsē´nishə bəhänt´lōōng] 160
medicinal spring Heilquelle [hīl´-
kvelə] 175
medicine Medikament [med`ikä-
ment´] 159, 161; (discipline) Medizin
[mä`ditsēn´] 39
meditation Andacht [än´däht] 125
medium halbdurch [hälp´dōōrsh`],
medium [mē´dē-ōōm] 100
meet treffen [tref´ən] 14, 15, 118,
184;**~again**(sich)wiedersehen[(zish)
vē´dərzä-ən] 16, 183
melon Melone [melō´nə] 102, 110;
honeydew ~ Honigmelone [hō´nish-
melō´nə] 110; **water~** Wassermelo-
ne [väs´ərmelō´nə] 110
membership card Mitgliedskarte
[mit´glētskär`tə] 95
memorial Gedenkstätte [gədenk´-
shtetə] 119, 121
men's room Herrentoilette [her´ən-
tō-älet`ə] 92
menstruation Menstruation [men`-
strōō-ätsyōn´], Monatsregel [mō´-
nätsrä`gəl] 167

mention: Don't ~ it Keine Ursache [kī´nə ōōr´zähə] 21

menue Speisekarte [shpī´zəkärtə] 96

meringue Sahnebaiser [zä´nəbäzä´] 113

metabolism Stoffwechsel [shtôf´veksəl] 167

metalworker Schlosser [shlôs´ər] 37

meter Meter [mā´tər] 192

Methodist Methodist [met`ōdist´] 124

middle Mitte [mit´ə] 65, 176; **~ ear inflammation** Mittelohrentzündung [mit´əlōrentsin´dōōng] 171

midfield man Mittelfeldspieler [mi´təlfeltshpē´ələr] 190

midnight Mitternacht [mit´ərnäht] 31

midwife Hebamme [hāb´ämə] 37

mile Meile [mī´lə] 193; **nautical ~** Seemeile [zā´mīlə] 193

mileage indicator Kilometerzähler [kēlōmā´tərtsä´lər] 54

military base Kaserne [käzer´nə] 121

milk Milch [milsh] 98, 114; **evaporated ~** Kondensmilch [kôndens´milsh] 114; **condensed ~** Kondensmilch [kôndens´milsh] 98; **~ shake** Milchmixgetränk [milsh´miksgətrengk´] 112

millimeter Millimeter [milēmā´tər] 193

mine mein [mīn] 80

miner Bergmann [berk´män] 37

minerals Mineralien [min`erä´lē·ən] 175

miniature golf Minigolf [min´ēgôlf] 180; **~ course** Minigolfanlage [min´ēgôlfän´lägə] 180

ministry Ministerium [min`istär´ē-ōōm] 121

minute Minute [minōō´tə] 30, 86; **just a ~** einen Augenblick [ī´nən ou´gənblik] 16

mirror Spiegel [shpē´gəl] 55, 92, 141

miss fehlen [fā´lən] 23, 63; *(motor)* stottern [shtôt´ərn] 54

Miss ... Fräulein ... [froi´līn ...] 13

mist Nebel [nā´bəl] 27

misty neblig [nāb´lish] 25

molar Mahlzahn [mäl´tsän] 174

mole Mole [mō´lə] 76

moment Moment [mōment´] 87; **at the ~** zur Zeit [tsōōr tsīt] 32

monastery Kloster [klōs´tər] 125

Monday Montag [mōn´täk] 33

money Geld [gelt] 85, 151, 153; **~ exchange** Wechselstube [vek´səlshtōō´bə] 60, Geldwechsel [gelt´veksəl] 152; **~ order** Zahlkarte [tsäl´kärtə] 146

month Monat [mō´nät] 32

monument Denkmal [dengk´mäl] 119, 121

moon Mond [mōnt] 27

moped Moped [mō´pet] 41

morning Morgen [môr´gən] 31; **Good ~!** Guten Morgen! [gōō´tən môr´gən] 12; **in the ~** morgens [môr´gəns] 31; **this ~** heute morgen [hoi´tə môr´gən] 31

mortal danger Lebensgefahr [lā´bənsgəfär] 191

mortgage Hypothek [hēpōtāk´] 152

mosaic Mosaik [mōzä·ēk´] 125

Moslem Moslem [môs´lem], Muslim [mōōs´lim] 124

mosque Moschee [môshā´] 125

motel Motel [mōtel´] 81

mother Mutter [mōō´tər] 35

mother-in-law Schwiegermutter [shvē´gərmōōtər] 35

motion picture theater Kino [kē´nō] 121, 179

motor Motor [mō´tôr] 54; **~ scooter** Motorroller [mō´tôrôl`ər] 41; **~ oil** Motoröl [mō´tôräl´] 46

motorail service Autoreisezug [ou´tōrī´zətsōōk´] 60

motorboat Motorboot [mō´tôrbōt] 75, 186

motorcycle Motorrad [mō´tōrät] 41, 42, 73

mountain Berg [bärk] 121; **~ range** Gebirge [gəbir´gə] 121; **~ climber** Bergsteiger [berk´shtīgər] 189; **~ climbing** Bergsteigen [berk´shtīgən] 189

mountains Gebirge [gəbir´gə] 70

mousse Mousse [mōōs] 109

moustache Schnurrbart [shnōōr´bärt] 157

mouth Mund [mōōnt] 165, 167

mouthwash Mundwasser [mŏŏnt'vä-sər] 141, 161

move *(verb)* bewegen [bəvā'gən] 164; *(e. g. apartment)* umziehen [ŏŏm'tsē·ən] 92; ~ **in** einziehen [īn'tsē·ən] 92; ~ **out** ausziehen [ous'tsē·ən] 92; ~ *(noun; games)* Zug [tsŏŏk] 182

movie Film [film] 179; ~ **house** Kino [kē'nō] 179

movies Kino [kē'nō] 179

Mr. ... Herr ... [her ...] 13

Mrs. ... Frau ... [frou ...] 13

much viel [fēl] 127; **too** ~ zuviel [tsŏŏ-fēl'] 127; **how** ~ wieviel [vēfēl'] 18, 19, 41, etc.; **how** ~ **is ...** was kostet ... [väs kôs'tət ...] 62, 68

mud Schlamm [shläm] 175; ~ **bath** Moorbad [mōr'bät] 175; ~ **pack** Packung [päk'ŏŏng] 175

muggy schwül [shvēl] 25

mumps Mumps [mŏŏmps] 171

murder Mord [môrt] 153

Muscatel Muskatellerwein [mŏŏs'-kätel'ərvīn] 111

muscle Muskel [mŏŏs'kəl] 168

museum Museum [mŏŏzā'ŏŏm] 116, 119, 121

mushroom Pilz [pilts] 101, 108, Champignon [shäm'pinyōN'] 101

music Musik [mŏŏzēk'] 177; **piece of** ~ Musikstück [mŏŏzēk'shtĭk] 178

musical Musical [myŏŏ'zikəl] 177

musician Musiker [mŏŏ'zikər] 37

musicology Musikwissenschaft [mŏŏ-zēk'vis'ənshäft] 39

mussel Muschel [mŏŏsh'əl], Miesmuschel [mēs'mŏŏshəl] 105

must müssen [mĭs'ən] 22

mustard Senf [zenf] 101; ~ **jar** Senfglas [zenf'gläs] 97

mutton Hammelfleisch [häm'əlflīsh] 106

my mein(e) [mīn('ə)] 48, etc.

N

nail Nagel [nä'gəl] 141, 156, 168; ~ **file** Nagelfeile [nä'gəlfīlə] 141; ~ **polish** Nagellack [nä'gəläk] 141,

156; ~ **polish remover** Nagellackentferner [nä'gəläkentfer'nər] 141; ~ **scissors** Nagelschere [nä'gəlshärə] 141

name Name [nä'mə] 14, 19, 48, 79; **first** ~ Vorname [fōr'nämə] 79; **last** ~ Familienname [fämē'lē·ən·nämə] 79

napkin Serviette [zervē·et'ə] 97

narcotics Rauschgift [roush'gift] 154

narrow schmal [shmäl] 127

national park Naturschutzgebiet [nätŏŏr'shŏŏtsgəbēt'] 121

nationality Nationalität [nätsyōnälität'] 79; ~ **plate** Nationalitätskennzeichen [nätsyōnälitäts'kentsī·shən] 54, 79

nausea Übelkeit [ē'bəlkīt] 171

nauseate ekeln [ā'kəln] 164

nave Schiff [shif] 125

near nahe [nä'ə]; ~ **here** in der Nähe [in där nä'ə] 44

nearest nächste(r) [nä*sh*'stə(r)] 19, 45, 50

near-sighted kurzsichtig [kŏŏrts'-zi*sh*tish] 138

neck Hals [häls] 168; **back of the** ~ Genick [gənik'] 168; **nape of the** ~ Nacken [näk'ən] 168

necklace (Hals)kette [(häls')ket'ə] 133, 153

need brauchen [brou'hən] 18, etc.

needle Nadel [nä'dəl] 136; **sewing** ~ Nähnadel [nä'nädəl] 136

negative Negativ [nä'gätēf] 131

nephew Neffe [nef'ə] 35

nephritis Nierenentzündung [nē'-rənents*in*'dŏŏng] 71

nerve Nerv [nerf] 168, 174

nerves Nerven [ner'fən] 168

neuralgia Neuralgie [noirälgē'] 171

neurologist Nervenarzt [ner'fənärtst], Neurologe [noi'rōlō'gə] 162

neutral (gear) Leerlauf [lār'louf] 53

never niemals [nē'mäls] 21

new neu [noi] 50

news Nachrichten [näh'rishtən] 182

newsdealer Zeitungshändler [tsī'-tŏŏngs·hend'lər] 129

newspaper Zeitung [tsī'tŏŏng] 86, 182

next nächste(r) [näsh´stə(r)] 32, etc.
nice nett [net] 184
niece Nichte [nish´tə] 35
night Nacht [näht] 82; **Good ~!** Gute Nacht! [gōō´tə näht] 17; **at ~** nachts [nähts] 31; **all ~** die ganze Nacht [dē gän´tsə näht] 44; **~ club** Nachtklub [näht´klōōp] 180; **~ duty** Nachtdienst [näht´dēnst] 159; **~ rate** Nachttarif [näht´tärēf] 148; **~ shirt** Herrennachthemd [her´ən·näht´hemt] 134
nightie Nachthemd [näht´hemt] 134
night's lodging Übernachtung [ēbərnäh´tōōng] 92
nine neun [noin] 28
ninepins Kegeln [kā´gəln] 189
no nein [nīn] 21; **~ admittance** kein Eintritt [kīn īn´trit] 191
nobody niemand [nē´mänt] 49
non-swimmer Nichtschwimmer [nisht´shvimər] 186
noodle Nudel [nōō´dəl] 103; **flat ~s** Bandnudeln [bänt´nōōdəln] 103
noon Mittag [mit´äk]; **at ~** mittags [mit´äks] 31; **this ~** heute mittag [hoi´tə mit´äk] 32
nose Nase [nä´zə] 162, 168
nosebleed Nasenbluten [nä´zənblōōtən] 171
notary Notar [nōtär´] 37
note Note [nō´tə] 177
nothing nichts [nishts] 21, 99, 154, etc.
novel Roman [rōmän´] 130; **detective ~** Kriminalroman [krim´inäl´rōmän`] 130
November November [nōvem´bər] 33
now jetzt [yetst] 32, 66, 70; **~ and then** ab und zu [äp ōōnt tsōō] 32
nude nackt [näkt] 185; **~ beach** FKK-Strand [ef´kä´kä´shtränt] 186
number Nummer [nōōm´ər] 64, 79, 85, 148
nurse *(female)* (Kranken)schwester [(kräng´kən)shves`tər] 37, 172; *(male)* Krankenpfleger [kräng´kənpflā`gər] 37; **night ~** Nachtschwester [näht´shvestər] 172
nursery Kinderzimmer [kin´dərtsimər] 93

nut braid Nußzopf [nōōs´tsôpf] 109
nutmeg *(powder)* Muskat [mōōskät´] 101
nuts Nüsse [nis´ə] 110
nylon Nylon [nī´lôn] 137

O

oarsman Ruderer [rōō´dərər] 189
observatory Observatorium [ôp`zervätōr´ēōōm] 121
occupation Beruf [bərōōf´] 79
occupied besetzt [bəzetzt´] 66
ocean Ozean [ō´tsä·än] 77
October Oktober [ôktō´bər] 33
offer anbieten [än´bētən] 16
office Büro [bērō´] 121; **lost and found ~** Fundbüro [fōōnt´bērō] 121; **~ hours** Sprechstunde [shpresh´shtōōndə] 162
officer Offizier [ôfitsēr´] 74, 76; **deck ~** Deckoffizier [dek´ôfitsēr`] 74; **first ~** erster Offizier [ers´tər ôfitsēr´] 76
off-side abseits [äp´zīts] 190
often oft [ôft] 72; **how ~** wie oft [vē ôft] 72
oil Öl [äl] 45, 46, 101; **~ can** Ölkanne [äl´känə] 46; **~ change** Ölwechsel [äl´veksəl] 46; **~ level** Ölstand [äl´shtänt] 46; **~ filter** Ölfilter [äl´filtər] 54; **~ pump** Ölpumpe [äl´pōōmpə] 54
ointment Salbe [zäl´bə] 161; **boric acid ~** Borsalbe [bōr´zälbə] 160; **burn ~** Brandsalbe [bränt´zälbə] 160; **eye ~** Augensalbe [ou´gənzälbə] 160
old alt [ält] 34
older älter [el´tər] 35
olive Olive [ōlē´və] 101
on *(date)* am [äm] 34
one eins [īns] 28; ein(e); ein(e) [ī´n(ə)] 78; **~ way street** Einbahnstraße [īn´bänshträsə] 58
one-way ticket einfache Fahrkarte [īn´fähə fär´kär`tə] 62
onion Zwiebel [tsvē´bəl] 101
open *(adj.)* offen [ôf´ən] 118; geöffnet [gə·ef´nət] 44; **open** *(verb)* öffnen [ef´nən] 18, 65, 80, 165, 191; **do**

not ~ nicht öffnen [nisht ef'nən] 191; ~ **market** Markt [märkt] 121

opera Oper [ō'pər] 177; ~ **glasses** Opernglas [ō'pərngläs] 177

operate operieren [ōpərē'rən] 172

operating room Operationssaal [ōp`-ərätsyōns'zäl] 172

operation Operation [ōpərätsyōn'] 165, 172

operator Telefonistin [tā`läfōnis'tin] 150

operetta Operette [ōpəret'ə] 177

ophthalmologist Augenarzt [ou'gənärtst] 162

optician Optiker [ōp'tikər] 37, 129, 138

oral surgeon Kieferchirurg [kē'fərshirōōrk'] 174

orange *(noun; South German)* Orange [ōräN'zhə], *(North German)* Apfelsine [äpfəlzē'nə] 102, 109, 110; ~ **juice** Orangensaft [ōräN'zhənzäft'] 102; ~ *(adj.)* orangefarben [ōräN'zhəfär'bən] 194; ~ **stick** Nagelreiniger [nä'gəlrīnigər] 141

orangeade Orangeade [ōräNzhä'də] 112

orchestra Orchester [ōrkes'tər] 177; ~ **seats** Parkett [pärket'] 178

orchid Orchidee [ōr'shidä'ə] 130

order *(verb)* bestellen [bəshtel'ən] 89, 96, 115; ~ *(noun)* Ordnung [ōrd'nōōng] 23; **out of** ~ außer Betrieb [ou'sər bətrēp'] 23, defekt [dāfekt'] 50

organ Orgel [ōr'gəl] 125

orthopedist Orthopäde [ōr'tōpä'də] 163

otolaryngologist Hals-, Nasen- und Ohrenarzt [häls nä'zən ōōnt ōr'-ənärtst] 163

ounce Unze [ōōn'tsə] 193

ouverture Ouvertüre [ōōvertē'rə] 178

over über [ē'bər] 34

overpass Übergang [ē'bərgäng] 65

oyster Auster [ou'stər] 102, 104

P

pack Päckchen [pek'shən] 126

package Paket [päkät'] 150; ~ **card** Paketkarte [päkät'kärtə] 150

packet Packung [päk'ōōng] 193, Päckchen [pek'shən] 126

pad Block [blōk] 138; **scratch** ~ Notizblock [nōtēts'blōk] 138; **sketch** ~ Zeichenblock [tsī'shənblōk] 138

pail Eimer [ī'mər] 92

pain Schmerz [shmerts] 163, 171; ~ **killer** Schmerzmittel [shmerts'mitəl] 173; ~ **pills** Schmerztabletten [shmerts'täblet'ən] 161

paint *(noun)* Farbe [fär'bə]; ~ *(verb)* malen [mä'lən] 119; ~ **job** Lackierung [läkē'rōōng] 54

painter Maler [mä'lər] 37

painting Malerei [mä'lərī'] 39

pair Paar [pär] 126, 139, 193

pajamas Pyjama [pijä'mä] 134

palace Palast [päläst'] 119, 121

palate Gaumen [gou'mən] 168

pale hell [hel] 127

pancreas Bauchspeicheldrüse [bouh'shpīshəldrē'zə] 168

panties Schlüpfer [shlipf'ər], Slip [slip], Höschen [hœs'shən] 134

pants Hose [hō'zə] 134; ~ **suit** Hosenanzug [hō'zənän'tsōōk] 134

paper Papier [päpēr'] 132

paperback Taschenbuch [täsh'ənbōōh] 130

paper napkin Papierserviette [päpēr'-zärvē-et'ə] 144

papers Papiere [päpē'rə] 78

paprika Paprika [päp'rikä] 101

parallel bars Barren [bär'ən] 188

paralysis Lähmung [lä'mōōng] 171

parcel Paket [päkät'] 145, 150; **small** ~ Päckchen [pek'shən] 145, 150; **registered** ~ **with declared value** Wertpaket [värt'päkät] 150

pardon: Beg your ~? Wie bitte? [vē bit'ə] 20, 24; **I beg your** ~! Verzeihung! [fertsī'ōōng] 22

parent Elternteil [el'tərntīl] 35

parents Eltern [el'tərn] 35

park *(verb)* parken [pär'kən] 43, 44,

95; **~** *(noun)* Park [pärk], Grünanlage [grēn'änlägə] 122
parka Anorak [än'ōräk] 134
parking Parkplatz [pärk'pläts] 58; **no ~** Parkverbot [pärk'ferbōt'] 42; **~ disk** Parkscheibe [pärk'shībə] 42; **~ lot** Parkplatz [pärk'pläts] 42, 44; **~ meter** Parkuhr [pärk'ōōr] 42; **~ lights** Standlicht [shtänt'lisht] 53; **~ lot** Parkplatz [pärk'pläts] 84; **~ space** Box [bōks] 44
parsley Petersilie [pā'tərzēl'yə] 101
part Teil [tīl]; *(on stage)* Rolle [rōl'ə], Partie [pärtē'] 178; *(hair)* Scheitel [shī'təl] 157; **~ of town** Stadtteil [shtät'tīl] 122
partridge Rebhuhn [rāp'hōōn] 105
party Party [pär'tē] 183; **~ games** Gesellschaftsspiele [gəzel'shäfts-shpē'lə] 182
pass *(noun)* Paß [päs] 42; **~** *(verb)* reichen [rī'shən] 99; **~ (on the road)** überholen [ēbərhō'lən] 43
passenger Passagier [päsäzhēr'] 77; Reisende(r) [rī'zendə(r)] 66; Fahrgast [fär'gäst] 67; **~ car** Personenwagen [perzō'nənvä'gən] 41
passing Überholen [ēbərhō'lən]; **no ~** Überholverbot [ēbərhōl'ferbōt'] 42; **~ out** Ohnmacht [ōn'mäht] 171
passport Paß [päs] 78, 84; **~ control** Paßkontrolle [päs'kôntrôlə] 78
past *(time)* nach [näh] 30
pasta Teigwaren [tīk'värən] 104
pastime Zeitvertreib [tsīt'fertrīp] 180, 182
pastor Pastor [päs'tôr] 125
pastry chef Konditor [kôndē'tôr] 37
patch flicken [flik'ən] 46
path Weg [vāk] 19, 42, 122
patient Patient [pätsyent'] 172
patio Terrasse [teräs'ə] 92
patterned gemustert [gəmōōs'tərt] 137
pavilion Pavillon [pä'vilyôN] 122
pawn *(chess)* Bauer [bou'ər] 181
pay zahlen [tsä'lən] 115, 80; **~ for** bezahlen [bətsä'lən] 41; **~ out** auszahlen [ous'tsälən] 152
payment Zahlung [tsä'lōōng] 152

pea Erbse [är'psə] 107
peach Pfirsich [pfir'zish] 110; **~ melba** Pfirsich Melba [pfir'zish mel'bä] 114
peanuts Erdnüsse [ärt'nisə] 110
pear Birne [bir'nə] 109
pearls Perlen [per'lən] 133
pedal Pedal [pədäl'] 54
pedestrian Fußgänger [fōōs'gengər] 122; **~ crossing** Fußgängerübergang [fōōs'gengərē'bərgäng] 122
pediatrician Kinderarzt [kin'dərärtst] 163
pedicure Pediküre [pedikē'rə] 156, 158
pelvis Unterleib [ōōn'tərlīp] 168
pen Stift [shtift] 138; **ball point ~** Kugelschreiber [kōō'gəlshrībər] 138; **fountain ~** Füllfederhalter [fil'fädərhältər] 138
penalty kick Strafstoß [shträf'shtōs] 190
pencil Bleistift [blī'shtift] 138
pendant Anhänger [än'hengər] 133
penis Penis [pā'nis] 168
pension Pension [päNsyôn'] 81, 92
people Personen [perzō'nən] 41
pepper Pfeffer [pfef'ər] 97, 101; **~ mill** Pfeffermühle [pfef'ərmēlə] 97; **~ shaker** Pfefferstreuer [pfef'ərshtroi'ər] 97; **peppermint** Pfefferminze [pfef'ərmintsə] 161
peppers Paprikaschoten [päp'rikäshō'tən] 108
peptic ulcer Magengeschwür [mä'gəngəshvēr] 171
perch Barsch [bärsh] 104
performance Vorstellung [fōr'shtelōōng] 176, Aufführung [ouf'fērōōng] 178
perfume Parfum [pärfēm'] 80, 141
perhaps vielleicht [fillīsht'] 21
period Epoche [epô'hə] 119
permanent wave Dauerwelle [dou'ərvelə] 155, 158
personal persönlich [perzän'lish] 80
petticoat Unterrock [ōōn'tərôk] 171
pharmacist Apotheker [äpōtā'kər] 37
pharmacy Apotheke [äpōtā'kə] 159; Pharmazie [fär'mätsē'] 39

pheasant Fasan [fäzän´] 105

phone (verb) telefonieren [tä´läfōnēr´ən] 78; ~ (noun) Telefon [tälä-fōn´] 48, 147; ~ **booth** Telefonzelle [täläfōn´tselə] 147; ~ **call** Telefongespräch [täläfōn´gəshpräsh] 85, 147; ~ **book** Telefonbuch [täläfōn´bōōh] 147; **pay** ~ Münzfernsprecher [mïnts´fernshpresh´ər] 148

photo Foto [fō´tō] 132

photocopy Fotokopie [fō´tōkōpē´] 138

photograph (verb) fotografieren [fōtōgräfē´rən] 132

photographer Fotograf [fōtōgräf´] 74, 129

physics Physik [fïzēk´] 39

pianist Pianist [pē´änist´], Pianistin [pē`änis´tin] 178

piano recital Klavierabend [klävēr´äbənt] 178

pick up abholen [äp´hōlən] 41

pickle Salzgurke [zälts´gōōrkə] 108

pickled (meat) gepökelt [gəpā´kəlt] 100, 107

pickles Gewürzgurken [gəvïrts´gōōr´kən] 101

picture Bild [bilt] 119, 132, 144; (Film-) Vorführung [(film´)fōr´fēroͦong] 179

piece Stück [shtïk] 57, 126, 193; (chess) Stein [shtīn] 182

pier Mole [mō´ə] 77

pike Hecht [hesht] 104

pike-perch Zander [tsän´dər] 104

piles Hämorrhoiden [hem´ôrô-ē´-dən] 171

pill Pille [pil´ə] Tablette [täblet´ə] 161

pillar Säule [zoi´lə] 125

pillow Kopfkissen [kôpf´kisən] 87, 90

pillowcase Kopfkissenbezug [kôpf´-kisənbətsōōk´] 90

pilot Pilot [pilōt´] 71

pin (noun) Stecknadel [shtek´nädəl] 136; **bobby** ~**s** Haarklemmen [här´-klemən] 140; ~ **up** (verb) aufstecken [ouf´shtekən] 155

pincers Kneifzange [knīf´tsängə] 57

pinch drücken [drik´ən] 139

pineapple Ananas [än´änäs] 109; ~ **juice** Ananassaft [än´änäs·zäft´] 102

ping pong Tischtennis [tish´tenis] 180, 182, 190

pink rosarot [rō´zärōt] 194

pipe Leitung [lī´toͦong] 54, 88; **tobacco**~ Pfeife [pfī´fə] 140; ~ **cleaner** Pfeifenreiniger [pfī´fənrī´nigər] 140

pitcher Kännchen [ken´shən] 97; **cream** ~ Milchkännchen [milsh´ken-shən] 97

pity: what a ~! (wie) schade! [(vē) shä´də] 22

place Platz [pläts] 66; ~ **of birth** Geburtsort [gəbōōrts´ôrt] 79; ~ **of residence** Wohnort [vōn´ôrt] 79

plaice Scholle [shôl´ə] 104

plane Flugzeug [flōōk´tsoik] 71; Maschine [mäshē´nə] 68, 71

plate Platte [plät´ə] 174; Teller [tel´-ər] 97; **bread** ~ kleiner Teller [klī´-nər tel´ər] 97; **soup** ~ Suppenteller [zōōp´əntelər] 97

platform Gleis [glīs], Bahnsteig [bän´-shtīk] 60, 61, 64, 65, 67

play (verb) spielen [shpē´lən] 182, 187; ~ (noun) Theaterstück [tä·ä´tər-shtïk] 178

player Spieler [shpē´lər] 189

playground Spielplatz [shpēl´pläts] 95

playing cards Spielkarten [shpēl´kär-tən] 144

playroom Kinderspielzimmer [kin´-dərshpēltsim´ər] 97

please bitte [bit´ə] 20, etc.

pleasure: With ~! Mit Vergnügen! [mit fergnē´gən] 21

plenty reichlich [rīsh´lish] 127

pleurisy Rippenfellentzündung [rip´-ənfelentsin´doͦong] 171

pliers Zange [tsäng´ə] 57

plug Stecker [shtek´ər] 92

plum (North German) Pflaume [pflou´mə], (South German) Zwetschge [tsvetsh´gə] 110

plumber Installateur [in´stälätär´], Klempner [klemp´nər] 37

P.M.: at five ~ um fünf Uhr nachmittags [oͦom fïnf ōōr näh´mitäks´] 30

pneumonia Lungenentzündung [loͦong´ənentsin´doͦong] 171

point Punkt [poͦongkt] 188

poisoning Vergiftung [fergif´toͦong] 171

police Polizei [pōlitsī′] 49, 122, 153; ~ **car** Polizeiwagen [pōlitsī′vägən] 154; Funkstreifenwagen [foŏngk′-shtrīfənvä′gən] 154; ~ **station** Polizeirevier [pōlitsī′revēr] 116, 122, 154

policeman Polizist [pōlitsist′] 122

polish polieren [pōlēr′ən] 156

political science Politologie [pōl′itōlōgē′] 39

pool hall Billardraum [bil′yärtroum] 180

poppy seed cake Mohnkuchen [mōn′kōōhən]109

pork Schweinefleisch [shvī′nəflīsh] 107; ~ **hock** Schweinshaxe [shvīns′-häksə] 107

port (land) Hafen [hä′fən] 72, 77, 122; (side) Backbord [bäk′bôrt] 77; ~ **fees** Hafengebühr [hä′fəngəbēr] 77

portal Portal [pôrtäl′] 125

porter Gepäckträger [gəpek′trä′gər] 64

portion Portion [pôrtsyōn′] 96, 115

possible möglich [mäk′lish] 22

post no bills Ankleben verboten [än′-kläbən ferbō′tən] 191

post office Post [pôst] 122, Postamt [pôst′ämt] 116, 122, 145; ~ **box** Postfach [pôst′fäh] 150

postage Porto [pôr′tō] 145

postal clerk Postbeamte(r) [pôst′-bə·ämtə(r)] 37, 150

postal savings book Postsparbuch [pôst′shpärbōōh] 150

postal transfer Postanweisung [pôst′änvīzōōng] 146

postcard Postkarte [pôst′kärtə] 85; **picture ~** Ansichtskarte [än′zishtskär′tə] 85

postman Briefträger [brēf′trägər] 150

pot Topf [tôpf] 92, Kännchen [ken′-shən] 96, Kanne [kän′ə] 97; **coffee ~** Kaffeekanne [käf′äkän′ə] 97; **tea ~** Teekanne [tä′känə] 97

potatoes Kartoffeln [kärtôf′əln] 108; **home-fried ~** Bratkartoffeln [brät′-kärtôf′əln] 108; **baked ~** gebackene Kartoffeln [gəbäk′ənə kärtôf′-əln], Pellkartoffeln [pel′kärtôf′əln]

108; **mashed ~** Kartoffelbrei [kärtôf′-əlbrī], Kartoffelpüree [kärtôf′əlpi-rä′] 108; **French-fried ~** Pommes frites [pômfrit′] 108; **boiled ~** Salzkartoffeln [zälts′kärtôf′əln] 108

poultry Geflügel [gəflē′gəl] 105

pound (approx.) Pfund [pfōont] 126, 193; **quarter ~** (approx.) hundert Gramm [hōon′dərt gräm] 126

powder Puder [pōō′dər], 141, Pulver [pōol′fər] 161; ~ **puff** Puderquaste [pōō′dərkvästə] 141

power Kraft [kräft]; ~ **brake** Servobremse [zer′vōbrem′zə] 54; ~ **station** Kraftwerk [kräft′värk] 122; ~ **steering** Servolenkung [zer′vō-leng′kōōng] 54

practice Training [trä′ning] 188

prawn Garnele [gärnä′lə] 104

preach predigen [prä′digən] 123

precipitation Niederschlag [nē′dər-shläk] 27

pregnancy Schwangerschaft [shväng′ərshäft] 168

premium Superbenzin [zōō′pərben-tsēn′] 45

prepaid vorbezahlt [vōr′bətsält] 147

prescribed verschrieben [fershrē′-bən] 159

prescription Rezept [retsept′] 159, 164

present Geschenk [gəshengk′] 80

press bügeln [bē′gəln] 137

press-stud Druckknopf [drōŏk′-knöpf] 136

preview Trailer [trä′lər], Programmvorschau [prōgräm′fôrshou] 179

previously vorher [fôr′här] 32

price Preis [prīs] 92

priest Priester [prēs′tər] 123

print Abzug [äp′tsōōk] 131

printed matter Drucksache [drōŏk′-zähə] 145, 150

priority road: (end of) ~ (Ende der) Vorfahrtsstraße [(en′də där) fōr′-färts·shträ′sə] 58

prison Gefängnis [gəfeng′nis] 154

probably wahrscheinlich [värshīn′-lish] 21

procession Prozession [prō′tse-syōn′] 125

producer Produzent [prōdōōtsent'] 178

production Inszenierung [instsänēr'ōōng] 178

program Programmheft [prōgräm'heft] 178; ~ Sendung [zen'dōōng] 182; ~ **schedule** Programm [prōgräm'] 182

pronounce aussprechen [ous'shpreshən] 24

prophylactics Präservative [prä'zervätē'və] 141, 161

Protestant Protestant [prō'testänt'] 124

psychiatrist Psychiater [psē'shēät'ər] 163

psychologist Psychologe [psē'shōlō'gə] 163

psychology Psychologie [psēsh'ōlōgē'] 39

public garden Grünanlage [grēn'änläg'ə] 122

public notices öffentliche Bekanntmachungen [ē'fəntlishə bəkänt'mähōōngən] 191

public rest room Bedürfnisanstalt [bədirf'nisänshtält] 122

pull ziehen [tsē'ən] 173, 191

pulpit Kanzel [kän'tsəl] 125

pump room Trinkhalle [tringk'hälə] 175

pumpkin Kürbis [kir'bis] 107

punch Punsch [pōōnsh] 112

puncture Reifenpanne [rī'fənpänə] 47

pupil Schüler [shē'lər] 37

purple purpur [pōōr'pōōr] 194

purse Handtasche [hänt'täshə], Portemonnaie [pōrt'mônä'] 144, 153

purser Zahlmeister [tsäl'mīstər] 74

push drücken [dri'kən], stoßen [shtō'sən] 191

Q

quai Kai [kī] 77

quail Wachtel [väh'təl] 105

quart (approx.) Liter [lē'tər] 126

quarter Viertel [fir'təl] 30; Vierteljahr [fir'təlyär'] 32; ~ **to nine** drei Viertel neun [drī fir'təl noin] 30

queen (chess) Dame [dä'mə] 181

question Frage [frä'gə]; **Out of the ~!** Kommt gar nicht in Frage! [kômt gär nisht in frä'gə] 21

quick(ly) schnell [shnel] 48

quinine Chinin [shinēn'] 161

R

rabbi Rabbiner [räbē'nər] 125

rabbit Kaninchen [känēn'shən] 106

race Rennen [ren'ən] 187; ~ **car driver** Rennfahrer [ren'färər] 187

racing boat Rennboot [ren'bōt] 187

racing car Rennwagen [ren'vägən] 187

radiation therapy Bestrahlung [bəshträ'lōōng] 175

radiator Heizkörper [hīts'kərpər] 92; ~ Kühler [kē'lər] 53; ~ **grill** Kühlergrill [kē'lərgrill] 54

radio Radio [rä'dē·ō] 180, 182; ~ **play** Hörspiel [hər'shpēl] 182; ~ **room** Funkraum [fōōngk'roum] 74

rag Lappen [läp'ən] 57

ragout Ragout [rägōō'] 106

rail car Triebwagen [trēp'vägən] 60

railroad Eisenbahn [ī'zənbän] 67, 72, 192; ~ **man** Eisenbahner [ī'zənbänər] 37; ~ **crossing** (beschrankter) Bahnübergang [(bəshrängk'tər) bän'ēbərgäng] 42, 58; ~ **station** Bahnhof [bän'hōf] 72

rain (noun) Regen [rāg'ən] 88; ~ (verb) regnen [rāg'nən] 25; **it's raining** es regnet [es rāg'nət] 27

raincoat Regenmantel [rā'gənmäntəl] 135

raisins Rosinen [rōzē'nən] 101

ranch wagon Kombiwagen [kôm'bēvä'gən] 41

rare (meat) englisch [eng'lish] 100

rash Ausschlag [ous'shläk] 171

raspberries Himbeeren [him'bārən] 110

rather: I'd ~ have ... Ich möchte lieber ... [ish mesh'tə lē'bər ...] 20

raw roh [rō] 100, 107

razor Rasierapparat [räzēr'äpärät'] 141; **safety ~** Naßrasierer [näs'räzērər] 141; **straight** ~ Rasiermesser [rä́zēr´mesər] 141; ~ **blade** Rasierklinge [räzēr´klingə] 141; ~ **cut** Messerformschnitt [mes´ərfôrm`shnit] 157

reading room Leseraum [lā´zəroum] 74

ready fertig [fer´tish] 50, 87

real estate agency Immobilienhändler [imōbēl´ē-ənhend`lər] 129

rear hinten [hin´tən]; **(at the)** ~ am Ende [äm en´də] 65, 66; **the** ~ **...** hinten [hin´tən] 46; ~ **lights** Schlußlichter [shlōōs´lishtər] 53; ~ **motor** Heckmotor [hek´mōtôr] 54; ~ **view mirror** Rückspiegel [rik´shpēgəl] 55; ~**end collision** Auffahrunfall [ouf´fär-ōōn`fäl] 49

receipt Quittung [kvit´ōōng] 150

recently neulich [noi´lish] 32

reception desk Empfang [empfäng´], Rezeption [rätseptsyōn´] 92

recommend empfehlen [empfā´lən] 81

record Schallplatte [shäl´plätə] 130, 182; ~ **player** Plattenspieler [plä´tənshpēlər] 182; ~ **phonograph** ~ Schallplatte [shäl´plätə] 144

recording tape Tonband [tōn´bänt] 144, 182

recreation room Tagesraum [tä´gəsroum] 95

red rot [rōt] 194; **bright** ~ hellrot [hel´rōt] 194; **fire engine** ~ knallrot [knäl´rōt] 194; **dark** ~ dunkelrot [dōōng´kəlrōt] 194; ~ **cabbage** Rotkohl [rōt´kōl] 108; ~ **currants** rote Johannisbeeren [rō´tə yōhän´isbārən] 110

reduced fare ticket ermäßigte Fahrkarte [ermä´sishtə fär´kär`tə] 62

reduced rates Ermäßigung [ermä´sigōōng] 83

refer überweisen [ēbərvī´zən] 165

referee Schiedsrichter [shēts´rishtər] 189

reference Verweisung [fervī´zōōng] 192; **with** ~ **to** bezüglich [bətsēk´lish] 192

refill auffüllen [ouf´filən] 140

refrain (from smoking) (das Rauchen) einstellen [(däs rouh´ən) īn´shtelən] 70

refreshments Erfrischungen [erfrish´-ōōngən] 65, 191

refrigerator Kühlschrank [kēl´shrängk] 92

regard: send one's ~**s** grüßen lassen [grē´sən läs`ən] 16; **Give ... my best** ~**s** Grüßen Sie ... von mir [grē´sən zē ... fôn mēr] 16

register anmelden [än´meldən] 84; ~ einschreiben [īn´shrībən] 150

registered letter Einschreibebrief [īn´shrībəbrēf] 150

registration Zulassung [tsōō´läsōōng] 43; Anmeldung [än´meldōōng] 84, 92; ~ **form** Anmeldeformular [än´meldəfôrmōōlär`] 84

regret Bedauern [bədou´ərn] 22

regular Normalbenzin [nôrmäl´bentsēn`] 45

religion Religion [reli´gyōn´] 123, 125

religious religiös [reli´gyäs´] 125

remedy Mittel [mit´əl] 70, 161

renew verlängern [ferleng´ərn] 79

rent *(noun)* Miete [mē´tə] 92; ~ *(verb)* mieten [mē´tən], ausleihen [ous´lī-ən] 41, 85, 92, 95, 185

repair *(verb)* reparieren [repärē´rən] 46; ~ *(noun)* Reparatur [repärätōōr´] 55, 137, 142; ~ **shop** Reparaturwerkstatt [repärätōōr´verk`shtät] 48

replace ersetzen [erzets´ən] 138

reply Rückantwort [rik´äntvôrt] 147

report anzeigen [än´tsīgən] 153

reservation Buchung [bōō´hōōng] 71

reserve bestellen [bəshtel´ən] 82; reservieren [rezervēr´ən] 62, 96, vorbestellen [fōr´bəshtelən] 62; ~ **tank** Reservetank [rezer´vətängk] 45; ~ **fuel can** Reservekanister [rezer´vəkänis`tər] 55; ~ **wheel** Reserverad [rezer´vərät`] 47

respiration Atmung [ät´mōōng] 168

rest Pause [pou´zə]; ~ **room** Toilette [tō-älet´ə] 60, 65, 66, 92, 94

restaurant Restaurant [restōräN´] 60, 96; **Chinese** ~ chinesisches Restaurant [shinä´zishəs restōräN´] 96; **fish** ~ Fischrestaurant [fish´restô-räN`] 96

result Ergebnis [ergäp´nis] 188

retailer Kaufmann [kouf´män] 37

retiree Rentner [rent´nər] 37

return flight Rückflug [rĭk´flo͞ok] 71

return postage Rückporto [rĭk´pôrtō] 150

reverse (gear) Rückwärtsgang [rĭk´-vertsgäng´] 53

rheumatism Rheuma [roi´mä] 171

rhubarb Rhabarber [räbär´bər] 110

rib Rippe [rĭp´ə] 168

ribbon Band [bänt] 136

rice Reis [rīs] 103

ricotta Quark [kvärk] 108

ride fahren [fä´rən] 66; reiten [rī´-tən] 189

rider Reiter [rī´tər] 189

riding Reitsport [rīt´shpôrt] 189; ~ **stable** Reitschule [rīt´sho͞olə] 180

rifle range Schießstand [shēs´shtänt] 189

right richtig [rĭsh´tĭsh] 21, 31; rechts [reshts] 40, 116; ~ **of way** Vorfahrt [fōr´färt] 43, 49; ~ **away** sofort [zō-fōrt´] 96

ring Ring [rĭng] 133, 153, 188; **wedding** ~ Ehering [ā´əring], Trauring [trou´ring] 133

rise steigen [shtī´gən] 25

river Fluß [flo͞os] 70, 122

road Straße [shträ´sə] 19, 40, 122, 191; ~ **sign** Verkehrsschild [ferkärs´-shilt] 43, 122; ~ **conditions** Straßenzustand [shträ´səntso͞o´shtänt] 25; **private** ~ Privatstraße [prĭvät´shträ-sə], Durchgang verboten [do͞orsh´-gäng ferbō´tən] 191; ~ **under construction** Baustelle [bou´shtelə] 43

roast Braten [brä´tən] 105; **pickled pot** ~ Sauerbraten [zou´ərbrätən] 106; ~ **chestnuts** Maroni [märō´nē] 110

roasted geröstet [gərös´tət], im Ofen gebraten [im ō´fən gəbrä´-tən] 100

rock Felsen [fel´zən]

rod Stange [shtäng´ə]

rôle Rolle [rôl´ə], Partie [pärtē´] 178; **leading** ~ Hauptrolle [houpt´rō-lə] 178

roll Brötchen [brät´shən], Semmel [zem´əl] 98; Rolle [rôl´ə] 126

Romanesque romanisch [rōmä´nish] 125

roof Dach [däh]; (car) Verdeck [ferdek´] 55

rook (chess) Turm [to͞orm] 181

room Platz [pläts] 94; ~ Zimmer [tsim´ər] 82; ~ **referral office** Zimmernachweis [tsim´ərnäh´vīs] 60; **single** ~ Einzelzimmer [īn´tsəltsimər] 82; **double** ~ Doppelzimmer [dôp´əltsimər] 82; **quiet** ~ ruhiges Zimmer [ro͞o´igəs tsim´ər] 82

root Wurzel [vo͞or´tsəl] 174; ~ **canal work** Wurzelbehandlung [vo͞or´tsəl-bəhänd`lo͞ong] 174

rope Seil [zīl] 77

rose Rose [rō´zə] 130

rosemary Rosmarin [rōs´märēn] 101

rouge Rouge [ro͞ozh] 142

rough seas Seegang [zā´gäng] 77

round rund [ro͞ont] 156

round-trip Rundreise [ro͞ont´rīzə] 73; ~ **ticket** Rückfahrkarte [rĭk´fär-kär`tə] 59, 62, Hin- und Rückflug [hin o͞ont rĭk´flo͞ok] 69

route Fahrtroute [färt´ro͞otə] 43, (Bus)Linie [(bo͞os`)lē´nē·ə] 59, Strecke [shtrek´ə] 67, 71

row Reihe [rī´ə] 176

rowing Rudern [ro͞o´dərn] 189

rubber boots Gummistiefel [go͞om´ē-shtē´fəl] 139

ruby Rubin [ro͞obēn´] 133

rucksack Rucksack [ro͞ok´zäk] 144

rudder Ruder [ro͞o´dər] 77

ruin Ruine [ro͞o·ē´nə] 122

rum Rum [ro͞om] 112

run laufen [lou´fən] 51, 186

S

sacristan Mesner [mes´nər], Kirchendiener [kir´shəndēnər] 125

sacristy Sakristei [zäkristī´] 125

saddle (Berg)Rücken [(berk´)rĭk´-ən] 106

safety pin Sicherheitsnadel [zish´ər-hītsnä`dəl] 136

sail (noun) Segel [zā´gəl] 77, 189; ~ (verb) segeln [zā´gəln] 189

sailboat Segelboot [zä´gəlbōt] 75, 186, 188
sailing Segelsport [zä´gəlshpôrt] 189; **~ school** Segelschule [zä´gəlshōōlə] 180
sailor Matrose [mätrō´zə] 77
salad Salat [zälät´] 108
salesperson Verkäufer [ferkoi´fər] 37
salmon Lachs [läks] 102, 104, Salm [zälm] 104; **smoked ~** Räucherlachs [roi´shərläks´] 102
salt Salz [zälts] 97, 101; **~ shaker** Salzstreuer [zälts´shtroiər] 97
salted gesalzen [gəzäl´tsən] 100
salty salzig [zäl´tsish] 115
salve Salbe [zäl´bə] 161
sanatorium Sanatorium [zän´ätōr´-ē-ōōm] 175
sandals Sandalen [zändä´lən] 139; **beach ~** Badeschuhe [bä´dəshōō-ə], Strandschuhe [shtränt´-shōō-ə] 139
sandpaper Schmirgelpapier [shmir´-gəlpäpēr´] 57
sanitary napkin Damenbinde [dä´-mənbində] 142, 161
sardines Sardinen [zärdē´nən] 102
Saturday Sonnabend [zôn´äbənt], Samstag [zäms´täk] 33, 155
sauce Soße [zō´sə] 101; **cream ~** Rahmsoße [räm´zōsə] 101
saucer Untertasse [ōōn´tərtäsə] 97
sauerkraut Sauerkraut [zou´ərkrout] 108
sauna Sauna [zou´nä] 175
sausage Wurst [vōōrst] 98, 107; **~ salad** Wurstsalat [vōōrst´zälät´] 102
savings book Sparbuch [shpär´-bōōh] 152
Savoy cabbage Wirsingkohl [vir´-zing-kōl´] 108
say sagen [zä´gən] 24
scarf Schal [shäl], Halstuch [häls´-tōōh] 135
scarlet fever Scharlach [shär´läh] 171
scenery Bühnenbild [bē´nənbilt] 178
scheduled flight Linienflug [lē´-nē-ənflōōk] 71
scholar Wissenschaftler [vis´ən-shäft´lər] 37

school Schule [shōō´lə] 38, 122
sciatica Ischias [ish´ē-äs] 171
scientist Wissenschaftler [vis´ən-shäft´lər] 37
scissors Schere [shā´rə] 136, 142
score Spielstand [shpēl´shtänt] 187
Scotch tape Klebeband [klā´bəbänt] 144
screen Leinwand [līn´vänt] 179
screenplay Drehbuch [drā´bōōh] 179
screw Schraube [shrou´bə] 55, 57
screwdriver Schraubenzieher [shrou´bəntsē´ər] 57
scuba diving Tauchen [tou´hən] 186
scuba equipment Taucherausrüstung [tou´hərous´ristōōng] 186
scull Ruderboot [rōō´dərbōt] 189
sculptor Bildhauer [bilt´hou-ər] 37
sea See [zā] 77; **~ water** Meerwasser [mär´väsər] 175
seasickness Seekrankheit [zā´-krängk-hīt] 75, 77, 171
season Saison [zezôN´] 93
seasoned gewürzt [gəvirtst´] 100
seasoning Gewürze [gəvirts´ə] 101
seat Platz [pläts] 16, 62, 65, 68, 96, 176, Sitz [zits] 55; **~ belt** Sicherheitsgurt [zish´ərhītsgōort´] 55, Anschnallgurt [än´shnälgōort´] 71; **~ reservation** Platzkarte [pläts´kär´tə] 62
second (noun) Sekunde [zəkōōn´-də] 32; **~** (adj.) zweite(r) [tsvī´tə(r)] 29; **~ class** zweite Klasse [tsvī´tə kläs´ə] 62
secretary (male) Sekretär [zekrätär´] 37
security Wertpapier [vārt´päpēr´] 152
see besichtigen [bəzish´tigən] 118; sehen [zā´ən]; **~ you soon!** Bis bald! [bis bält´] 17; **~ you tomorrow!** Bis Morgen! [bis môr´gən] 17
self-service Selbstbedienung [selpst´bədēnōōng] 129
send schicken [shik´ən]; (luggage) aufgeben [ouf´gäbən] 63, 147
sender Absender [äp´zendər] 150
separate getrennt [gətrent´] 115
September September [septem´bər] 33
serious schlimm [shlim] 164
sermon Predigt [prä´disht] 123

service Gottesdienst [gôt'əsdēnst] 123; Bedienung [bədē'nŏŏng] 83, 93; **~ charge** Bedienungszuschlag [bedē'nŏŏngs·tsŏŏ'shläk] 93; **~ station** Reparaturwerkstatt [repärä-tŏŏr'verk`shtät] 48

serving dish Platte [plät'ə] 97

set legen [lā'gən] 158

setting lotion Festiger [fes'tigər] 156

settings Bühnenbild [bē'nənbilt] 178

seven sieben [zē'bən] 28, 86

severe stark [shtärk] 163

sew nähen [nä'ən] 137

shampoo Haarwaschmittel [här'väsh-mitəl], Shampoo [shämpŏŏ'] 142, 157

shape Form [fôrm] 127

sharp stechend [shtesh'ənt] 163; scharf [shärf] 163; **at eleven ~** pünktlich um elf [pingkt'lish ŏŏm elf] 30

shave rasieren [räzēr'ən] 157, ausrasieren [ous'räzērən] 156

shaving brush Rasierpinsel [räzēr'-pinzəl] 142

shaving cream Rasiercreme [räzēr'-kräm] 142

shaving foam Rasierschaum [räzēr'-shoum] 142

shaving soap Rasierseife [räzēr'zīfə] 142

she sie [zē]

sheet Laken [lä'kən] 90

shell Muschel [mŏŏsh'əl] 186

sherbet Wassereis [väs'ər·īs] 114; **lemon ~** Zitroneneis [tsitrō'nən·īs] 114; **orange ~** [ôräN'zhən·īs] 114

sherry Sherry [sher'ē] 111

shin Schienbein [shēn'bīn] 168

shine scheinen [shī'nən] 26

ship Schiff [shif] 72, 77; **passenger ~** Passagierschiff [päsäzhēr'shif] 77

shipboard party Bordfest [bôrt'fest] 77

shipping agency Schiffsagentur [shifs'ägentŏŏr] 77

shipping company Reederei [rādə-rī'] 73, 77

ship's doctor Schiffsarzt [shifs'ärtst] 75, 77

shirt Hemd [hemt], Oberhemd [ō'bərhemt] 135

shock Schock [shôk] 171; **~ absorber** Stoßdämpfer [shtōs'dempfər] 55

shoe Schuh [shŏŏ] 139; **~ horn** Schuhlöffel [shŏŏ'lefəl], Schuhanzieher [shŏŏ'äntse·ər] 139; **~ laces** Schnürsenkel [shnēr'zengkəl] 139

shoemaker Schuster [shŏŏ'stər] 37

shoot schießen [shē'sən] 189

shop Geschäft [gəsheft'], Laden [lä'dən] 122, 128; **antique ~** Antiquitätenhändler [än`tikvitä'tən-hend`lər] 128; **barber ~** (Herren)Friseur [(her'ən)frizőr'] 128; **textile ~** Textilwarengeschäft [tekstēl'värən-gəsheft`] 129; **watchmaker's ~** Uhrmacher [ŏŏr'mähər] 129; **wine ~** Weinhandlung [vīn'händlŏŏng] 129; **butcher ~** Metzgerei [metsgərī'], Fleischerei [flīshərī'] 128; **china ~** Porzellangeschäft [pôr'tselän·gə-sheft`] 128; **cobbler ~** Schuhmacherei [shŏŏ'mähərī'] 128; **dressmaker's ~** (Damen)Schneiderei [(dä'mən)shnīdərī'] 128; **electrical ~** Elektrohandlung [ālek'trōhänd`-lŏŏng] 128; **flower ~** Blumenhandlung [blŏŏ'mənhänd`lŏŏng] 128; **hat ~** Hutgeschäft [hŏŏt'gəsheft`] 129; **lingerie ~** Wäschegeschäft [vesh'əgəsheft`] 129; **perfume ~** Parfümerie [pärfēmərē'] 129; **pet ~** Tierhandlung [tēr'händ`lŏŏng] 129; **photo ~** Fotogeschäft [fō'tōgə-sheft`] 129, 131; **shoemaker's ~** Schuhmacher [shŏŏ'mähər] 129; **souvenir ~** Souvenirladen [zŏŏvə-nēr'lädən] 129; **tailor ~** (Herren)Schneiderei [(her'ən)shnīdə-rī'] 129

shopping Einkauf [īn'kouf] 118, 126; **~ mall** Einkaufszentrum [īn'-koufs·tsen'trŏŏm] 122

shore Ufer [ŏŏ'fər] 77

short kurz [kŏŏrts] 133, 155; **~ circuit** Kurzschluß [kŏŏrts'shlŏŏs] 55; **~ sleeved** kurzärmlig [kŏŏrts'erm-lish] 135; **~ subject** Kurzfilm [kŏŏrts'film] 179; **~ wave** Kurzwelle [kŏŏrts'velə] 175, 182

shorten kürzen [kir'tsən] 137

shortly kurz [koŏrts] 31

shorts Shorts [shŏrts], kurze Hose [koŏrt´sə hō´zə] 135

shoulder Schulter [shoŏl´tər] 107, 168

show zeigen [tsī´gən] 20, 40, 83, 126

shower Dusche [doŏsh´ə] 82, 93, 186; Regenschauer [rā´gənshou´-ər] 27

shrimps Garnelen [gärnā´lən] 102

shuffle mischen [mish´ən] 181

shut schließen [shlē´sən] 88

shutter Verschluß [fershloŏs´] 132; ~ **release** Auslöser [ous´lāzər] 132; **automatic** ~ Selbstauslöser [zelpst´-ouslāzər] 132

sick krank [krängk] 12, 162; **I feel** ~ mir ist schlecht [mēr ist shlesht] 70; ~ **bay** Schiffshospital [shifs´hóspitäl´] 74

side Seite [zī´tə] 176; ~ **road** Nebenstraße [nā´bənshträsə] 122; ~ **wind** Seitenwind [zī´tənvint] 43

sideburns Koteletten [kótlet´ən] 158

sidewalk Gehsteig [gā´shtīk], Bürgersteig [bér´gərshtīk] 122

sights Sehenswürdigkeiten [zā´ənsvirdishkī´tən] 117

sightseeing Besichtigung [bəzisht´-tigoŏng] 118, 122

sign (noun) Zeichen [tsī´shən] 191; ~ (verb) unterschreiben [oŏntərshrī´bən] 146; ~ **up** anmelden [än´-meldən] 85

signature Unterschrift [oŏn´tərshrift´] 79, 84, 152

silk Seide [zī´də] 137; **artificial** ~ Kunstseide [koŏnst´zīdə] 137; ~ **thread** Nähseide [nā´zīdə] 136

silver (adj.) silbern [zil´bərn] 194; ~ (noun) Silber [zil´bər] 133; ~ **plated** versilbert [ferzil´bərt] 133

silverware Besteck [bəshtek´] 97

since seit [zīt] 32

sincere aufrichtig [ouf´rishtish] 23; **Yours sincerely** Mit freundlichen Grüßen [mit froint´lishən grē´-sen] 13

sinew Sehne [zā´nə] 168

singer Sänger [zeng´ər], Sängerin [zeng´ərin] 178

singing Gesang [gəzäng´] 178

single ledig [lā´dish] 79

singles (tennis) Einzel [īn´tsəl] 190

sink Waschbecken [väsh´bekən] 93

sister Schwester [shves´tər] 35; ~ **in-law** Schwägerin [shvā´gərin] 35

site Platz [pläts] 94

six sechs [zeks] 28, 82

size Größe [grā´sə] 133, 139

skate eislaufen [īs´loufən] 188

skater Schlittschuhläufer [shlit´shoŏ-loi´fər] 188

skates Schlittschuhe [shlit´shoŏ·ə] 188

ski (verb) skilaufen [shē´loufən] 189; ~ (noun) Ski [shē] 189; ~ **binding** Skibindung [shē´bindoŏng] 189; ~ **jump** Sprungschanze [shproŏng´-shäntsə] 189; ~ **lift** Skilift [shē´lift] 189; ~ **pants** Skihose [shē´hōzə] 135

skiing Skisport [shē´shpórt] 189

skin Haut [hout] 168, 171; ~ **disease** Hauterkrankung [hout´erkräng´-koŏng] 171; ~ **lesion** Hautabschürfung [hout´äpshür´foŏng] 171

skirt Rock [rók] 135

skull Schädel [shā´dəl] 168

sky Himmel [him´əl] 26

slack locker [lók´ər] 51

slacks Hose [hō´zə] 135

sled Schlitten [shlit´ən] 144

sleep schlafen [shlä´fən] 12, 164

sleeper Schlafwagen [shläf´vägən] 60,61; ~ **reservation** Schlafwagenkarte [shläf´vägənkär´tə] 62

sleeping bag Schlafsack [shläf´zäk] 95

sleeping car Schlafwagen [shläf´vägən] 60, 64, 66

sleeping pill Schlafmittel [shläf´mi-təl] 173, Schlaftablette [shläf´tä-blet´ə] 161

slice Scheibe [shī´bə] 98

slide Dia [dē´ä] 131; ~ **frame** Diarahmen [dē´ärämən] 132

sliding roof Schiebedach [shē´bə-däh] 55

slip rutschen [roŏtsh´ən] 53

slippers Pantoffel [päntóf´əl] 139; **bedroom** ~ Hausschuhe [hous´-shoŏ·ə] 139

slippery glatt [glất] 25, 43

slow langsam [láng´zäm] 24, 31, 42, 51

small klein [klīn] 127

smallpox Pocken [pók´ən] 78, 171

smear schmieren [shmē´rən] 55

smoke rauchen [rouh´ən] 70, 165

smoked geräuchert [gəroi´shərt] 100, 107

smoking Rauchen [rouh´ən] 191; ~ *(sign)* Raucher [rouh´ər] 66; **no** ~ Rauchen verboten [rouh´ən ferbō´tən] 191; **no** ~ *(sign)* Nichtraucher [nisht´rouh ər] 66

smuggling Schmuggel [shmo͞og´əl] 154

snails Weinbergschnecken [vīn´berkshnek`ən] 102

snapshot Schnappschuß [shnäp´sho͞os] 132

sneakers Turnschuhe [to͞orn´sho͞o-ə] 139

snow *(verb)* schneien [shni´ən] 25, 27; ~ *(noun)* Schnee [shnā] 27; ~ **flurries** Schneegestöber [shnā´gəshtöbər] 27; ~ **chains** Schneeketten [shnā´ketən] 52

soap Seife [zī´fə] 87, 142; **cake of** ~ ein Stück Seife [īn shtik zī´fə] 87

soccer Fußball [fo͞os´bäl] 189; ~ **field** Fußballplatz [fo͞os´bälpläts`] 186; ~ **game** Fußballspiel [fo͞os´bälshpēl] 187; **play** ~ Fußball spielen [fo͞os´bäl shpē´lən] 190

socket Steckdose [shtek´dōzə] 88, 93; ~ **wrench** Steckschlüssel [shtek´-shlisəl] 57

socks Socken [zōk´ən], Strümpfe [shtrim´pfə] 135

soda Soda [zō´dä] 160; **bicarbonate of** ~ doppeltkohlensaures Natron [dóp´əltkō`lənzou´rəs nä´trōn] 160

soft weich [vīsh] 100; ~ **drink** Limonade [limōnä´də] 112

solder löten [lö´tən] 55

sole *(verb)* besohlen [bəzō´lən] 139; ~ *(noun)* Sohle [zō´lə] 139; **crepe** ~ Kreppsohle [krep´zōlə] 139; **leather** ~ Ledersohle [lā´dərzōlə] 139; **rubber** ~ Gummisohle [go͞om´ē-

zōl´ə] 139; ~ Fußsohle [fo͞os´zōlə] 168; ~ Seezunge [zā´tso͞ongə] 104

solid color einfarbig [īn´färbish] 137, 194

soloist Solist [zōlist´], Solistin [zōlis´tin] 178

somebody jemand [yā´mänt] 41, 184

something etwas [et´väs] 183

sometimes manchmal [mänsh´mäl] 32

son Sohn [zōn] 14, 35

song Lied [lēt] 178; **folk** ~ Volkslied [fōlks´lēt] 178; ~ **recital** Liederabend [lē´dərräbənt] 178

soon bald [bält] 16, 32

soprano Sopran [zōprän´], Sopranistin [zōpränis´tin] 178

sore throat Halsschmerzen [häls´smertsən] 171

sorry: I'm very ~ Es tut mir sehr leid [es to͞ot mēr zär līt] 22

soup Suppe [zo͞op´ə] 103; **bean** ~ Bohnensuppe [bō´nənzo͞opə] 103; **cream of mushroom** ~ Champignoncremesuppe [shäm´pinyoNkrämzo͞op´ə] 103; **cream of chicken** ~ Hühnercremesuppe [hē´nərkrämzo͞op´ə] 103; **potato** ~ Kartoffelsuppe [kärtóf´əlzo͞op´ə] 103; **clear** ~ klare Suppe [klä´rə zo͞op´ə] 103; **leek** ~ Lauchsuppe [louh´zo͞opə] 103; **onion** ~ Zwiebelsuppe [tsvē´bəlzo͞opə] 103; **pea** ~ Erbsensuppe [erp´sənzo͞opə] 103; **fish** ~ Fischsuppe [fish´zo͞opə] 103; **vegetable** ~ Gemüsesuppe [gəmē´zəzo͞opə] 103; **thick** ~ legierte Suppe [lāgēr´tə zo͞op´ə] 103; **lentil** ~ Linsensuppe [lin´zənzo͞op´ə] 103; **oxtail** ~ Ochsenschwanzsuppe [ók´sənshvänts-zo͞op´ə] 103; **turtle** ~ Schildkrötensuppe [shilt´krätənzo͞op´ə] 103; **cream of asparagus** ~ Spargelcremesuppe [shpär´gəlkrämzo͞op´ə] 103; **tomato** ~ Tomatensuppe [tōmä´tənzo͞opə] 103

sour sauer [zou´ər] 115

souvenir Reiseandenken [rī´zəändeng`kən] 80

spa Badeort [bä´də-ôrt`] 175

space Platz [pläts] 44

spades Pik [pĕk] 181

spaghetti Spaghetti [shpäget'ē] 104

spare part Ersatzteil [erzäts'tīl] 50, 55

spare wheel Ersatzrad [erzäts'rät] 55

spark Funke [fŏŏng'kə] 55; ~ plug Zündkerze [tsínt'kertsə] 45, 55

speak sprechen [shpresh'ən] 15, 23, 74, 88

speaking! am Apparat! [äm äpärät'] 148

special spezial [shpetsē·äl'] 46; ~ delivery durch Eilboten [dŏŏrsh īl'bōtən] 150; ~ delivery letter Eilbrief [īl'brēf] 150; ~ issue Sondermarke [zōn'dərmärkə] 146; ~ issue stamp Sondermarke [zōn'dərmärkə] 150

specialist Facharzt [fäh'ärtst] 162; ear, nose and throat ~ Hals-, Nasen- und Ohrenarzt [häls na'zən ōōnt ōr'ənärtst] 162

spectacles Brille [bril'ə] 138

speed Geschwindigkeit [gəshvin'dishkīt]; ~ limit Geschwindigkeitsbegrenzung [gəshvin'dishkītsbəgren'tsŏŏng] 43, zulässige Höchstgeschwindigkeit [tsŏŏ'lesigə häshst'gəshvin'dishkīt] 58

speedometer Tachometer [tähōmä'tər] 55

spell buchstabieren [bŏŏh'shtäbē'rən] 24

spices Gewürze [gəvirts'ə] 101

spinach Spinat [shpinät']108

spinal cord Rückenmark [rik'ənmärk] 168

spine Rückgrat [rik'grät], Wirbelsäule [vir'bəlzoilə] 168

spleen Milz [milts] 168

spoke Speiche [shpī'shə] 55

sponge Schwamm [shväm] 142

spoon Löffel [lef'əl] 97; soup ~ Suppenlöffel [zŏŏp'ənlefəl] 97; tea-Teelöffel [tā'lefəl] 97

sport shirt Freizeithemd [frī'tsīthemt], Sporthemd [shpôrt'hemt] 135

sports Sport [shpôrt] 186, 190; ~ event Sportveranstaltung [shpôrt'feränshtältŏŏng] 186; ~ fan Sportsfreund [shpôrts'froint] 190

sportswear Sportkleidung [shpôrt'-klīdŏŏng] 135

spot remover Fleckenwasser [flek'-ənväsər], Fleckentferner [flek'entfer'ner] 144

sprain (verb) verstauchen [fershtou'-hən] 164; ~ (noun) Verstauchung [fershtou'hŏŏng] 171

spring Feder [fā'dər] 55, 143; Frühling [frē'ling] 33

squab Taube [tou'bə] 105

square (adj.) Quadrat... [kvädrät'...] 193; ~ (noun) Platz [pläts] 122, 192; Feld [felt] 181

squash Kürbis [kir'bis] 107

stadium Stadion [shtä'dē·ōn] 122, 186

stage Bühne [bē'nə] 178; ~ director Regisseur [rezhisər'] 178

stain Fleck [flek] 137

staircase Treppe [trep'ə] 93

stairwell Treppenhaus [trep'ənhous] 93

stake Einsatz [īn'zäts] 182

stall aussetzen [ous'zetsən] 54

stamp (noun) Briefmarke [brēf'märkə] 85, 146, 150; ~ machine Briefmarkenautomat [brēf'märkənoutōmät'] 150; set of ~s Briefmarkenblock [brēf'märkənblôk] 146; ~ (verb) frankieren [frängkēr'ən] 150

standard (oil) normal [nôrmäl'] 46

star Stern [shtern] 27

starboard Steuerbord [shtoi'ərbôrt] 77

start beginnen [bəgin'ən] 176, 188

starter Anlasser [än'läsər] 55

station Bahnhof [bän'hôf] 60, 67, 72, 84, 89, 116; Station [shtätsyōn'] 66; Sender [zen'dər] 180; ~ master Aufsicht [ouf'zisht] 65; Bahnhofsvorsteher [bän'hôfsfôr'shtä·ər] 67; ~ wagon Kombiwagen [kôm'bēvä'gən] 41

stationery Schreibwaren [shrīp'värən] 138

Stations of the Cross Kreuzweg [kroits'vāk] 125

statue Statue [shtä'tŏŏ·ə] 119, 125

stay bleiben [blī'bən] 186

steak Steak [stāk] 106; rump ~ Rumpsteak [rŏŏmp'stāk] 106

steal stehlen [shtä´lən] 153

steamed gedämpft [gədempft´], gedünstet [gəd*i*ns´tət] 100, 106

steamer Dampfschiff [dämpf´shif] 77

steep downgrade Gefälle [gəfel´ə] 43

steep upgrade Steigung [shtī´gŏŏng] 43

steering Lenkung [leng´kŏŏng] 56; **~ wheel** Lenkrad [lengk´rät] 56

stern Heck [hek] 77

stew Eintopf [īn´tôpf] 105

steward Steward [styŏŏ´ərt] 74, 77; **chief ~** Obersteward [ō´bərstyŏŏ´ərt] 74

stewed geschmort [gəshmôrt´] 100, 107

still noch [nôh] 31, 44, 50

stock Aktie [äk´tsyə] 152

stockings Strümpfe [shtr*i*m´pfə] 135

stole Stola [shtō´lä] 135

stomach Magen [mä´gən] 159, 163, 168; **~ pains** Magenschmerzen [mä´gənshmertsən] 171

stop (noun) Haltestelle [häl´təshtelə] 59, 117, 122, 191; Aufenthalt [ouf´enthält] 66; **~** (verb) aufhören [ouf´hœrən] 26; anhalten [än´häl-tən] 43, 59, 61, 117

stopover Zwischenlandung [tsvish´ənländŏŏng] 68, 71

stopped up verstopft [fershtôpft´] 88

stopping Halten [häl´tən]; **no ~** Halteverbot [häl´təferbōt´] 42, 58

store Geschäft [gəsheft´] 128; Laden [lä´dən] 122; **candy ~** Süßwarengeschäft [zēs´värəngəsheft´] 128; **cigar ~** (Germany) Tabakladen [täb´äklädən] 140, (Austria) Trafik [träfik´] 128; **department ~** Kaufhaus [kouf´hous], Warenhaus [vä´rənhous] 128; **drug ~** (cosmetics and sundries) Drogerie [drōgərē´], (prescription pharmacy) Apotheke [äpōtā´kə] 128; **furniture ~** Möbelgeschäft [mä´bəlgəsheft´] 128; **grocery ~** Lebensmittelgeschäft [lä´bənsmitəlgəsheft´] 128; **hardware ~** Eisenwarengeschäft [ī´zənvärəngəsheft´] 129; **jewelry ~** Juwelier [yŏŏvelēr´] 129; **leather goods ~** Le-

derwarengeschäft [lä´dərvärəngəsheft´] 129; **liquor ~** Spirituosengeschäft [shpir´itŏŏ-ō´zəngəsheft´] 129; **music ~** Musikalienhandlung [mŏŏzikä´lē-ənhänd´lŏŏng] 129; **shoe ~** Schuhgeschäft [shŏŏ´gəsheft´] 129; **record ~** Schallplattengeschäft [shäl´plätəngəsheft´] 129; **sporting goods ~** Sportwarengeschäft [shpôrt´värəngəsheft´] 129; **stationery ~** Schreibwarengeschäft [shrīp´värəngəsheft´] 129; **toy ~** Spielwarengeschäft [shpēl´värəngəsheft´] 129

storekeeper Kaufmann [kouf´män] 37

storm Sturm [shtŏŏrm] 26

stormy stürmisch [shtīr´mish] 25

stove Ofen [ō´fən] 93

straight ahead geradeaus [gərä´də-ous´] 40, 116

straighten out geradebiegen [gərä´dəbēgən] 56

strait Straße [shträ´sə] 77

strand Strähne [shträ´nə] 158

strawberries Erdbeeren [ārt´bārən] 110

street Straße [shträ´sə] 116, 192, 192

strict streng [shtreng] 165

string Bindfaden [bint´fädən] 57, 144

stroke Gehirnschlag [gəhirn´shläk], Schlaganfall [shläk´änfäl] 171

strudel Strudel [shtrŏŏ´dəl] 109; **apple ~** Apfelstrudel [äp´fəlshtrŏŏdəl] 109; **cheese ~** Topfenstrudel [tôpf´ənshtrŏŏdəl] 109

student Student [shtŏŏdent´] 37

study studieren [shtŏŏdē´rən] 15, 38

stuffed gefüllt [gəf*i*lt´] 100; **~ animal** Stofftier [shtôf´tēr] 144

subtitled mit Untertiteln [mit ŏŏn´tərtētəln] 179

suburb Vorort [fōr´ôrt] 122

suburban train Vorortzug [fōr´-ôrt-tsŏŏk´] 60

subway Untergrundbahn [ŏŏn´tərgrŏŏntbän´], U-Bahn [ŏŏ´bän] 117

success Erfolg [erfôlk´] 23

suddenly plötzlich [plets´lish] 54

suède Wildleder [vilt´lädər] 139; **~ coat** Wildledermantel [vilt´lädərmäntəl] 135; **~ jacket** Wildlederjacke [vilt'lädəryäk'ə] 135

sugar Zucker [tsŏok'ər] 97, 114; **cube ~** Würfelzucker [vér'fəl·tsŏo̅kər] 114; **~ bowl** Zuckerdose [tsŏok'ərdōzə] 97

suit *(lady's)* Kostüm [kôstēm'], *(man's)* Anzug [än'tsŏok] 135

suitcase Koffer [kôf'ər] 63, 80, 144, 153

summer Sommer [zôm'ər] 135; **~ dress** Sommerkleid [zôm'ərklīt] 135

sun Sonne [zôn'ə] 26; **~ tan cream** Sonnencreme [zôn'ənkräm] 142; **~ tan lotion** Sonnenmilch [zôn'ənmilsh] 142; **~ tan oil** Sonnenöl [zôn'ənöl'] 142; **~ roof** Schiebedach [shē'bədäh] 55

sunbath Sonnenbad [zôn'ənbät] 186

sunburn Sonnenbrand [zôn'ənbränt] 171

sundae Eisbecher [īs'beshər] 114

Sunday Sonntag [zôn'täk] 33

sundries Verschiedenes [fershē'dənəs] 143

sunglasses Sonnenbrille [zôn'ənbrilə] 138

sunlamp Höhensonne [hö'ənzônə] 175

sunrise Sonnenaufgang [zôn'ənouf'gäng] 27

sunset Sonnenuntergang [zôn'ənŏon'tərgäng] 27

sunstroke Sonnenstich [zôn'ənshtish] 171

supermarket Supermarkt [zŏo'pərmärkt] 129

supplement: pay the ~ nachlösen [näh'läzən] 66

supplemental fare ticket Zuschlagkarte [tsŏo'shläk·kär'tə] 62

supplemental fare payable zuschlagpflichtig [tsŏo'shläkpflish'tish] 60

suppository Zäpfchen [tsepf'shən] 161

suppuration Vereiterung [fer·ī'tərŏong] 171

surcharge Zuschlag [tsŏo'shläk] 83; **seasonal ~** Saisonzuschlag [zezôN'tsŏo'shläk] 83

surgeon Chirurg [shirŏork'] 163, 172; **plastic ~** plastischer Chirurg [pläs'tishər shirŏork'] 163

surroundings Umgebung [ŏomgā'bŏong] 122

suspenders Hosenträger [hō'zəntrā'gər] 135

sweater Pullover [pŏolō'vər] 135

sweatshirt Sweatshirt [svet'shärt] 135

sweets Süßigkeiten [zē'sishkī'tən] 114

swelling Schwellung [shvel'ŏong] 171

swim schwimmen [shvim'ən], baden [bä'dən] 95, 185

swimmer Schwimmer [shvim'ər] 186, 190

swimming Schwimmen [shvim'ən] 190; **~ pier** Badesteg [bä'dəshtäk] 186; **no ~ allowed** Baden verboten [bä'dən ferbō'tən] 191; **~ area** Badegelegenheit [bä'dəgəlā'gənhīt] 122

swimming pool Swimmingpool [svim'ingpŏol'] 74, 93, Schwimmbecken [shvim'bekən] 187; **outdoor ~** Freibad [frī'bät] 187; **indoor ~** Hallenbad [häl'ənbät] 187

swimsuit Badeanzug [bä'dəäntsŏok] 135

Swiss schweizerisch [shvī'tsərish] 152; **~ Francs** Schweizer Franken [shvī'tsər fräng'kən] 152

switch (Licht)Schalter [(lisht')shäl'tər] 56, 93

swollen geschwollen [gəshvôl'ən] 164

sympathy Anteilnahme [än'tīlnä'mə] 23

symphony concert Symphoniekonzert [zimfōnē'kôntsert'] 178

synagogue Synagoge [zin'ägō'gə] 116, 123

synthetic thread synthetisches Nähgarn [zintä'tishəs nä'gärn] 136

system time table *(railroad)* Kursbuch [kŏors'bŏoh] 61, 67; *(plane)* Flugplan [flŏok'plän] 71

T

table Tisch [tish] 93; **~ tennis** Tischtennis [tish'tenis] 182

tablecloth Tischdecke [tish′dekə] 93, 97

tablet Tablette [täblet′ə] 161

tailor Schneider [shnī′dər] 37

take (bringen [bring′ən] 17; holen [hō′lən] 44; dauern [dou′ərn] 19, 72; nehmen [nā′mən] 83, 127

taken besetzt [bəzetst′] 96

take-off Abflug [äp′flook] 71

talcum powder Talkumpuder [täl′-koōmpoōdər] 161

tampon Tampon [täm′pôn] 142

tangerine Mandarine [mändärē′nə] 110

tape Band [bänt] 136; ~ **measure** Zentimetermaß [tsentimä′tərmäs] 136; ~ **recorder** Tonbandgerät [tōn′-böntgərät′] 182

target Zielscheibe [tsēl′shībə] 189

tart Torte [tôr′tə] 114; **fruit** ~ Obsttorte [ōpst′tôrtə] 114

taxi Taxi [täk′sē] 64, 89, 117, 129; ~ **stand** Taxistand [täk′sēshtänt] 116, 123, 191

tea Tee [tā] 98, 113, 183; ~ **with lemon** Tee mit Zitrone [tā mit tsitrō′nə] 98; ~ **with milk** Tee mit Milch [tā mit milsh] 98

teacher Lehrer [lā′rər] 37

tease toupieren [toōpēr′ən] 156

technical technisch [tesh′nish]; ~ **college** Technische Hochschule [tesh′nishə hōh′shoōlə] 39

technician Techniker [tesh′nikər] 38

telegram Telegramm [tälägräm′] 147, 150; ~ **form** Telegrammformular [täläg-räm′fôrmoōlär′] 147

telegraphic telegraphisch [tälägrä′-fish] 152

telephone Telefon [täläfôn′] 93, 150; **pushbutton** ~ Tastentelefon [täs′-təntäläfôn′] 150

television Fernsehen [fern′zā·ən] 180, 182, 192; ~ **play** Fernsehspiel [fern′zäshpēl] 182

tell sagen [zä′gən] 20

teller Schalterbeamter [shäl′tər-bə·ämtər] 152

temperature Temperatur [tempərä-toōr′] 25, 27; Fieber [fē′bər] 172; ~ **chart** Fieberkurve [fē′bərkoōrvə] 172

temple Schläfe [shlä′fə] 168; Tempel [tem′pəl] 123

temporarily vorläufig [fôr′loifish] 32

temporary provisorisch [prōvizōr′ish] 173

ten zehn [tsān] 28, 87

tender zart [tsärt] 100

tenderloin Lende [len′də] 106

tendon Sehne [zā′nə] 168; **pulled** ~ Sehnenzerrung [zā′nəntser′oōng] 171

tennis Tennis [ten′is] 190; **play** ~ Tennis spielen [ten′is shpē′lən] 190; ~ **ball** Tennisball [ten′isbäl] 190; ~ **court** Tennisplatz [ten′ispläts] 180, 190

tenor Tenor [tenôr′] 178

tent Zelt [tselt] 95

terrace Terrasse [teräs′ə] 82, 93

terrific! Prima! [prē′mä] 21

tetanus Tetanus [tet′änoōs] 172

thank you danke [däng′kə], ~ **very much** danke sehr [däng′kə zär], danke schön [däng′kə shön] 21

thanks danke [däng′kə] 12, 21; ~ **very much!** Vielen Dank! [fē′lən dängk] 17, 49; ~ **a lot!** Vielen herzlichen Dank! [fē′lən herts′lishən dängk] 21

thaw tauen [tou′ən]; Tauwetter [tou′vetər] 27

theatre Theater [tā·ä′tər] 121, 176, 178; ~ **schedule** Spielplan [shpēl′-plän] 178

theft Diebstahl [dēp′shtäl] 153

there dort [dôrt] 40, 65, etc.

thermometer Thermometer [ter′mō-mä′tər] 144, 161

thermos bottle Thermosflasche [ter′-mōsflôshə] 144

thermostat Thermostat [ter′mōstät′] 56

thief Dieb [dēp] 154

thigh Oberschenkel [ō′bərsheng-kəl] 167

thimble Fingerhut [fing′ərhoōt] 136

third dritte(r) [drit′ə(r)] 29

thorax Brustkorb [broōst′kôrp] 168

thread Garn [gärn], Faden [fä′dən], Zwirn [tsvirn] 136; **screw** ~ Gewinde [gəvin′də] 56

three drei [drī] 28

thriller Kriminalroman [krim′inäl′rō-män] 130

throat Hals [häls], Rachen [räh′ən] 162, 168

through car Kurswagen [kōōrs′vä-gən] 61, 64

throughway Durchgang [dōōrsh′-gäng] 123

throw up erbrechen [erbresh′ən] 163

throw-in Einwurf [īn′vōōrf] 190

thumb Daumen [dou′mən] 167

thunder Donner [dôn′ər] 27

thunderstorm Gewitter [gəvit′ər] 26, 71

Thursday Donnerstag [dôn′ərstäk] 33

thyme Thymian [tēm′i·än] 101

ticket Fahrschein [fär′shīn] 59, 117, 185, (Fahr)Karte [(fär′)kär′tə] 62, 67, 72, 176, 178; Flugschein [flōōk′-shīn], Ticket [tik′ət] 71; **one way ~** einfacher Fahrschein [īn′fähər fär′-shīn] 117; **transfer ~** Umsteigefahrschein [ōōm′shtīgəfär′shīn] 117; **~ sales** Kartenverkauf [kär′tənferkouf′] 178; **~ window** Fahrkartenschalter [fär′kärtənshäl′tər] 60

tie Krawatte [krävät′ə] 135

tight fest [fest] 51; knapp [knäp] 133, 139

tighten anziehen [än′tsē·ən] 55

tights Strumpfhose [shtrōōmpf′hō-zə] 135

time Zeit [tsīt] 15, 20, 30, 32, 192; **what ~** wann [vän] 18; **any ~** jederzeit [yā′dərtsīt′] 32; **on ~** pünktlich [pingkt′lish] 32, 66; **~ table** Fahrplan [fär′plän] 60

tincture Tinktur [tingktōōr′] 161

tint tönen [tā′nən] 158

tiny shrimp Krabben [kräb′ən] 102

tire Reifen [rī′fən] 46, 47; **~ change** Reifenwechsel [rī′fənvek′səl] 47; **~ pressure** Reifendruck [rī′fən-drōōk′] 46, 47

tires Bereifung [bərī′fōōng] 47

tissue Papierhandtuch [päpēr′hänt-tōōh] 140

to *(time)* vor [fōr] 30; *(place)* nach [näh] 59, 61, etc.

to let zu vermieten [tsōō fermē′tən] 191

toast Toast [tōst] 98

tobacco Tabak [täb′äk] 140

toboggan Schlitten [shlit′ən] 190

today heute [hoi′tə] 31, 68, 123, 180, 187

toe Zehe [tsā′ə], Zeh [tsā] 168

together zusammen [tsōōzäm′ən] 115

toilet Toilette [tô·älet′ə] 82, 88; **~ articles** Toilettenartikel [tōälet′ənärtik′əl] 142; **~ kit** Reisenecessaire [rī′zə·nesesär′] 142; **~ paper** Toilettenpapier [tô·älet′ənpäpēr′] 93, 142

toiletry Toilettenartikel [tô·älet′ən-ärtikəl] 140

tomato *(German)* Tomaten [tōmä′tən], *(Austrian)* Paradeiser [pärädī′zər] 108; **~ juice** Tomatensaft [tō-mä′tənzäft] 102

tomb Grab [gräp] 123

tomorrow morgen [môr′gən] 17, 31, 68, 73, 86, 89, 155, 176; **the day after ~** übermorgen [ē′bərmôrgən] 31; **~ morning** morgen früh [môr′gən frē] 31, 44

ton *(measure)* Tonne [tôn′ə] 193

tongue Zunge [tsōōng′ə] 107, 165, 168

tonic Stärkungsmittel [shter′-kōōngsmit′əl] 161; Tonicwasser [tô′nikväsər] 112

tonight heute nacht [hoi′tə näht] 31; heute abend [hoi′tə ä′bənt] 176

too gleichfalls [glīsh′fäls] 21; auch [ouh] 47; *(degree)* zu [tsōō] 31, 51

tool Werkzeug [verk′tsoik] 57; **~ box** Werkzeugkasten [verk′tsoik·käs′-tən] 57; **~ kit** Werkzeugkasten [verk′tsoik·käs′tən] 57

tooth Zahn [tsän] 168, 174; **~ brush** Zahnbürste [tsän′birstə] 142; **~ paste** Zahnpasta [tsän′pästä] 142; **~ powder** Zahnpulver [tsän′pōōlfər] 142; **~ cervix** Zahnhals [tsän′häls] 174; **wisdom ~** Weisheitszahn [vīs′-hītstsän′] 174

toothache Zahnschmerzen [tsän′-shmertsən] 173

toothpick Zahnstocher [tsän´shtô-hər] 97

top *(car)* Verdeck [ferdek´] 56

topless oben ohne [ō´bən ō´nə] 185

touch berühren [bərē´rən] 191; **do not ~** nicht berühren [nisht bərē´rən] 191

tough zäh [tsä] 100, 115

toupé Toupet [tōōpā´] 158

tour: guided ~ Führung [fē´rōōng] 118; **~ guide** Reiseleiter [rī´zəlī-tər] 74, 93

tour guide's office Reiseleitung [rī´-zəlī´tōōng] 74

tow abschleppen [äp´shlep`ən] 48; **~ truck** Abschleppwagen [äp´shlep-vä`gən] 48; **~ line** Abschleppseil [äp´shlepzīl`] 49

towel Handtuch [hän´tōōh] 87, 142; **bath ~** Badetuch [bä´dətōōh] 142

tower Turm [tōōrm] 123

towing service Abschleppdienst [äp´-shlepdēnst`] 49

town Stadt [shtät] 40, 86, 121, 123; **old ~** Altstadt [ält´shtät] 121

toy Spielzeug [shpēl´tsoik] 144

track Gleis [glīs], Bahnsteig [bän´-shtīk] 61, 65, 67; **~ and field** Leichtathletik [līsht´ätlā`tik] 190; **~ suit** Trainingsanzug [trä´ningsän`tsōōk] 135

traffic (Straßen)Verkehr [(shträ´-sən)ferkär´] 43, 123; **~ light** Ampel [äm´pəl] 43, 123; **~ regulations** Verkehrsregeln [ferkärs´rā`gəln] 43

tragedy Tragödie [trägœ´dē-ə] 178

trailer Anhänger [än´hengər] 41; Wohnwagen [vōn´vägən] 41

train Zug [tsōōk] 61, 64, 67, 89; **(regional)suburbanexpresss~**Schnellbahn [shnel´bän], S-Bahn [es´bän] 117

trainee Lehrling [lār´ling], Auszubildender [ous´tsōōbil`dəndər] 38

tranquilizer Beruhigungsmittel [bə-rōō´igōōngsmit`əl] 161

transfer Umsteigefahrschein [ōōm´-shtīgəfär`shīn] 63; **~ Überweisung** [ēbərvī´zōōng] 152

translate übersetzen [ēbərzets´ən] 24

translation Übersetzung [ē´bər-zets´ōōng] 130

translator Dolmetscher [dôl´met-shər] 37; Übersetzer [ēbərzets´ər] 38

transmission Getriebe [gətrē´bə] 56

travel agency Reisebüro [rī´zəbē-rō`] 82, 93, 123, 129

traveler's cheque Reisescheck [rī´-zəshek] 127

travel reading Reiselektüre [rī´zəlek-tē´rə] 130

traveling reisen [rī´zən] 78; **~ group** Reisegruppe [rī´zəgrōōpə] 78

tray Tablett [täblet´] 97

trick Stich [shtish] 181

trim stutzen [shtōōts´ən] 155, 157

trip Fahrt [färt] 43, 61; Reise [rī´zə] 12, 17

tripe Kutteln [kōōt´əln] 106

tripod Stativ [shtätēf´] 132

trotting race Trabrennen [träp´re-nən] 189

trouble Bemühungen [bəmē´-ōōngən] 21; Umstände [ōōm´-shtendə] 16

trousers Hose [hō´zə] 135

trout Forelle [fôrel´ə] 104

truck Lastwagen [läst´vägən] 41; **~ driver** LKW-Fahrer [el`kävä´fā`rər] 38

trump Trumpf [trōōmpf] 181

trunk Kofferraum [kô´fəroum] 56

tube Schlauch [shlouh] 56; Tube [tōō´bə] 126

tubeless *(tire)* schlauchlos [shlouh´-lōs] 47

tuberculosis Tuberkulose [tōō`berkōōlō´zə] 172

Tuesday Dienstag [dēns´täk] 33

tug Schlepper [shlep´ər] 77

tulip Tulpe [tōōl´pə] 130

tumor Geschwulst [gəshvōōlst´] 172

tuna fish Thunfisch [tōōn´fish] 104

turbot Steinbutt [shtīn´bōōt] 104

turkey *(hen)* Pute [pōō´tə] 105; *(tom)* Truthahn [trōōt´hän] 105

turn (sich) umdrehen [(zish) ōōm´-drā`ən]; **~ (the car)** wenden [ven´-dən] 43; **~ into a road** einbiegen [īn´-bēgən] 43; **~ off (a road)** abbiegen [äp´bēgən] 43; **~ off** ausschalten [ous'shältən] 182; **~ on** anschalten [än'shältən] 182

turnips weiße Rüben [vī'sə rē'bən] 108

tweezers Pinzette [pin'tsetə] 142

two zwei [tsvī] 28, 73, 78; **~-piece** Jakkenkleid [yäk'ənklīt] 135; **~-stroke motor** Zweitaktmotor [tsvī'täktmō'tôr] 54

typewriter Schreibmaschine [shrīp'-mäshēnə] 138; **~ paper** Schreibmaschinenpapier [shrīp'mäshē'nən-päpēr'] 138

typhoid fever Typhus [tē'foos] 172

U

ulcer Geschwür [gəshvēr'] 172

ultrasonics Ultraschall [ool'träshäl] 175

umbrella (Regen)Schirm [(rā'gən)-shirm] 91, 144, 153; **garden ~** Sonnenschirm [zôn'ənshirm] 91, 185

umpire Schiedsrichter [shēts'rishtər] 190

uncle Onkel [ông'kəl] 35

under unter [oon'tər] 34

underpants Unterhose [oon'tər-hōzə] 135

underpass Unterführung [oontər-fē'roong] 65

undershirt Unterhemd [oon'tər-hemt] 135

understand verstehen [fershtā'ən] 24

undertow Strömung [shtrā'moong] 185

underwear Unterwäsche [oon'tər-veshə] 135

undisturbed ungestört [oon'gə-shtärt] 183

university Universität [oon'iverzi-tät'] 38, 123

unlock aufschließen [ouf'shlēsən] 92

unstamped unfrankiert [oon'fräng-kērt] 150

until bis [bis] 32, 44

urgent dringend [dring'ənd] 147

urine Urin [oorēn'], Harn [härn] 168

urologist Urologe [oorōlō'gə] 163

us uns [oons] 87

use Gebrauch [gəbrouh'] 80

usher Platzanweiser [pläts'änvīzər] 179

uterus Gebärmutter [gəbär'-mootər] 168

V

vacant frei [frī] 66

vacation Urlaub [oor'loup] 14

vaccinate impfen [impf'ən] 164

vaccination Impfung [impf'oong] 78; **~ certificate** Impfschein [impf'shīn] 78, 79

vagina Vagina [vägē'nä], Scheide [shī'də] 168

valerian drops Baldriantropfen [bäl'-drē-äntröpf'ən] 161

valid gültig [gil'tish] 62, 68, 79

valley Tal [täl] 123

valuables Wertsachen [vārt'zähən] 84

value declaration Wertangabe [vārt'-ängäbə] 150

valve Ventil [ventēl'] 47, 56

vanilla Vanille [vänil'yə] 101

vase Vase [vä'zə] 130, 144

vaseline Vaseline [väzəlē'nə] 161

veal Kalbfleisch [kälp'flīsh] 106; **~ knuckle** Kalbshaxe [kälps'häksə] 106

vegetable Gemüse [gəmē'zə] 107; **~ market** Gemüsehandlung [gəmē'-zəhänd'loong] 129

vehicle Fahrzeug [fär'tsoik] 41, 58

vein Ader [ä'dər], Vene [vä'nə] 168

velvet Samt [zämt] 137

venereal disease Geschlechtskrankheit [gəshleshts'krängkhīt] 172

venison Hirsch [hirsh], Reh [rā] 106

ventilation Lüftung [lif'toong] 93

verdict Urteil [oor'tīl] 154

vermicelli Fadennudeln [fä'dən·noo-dəln] 103

vermouth Wermut [vär'moot] 111

very sehr [zār] 21

vest Weste [ves'tə] 135

veterinarian Tierarzt [tēr'ärtst], Tierärztin [tēr'ärts`tin] 38

veterinary medicine Tiermedizin [tēr´mäditsēn`] 39
victory Sieg [zēk] 188
video cassette Videokassette [vē´-dā·ōkäset`ə] 144
village Dorf [dôrf] 123
vinegar Essig [es´ish] 101
vintage Jahrgang [yär´gäng] 111
violet *(adj.)* violett [vē´ōlet´] 194; ~ *(noun)* Veilchen [fīl´shən] 130
violin recital Violinabend [vē·ōlēn´-äbənt] 178
visa Visum [vē´zōōm] 78
visit besuchen [bəzōō´hən] 78, 183; *(chat)* sich unterhalten [zish ōōntərhäl´tən] 183
visiting hours Besuchszeit [bə-zōōhs´tsīt] 172
vitamin pills Vitamintabletten [vitä-mēn´täblet`ən] 161
vocational school Berufsschule [bə-rōōfs´shōōlə] 39
vodka Wodka [vôt´kä] 112
volleyball Volleyball [vôl´ēbäl] 190
voltage Stromspannung [shtrōm´-shpän`ŏong] 75, 86, 93
volume Band [bänt] 130
vomiting Erbrechen [erbresh´ən] 172
voyage Schiffsreise [shifs´rīzə], See-reise [zā´rīzə] 77

W

wafer Eiswaffel [īs´väfəl] 114
wait warten [vär´tən] 87, 117, 155
waiter Kellner [kel´nər] 38, Ober [ō´bər] 96
waiting room Wartesaal [vär´təzäl] 60, 65; Warteraum [vär´təroum] 69, 71; Wartezimmer [vär´tətsimər] 163
waitress Kellnerin [kel´nərin] 38, 96
wake wecken [vek´ən] 86, 89
walk gehen [gā´ən] 184; **take a** ~ spazierengehen [shpätsē´rəngā·ən] 183
walking shoes Halbschuhe [hälp´-shōō·ə] 139
wall Mauer [mou´ər] 123; Wand [vänt] 93

wallet Brieftasche [brēf´täshə], Portemonnaie [pôrt´mônä`] 144, 153
walnuts Walnüsse [väl´nisə] 110
want wollen [vôl´ən] 21
ward Station [shtätsyōn´] 173
warm warm [värm], heiß [hīs] 25, 67, 185; herzlich [herts´lish] 23
warning triangle Warndreieck [värn´-drī`ek] 56
warship Kriegsschiff [krēks´shif] 77
wash waschen [väsh´ən] 47, 95, 155, 158; ~ **and set** waschen und legen [väsh´ən ŏont lā´gən] 155; ~ **cloth** Waschlappen [väsh´läpən] 142; ~ **room** Waschraum [väsh´-roum] 94
washer Dichtung [dish´tŏong] 56
washing line Wäscheleine [vesh´əlī-nə] 144
watch Uhr [ōōr] 142, 153; **wrist** ~ Armbanduhr [ärm´bäntōōr] 143, 153; **pocket** ~ Taschenuhr [täsh´ən-ōōr`] 143; **stop** ~ Stoppuhr [shtôp´-ōōr`] 143; ~ **band** Uhrenarmband [ōōr´ənärmbänt] 143
watchmaker Uhrmacher [ōōr´mä-hər] 38, 142
water Wasser [väs´ər] 45, 82, 93, 112, 186; **soda** ~ Sodawasser [zō´dävä-sər] 112; **mineral** ~ Mineralwasser [minəräl´väsər] 112; **carbonated** ~ Mineralwasser mit Kohlensäure [minəräl´väsər mit kō´lənzoirə] 112; **non-carbonated** ~ Mineralwasser ohne Kohlensäure [minəräl´väsər ō´nə kō´lənzoirə] 112; ~ **glass** Wasserglas [väs´ərgläs] 93; **drinking** ~ Trinkwasser [tringk´väsər] 95; **cooling** ~ Kühlwasser [kēl´väsər] 45; ~ **temperature** Wassertemperatur [väs´ərtempərätōōr`] 186; **hot and cold running** ~ fließend Kalt- und Warmwasser [flē´sənt kält ŏont värm´väsər] 82; ~ **skiing** Wasserski fahren [väs´ərshē` fä´rən] 185
waterfall Wasserfall [väs´ərfäl] 123
wave Welle [vel´ə] 77, 186
way Weg [vāk]; **this** ~ in dieser Richtung [in dē´zər rish´tŏong] 40; **by** ~ **of** über [ē´bər] 61; **no** ~! Auf keinen Fall! [ouf kī´nən fäl] 21

we wir [vēr]
weather Wetter [vet'ər] 25, 70; **~ report** Wetterbericht [vet'ərbərisht] 25; **~ prediction** Wettervorhersage [vet'ərförhär'zägə] 27
wedding Trauung [trou'ōōng] 123
Wednesday Mittwoch [mit'vôh] 33
week Woche [vô'hə] 31, 78, 82
weekend Wochenende [vô'hənən`də] 32
weekly jede Woche [yā'də vô'hə] 32
welcome Empfang [empfäng'] 12; willkommen [vilkôm'ən] 21
well gut [gōōt] 12, 20; **~ done** durchgebraten [dŏŏrsh'gəbrä'tən] 100
wet naß [näs] 155; **~ paint** frisch gestrichen [frish gəshtrish'ən] 191
what was [väs] 15, 18; **~ for** wozu [vōtsōō'] 18
wheel Rad [rät] 47, 56
when wann [vän] 18, 30, 41, 72; wenn [ven] 41
where wo [vō] 18, 19, 40, 72; wohin [vōhin'] 59; **~ from** woher [vō'här] 14, 18; **~ to** wohin [vōhin'] 18, 40; **~ is there ...?** Wo gibt es ...? [vō gēpt es ...] 19
which welche(r) [vel'shə(r)] 18, 59, 116
whiskey Whisky [vis'kē] 112
white weiß [vīs] 194
who wer [vār] 18
wholesaler Großhändler [grōs'hendlər] 38
whom wen [vān] 18; **to ~** wem [vām] 18; **with ~** mit wem [mit vām] 18
whose: ~ is that? Wem gehört das? [vām gəhört däs] 18
why warum [väröōm'], weshalb [veshälp'] 18
wide breit [brīt] 127, 133, 139
widowed verwitwet [fervit'vət] 79
wife Frau [frou], Gattin [gät'in] 13, 14; Ehefrau [ā'əfrou] 35, 162
wig Perücke [perik'ə] 156, 158
win gewinnen [gəvin'ən] 188
wind Wind [vint] 26; **north (east) ~** Nord(Ost)-Wind [nôrt'(ôst')vint] 27; **south (west) ~** Süd(West)-Wind [zēt'(vest')vint] 27; **~ breaker** Windjacke [vint'yäkə] 135

winding road Serpentine [zer`pentē'nə] 43
window Fenster [fens'tər] 65, 88, 93, 191; Scheibe [shī'bə] 47; **~pane** Fensterscheibe [fens'tərshībə] 93; **~ seat** Fensterplatz [fens'tərpläts] 67
windshield Windschutzscheibe [vint'shōōts-shī'bə] 47, 56; **~ wiper** Scheibenwischer [shī'bənvishər] 55; **~ washer** Scheibenwaschanlage [shī'bənväsh'änlä'gə] 56
windy windig [vin'dish] 25
wine Wein [vīn] 96, 111; **Baden ~** badischer Wein [bä'dishər vīn] 111; **dessert ~** Dessertwein [desär'vīn] 111; **Franconian ~** Frankenwein [fräng'kənvīn] 111; **~ list** Weinkarte [vīn'kärtə] 96; **fruity ~** fruchtiger Wein [frōōh'tigər vīn] 111; **sweet ~** süßer Wein [zē'sər vīn] 111; **Moselle ~** Moselwein [mō'zəlvīn] 111; **mulled ~** Glühwein [glē'vīn] 111; **red ~** Rotwein [rōt'vīn] 111; **Rhine ~** Rheinwein [rīn'vīn] 111; **white ~** Weißwein [vīs'vīn] 111; **dry ~** trockener Wein [trôk'ənər vīn], herber Wein [här'bər vīn] 111
wing *(plane)* Tragfläche [träk'fleshə], Flügel [flē'gəl] 71
winter Winter [vin'tər] 33
wire Draht [drät] 57; Telegramm [tālāgräm'] 147
wish wünschen [vin'shən] 20, 23
wisp Strähne [shträ'nə] 158
withdraw abheben [äp'hābən] 152
within innerhalb [in'ərhälp] 32
witness Zeuge [tsoi'gə] 49
wood carving Holzschnitzerei [hôlts'shnitsərī] 144
wool Wolle [vôl'ə] 136; **pure ~** reine Wolle [rī'nə vôl'ə] 137; **pure virgin ~** reine Schurwolle [rī'nə shōōr'vôlə] 137
word Wort [vôrt] 24, 147
work *(verb)* arbeiten [är'bītən] 15; funktionieren [fōōngk'tsyōnēr'ən] 19, 23, 48, 50, 51, 87; **~** *(noun)* Werk [verk] 178
worker Arbeiter [är'bītər] 38
worsted Kammgarn [käm'gärn] 137

wound Wunde [vōōn′də] 172; ~ **salve** Wundsalbe [vōōnt′zälbə] 161
wrapping paper Packpapier [päk′päpēr] 138
wrench Schraubenschlüssel [shrou′bənshlísəl] 57
wrestle ringen [ring′ən] 190
wrestler Ringer [ring′ər] 190
wrestling Ringkampf [ring′kämpf] 190
wrist Handgelenk [hänt′gəlengk] 168
write schreiben [shrī′bən]; ~ **something down** etwas aufschreiben [et′väs ouf′shrībən] 24
writer Schriftsteller [shrift′shtelər] 38
writing paper Schreibpapier [shrīp′päpēr] 138
wrong falsch [fälsh] 148

X

x-ray *(noun)* Röntgenaufnahme [rent′gənoufnä`mə] 173; ~ *(verb)* durchleuchten [dōōrshloish′tən] 173

Y

yacht Jacht [yäht] 77
yard *(approx.)* Meter [mā′tər] 126, 193

year Jahr [yär] 23, 32
yellow gelb [gelp] 132, 194
yes ja [yä] 21
yesterday gestern [ges′tərn] 31; **the day before** ~ vorgestern [fōr′gestərn] 31
yield right of way *(sign)* Vorfahrt gewähren [fōr′färt gəvä′rən] 58
you du [dōō], Sie [zē]
young jung [yŏŏng] 35
younger jünger [ying′ər] 35
your Ihr [ēr], dein [dīn]
youth Jugend [yŏŏ′gənt] 95; ~ **group** Jugendgruppe [yŏŏ′gəntgrōŏpə] 95; ~ **hostel** Jugendherberge [yŏŏ′gənt·her`bergə] 81, 94, 95; ~ **hostel card** Herbergsausweis [här′bärksous`vīs] 95

Z

zebra crossing Zebrastreifen [tsä′bräshtrī`fən] 43, 123
zero null [nŏŏl] 28; Null [nŏŏl] 25
zipper Reißverschluß [rīs′fershlŏŏs] 136
zoo Zoo [tsō] 119, 123
zoology Zoologie [tsō·ōlōgē′] 39

SIZES AND MEASUREMENTS

Men's Ready-made Suits

American	34	35	36	37	38	39	40	41	42
German	42	44	46	46–47	48	50	50–52	52	54

Ladies' Dresses, Suits, Blouses

American	10	12	14	16	18	20
German	38	40	42	44	46	48

Shirts

American	14	$14\frac{1}{2}$	15	$15\frac{1}{2}$	$15\frac{3}{4}$	16	$16\frac{1}{2}$	17
German	35–36	37	38	39	40	41	42	43

Men's Socks

American	10	$10\frac{1}{2}$	11	$11\frac{1}{2}$	12
German	39–40	40–41	42	42–43	43–44

Measurements

Inches	22	24	26	28	30	32	34	36	38	40	42	44	46	48	50
Centimeters	56	61	66	71	76	81	86	91	97	102	107	112	117	122	127

Shoes

American	4	5	6	7	8	9	10	11	12	13
German	$36\frac{1}{2}$	$37\frac{1}{2}$	39	40	$41\frac{1}{2}$	$42\frac{1}{2}$	44	$45\frac{1}{2}$	$46\frac{1}{2}$	48

Ladies' Shoes

American	6	7	8	9
German	37	$38\frac{1}{2}$	40	41